Capital Adequacy Beyond Basel

CAPITAL ADEQUACY BEYOND BASEL
Banking, Securities, and Insurance

Edited by
Hal S. Scott

OXFORD
UNIVERSITY PRESS

2005

OXFORD

UNIVERSITY PRESS

Oxford   New York

Auckland   Bangkok   Buenos Aires   Cape Town   Chennai
Dar es Salaam   Delhi   Hong Kong   Istanbul   Karachi   Kolkata
Kuala Lumpur   Madrid   Melbourne   Mexico City   Mumbai   Nairobi
São Paulo   Shanghai   Taipei   Tokyo   Toronto

Copyright © 2005 by Oxford University Press, Inc.

Published by Oxford University Press, Inc.
198 Madison Avenue, New York, New York 10016

www.oup.com

Oxford is a registered trademark of Oxford University Press

MK

Library of Congress Cataloging-in-Publication Data
Capital adequacy beyond Basel : banking, securities, and insurance /
edited by Hal S. Scott.
p.   cm.
Includes bibliographical references and index.
ISBN-13 978-0-19-516971-3
ISBN 0-19-516971-9
1. Bank reserves—Government policy.
2. Insurance—Reserves—Government policy.
3. Banks and banking—State supervision.
4. Financial institutions—State supervision.
5. Bank loans.   I. Scott, Hal S.
HG1656.A3C278   2005
332.1′068′1—dc22   2004004468

1 3 5 7 9 8 6 4 2

Printed in the United States of America
on acid-free paper

Acknowledgments

The opinions shared in this book are those of the authors and not necessarily those of the institutions for which they work.

The contributors would like to thank Swiss Reinsurance Company, without whose financial support this research project would not have been possible; Jens Drolshammer, for helping to formulate the idea for this project; Jenepher Moseley, for her amazing editing skills and dedication; Paul Donnelly and Karen Capria at Oxford University Press for seeing the book through to production; and from the Program on International Financial Systems, Melissa Greven, our in-house editor, and J Weinstein, who managed this project every step of the way.

Contents

Contributors

Michel Crouhy is partner at BlackDiamond Consulting and formerly Senior Vice President, Business Analytic Solutions, Treasury Balance Sheet and Risk Management Division at CIBC (Canadian Imperial Bank of Commerce). His responsibilities included the approval of all pricing, balance sheet, risk, and capital-related models, the development of risk measurement methodologies and models for market, credit (corporate and retail), and economic capital attribution, as well as customer behavior analytics.

Prior to his current position at CIBC, Michel Crouhy was a Professor of Finance at the HEC School of Management in Paris, where he was also Director of the M.S. HEC in International Finance. He has been a visiting professor at the Wharton School and at UCLA. Dr. Crouhy holds a Ph.D. from the Wharton School and is Doctoris Honoris Causa from the University of Montreal.

He is coauthor of *Risk Management* and has published extensively in academic journals in the areas of banking, options, and financial markets. He is also associate editor of the *Journal of Derivatives*, the *Journal of Banking and Finance*, and is on the editorial board of the *Journal of Risk*.

Mark J. Flannery is the BankAmerica Eminent Scholar in Finance at the Warrington College of Business, University of Florida. Professor Flannery teaches corporate finance and financial management of financial institutions in the graduate program. He has consulted with various federal banking agencies and the two housing GSEs. His published work deals primarily with the management and regulation of financial institutions, but it also includes work on asset pricing and corporate finance. Flannery's current research focuses on the information content of security prices. He is an Editor of the *Journal of Money, Credit and Banking*, and the outside Director of the FDIC's Center for Financial Research. Professor Flannery has served on the faculty of the University of Pennsylvania and the University of North Carolina, and as a visiting professor at the London Business School and the University of New South Wales.

Dan Galai is the Abe Gray Professor of Finance and Business Administration at the Hebrew University School of Business Administration in Jerusalem. He was a visiting professor of finance at INSEAD and at the University of California, Los Angeles, and has also taught at the University of Chicago and at the University of California, Berkeley. Dr. Galai holds a Ph.D. from the University of Chicago and undergraduate and graduate degrees from the Hebrew University. He has served as a consultant for the Chicago Board of Options Exchange and the American Stock Exchange as well as for major banks. He has published numerous articles in leading business and finance journals, on options, risk management, financial markets and institutions, and corporate finance. He is a coauthor of *Risk Management*.

He was a winner of the first annual Pomeranze Prize for excellence in options research presented by the CBOE. Dr. Galai is a principal in Sigma P.C.M., which is engaged in portfolio management and corporate finance.

Scott E. Harrington is the W. Frank Hipp Professor of Insurance and Professor of Finance in the Moore School of Business at the University of South Carolina. During 1978–1988, he was on the faculty of the Wharton School at the University of Pennsylvania. A former President of both the American Risk and Insurance Association and the Risk Theory Society, he has published articles in numerous academic and policy journals, including the *Journal of Business*, the *Journal of Law and Economics*, the *Review of Economics and Statistics*, the *Journal of Risk and Insurance*, the *Journal of Banking and Finance*, the *Journal of Financial Intermediation*, the *Journal of Risk and Uncertainty*, the *Journal of Insurance Regulation*, and *Science*. He has contributed articles to books published by the American Enterprise Institute, the Brookings Institution, the Federal Reserve Bank of Boston, the Federal Reserve Bank of Chicago, Oxford University Press, W.W. Norton, and other publishers. He is coauthor or coeditor of numerous scholarly books, including *Cycles and Crises in Property/Casualty Insurance* and *Rate Regulation of Workers' Compensation Insurance: How Price Controls Increase Costs*, and coauthor of the textbook *Risk Management and Insurance*. Dr. Harrington currently serves on the Shadow Financial Regulatory Committee. He is an Associate Editor of the *Journal of Risk and Insurance* and a member of the editorial advisory board for *Regulation* magazine.

Richard Herring is Jacob Safra Professor of International Banking, Director of The Lauder Institute of Management & International Studies, and

Co-Director of the Wharton Financial Institutions Center. He served as Undergraduate Dean of the Wharton School from 1995–2000.

Dr. Herring is an expert on financial institutions and international finance. He has advised numerous U.S. government agencies as well as several multilateral lending institutions and international financial institutions. He is cochair of the Shadow Financial Regulatory Committee and the Biennial Multinational Banking Seminar, and has been a fellow of the World Economic Forum in Davos, Switzerland. Dr. Herring is the author of more than 80 articles and books. He serves on the editorial boards of several leading journals and is coeditor of *The Brookings-Wharton Papers on Financial Services*. His current research interests include financial conglomerates, liquidity and financial regulation.

Before coming to Wharton in 1972, Dr. Herring taught at Princeton University. He received his AB from Oberlin College (1968) and his MA (1970) and Ph.D. (1973) from Princeton University.

Howell E. Jackson is Associate Dean for Research and the Finn M.W. Caspersen and Household International Professor at Harvard Law School, where he teaches courses on the regulation of financial institutions, securities regulation, pension law, international finance, and analytical methods for lawyers. His research currently deals with the regulation of international securities market, reform of the social security system, problems in consumer finance, and comparative cost-benefit analyses of financial regulation. He is coauthor of the *Regulation of Financial Institutions* and *Analytical Methods for Lawyers* and author of numerous scholarly articles. Professor Jackson has served as a consultant to the U.S. Treasury Department in connection with the Gramm-Leach-Bliley Act and also as an adviser to the United Nations Development Programme, the World Bank/International Monetary Fund, and the Harvard Institute for International Development in connection with various projects involving the reform of financial systems in other countries. Prior to joining the Harvard Law School faculty in 1989, Professor Jackson served as a law clerk to U.S. Supreme Court Justice Thurgood Marshall and practiced law in Washington, D.C.

Paul Kupiec is Associate Director of the Division of Insurance and Research at the Federal Deposit Insurance Corporation in Washington, D.C. Former positions include: Deputy Chief of the Banking Supervision and Regulation Division in the Monetary and Exchange Affairs Department of the International Monetary Fund; Director in the Finance Division at Freddie Mac; Vice-President at J.P. Morgan's RiskMetrics group, and Senior Economist in Trading Risk Analysis and Capital Markets sections at the Federal Reserve Board. He has also served as a visiting Economist at the Bank for International Settlements, an Assistant Professor of Finance at North Carolina State University, and as a consultant on financial market issues for the OECD.

Andrew P. Kuritzkes is a Managing Director at Mercer Oliver Wyman. He joined Oliver, Wyman & Company in 1988, was a Managing Director in the firm's London office from 1993 to 1997, and served as Vice Chairman of Oliver, Wyman & Company globally from 2000 until the firm's acquisition by Mercer, Inc. (a division of Marsh & McLennan Companies) in 2003.

Mr. Kuritzkes has consulted on a broad range of strategy, risk management, regulatory, and organizational issues for financial institutions and regulators in the United States, Canada, the United Kingdom, Switzerland, Germany, the Netherlands, Hong Kong, and Singapore. He has worked extensively with organizations, at the Board and senior executive levels, on a number of issues relating to corporate banking strategy and finance and risk management, including the link between risk measurement and strategy, the impact of regulation, active portfolio management, and the evolution of wholesale lending.

Mr. Kuritzkes has written and spoken widely on a broad range of risk, financial structuring, and regulatory topics. His articles have appeared in *Strategic Finance, Risk, Die Bank, Banking Strategies, Journal of Applied Corporate Finance, Journal of Risk Finance*, and the *Brookings-Wharton Papers on Financial Services.*

Before joining Oliver, Wyman & Company, Mr. Kuritzkes worked as an economist and lawyer for the Federal Reserve Bank of New York from 1986 to 1988.

Robert M. Mark is the CEO of Black Diamond, which provides corporate governance, risk management consulting, and transaction services. He serves on several boards and is the Chairperson of The Professional Risk Managers' International Association's Blue Ribbon Panel. In 1998, he was awarded the Financial Risk Manager of the Year by the Global Association of Risk Professionals.

Prior to his current position, he was the Senior Executive Vice-President, Chief Risk Officer, and a member of the Management Committee at the Canadian Imperial Bank of Commerce (CIBC). Dr. Mark's global responsibility covered credit, market, and operating risks for all of CIBC and its subsidiaries.

Prior to CIBC, he was the partner in charge of the Financial Risk Management Consulting practice at Coopers & Lybrand. Prior to his position at C&L, he was a managing director in the Asia, Europe, and Capital Markets Group at Chemical Bank. Before he joined Chemical Bank, he was a senior officer at Marine Midland Bank/Hong Kong Shanghai Bank where he headed the technical analysis trading group within the Capital Markets Sector.

He earned his Ph.D. from NYU's Graduate School of Engineering and Science. Subsequently, he received an Advanced Professional Certificate in accounting from NYU's Stern Graduate School of Business, and is a graduate of Harvard Business School's Advanced Management Program. He is an Adjunct Professor and coauthor of *Risk Management*.

Til Schuermann is currently a Senior Economist at the Federal Reserve Bank of New York's Research Department where he focuses on risk measurement and management in financial institutions and capital markets. He is also a Sloan Research Fellow at the Wharton Financial Institution Center and teaches at Columbia University. Prior to joining the New York Fed in May of 2001 he spent five years at the management consulting firm Oliver, Wyman & Company, where he was a Director and Head of Research. Til spent 1993 to 1996 at Bell Laboratories working on combining techniques from statistics and artificial intelligence to build models for bad debt prediction as well as developing risk-based management decision support tools. Til has numerous publications in the area of risk modeling and applied econometrics and has edited *Simulation-Based Inference in Econometrics*. He received his Ph.D. in economics in 1993 from the University of Pennsylvania.

Hal S. Scott is the Nomura Professor of International Financial Systems and the Director of the Program on International Financial Systems at Harvard Law School. He teaches courses on Banking Regulation, Securities Regulation, International Finance, and the Payment System. He joined the Harvard faculty in 1975 after serving for a year as a clerk to Supreme Court Justice Byron R. White. Professor Scott served as Reporter to the 3-4-8 Committee of the Permanent Editorial Board of the Uniform Commercial Code from 1978–1983 to revise the law for payment systems.

His books include *International Finance: Transactions, Policy and Regulation* (11th ed.) and *Asian Money Markets* (Oxford 1995). He has served as a consultant to financial institutions, foreign governments, and the World Bank and OECD. He is past President of the International Academy of Consumer and Commercial Law and is currently a member of the Board of Governors of the American Stock Exchange and a member of the Shadow Financial Regulatory Committee.

Philip A. Wellons was Associate Director of the Program on International Financial Systems at Harvard Law School. He joined the Harvard University faculty in 1976, teaching first at Harvard Business School, in business strategy and comparative political economy, specializing in global finance. In 1987, he moved to Harvard Law School, where he taught courses about the world debt crisis and international finance.

His fields are comparative government policy and financial markets, as well as law and financial reform in developing and transition countries. The work involves research, consulting, and training, in Asia, Europe, North America, and Africa. He coauthored a textbook with Hal S. Scott on international finance and law, in its tenth edition. He has consulted for governments, major banks, the OECD, the World Bank, the International Legal Center, various agencies of the United Nations, the USAID, the European Bank for Reconstruction and Development, and the Asian Development Bank. He has testified before Congress.

Capital Adequacy Beyond Basel

Introduction

LOOKING BEYOND BASEL

This book appears at a time when the Bank for International Settlements in Basel is revising its rules for the regulation of capital adequacy, as developed by the Basel Committee on Banking Supervision (BCBS or Basel Committee). These rules were originally issued in 1988 to ensure adequate capital for credit risk in internationally active G-10 banks and were then added to, in 1996, to require capital for market risk. They have since been adopted by more than 100 countries in some form. This book looks beyond Basel in two ways. First, it calls into question many aspects of the Basel Committee's proposed revisions of its credit risk rules and the creation of new capital requirements for operational risk. Second, it shows that the Basel rules may not be appropriate for securities firms and insurance companies and thus calls into question the proposed use of these rules for the consolidated capital requirements of financial service holding companies—holding companies that own banks, securities firms, and insurance companies. This book is a collection of essays by experts in the field that bring together the disciplines of business, economics, and law to examine what the best approach to capital adequacy will be in the future.

In the United States, the current Basel rules have been extended to financial service holding companies at the consolidated holding company level and to all banks; the capital rules of the Securities and Exchange Commission (SEC) apply to securities firms, and the rules of state regulators apply to insurance companies, whether or not these companies are part of a financial service holding company. The European Union has extended the Basel rules to all securities firms and banks, but special rules continue to

3

apply to insurance companies. Japan's approach is more like that of the United States. Switzerland, a key financial center in Europe, that is not part of the European Union, applies the Basel rules to banks and different rules to securities firms and insurance companies. Suffice it to say that capital adequacy rules are not exclusively set by the Basel Committee.

In addition to proposed revisions of the credit risk rules, the Basel Committee for the first time has proposed that capital be required for operational risk and that all capital requirements be applied to financial holding companies of internationally active banks. These proposals are collectively referred to as Basel II throughout the book. They have triggered widespread criticism and may jeopardize continued acceptance of the Basel rules. The United States, for example, announced in 2003 that it would apply Basel II only to its biggest banks, 10 on a mandatory basis, and perhaps another 10 on a voluntary basis, assuming they qualify. And this application will apply only to that part of the Basel methodology that relies less on Basel commands and more on bank models. This will leave most banks in the United States with Basel I at both the bank and the bank holding company levels. Although the European Union plans to apply Basel II to all of its banks (European Commission 2003), the U.S. rejection of major portions of the Basel rules does not augur well for their continued acceptance worldwide. The world will be looking for alternative approaches, and this book, it is hoped, will help in that search. In looking beyond the Basel Committee, the book suggests that there should be more reliance on market discipline and bank models, rather than compulsory rules.

DIFFERENCES AMONG FINANCIAL INSTITUTIONS

One important conclusion reached in this study is that the three different financial institutions examined should not have the same capital rules because they have different risks and raise different regulatory concerns. This suggests that the continued U.S. practice of extending the Basel rules to the financial services holding company level, now mandated by Basel II, and the E.U. practice of extending the rules to securities firms is wrongly conceived. As Richard Herring and Til Schuermann and Scott Harrington point out in chapters 1 and 2, the risks of financial institutions differ significantly. Most important, neither securities nor insurance firms pose systemic risk concerns since they have no immediately withdrawable deposits and weak, if any, public safety nets such as deposit insurance or lender-of-last-resort protection of banks. In addition, the risk of the failure of these firms is less than that of banks. Securities firms do not suffer from the uncertainty of asset values, apart from their more exotic derivative positions, which are the hallmark of the lending operations of commercial banks. Insurance companies have more problems with the opaqueness of some assets, for example, commercial real estate, but a significant portion of their assets are market-priced securities. Both securities and insurance firms are able to mark to market most of their assets, although insurance companies do not do so under their special accounting rules.

The differences between these institutions are reflected in different purposes of capital regulation. In the case of a securities firm, the primary objective is to have enough capital to liquidate without losses to the customers. Absent fraud, this is relatively easy, since customer funds and securities are segregated. Unlike depositors, retail customers of securities firms are not generally an important funding source. In the case of insurance companies, the major risk is that premiums and reserves, and earnings on investments, will not be adequate to cover the underwriting risk, the obligation to policyholders. This is more of a risk for property and casualty insurance, where the underwriting risk cannot be calculated with the same certainty as it can for life insurance. In a sense, the uncertainty of the value of liabilities of insurance companies is like the uncertainty of asset value in banks. But, even though insurance companies have such uncertainty, policyholder liabilities are long-term, giving firms a long period of time to take remedial measures. Also, insurance companies are able to decrease liability risk through reinsurance, probably more effectively than banks can reduce asset risk through credit derivatives or securitization, although these and other advances in risk management techniques are narrowing the gap.

HOW TO ENSURE ADEQUATE CAPITAL

There are three basic ways to deal with capital adequacy: market discipline, supervisory review of firm economic models used to determine capital, and command and control regulation.

Market Discipline

For most firms, the world relies entirely on market discipline to determine capital because it works best. There is a reluctance to rely on this technique for banks because of the concern with systemic risk and the lack of transparency of bank risks—that is, the lack of clearly ascertainable values for loans. However, one can seriously question the extent of systemic risk in today's banking system, at least in most advanced economies.

Systemic risk in the payment system, which used to be the core of systemic risk arguments, has been greatly reduced or eliminated. Net settlement systems, with their risk of deleting transactions of failed banks and recalculating settlement positions (so-called delete and unwind), which stood to cause a chain reaction of bank failures, have been modified to mitigate the risks of bank failure. For example, in the United Kingdom, the net settlement system has been converted into a real-time gross settlement system, or risk has been greatly reduced through more continuous settlement and algorithm techniques that permit efficient settlement sequencing, as in the case of the New York Clearinghouse Interbank Payment System (CHIPS). Interbank exposures through placements or clearing accounts, a concern in such failures as Continental Illinois in the mid-1980s, are now controlled by regulation that limits placement exposures, Section 308 of the Federal Deposit Insurance Corporation Improvement Act (FDICIA) of 1991, implemented by Regulation F of the Federal Reserve Board, 12 C.F.R. § 206.1 et seq., or by more effective monitoring of their correspondent accounts by bank respondents. The irrational runs on banks are limited by deposit insurance and lender-of-last-resort powers. Moreover, the lack of market discipline induced by reliance on public safety net bailouts has been greatly reduced in the United States by Section 142 of FDICIA, limiting the Fed's use of its lender-of-last-resort power, and by Section 302 of FDICIA, requiring that deposit insurance be priced in such a way as to ensure that the banks and not the public pay the freight. If safety nets differ substantially among countries, as they well might (see Scott and Iwahara 1994), then the case for international capital standards is considerably weaker.

It may be argued that the lower level of systemic risk is due to efficacious supervision and regulation, including that of capital. Under this view, if capital regulation were abolished, systemic risk would increase. This logic is flawed. Systemic risk deals with mechanisms through which one bank's failure is transmitted to others. If no such mechanisms exist or if they are rarely of concern, then the lack of capital regulation would not imply that the possible failure of one bank would lead to the failure of others. We are certainly troubled when a person dies from the failure to take medicine against a noninfectious disease, but only if the disease were infectious would we regulate an individual's ex ante behavior, for example, by requiring that person to be vaccinated, or the person's ex post behavior, by requiring her to be quarantined.

The term "systemic risk" in the banking system is often used today to refer to the possibility that a major bank failure or failures could disrupt an economy or have contagion effects on other economies. It is hard to see how this could occur through a single bank failure in most major economies, given the relative lack of concentration within domestic banking systems[1] and the increasing internationalization of banking markets. The Asian crisis is often used as an example of the contagion problem but the relative role of inadequately capitalized banks in producing the crisis and the extent to which contagion occurred as a result of that problem, are a matter of great debate. Nor is it clear that contagion could spread as easily among advanced economies. Indeed, the very existence of contagion is hotly contested (Karolyi 2003). Moreover, it is far from clear that bank failure is the only serious potential source for serious economic shocks. Potential effects from the collapse of major employers, or of energy or commodity suppliers, have not resulted in the capital regulation of these firms.

Nonetheless, the entire system of banking regulation is predicated on the possibility of systemic risk as a result of a substantial fear of the unknown, the supposed lessons of the past, and the bureaucratic imperative to preserve power.

Two chapters in our volume discuss potential improvements in market discipline for banks through the creation of instruments that can give valuable signals to regulators and reduce the risks of bank failure. Both chapters suggest that market discipline may be a preferable alternative to regulation.

Of the two, Paul Kupiec, in his chapter "Subordinated Debt as an Alternative to the Internal Models Approach" (chapter 4), discusses the virtues of mandatory subordinated debt requirements. Sophisticated holders of such instruments would demand adequate levels of equity protection, and information in the form of benchmarked yields would be available to the market, as well as regulators, to serve as a discipline to bank issuers. Adequate disclosure is a key premise of market discipline. Subordinated debt holders, along with the rating agencies, would presumably demand adequate disclosure, as sophisticated holders of securities do generally. The United States now requires banks to hold a certain amount of subordinated debt, but these requirements could be greatly strengthened along the lines suggested by the U.S. Shadow Financial Regulatory Committee, a group of legal and economic experts on financial regulation. This committee proposed that banks be required to issue subordinated debt equal to 2% of assets and off-balance sheet obligations on a periodic basis in large denominations, that is, to sophisticated holders.

Mark Flannery, in his chapter "Market Discipline via Reverse Convertible Debentures" (chapter 5), suggests another instrument that could serve a similar purpose, a reverse convertible debenture (RCD). This is a subordinated debt instrument that would convert into equity when capital ratios deteriorated below a set point. Unlike subordinated debt instruments, RCDs avert bankruptcy by providing more equity when needed.

The key problem with both these proposals is the cost and practicality of issuing sufficient amounts of such instruments and the lack of investor appetite for them. Recent studies seem to indicate, however, that they could furnish potential valuable signals to regulators. It is also possible that equity prices could serve to provide market discipline and signals, without the cost and practical problems raised by subordinated debt and RCDs (Gunther, Levonian, and Moore 2001). See also Krainer and Lopez (2003), who look at equity market information as being informative for predicting supervisory rating changes for U.S. bank holding companies. They find the information is indeed predictive but that it helps only a little.

As has already been stated, the case for market discipline, rather than regulatory command, is stronger for securities firms and insurance companies, whose failure raises much less concern with systemic risk. Scott Harrington, in his chapter titled "Capital Adequacy in Insurance and Reinsurance" (chapter 2), makes the case that for property and casualty companies, market discipline is effective in ensuring adequate levels of capital. Policyholders are sophisticated and risk sensitive and are advised by sophisticated parties—agents, brokers, and rating agencies. Similar observations are made about securities firms by Richard Herring and Til Schuermann in chapter 1, "Capital Regulation for Position Risk."

Models

Various chapters discuss the use of bank models to deal with risk. As Kupiec points out, bank models may be inferior to market discipline as a control device because models do not incorporate the external costs of bank failure and because they can be manipulated by their operators. But the general conclusion is that they do a better job than Basel command and control regulations in providing for adequate capital to deal with risk.

As the Herring-Schuermann chapter points out, models have been accepted by the Basel Committee for market risk since 1996, subject to some rather strict, perhaps overly strict, parameters. And as chapter 7, by Andrew Kuritzkes and Hal Scott ("Sizing Operational Risk and the Effect on Insurance Implications for the Basel II Capital Accord"), points out, models are acceptable under the Basel II proposals for operational risk for the most sophisticated banks (the advanced management approach, or AMA), albeit with an artificially low limit of 20% capital reduction attributable to insurance. The decision to allow banks to use models for operational risk is truly remarkable because there is virtually no track record for the actual use of such models. This is ironic insofar as Basel's opposition to credit models is based on claims that they cannot be verified.

Although models for credit risk have not been acceptable to Basel, chapter 6, "The Use of Internal Models," by Michel Crouhy, Dan Galai, and Robert Mark, shows that the credit risk models seem to set more appropriate levels of capital than the standardized Basel methodology. Compared to credit models, Basel II, like Basel I, requires too much capital for low-risk assets and too little for high-risk assets, continuing to give banks the perverse incentive to hold higher risk assets and providing no credit for diversification. Basel is probably right in observing that credit models are hard to verify. As shown by Crouhy, Galai, and Mark, a major part of the difficulty is that default is a relatively rare event and that validation of portfolio loss probabilities over a one-year period at the 99% confidence level implies 100 years of data. Nonetheless, it seems extreme to completely ignore the value of diversification. The problems of verification cannot justify treating the risks of a bank with 100 $1 million loans the same as a bank with one $100 million loan. Bank models are no less verifiable than the "Basel model" standardized methodology.

Basel is actually a bit hypocritical when it comes to credit models. While prohibiting banks from using them, it calibrates its own credit risk rules by using bank models. The calibration exercise involves a determination of what percentage of risk-weight assets to require in capital. In making this determination, BCBS has sought to use as a benchmark the percentage of risk-weight assets that the bank models require. This is back-door acceptance of modeling. If modeling is reliable for calibration, it is hard to understand why it is not acceptable for directly setting capital requirements.

As described by Herring and Schuermann and by Harrington, securities and insurance regulators generally do not permit their firms to use models. Neither the SEC net capital rule for securities firms nor the National

Association of Insurance Commissioners (NAIC) rules for insurance companies permit models. In the European Union, however, models are permitted for market risk of securities firms, since such firms are subject to the Basel market risk rules that permit models. The case for allowing models for securities and insurance firms seems particularly strong given the lower level concern with their failure. Herring and Schuermann show that the Basel and the NAIC rules produce substantially higher capital requirements in some instances for position risk than do models. The SEC has experimented with models for derivative dealers but has yet to propose their use. Kupiec's concern with the problem of moral hazard externalities in the use of bank models is much less important when it comes to firms that pose less systemic risk and do not enjoy a public safety net.

Regulation

There are numerous and good reasons for saying that command-and-control regulation by bank regulators is the least justified strategy for dealing with capital adequacy. First, it often gets the basics wrong, requiring too much capital for the best credit risks, and, as Kuritzkes and Scott show, defining operational risk to exclude the biggest source of risk, business risk, which is the only type of operational risk that can be handled only by capital. The risks they do include, control failures (e.g., embezzlement) and event risk (e.g., 9/11), can be dealt with by better controls or insurance. There is substantial and mounting opposition to the imposition of capital requirements for operational risk. Harrington regards the NAIC risk-based capital standards and the E.U. standards based on simple proportions of premiums, claims, or related liabilities as crude measures of risk. It is not surprising that firms with different risk profiles and controls, and with their own money at stake, might do a better job in determining needed capital than regulators promulgating standardized rules.

Second, enforcement of mandatory requirements is weak in the United States, as Philip Wellons shows in his chapter, "Enforcement of Risk-Based Capital Rules" (chapter 8), and in Japan, where undercapitalized banks have been permitted to stay afloat. The level of regulatory capital is highly dependent on recognition of losses; this is within the control of supervisors, who, as Wellons notes, may have incentives to avoid requiring such recognition.

Third, it is very difficult to have consistent application of mandatory capital adequacy rules or enforcement across borders. Basel II, which is significantly more complex than Basel I, gives much more reign to supervisory discretion. It wrongly assumes that risks are the same in all countries, despite significant variations in macroeconomies, taxation, law, and accounting (Scott and Iwahara 1994). As Kuritzkes and Scott point out, legal risk, a major component of operational risk, is significantly different among individual states within the United States, let alone among countries.

Consistency of application will suffer further in the future as the United States applies Basel I and Europe applies Basel II to most of its banks.

Further, some U.S. banking organizations operating in Europe—those other than the top 10 or 20—will face the prospect of having Basel I applicable to their holding company and domestic bank subsidiaries, while Basel II is applied to their European subsidiaries.

Fourth, Basel requirements encourage inefficient regulatory arbitrage. While it may be efficient for banks to make and hold loans to good credits, excessive capital requirements could force banks to dispose of them through securitization. Or, rules on the amount of capital required to be held by banks selling protection on credit derivatives could force such business away from banks and toward securities or insurance firms subject to lower capital requirements. Another striking example, noted by Herring and Schuermann, is that no capital is imposed on E.U. insurance companies for position risk, even though insurance companies hold more marketable securities than banks or insurance firms. Their scenario studies show that the same portfolio leads to substantially different required capital under the Basel and the NAIC rules than is required under SEC rules. This is a concern not only because capital regulation can significantly affect competition but also because the distorting effects of regulation may force business into the hands of the least efficient competitors.

Fifth, consolidated capital regulation of the holding company is fraught with difficulty. This is vividly demonstrated by Howell Jackson in chapter 3, "Consolidated Capital Regulation for Fiscal Conglomerates." Banks, securities firms, and insurance companies are each subject to different capital regimes—with good reason, given their different risks. When such firms, with their different capital structures, are consolidated under a holding company, it makes little sense to subject them to consolidated capital requirements under a single regime designed for banks. This then leads to exceptions to consolidation, which in turn raise problems. For example, Basel II does not consolidate insurance subsidiaries in recognition of the fact that it makes no sense to apply consolidated bank risk rules to such companies' activities. Instead, Basel requires the holding company to deduct its investment in the insurance company in calculating its own capital. This deduction requirement, too, makes little sense in many cases. The insurance company subsidiary may have a significant value, even an ascertainable market value, yet the holding company is unable to count this as capital.

Despite the weakness in the application of consolidated capital requirements, defenders point to the need to avoid two problems, excessive leverage and double gearing.[2] The excessive leverage problem is based on a concern that an overleveraged holding company that is in trouble may raid bank capital. But this can be prevented by prohibiting the raiding and by making sure that banks are always adequately capitalized. Such prohibitions may not be always observed, but if one posits noncompliance with rules, even rules against excessive holding company leverage could be breached.

The double-gearing problem is lucidly explained by Professor Jackson. The concern here is that a bank's investment in a subsidiary, through the downstreaming of cash, may be quite risky. Consolidated capital requirements attempt to remedy this problem by prohibiting the investing bank from counting its investment in a subsidiary as capital. As Jackson explains, consolidated capital requirements effectively risk-weight investments by banks in subsidiaries at 1250%. But this seems quite extreme—it cannot be the case that investments in all subsidiaries are equally risky, nor is there evidence that 1250% is the right riskweight. After all, even if the market rates the subsidiary as AAA, the 1250% risk weight still applies. Furthermore, banking organizations in many countries, such as the United States, do not make major investments through subsidiaries of banks. Such investments are made instead through the holding company. Indeed, U.S. legislation requires this result in many cases.

Professor Jackson's essay does cite an advantage to consolidated capital requirements; they permit the holding of capital against the total risk of a financial company. Firms themselves consolidate operations across affiliates in determining their own economic capital. Indeed, in determining economic capital, firms make this determination only on a consolidated basis. As Jackson also points out, however, firms take into account the risk-reducing effects of diversification in making such calculations. As already discussed, Basel does not permit taking diversification into account at the bank level for credit risk, and only to a very limited extent for market risk, and this obtains for consolidated capital, as well. This is understandable for regulators. Firms determining economic capital—only on a consolidated basis—implicitly assume that there are no organizational boundaries between firm units; it is all for one and one for all. Regulators would never permit this because, in effect, it requires cross-guarantees among all the units in the banking organization. Bank regulators would not permit the bank to extend such guarantees.

Excess Capital

Many of the chapters observe that the various capital requirements proposed by Basel II should not be considered binding because so many financial institutions already hold much more capital than they are required to do through regulation. Some firms hold excess capital to avoid any supervisory intervention or to qualify for certain activities—for example, only well-capitalized U.S. banking companies can engage in certain merchant banking, securities, or insurance activities—but the level of capital held seems to exceed these levels, as well. Harrington reports that banks hold 178% of required capital, while nonlife insurance companies hold 327%. Herring and Schuermann cite the Joint Forum Survey (Joint Forum 2001) data that show that banks hold between 1.3 and 1.8 times the required capital, while securities firms hold 1.2 to 1.3 and insurance firms hold 5 times the required capital.

Nevertheless, these percentages do not necessarily mean that banks are holding excess regulatory capital. A possible explanation, offered by Kuritzkes and Scott, is that banks, like other firms, generally hold a substantial percentage of their capital, roughly 25% to 30%, to protect against business risk, which, as noted earlier, is not included by Basel in the categories of risk for which regulatory capital is required. In addition, neither Basel I nor Basel II requires capital for interest-rate risk. If one is interested in requiring enough capital to provide a comfortable cushion against failure, Basel's regulatory capital requirements are critically deficient, since they omit requiring capital for the most important risks. Obviously, both the market and the bank economic capital models would require capital for business risk and interest-rate risk.

To illustrate, suppose a bank has 100 in capital but Basel requires only 70 for credit, market, and operational (nonbusiness) risk. Further suppose that the bank's internal model suggests that it should have 40 in capital for business risk and 10 for interest rate risk. The bank should hold 120 in total capital to cover all of its risks but holds only 100. While it appears to have excess capital for Basel purposes, it may actually be undercapitalized. The 100 capital may fully cover its business and interest rate risk but only 50 of its required 70 of regulatory capital.

CONCLUSIONS

The chapters in this book show that securities firms, insurance companies, and banks should be subject to different capital requirements. The effect, therefore, is also to call into question the use of bank-style consolidated capital requirements for financial service holding companies.

The study further shows that market discipline is better than capital regulation, particularly for securities and insurance firms. It also shows that models-based regulation is preferable to command and control regulations.

Basel faces an uncertain future. Its Basel II command-and-control proposals have already been rejected by the United States as too complex and unreliable. It is to be hoped that this rejection will stimulate a rethinking of the approach for all types of financial institutions and give new momentum to the trend toward placing more reliance on market discipline and models-based regulation.

Notes

1. The market share in total assets of the top three banks on average over the 1990–97 period was France, 41%; Germany, 45%; Italy, 35%; Japan, 21%; the United Kingdom, 55%; and the United States, 19% (Cetorelli 2003).

2. Fears of contagion are also used to justify a consolidated capital requirement. The idea is that if the holding company, or any nonbank unit within it, fails, there could be a run on the bank. This is, of course, the same argument that was used for many years to justify limitations on the activities of bank affiliates. This scenario can be stopped in its tracks by proper use of a central bank's lender-of-last-resort authority. It is interesting that neither insurance nor securities supervisors pay any heed to consolidated capital regulation; they do not view the risk of a contagious collapse or systemic risk as a serious problem.

References

Basel Committee on Banking Supervision (BCBS). 2001. Joint Forum Survey on Risk Management Practices and Regulatory Capital, Cross-Sectoral Comparison (November). Available at: www.bis.org/publ/joint03.pdf.

Cetorelli, Nicola. 2003. Real Effects of Bank Concentration and Competition in Europe. Paper for the World Bank Conference on Bank Concentration and Competition (April). Available at: www.worldbank.org/research/interest/confs/042003/europe_cetorelli2.pdf.

European Commission. 2003. Third Consultation Paper: Review of Capital Requirements for Banks and Investment Firms (July 1). Available at: http://europa.eu.int/comm/internal_market/regcapital/index_en.htm#cp3.

Gunther, Jeffery W., Mark E. Levonian, and Robert R. Moore. 2001. Can the Stock Market Tell Bank Supervisors Anything They Don't Already Know? *Federal Reserve Bank of Dallas Economic and Financial Review* 2: 2–9. Available at: www.dallasfed.org/research/efr/2001/efr0102a.pdf.

Joint Forum. 2001. Risk Management Practices and Regulatory Capital, Cross-Sectoral Comparison. Basel Committee Joint Publication No. 4. Available at: www.bis.org/publ/joint04.pdf.

Karolyi, G. Andrew. 2003. Does International Financial Contagion Really Exist? Dice Center Working Paper No. 2003-12. Available at: www.cob.ohio-state.edu/fin/dice/papers/2003/2003-12.pdf.

Krainer, John, and Jose A. Lopez. 2003. Using Equity Market Information to Monitor Banking Institutions. *Federal Reserve Bank of San Francisco Economic Letter* 2003-01. Available at: www.frbsf.org/publications/economics/letter/2003/el2003-01.pdf.

Scott, Hal S., and Shinsaku Iwahara. 1994. In Search of a Level Playing Field: The Implementation of the Basel Accord in Japan and the United States. Washington, D.C.: Group of Thirty Occasional Paper No. 46.

1

Capital Regulation for Position Risk in Banks, Securities Firms, and Insurance Companies

RICHARD HERRING AND TIL SCHUERMANN

We examine why these regulatory differences exist and what they imply for differences in minimum capital requirements for position risk. We consider differences in the definition and measurement of regulatory capital, and we quantify differences in the capital charges for position risk by reference to a model portfolio that contains a variety of financial instruments, including equity, fixed income instruments, swaps, foreign exchange positions, and options—instruments that may appear in the portfolios of securities firms, banks, or insurance companies. For most leading firms in the financial services industry, however, market forces, not minimum regulatory capital requirements, appear to play the dominant role in firms' capital decisions. Thus we conclude by considering measures to enhance market discipline.

This chapter demonstrates an important finding of this book: that banks, securities firms, and insurance companies each need to set capital differently. Although banks and securities firms do engage in similar businesses, credit risk is a much more significant consideration for banks. In addition, securities firms pose less danger of systemic risk. The chapter shows that market discipline, rather than regulatory requirements, already drives capital decisions by securities firms.

INTRODUCTION

Currently, banks, securities firms, and insurance companies conduct trading businesses that involve many of the same financial instruments and several of the same counterparties but that are subject to very different capital regulations. In this chapter, we examine why these regulatory differences exist and what they imply for differences in minimum capital requirements for position risk, one of the key risks that confronts financial institutions.

We consider differences in the definition and measurement of regulatory capital, and we quantify differences in the capital charges for position risk by reference to a model portfolio that contains a variety of financial instruments, including equity, fixed-income instruments, swaps, foreign exchange positions, and options that may appear in the portfolios of securities firms, banks, or insurance companies. For most leading firms in the financial services industry, however, market forces, not minimum regulatory capital requirements, appear to play the dominant role in firms' capital decisions. Thus, we conclude by considering measures to enhance market discipline.

Position Risk in Securities Firms, Banks, and Insurance Companies

"Market risk" is "the risk of losses in on- and off-balance-sheet positions arising from movements in market prices." (See BCBS 1996a.) "Asset liquidity risk" is generally combined with market risk and represents "the risk that an entity will be unable to unwind a position in a particular financial instrument at or near its market value because of a lack of depth or disruption in the market for that instrument" (Joint Forum 2001, p. 17). In what follows, we use the term "position risk" to refer to the combination of market risk and asset liquidity risk.

Position risk that is large relative to an institution's capacity to bear loss can seriously injure or even destroy a financial institution. Over the past thirty years, the list of financial institutions that have been severely harmed by excessive position risks includes Franklin National Bank, Bankhaus Herstatt, Barings Bank, Piper Jaffray, Banesto, Credit Lyonnais, Daiwa Bank, Long Term Capital Management, and Allied Irish Bank. (See inter alia Crouhy, Galai, and Mark 2001; Jorion 2001.) A much longer list of firms, including many of the most active international financial institutions, has incurred trading losses that have exceeded at least one quarter's earnings.

Position risk is the most important category of risk faced by securities firms because proprietary positions in a wide range of financial instruments are closely allied with the core activities of underwriting, trading, and dealing in securities. Consequently, position risk has been the principal focus of capital regulation among securities regulators. Although the International Organization of Securities Commissions (IOSCO) has tried to harmonize capital requirements for securities firms internationally,[1] substantial differences remain among even the Group of Ten (G-10) countries that make up the Basel Committee on Banking Supervision (Basel Committee or BCBS). The members of the European Union (E.U.) have harmonized the regulation of position risk in securities firms (as well as banks) with the adoption of the Capital Adequacy Directive (CAD) in 1993,[2] but securities regulators in Canada, Japan, the United States, and other non-E.U. countries rely on a different framework that requires securities firms to maintain minimum levels of highly liquid assets to meet promptly all obligations to customers and other market participants. In the quantitative analysis that follows, we focus on the E.U. CAD approach and the U.S. SEC (Securities and Exchange Commission) net capital approach (NCA) because the securities firms that conduct the largest volume of cross-border activities are headquartered in these countries.

Credit risk is the most important category of risk for most banks and so the main focus of bank capital regulation has been credit risk.[3] Indeed, capital regulation for credit risk was the subject of the first internationally coordinated attempt to harmonize capital regulation in the financial services industry, the Basel Capital Accord (BCBS 1988).

Large internationally active banks have always been active participants in some financial markets, particularly foreign exchange markets,[4] to serve the needs of their clients and to conduct their own proprietary trading operations. But, as many of the banks' most creditworthy clients began to substitute capital market instruments for bank loans, banks began to serve these clients more actively in their trading rooms than on their balance sheets. Position risk became an increasingly important factor at these banks, and so the regulatory authorities responded with an Amendment to the Capital Accord to encompass position risk in capital regulation (BCBS1996a). The amendment provided internationally active banks with a choice between a standardized approach (similar in spirit but significantly different in detail from the NCA) and the supervised use of the banks' own internal models for setting capital charges for position risk. In the quantitative analysis we focus on the standardized approach and three different kinds of internal models used in internationally active banks. These Basel approaches to setting capital charges for position risk provide the framework within which internationally active banks and European securities firms operate.

In contrast to banks and securities firms, the main risk to insurance companies springs from the liability side of the balance sheet, rather than from the asset side. The fundamental risk facing insurance companies is "underwriting risk," the risk that they will be unable to pay their contractual obligations to policyholders. This may occur because estimates of future payouts under the terms of insurance contracts are too low relative to the premiums charged so that technical provisions are inadequate to meet the claims of policyholders.[5] Capital regulation in the insurance industry has focused mainly on establishing a buffer to make sure that insurance obligations can be met even if technical provisions prove insufficient.[6] But the adequacy of technical provisions depends not only on estimates of payouts under insurance contracts and costs of dealing with claims but also on the returns on invested premiums, and so insurance companies are also subject to position risk (although the term is not generally used in the insurance industry). Insurance companies tend to characterize this as asset or investment risk (Joint Forum 2001, p. 17).

Insurance regulation has not generally focused on position risk per se, even though in most G-10 countries insurance companies hold larger amounts of financial securities than banks (IMF 2002, p. 33). E.U. rules do not make an explicit charge for position risk, although presumably it is implicitly taken into account in judging the adequacy of technical provisions.[7] Instead, countries in the European Union rely primarily on strict rules regarding permissible investments and limits on concentrations of investment. Nonetheless, many of the largest insurance companies in Europe sustained heavy losses during 2002 because of declining prices on world equity markets (*Economist* 2003). In the United States, however, the National Association of

Insurance Commissioners (NAIC) has developed a risk-based capital framework (RBC) that sets an explicit capital charge for investment risk as the weighted sum of assets where the weights implicitly reflect not only market risk but also credit risk and operational risk. Since this approach is more comparable to the regulation of position risk in banks and securities firms than the E.U. approach, we focus on the NAIC approach for insurance firms in the quantitative analysis.

THE RATIONALE FOR AND THE SCOPE OF CAPITAL REQUIREMENTS FOR POSITION RISK

The literature on the general rationale for capital regulation in financial institutions is extensive and has been the subject of several recent surveys (Ball and Stoll 1998; Benston 1999; Berger, Herring, and Szegö 1995; Dimson and Marsh 1995). Rather than review this literature, we highlight similarities and differences in the rationale for and consequent differences in the scope of capital regulation in the three sectors of the financial services industry—banks, securities firms, and insurance companies.

Consumer Protection

One common objective of capital regulation in each of the three sectors is the protection of consumers from exploitation by opaque and better informed financial institutions. In the banking sphere, the objective is depositor protection. In securities regulation, the objective is investor protection. And in insurance regulation, the objective is policyholder protection.[8] Capital regulation is not, of course, the only regulatory tool deployed to protect consumers, nor is it the most efficient regulatory tool for this purpose.[9] But consumer protection is one of the principal explicit reasons used to justify capital requirements for financial institutions in each of the three sectors.

Consumers of financial services—particularly unsophisticated consumers and investors—find it difficult to evaluate the quality of financial information, products, and services provided to them. In part, this is because payment for most financial products and services must be made in the current period in exchange for benefits that are promised far into the future. But even after the decision is made and financial results are realized, it is often difficult to determine whether an unfavorable outcome was the result of bad luck, incompetence, or dishonesty. Customers face a problem of asymmetric information in evaluating financial services. Consequently, they are vulnerable to *adverse selection*, the possibility that they will choose an incompetent or dishonest firm. They are also vulnerable to *moral hazard*, the possibility that firms or its agents will subordinate their interests to those of the firm itself or another customer or even engage in fraud.[10]

Capital requirements are intended to mitigate the risks of adverse selection by ensuring that the financial firm has at least some minimal level of resources to honor its commitments to its customers. Capital requirements are intended to mitigate moral hazard by ensuring that the owners of a financial institution have a stake in ensuring that the firm does not engage in fraud and conforms to conduct of business rules, if only to avoid fines or loss of equity value. To be effective in this role, capital requirements must be sensitive to the risks to which an institution is exposed. It follows that, if position risk is a significant factor, capital requirements should be sensitive to the position risks taken by a financial institution.

Systemic Risk

Systemic Risk and Banks

Although regulators in all three sectors emphasize consumer/investor protection, they differ with regard to the emphasis they place on preventing systemic risk. Bank regulators have long regarded the prevention of systemic risk as the fundamental rationale for imposing capital requirements on banks. Systemic risk may be defined as the risk of a sudden, unanticipated shock that would damage the financial system to such an extent that economic activity in the wider economy would suffer. The assumption is that shareholders will not take account of the social costs of systemic risk in their capital decisions and so will tend to hold less capital than if these spillover costs were considered.

Banks are often thought to be a source of systemic risk because of their central role in the payments system and in the allocation of financial resources, as well as because of the fragility of their financial structure.[11,12] Their financial structure is highly vulnerable to a loss in confidence because of the first-come, first-served nature of their short-term deposit liabilities, the illiquid nature of their loan portfolios, and the high degree of leverage they customarily maintain. Diamond and Dybvig (1983) have shown that bank runs can be self-fulfilling prophecies. If no one believes a bank run is about to occur, only those with immediate needs for liquidity will withdraw their funds, and, assuming that banks have sufficient liquid assets to meet these normal liquidity demands, there will be no panic. But this is a fragile equilibrium. If, instead, everyone believes a bank run is about to occur, depositors will race to be first in line in order to liquidate their deposits before the losses caused by the shock and the consequent rushed sale of illiquid assets exhaust their banks' capital positions. In the Diamond and Dybvig model, the shock may be essentially random (one well-known extension of the model characterizes the shocks as "sunspots"), or the shock may be information about a deterioration in business conditions that is expected to erode the bank's capital position.[13]

A shock from one bank may be contagiously transmitted to other banks. This may occur because other banks are exposed (or are thought to be exposed) to similar risks or because of *actual*, direct exposures to the damaged bank in interbank markets and/or the clearing and settlement process that underlies the payments system. More insidiously, this may also happen because of *suspected* exposures to the damaged bank. In the absence of clear and convincing evidence to the contrary, market participants are likely to assume that the institutions least able to withstand the shock have been damaged by it. They will attempt to protect themselves by liquidating their claims on the suspected, weaker institutions and reallocating their portfolios in favor of claims on institutions perceived to be stronger. The result is a flight to quality.

The real cost associated with a banking crisis is the spillover effect on the real economy. If banks are liquidated, the aggregate capabilities associated with the banks' teams of employees, who are able to distinguish successfully between good assets and bad, may be destroyed. In this case, total lending may be cut back a by a large amount, and a severe recession may ensue. Although in recent financial crises, such as those in Scandinavia in the early 1990s or in the United States in the 1980s, governments have prevented the widespread collapse of the financial system by extensive intervention, historically this has not been the case. Sometimes, banks have been allowed to fail in large numbers. In such cases, the recessions associated with banking crises were often severe. Recovery depended not only on rebuilding equity capital and reserves but also on rebuilding new teams of employees that could distinguish between good and bad assets.

The role of risk-sensitive capital regulation in guarding against systemic risk is twofold. First, capital is a buffer against loss, and so the larger an institution's capital relative to its risk exposure, the smaller the probability that it will be fatally damaged by a shock. Second, the larger an institution's capital relative to its risk exposure, the smaller the incentive for shareholders to take risks and therefore the smaller the probability that it will be fatally damaged by a shock (Herring and Vankudre 1987).

Bank regulators have demanded that capital requirements be applied on a consolidated basis. One of the first papers issued by the Basel Committee (BCBS 1979, p. 1) emphasized the importance of achieving consolidated supervision, arguing that supervisors must be "in a position to examine the totality of each bank's business worldwide." The principle is further refined in the recent proposed revision to the Basel Accord (BCBS 2001a, p. 11), which details procedures for consolidated corporate parents and siblings of banks.[14]

This emphasis on consolidation stems partly from a concern that banking groups should be constrained from double or multiple gearing by borrowing through one entity to increase the measured equity in a regulated entity. But it also stems from a concern about reputation risk and the assumption that banks are even more vulnerable to contagious transmission of shocks within a banking group than across banking groups. Thus, bank regulators insist on monitoring exposures to risk and capital adequacy on a groupwide basis not just an entity-by-entity (or solo) basis. This concern about taking a groupwide view in crisis prevention also extends to crisis management. Bank regulators believe that they need to have a consolidated view of the banking group in order to minimize the systemic consequences of a shock to the banking group, since an insolvency in one part of the group is expected to jeopardize the solvency of the banking entities in the group.

Systemic Risk and Securities Firms

In the United States, regulators of securities firms have not been given a mandate to guard against systemic risk. Since investor protection is the main regulatory objective, capital regulation for position risk extends only to the broker-dealer, the entity that deals with unsophisticated investors, not the consolidated securities firm, which may contain several other entities.

The rationale for this sharp difference in the objectives for and the scope of securities regulation flows from four key structural differences between banks and securities firms. First, securities firms segregate customer funds from the firms' own funds. Thus, bad news about the firms' own assets need not cause concern about the assets of the firms' clients.[15] Moreover, if a securities firm should fail, it is relatively easy to transfer the assets of that firm to another firm with minimal disruption in services to the client.

Second, liabilities of the securities firm are not deposit obligations payable on a first-come, first-served basis. Instead, they are generally dated debt instruments such as commercial paper, collateralized loans, or claims that have a payoff contingent on the performance of the firm. This liability structure protects securities firms from runs motivated by "sun spots" or other disturbances that become self-fulfilling prophecies.

Third, securities firms generally hold liquid, tradeable assets that are marked to market daily. This relatively transparent balance sheet reduces the vulnerability of the typical securities firm to the asymmetric information problems that arise from the opacity of a typical bank balance sheet. Moreover, in the event that a securities firm is subject to a loss in confidence and a consequent inability to borrow, it can reduce the size of its balance sheet relatively easily, without incurring fire-sale losses on the liquidation of assets.

Fourth, securities firms do not have direct access to large-value payment systems. Although securities firms generate very substantial payments in the course of conducting business for their clients and for their own, proprietary accounts, they rely on commercial banks to clear and settle such payments. Thus, the collapse of a securities firm will impact the payments system only to the extent that it causes the collapse of the bank that clears and settles payments on its behalf.

The upshot of these structural differences is that securities firms should be less vulnerable to shocks than banks. Moreover, in the event that a shock, nonetheless, causes a securities firm to become insolvent, the collapse of a securities firm is less likely to spread contagiously to the rest of the financial system and become a source of systemic risk.

In the United States, the most important test of these hypotheses to date is the collapse of the Drexel Burnham Lambert Group (DBLG). When DBLG filed for protection under Chapter 11 of the bankruptcy laws,[16] the authorities limited their role to facilitating an orderly unwinding of the affairs of DBLG and its regulated subsidiaries (Committee on Payments and Settlement Systems 1996, p. 6).[17] Client accounts at the regulated broker/dealer were transferred to other firms with minimal disruption of services. The anticipated flight to quality in the government securities market was slight and quickly reversed. Moreover, the Dow Jones average actually finished the day above the previous close.

Can one infer from the absence of systemic disturbances during the collapse of DBLG that securities firms do not pose a systemic threat to the financial system? Four trends in the international financial system over the decade since the collapse of DBLG suggest that such a conclusion may not be warranted.

First, leading securities firms have become increasingly international. Not only do they participate in securities markets around-the-clock and around the globe, but also they operate through a complex structure of affiliates in many different countries with differing bankruptcy regimes, and so it may be much more difficult to unwind the affairs of a leading securities firm without disrupting markets.

Second, securities firms have increasingly affiliated with commercial banks and/or insurance companies to form financial conglomerates. Universal banking countries have long integrated the securities business with traditional commercial banking, but over the past decade financial liberalization has enabled firms in the United States and Japan, which formerly required strict separation of commercial banking and the securities business, to combine the two activities. When the securities business is integrated with banking, then systemic concerns about banking may extend to the securities business, as well.

Third, securities firms have consolidated to form larger and larger entities. Partly, this is because the formation of financial conglomerates has often involved mergers and acquisitions, but the pace of consolidation has been even faster among firms in the same segment of the financial services industry. Although it is possible that larger financial firms will be less likely to fail, the occurrence of failure is more likely to be associated with systemic risk, since the spillover effects on the rest of the financial system are bound to be greater.

Fourth, the largest firms are becoming increasingly involved in global trading activities, particularly over-the-counter (OTC) derivatives. From 1992 to 1999, OTC derivatives markets quadrupled in notional value (Group of Ten 2001)). Moreover, the concentration of activity among the largest firms increased over the decade with the top 3 firms accounting for 27.2% and the top 10 accounting for 54.7% of the total OTC derivatives activities in the largest centers.[18] There is also a corresponding increasing concentration of risk in the clearing and settlement systems for payments and securities transactions.[19]

Regulators outside the United States have taken a different view of the likelihood that securities firms may be a source of systemic risk. Indeed, the IOSCO (1998, p. 4) report on the use of internal models to establish position risk requirements lists "the reduction of systemic risk" as the second rationale for minimum capital requirements.[20]

The narrow focus of U.S. capital regulation on the broker-dealer in U.S. securities firms also contrasts sharply with the tradition in Europe. Continental European supervisors have customarily applied consolidated supervision and capital regulation to the securities activities of the universal banks in their domain, just as if they were any other traditional banking activity. Indeed, the E.U. Capital Adequacy Directive requires consolidated supervision for institutions headquartered in the European Union and applies equally to banks and securities firms.

With the recent Directive on the Prudential Supervision of Financial Conglomerates, the European Union has gained potential leverage to subject U.S. securities firms to consolidated regulation and supervision. The directive may force securities firms that are not subject to consolidated supervision by a "competent" home country authority to form an E.U. holding company that will be subject to consolidated supervision in Europe or face substantially higher capital requirements on their European operations.[21]

The U.S. response is evolving. At the request of the Securities and Exchange Commission, the six U.S. securities firms most active in over-the-counter (OTC) securities markets formed the Derivatives Policy Group (DPG) and agreed to report to the SEC voluntarily on the activities of the unregulated affiliates of regulated broker/dealers in OTC derivatives markets.[22] In addition, the Gramm-Leach-Bliley Financial Modernization Act has given the SEC the authority to authorize an Investment Bank Holding Company that might, in principle, provide some sort of consolidated supervision and regulation of securities companies. The SEC, however, has not disclosed how or, indeed, whether it will implement this part of the legislation. The European Union has made clear that the DPG initiative is not sufficient to meet its concerns, and, while the formation of a Financial Services Holding Company under the supervision of the Federal Reserve Board by a securities firm would meet the criterion of competent consolidated supervision, none of the major, internationally active securities firms that is not affiliated with a bank has chosen to form a financial services holding company.

Systemic Risk and Insurance Companies

Systemic risk has not been a major preoccupation of insurance regulators, and there has been no evidence of the failure of an insurance company being a significant source of systemic risk.[24,25] Although failures of insurance companies can impose heavy private costs and can disrupt insurance markets, they do not appear to generate significant spillover impacts on other institutions and markets.[26] Nor does there appear to be significant contagion across members of a corporate family of insurance companies. For example, ING cut loose a failing insurance subsidiary in London without substantial repercussions for its ability to do business (Ladbury 1995).[27] Since policyholder protection is the primary regulatory objective, capital regulation has tended to be focused on individual insurance companies, on a solo basis, rather than on a consolidated basis.

The main reason for this difference from bank regulatory practice resides in the liability structure of insurance companies. Insurance companies are not reliant on first-come, first-served demand liabilities, and so they are not vulnerable to a loss of confidence and subsequent pressures to liquidate assets rapidly in order to meet the demands of creditors. Life insurance claims tend to be highly predictable, and property-casualty claims can often be paid off slowly (Kuritzkes and Scott 2002).[28] Indeed, property and casualty insurers may delay payments through investigative procedures and litigation. Thus, insurance companies are unlikely to find it necessary to incur fire-sale losses on the liquidation of their assets and exacerbate market dislocations by selling assets in markets with falling prices.[29]

In summary, capital regulation in each of the three sectors is motivated by a concern for protecting consumers of financial services. Banking regulation is distinctive, however, in its additional emphasis on capital regulation to safeguard against systemic risk. This concern leads banking regulators to insist on applying capital regulation on a consolidated basis. The differences in scope of capital regulation between securities regulators in the European Union and those in the United States reflect differences in history—the tradition of universal banking in continental Europe and the more segmented approach taken in the United States and the United Kingdom. The European Union applies the same capital regulation for market risk to banks and securities firms on a consolidated basis. The SEC, which lacks a mandate to safeguard the financial system against systemic risk, applies capital regulation to the registered broker-dealer only, not to the consolidated positions of the securities firm. Similarly, insurance regulators tend to apply capital regulation on a solo basis, to individual insurance companies, rather than to the consolidated position of insurance groups. The upshot is that most insurance groups and U.S. securities firms can take position risks that are not subject to regulatory capital charges.

DEFINITION OF CAPITAL AND THE REGULATORY
DISPOSITION OF FAILING FIRMS

Although position risk is subject to capital regulation in all three financial sectors, both the capital charges and the definition of capital eligible to meet these capital charges differs from sector to sector. In this section, we examine the rationale for differences in the definitions of eligible capital among the Basel Committee, the SEC, and the NAIC. In the next section, we consider differences in the capital charge for position risk.

Some of the differences in the definitions of regulatory capital stem from fundamental differences in the underlying business and in implicit assumptions about how long it would take to detect and merge or unwind a failing institution. Securities firms hold mainly marketable securities that can be valued daily—or even more frequently—and so they can be monitored at frequent intervals at relatively low cost. Moreover, because the positions of a securities firm are mainly marketable instruments, the authorities would expect to be able to achieve a prompt and orderly liquidation in which customer accounts could be transferred to another firm in the event of financial distress if a merger with a stronger firm was not possible. Since the primary objective of capital regulation is the protection of customers of the securities firm, the regulatory authorities are willing to count as regulatory capital a wide range of instruments that are subordinate to the claims of customers. Subordinated debt, moreover, enables firms to adjust their capital flexibly and at relatively low cost as their position risks fluctuate, because issuance costs are lower for debt than equity.

Although banks also hold substantial amounts of marketable securities, most bank assets do not trade in broad, deep secondary markets. Thus, it is relatively costly to monitor the banks daily, and so it is likely that a longer lag will occur before regulators can detect deterioration in a bank's condition. Moreover, because bank regulators are concerned with systemic risk as well as depositor protection, they place a strong emphasis on remediating a failing firm or finding a merger partner; the option of liquidating the bank is considered only as a last resort. For that reason, bank regulators place heavy emphasis on forms of "patient" capital that can permit the bank to continue operation while absorbing losses and without adding to debt servicing pressures in times of stress. By this logic, debt instruments are considered inferior forms of capital, if they qualify for regulatory capital at all. Even though suitably subordinated debt may protect depositors against loss, it imposes an additional debt-servicing burden on a bank and reduces the time regulators have to identify and attempt to remediate a faltering bank. Moreover, subordinated debt is available to absorb loss only after the bank is declared insolvent.[30]

Although insurance companies also hold substantial amounts of marketable instruments, their contractual obligations are much longer term than those of securities firms or banks. This gives insurance regulators a longer time than their counterparts in the other two sectors to detect and deal with financial distress. Rather than facing immediate pressure to deal with a faltering firm because of deposit runs or margin or collateral calls, insurance regulators face pressure mainly from the slower paced decisions of policy-holders to let their insurance contracts lapse or, in the case of some life insurance contracts, from policyholders who exercise options to withdraw funds. Since their primary objective is to protect policyholders, insurance regulators typically ring-fence the assets and liabilities of a faltering insurance company, effectively closing it to new business until its policy obligations can be transferred to another insurance company (Joint Forum 2001, p. 33). Insurance regulators place heavier emphasis on reserves than on capital to protect policyholders from loss (Joint Forum 2001, p. 12).

Net Worth

Each of the three definitions of capital has one element in common—net worth. But, even this element of regulatory capital is not directly comparable across the three sectors, because net worth is an accounting residual that depends on the accounting conventions used for the various elements of the balance sheet, and, reflecting historical differences in the underlying business, accounting conventions differ across the three sectors. In what follows we focus on differences across the three sectors in the United States with only passing reference to differences within sectors across countries.[31]

Figure 1.1 displays pro forma balance sheets for a securities firm, bank, and insurance company.[32] Securities firms are required to employ mark-to-market accounting practices because most of the assets and liabilities of securities firms are marketable securities. Positions are recorded at market or fair value, with unrealized gains and losses reflected in the income statement. Values are based on listed prices where possible; when listed prices are not available or when the firm believes that liquidating its position could affect market prices, fair values are used. Fair values are based on internal

Generic Bank (cost, accrual, and fair value)	
Assets	*Liabilities*
Cash reserves	Deposits
Trading account assets	Borrowings
Investment account securities	Trading liabilities
Fed funds sold and securities purchased under agreements to resell	Subordinated debt
Gross loans and leases	Net Worth
(less allowance for loan and lease losses)	Common stock
Other assets	Noncumulative perpetual preferred stock
	Other preferred stock
	Retained earnings
Generic Securities Firm (fair value)	
Assets	*Liabilities*
Cash and cash equivalents	Commercial paper and short-term debt
Securities and other financial instruments owned	Securities sold but not yet repurchased
Securities purchased under agreements to resell	Securities sold under agreements to repurchase
Receivables and accrued interest	Senior notes
Other assets	Subordinated debt
	Net Worth
	Common stock
	Preferred stock
	Retained earnings
Generic Insurance Company (statutory accounting principles)	
Assets	*Liabilities*
Cash and cash equivalents	Technical reserves (policy obligations)
Investments	Asset valuation reserves
Other assets	Other liabilities
	Surplus
	Common stock
	Borrowed surplus
	Unassigned surplus

Figure 1.1. Stylized Pro-Forma Balance Sheets. Source: Authors' compilation.

pricing models. They should reflect management's best judgment about the value of a financial instrument, and for that reason they are much more difficult to verify objectively than listed prices. As investigations of Enron's accounting practices have shown, the managerial discretion inherent in fair value procedures can be subject to abuse.[33]

Under the assumption that market prices are efficient, they are as likely to rise as fall, and so there is no rationale for a revaluation reserve for expected losses in a balance sheet that is drawn up according to fair value conventions. Consequently, U.S. securities firms are not permitted to maintain reserves except for probable losses due to pending litigation (Joint Forum 2001, p. 30).

Bank trading accounts are also subject to fair value accounting standards, but the banking book is subject to accrual accounting standards. Thus, the same financial instrument may be valued in two different ways depending on whether the bank has classified it as available for sale or in the trading book, or in the banking book as an investment asset to be held to maturity. (Bank supervisory authorities attempt to curb abuses of this discretion by monitoring shifts between the trading book and the banking book.)

Financial instruments in the banking book are recorded at cost so that capital gains are not recognized unless they are realized. This affords bank managers some degree of discretion over the recognition of capital gains that can be used to manage earnings (Carey 1993). Loans are reported at the principal amount outstanding, net of unearned income. The main rationale for using accrual accounting rather than fair value accounting is that many bank assets, particularly loans, are not traded in secondary markets, and it is assumed that they will be held to maturity. Although valuing individual loans is often difficult, the bank knows that, on average, some loans will not be fully repaid. This is reflected in an allowance for losses on loans and leases, which is a valuation allowance for probable losses inherent in the portfolio as of the balance sheet date. To some extent, the allowance for losses may be regarded as an attempt to mark the portfolio of loans and leases to market, but it is intended to reflect only the loss in the event of default, not changes in market value due to changes in the credit quality of the borrower (transition risk) or a change in the market price of credit risk (spread risk).[34] Similarly, reserves appear as a liability account to cover potential off-balance-sheet credit losses (Everett et al. 2002, p. 8).

These differences in accounting conventions mean that net worth in a securities firm is not directly comparable to net worth in a bank. The value of securities in the banking book do not reflect unrealized capital gains or losses, and the allowance for loss may be a very imprecise way of marking loans to market. Furthermore, bank regulators place additional restrictions on the components of net worth that may be counted as regulatory capital. Reflecting their emphasis on "patient money," bank regulators restrict the kind of preferred stock that may be counted as core capital to noncumulative perpetual preferred. Other, cumulative, fixed-charge preferred shares count only as supplementary capital (BCBS 1988, p. 6).

The NAIC capital requirements are based on statutory accounting principles (SAP), not on generally accepted accounting principles. "Policyholders' Surplus" is the statutory accounting term that corresponds to net worth or owners' equity, although it differs in fundamental respects from the net worth concepts used by the SEC and the bank regulatory authorities. Statutory accounting principles are intended to have a decidedly conservative bias. For the most part, SAP requires the lowest of several possible values for assets and the highest of several possible values for liabilities. Indeed, under SAP, some assets are omitted from the balance sheet altogether if they cannot be converted to cash at or near a known amount. But, in addition to making a conservative statement of the *level* of net worth, the rules of SAP are designed to prevent sharp *fluctuations* in net worth. This can lead to a decided departure from conservative valuation principles. Assets reported on the balance sheet—"admitted assets"—are valued according to NAIC rules. Equity claims are shown at their "association values," which usually correspond to year-end market values. On several occasions, the NAIC has authorized insurance companies to use association values that have been significantly above year-end closing prices in order to prevent "technical insolvencies caused by temporarily depressed market prices" (Troxel and Bouchie 1995, p. 8). Some European insurance regulators have exercised similar forbearance recently. For example, German insurers had to book equity losses in the year they occurred, but in the wake of the decline in equity markets after September 11, insurers were allowed "to create 'hidden losses' by postponing write-downs if the market value of their investments fell below the purchase value" (Hulverscheidt and Fromme 2003).

Another exception to the generally conservative bias of SAP is the valuation of bonds, which appear on the balance sheet at amortized cost under the (possibly optimistic) assumption that an insurance company is a going concern that will not have to liquidate bonds at depressed prices before they mature. This approach ignores, of course, any increase in interest rates or widening of credit spreads that would adversely affect the fair value of the bond before maturity.[35]

Insurance companies establish reserves to cover both policyholder claims and declines in asset value. These appear on the balance sheet as a liability and are known as underwriting reserves, or technical provisions, or reserves. In general, underwriting reserves do reflect the intended conservative bias of SAP and are subject to statutory minimums that may exceed the company's own estimates. In contrast to "reserves" under GAAP, insurance reserves are a true liability.

Reserves, Subordinated Debt, and Other Forms of Regulatory Capital

As noted, broker-dealers in the United States are prohibited from maintaining valuation reserves because their mark-to-market accounting discipline should make them unnecessary. Securities firms are permitted to

supplement net worth with subordinated debt to meet capital requirements.[36] Qualifying subordinated debt must have a minimum maturity of
one year and provide that the broker-dealer's obligation to repay will be
suspended if repayment would cause the broker-dealer to violate its minimum capital requirement. Broker-dealers generally rely heavily on subordinated debt to meet their capital requirements.

Under the original Basel Capital Accord, banks are permitted to issue
subordinated debt as supplementary (Tier 2) capital up to a limit of 50% of
core (Tier 1) capital. Qualifying subordinated debt must have an original
maturity of more than five years and is subject to a cumulative 20% discount
for each of its last five years of maturity (BCBS 1988, p. 20). With the
Amendment to the Capital Accord for Market Risk, the BCBS expanded the
role for subordinated debt by recognizing an additional kind of capital (Tier 3)
for the purpose of meeting the capital requirement for market risk. Tier 3
capital is subordinated debt with an original maturity of at least two years.
Like the SEC, the bank regulators require that such debt include a lock-in
clause precluding payment of either interest or principal if the payment would
cause the issuing bank's risk-based capital ratio to fall below the minimum.
Although broker-dealers make extensive use of short-term subordinated debt,
banks do not.[37] At yearend 2001, none of the U.S. banks subject to the capital
requirement for market risk had Tier 3 capital outstanding.

In addition to subordinated debt, banks in the United States, under Basel
I, are permitted to include, as Tier 2 capital, the allowance for loan loss
reserves up to a maximum of 1.25% of risk-weighted assets (USGAO 1998,
p. 119). The Basel Accord also permits the inclusion of a number of other
items in Tier 2 capital at the discretion of the national authorities, including
undisclosed reserves, revaluation reserves, and a variety of hybrid capital
instruments (BCBS 1988, pp. 18–19).

The NAIC permits the use of debt (borrowed reserves) and valuation
reserves in the computation of total adjusted capital (Joint Forum 2001,
p. 50). In practice, subordinated debt is often issued by the parent and
down-streamed as equity in the regulated insurance company.

In summary, definitions of eligible regulatory capital differ across the
three sectors. Even those components of eligible regulatory capital that
appear to be the same, such as net worth, are in fact quite different because
of fundamental accounting differences. These accounting differences in turn
reflect differences in the basic business of each sector and implicit assumptions about how to deal with a failing firm. Consequently, it is difficult to
make meaningful comparisons about the quantity of regulatory capital
across banks, securities firms, and insurance companies. We can only concur
with the Joint Forum's (2001, p. 5) conclusion that "comparisons of individual elements of the different capital frameworks are potentially inappropriate and misleading."

In the following section, we provide an overview of the different approaches to setting capital charges for position risk across the three sectors.
After contrasting the Basel Committee approach for internationally active

banks with the net capital approach of the SEC and risk-based capital approach of the NAIC, we attempt to quantify some of the differences by reference to a model portfolio.

REGULATORY APPROACHES TO CAPITAL

Rules Versus Internal Models

Perhaps the most important difference in regulatory approaches is between reliance on rules and the use of internal models to set capital charges. Rule-based systems rely on regulators to specify the capital charge for each position. For example, under the SEC's NCA, equity positions must have 15% capital set aside if they are considered liquid or 40% if they are considered illiquid (SEC rule 15c3-1). Rules do not take into account diversification benefits achieved through less than perfect correlation (the so-called portfolio effect). While they are relatively simple to understand and implement, rules have the disadvantage of being inflexible. They have difficulty dealing with product innovation, whether that innovation is designed to benefit clients or simply to circumvent the rules themselves.

Internal models are designed to take diversification effects into account. Moreover, regulators hope that by encouraging financial institutions to build their own comprehensive, portfolio-based models to measure risk, risk management will be strengthened and the incentives of regulators and firms will be more closely aligned. Hendricks and Hirtle (1997, p. 3) highlight this point: "By substituting banks' internal risk measurement models for broad, uniform regulatory measures of risk exposure, this approach should lead to capital charges that more accurately reflect individual banks' true risk exposures. And by including qualitative standards, the approach is consistent with the shift in supervisory interest from a focus on risk measurement to a more comprehensive evaluation of banks' overall risk management." Only the Basel Committee approach and the almost identical CAD of the European Union allow for an internal models approach for capital assessment.

Banking

The market risk amendment to the Basel Accord (BCBS 1996a) establishes a capital charge for market risk in a bank's trading book and for exposure to foreign exchange and commodity price risk in the banking book as well.[38] It assigns a capital charge for general and specific risk, although this distinction is not made for all types of risk factors. The separation between general and specific risk is similar to the distinction between systematic and idiosyncratic risk, although specific risk includes some notion of default likelihood as well.[39] Specific risk may also be incorporated in the internal models approach, subject to supervisory approval, through increasing the number of risk factors, stress testing, or scenario analysis. But it is usually subject to an add-on instead.

Banks with a *significant* market risk exposure are required to calculate a risk-based capital ratio that takes into account market risk in addition to credit risk. U.S. regulators deem market-risk exposure to be significant if the gross sum of trading assets and liabilities on the bank's balance sheet exceeds 10% of total assets or $1 billion (USGAO 1998, p. 121). At the end of 1996, 17 banks met this criterion, while at the end of 2001 the number was well above 40.[40]

Banking: Basic/Standardized Approach

The standardized approach (SA) to market risk measurement was proposed by the Basel Committee in April 1993 and updated in January 1996. The European Commission in its Capital Adequacy Directive (CAD) adopted something very similar known as the building block (BB) approach.[41] The main difference between the Basel Committee's SA approach and the European Union's BB approach is in the weights for specific risk. The capital charge is 8% (SA) or 4% (BB) for equities, reduced to 4% (SA) or 2% (BB) for well-diversified portfolios. The designation "well-diversified" seems to be at the discretion of the regulator. (See also Scott and Wellons 1999.) While some netting is allowed, diversification benefits achieved by holding less than perfectly correlated assets do not reduce capital charges. The overall capital charge for market risk is simply the sum of capital charges for each of the exposures. A full description of the rules is contained in BCBS (1996a), but we highlight in the next subsections some of the capital charges that are important for computing the capital requirement for our model portfolio.

Interest Rate Risk. Specific risk charges for debt instruments are differentiated by counterparty. There are three broad groups with five risk charges, as summarized in table 1.1. The "qualifying" category is broadly any issuer that is rated investment grade, plus government-sponsored enterprises and multilateral development banks.

The defining feature of general market risk is the broad allowance for full netting subject to so-called vertical (within maturity band) and horizontal (across maturity bands) disallowances, which reduce the netting offsets. Broadly, there are two approaches for calculating risk exposure: the maturity method and the duration method. The former is more formulaic, while the latter is designed to better reflect risk as function of yield curve volatility. In our model portfolio, we employ the simpler maturity approach for calculating required market risk capital. All interest rate derivatives and off-balance sheet instruments in the trading book are included in the risk calculation. Options are treated separately.

Equity Position Risk. All equity positions in the trading book are subject to the market risk capital calculation. Netting is allowed for positions in the same issue only. Specific risk is defined as the bank's *gross* equity position, while general risk applies only to *net* positions. The charge for specific risk is

Table 1.1. Specific Risk Charge, Interest Rate Risk,
BIS Standardized Approach

Issuer	% Capital Charge
Government	0
Qualifying	0.25 (< 6 months)
	1.00 (between 6 and 25 months)
	1.60 (> 24 months)
Other	8

Source: Authors' compilation based on BCBS (1996a).

4% if the portfolio is considered both liquid and well diversified; otherwise, the charge is 8%. The general market risk charge is 8%. Thus, the total market risk charge can be as much as 16%. As with interest rate instruments, equity derivatives and off-balance sheet positions held in the trading book should be included in the market risk calculation. Options are treated separately.

Foreign Exchange Risk. For foreign exchange (FX) and commodities, no distinction between general and specific risk is made. The FX calculation involves netting exposures in the same currency exposure and taking the maximum of the sum of the net short or long position across currencies. Gold is included in the FX risk calculation, rather than in commodities. The capital charge is then 8% for the overall position.

Treatment of Options. Options are required to be marked to market at the end of the trading day using market prices and, importantly, implied volatilities for valuation. The BCBS laid out several alternative approaches to calculating market risk capital charges for options. The simplified approach, available to banks that use only purchased options, are functions of the market value of the option (money-ness) and the market value of the underlying security. For banks that also write options, several intermediate approaches are available. These approaches involve the calculation of delta, gamma, and vega of the options (the delta-plus approach) or the somewhat more advanced scenario approach based on matrix values of the underlying position. (For additional discussion of the valuation of options, see appendix 1.) Both are approximations to the full Monte Carlo approach allowed (and advocated) under the internal models approach. In our model portfolio, we employ the intermediate, delta-plus approach to establish the capital charge for the options position. No credit is given to hedging an option position, since each instrument is treated separately.

Banking: Internal Models Approach

The 1996 amendment to the Capital Accord provided for the supervised use of internal models to establish capital charges, a revolutionary change in capital regulation. It was an implicit recognition of the complexity and the fast pace of innovation in financial instruments and institutions, where any rule written to set capital charges for a given set of instruments may spur innovations to reduce or avoid the charge. Only an internal models approach is likely to be able to address the portfolio of risks comprehensively and dynamically.

The internal models approach is designed to fully capture portfolio diversification effects that occur when assets that are less than perfectly correlated are combined in a portfolio. The goal is to more closely align the regulatory assessment of risk capital with the risks actually faced by the bank.[42] The approach starts from the presumption that similar risks should face similar capital charges.

General market risk is a direct function of the output from the internal value-at-risk (VaR) model initially developed by and for banks. It is used to answer the question, "Given the size of our positions, what is the most we should expect to lose over the next day due to market fluctuations?" The model is based on a probability distribution of returns for the positions, and this question can therefore be answered for a specified level of confidence. (See appendix 1 for a survey of VaR modeling techniques.) The capital requirement is based on a 10-day 99% VaR, which is often based practically on a 1-day 99% VaR, scaled up to reflect a 10-day holding period using a scaling factor,

$$99\% \text{ VaR} \times \sqrt{10} \times \kappa \tag{1.1}$$

where $\sqrt{10}$ is the liquidity factor to move from a 1-day to a 10-day holding period and κ is the supervisory add-on (3 to 4, depending on backtesting results). Market risk equivalent assets are then $\frac{1}{.08} = 12.5$ times the aggregated risk exposure (standardized) or charge (internal models).

Which banks are eligible to use the internal markets approach? This is left to the discretion of each country's supervisor, and the decision is based on a number of qualitative and quantitative criteria (BCBS 1996a). As of the fourth quarter of 2001, 18 of the largest 50 bank holding companies (by total assets) in the United States were reporting market risk equivalent assets from their internal models.

The resulting capital charge from the internal model, C^{FED}, is the maximum of yesterday's 99% 10-day adjusted ($\sqrt{10}$) daily VaR or the average of the daily VaR over the preceding 60 trading days multiplied by the regulatory capital multiplier $\kappa \in [3,4]$.[43]

$$C^{FED} = \max \left[VaR_{t-1}, \kappa \times \frac{1}{60} \sum_{i=1}^{60} VaR_{t-i} \right] \tag{1.2}$$

The calculations are to be based on data from at least one year (about 250 trading days).

Backtesting. How can a supervisor know whether the internal model of a bank accurately reflects the risk exposures of its portfolio? In stark contrast

Table 1.2. Backtesting VaR Models, Regulatory Color, and Capital Multipliers

# of Exceptions in 250 Days	Pr (Exceptions) if True 99% VaR[a]		BCBS Zones	Multiplier
0	8.1%		Green	3.0
1	20.5%			3.0
2	25.7%	89.2%		3.0
3	21.5%			3.0
4	13.4%			3.0
5	6.7%		Yellow	3.4
6	2.7%			3.5
7	1.0%	10.8		3.65
8	0.3%			3.75
9	0.08%			3.85
10 or more	0.01%		Red	4.0

[a]The percentages in the second column indicate the odds of observing the number of exceptions specified in the first column under the assumption that the VaR model is correct.
Source: BCBS (1996b).

to the situation with credit risk models, regulators have the luxury of rich and plentiful data to test market risk models. It is relatively straightforward to compare model outputs (forecasts) with actual outcomes (realizations). The BCBS requires banks to perform backtesting on a quarterly basis using one year (about 250 trading days) of data. This process simply counts the actual number of times in the past year that the loss on the profit and loss account (P&L) exceeded VaR. Over the course of a 250 trading-day year, we should expect 2.5 exceptions for 99% VaR, but the regulators allow four. Just because a bank has experienced four exceptions, however, does not mean the model is necessarily wrong. In fact, there is a 10.8% chance that the model will experience more than four exceptions even if VaR was calculated correctly. (The second column of table 1.2 shows the probability of observing the number of exceptions specified in the first column (Pr[exceptions]) over 250 days, if the VaR model is accurate. The BCBS has established color zones, shown in the third column, to indicate whether the bank will be subject to a penalty in the form of a higher multiplier [see column 4] because the number of exceptions is too high.)

The validity of backtesting rests on two questionable assumptions regarding the nature of portfolio changes and the associated profit and loss (P&L) account. First, VaR is usually an end-of-day measurement that is attributed to the P&L result of either the preceding day or the following day. In either case, the risk taken during the day may vary considerably from the end-of-day risk. The variation can be systematic, as would be the case if proprietary trading positions were taken intraday and then closed out by the end of the day. It can also be random, as would be the case if positions were taken temporarily and closed out frequently to facilitate customer orders. Significant differences between end-of-day VaR and intraday VaR can lead to systematic over- or underestimation of risk. This will result in a much weaker relationship between VaR and measured P&L volatility. Put another way, different intraday trading behaviors and strategies may appear identical to an end-of-day VaR system.

Second, the P&L result is assumed to be solely the result of movements in market prices. But, in addition to position-taking gains and losses, the P&L often contains fees, commissions, mark-ups, market-making spreads, and the results of intraday trading that are invisible to the standard batch VaR run once a night; all of these have a significant positive impact on P&L and add a modest amount of volatility to P&L that is unrelated to VaR. If the positive impact outweighs the increase in volatility, backtesting by means of exception counting may be undermined by fee, commission, or spread income that cloaks position-taking losses.

Securities Firms

The European Union applies the same capital rules to securities firms as to banks. These are virtually identical to the standardized and internal models approach of the BCBS. U.S. securities firms, however, are subject to an entirely different capital regulation regime, which we analyze in this subsection. (Japanese securities firms face a similar regime.)

The U.S. Net Capital Rule (Rule 15c3-1)

The Net Capital Rule and calculation is designed to ensure that if the business were forced to close its doors today, it would be able to return all customer-owned assets and complete customer transactions. Hence, liquidity is given primary importance in determining net capital. Let L^{sec} be the liabilities of the securities firm other than subordinated liabilities, and let R^{sec} be customer-related receivables. The Net Capital Rule has two standards: the basic method, which requires net capital to exceed $6\frac{2}{3}\%$ of aggregate indebtedness, and the alternative method, used by most of the large broker/dealers (and any with significant proprietary position taking), which requires net capital to exceed 2% of customer debit items. Because it applies to the most important U.S. securities firms, we focus on the alternative method in this section and apply it to the model portfolio in the following section.

- The capital requirement under the basic method is $C_{reg,1}^{SEC} \geq \frac{L^{sec}}{15}$ subject to certain exclusions such as fully collateralized obligations.[44]
- The capital requirement under the alternative method is $C_{reg,2}^{SEC} \geq \max\left[\frac{R^{sec}}{50}, \$250,000\right]$

Assets on the trading book are subject to haircuts—an industry term for valuating securities below market prices. They reflect the liquidity of the instrument and the credit quality of the counterparty as follows: the lower the liquidity and/or the lower the credit quality, the larger the haircut. In that sense, the SEC haircuts combine credit and liquidity risk with market risk. Final net (regulatory) capital for the firm is the sum of assets, adjusted for haircuts, less the liabilities:

$$C^{SEC} = A(1-h) - L$$

where $h = \frac{\sum A_i h_i}{A}$, a weighted average of the haircuts, h_i, for asset categories, A_i. A summary of haircuts is given in Ball and Stoll (1998).

Rule 15c3-1 applies a punitive haircut of 100% to swaps and OTC derivatives. For that reason, U.S. securities firms conduct most of their OTC derivatives operations in unregistered affiliates in the United States or in overseas offices, often in Europe, where they are subject to the European Union's CAD, rather than through the registered broker-dealer.[45]

Recently, the SEC has experimented with Basel-style internal models regulation for affiliates that deal in OTC derivatives. So far, only three firms have chosen to become regulated OTC dealers under this "SEC lite" regime.[46]

Capital Charges for Debt. For U.S. government and agency instruments, the haircuts are the most modest. They range from 0% for very short-term (0–3 months) to 6% for long-term (> 25 years) debt. Haircuts are applied to net positions, Investment-grade municipal bonds are treated similarly, though the top end is 7% for maturities of 20 years or longer. But the treatment of municipal bonds differs with respect to netting: the haircuts are applied to the maximum of long or short positions, not the net position.

For investment-grade nondomestic government and agency instruments, as well as for corporate debt, haircuts are applied to the maximum of long or short positions, not to the net position, and can climb as high as 9% for maturities of 25 years or more. Noninvestment grade debt receives a haircut of 30% under the basic method and 15% under the alternative approach.

Capital Charge for Equities. The haircut for liquid equities is 30% under the basic approach but only 15% under the alternative approach. A stock is considered liquid for net capital purposes if it traded on an exchange or has more than two market makers. For illiquid stocks, the haircut is 40%. If the position involves a combination of longs and shorts, it becomes a bit more complicated. Taking a liquid stock position as an example, a broker-dealer's haircut for equity securities is equal to 15% of the market value of the greater of the long or short equity position, plus 15% of the market value of the lesser position, but only to the extent this position exceeds 25% of the greater position (SEC 1997a).

Capital Charge for Foreign Currency. Haircuts are given to open, that is, unhedged, currency positions. In the spirit of assigning larger haircuts to less liquid asset types, currencies are grouped into major and other currencies, the former containing (as of 2001) the euro, the Japanese yen, the British pound, the Swiss franc, and the Canadian dollar. These positions receive a 6% haircut, while all other positions are subjected to a 20% haircut.[47]

Treatment of Options. Options receive treatment similar to the BCBS standardized approach under the SEC. They are required to be marked to market at the end of the trading day using market prices and implied volatilities for valuation. The SEC has two approaches: (1) the capital charge is based on the market value of the underlying asset, or (2) the capital charge is based on the market value of the option. The SEC amended the Net Capital Rule in February 1997 and made significant revisions to the treatment of options. For the first time, something akin to an internal models approach was allowed.[48] The amendment[49] requires that the options model calculate theoretical prices at 10 equidistant valuation points within a range consisting of an increase or a decrease of the following percentages of the daily market price of the underlying instrument for each kind of option: (1) 15% for equity securities with a ready market, narrow-based indexes, and nonhigh-capitalization diversified indexes; (2) 6% for major market currencies;[50] (3) 10% for high-capitalization diversified indexes; and (4) 20% for currencies other than major market currencies. The applicable haircut is the greatest loss at any one valuation point. We apply this option valuation approach to our model portfolio in the next section.

Like the BCBS standardized approach, this partial portfolio approach ignores hedging strategies designed to mitigate the risk. Typically an option position is at least hedged with respect to a change in price of the underlying position or delta hedged. But this is considered a separate position to which a haircut is applied. This increases the total required capital and thus actually discourages a firm from using a basic risk mitigation technique.

The Capital Adequacy Directive (CAD) of the European Union

The CAD (93/6/EEC; see Joint Forum 2001) applies to *both* banks and securities firms in the European Union. Market risks are defined to include all risks listed in the Market Risks Amendment to the Basel Accord (i.e., interest rate risk, equity position risk, foreign exchange risk, and commodity price risk) plus settlement risk. Two methods are proposed: (1) a building block approach that applies specified capital charges to the current market value of open positions (including derivatives) in fixed income and equities and the total currency and commodities positions and (2) an internal-models-based (VaR) approach. The resulting capital charge from the internal model is almost the same as the BIS charge.

Insurance

In contrast to the regulatory capital frameworks used by bank and securities regulators, insurance regulators make capital charges for both asset and liability risk (Webb and Lilly 1994; Kupiec and Nickerson 2001; Joint Forum 2001). In fact, a major source of market risk is the interest rate risk that results from the asset-liability mismatch (ALM). We focus on the risk-based capital (RBC) model for life insurance. The RBC model for property and casualty (P&C) insurance is based on the life model and is very similar.[51]

Table 1.3. Distribution of RBC Amounts by Risk Category
(all U.S. Insurers, 1991)

Risk Type	% Contribution
C1: Asset	70.5
C2: Insurance/underwriting	16.1
C3: Interest rate[a]	10.1
C3: Operational	3.3

[a]Reflected only in the life RBC formula.
Source: Webb and Lilly (1994), p. 48.

The RBC approach recognizes four classes of risk: (1) C1, or asset risk, which is analogous to credit risk in the Basel framework; (2) C2, or insurance risk or underwriting risk, which results from underpricing of insured risks; (3) C3, or interest rate risk, which results from the ALM problem; (4) C4, or business risk, which is analogous to operational risk in the Basel framework.[52]

RBC attempts to take account of concentration (or diversification) for each class of risk, For example, for C1 (asset risk), the risk factor for the 10 largest asset exposures is doubled, providing a strong incentive for diversifying the investment portfolio. C1 risk makes up the bulk of insurance-risk-based capital in the United States, as table 1.3 makes clear.

The final RBC, adjusted for covariance, is

$$C_{reg}^{ins} = RBC = \sqrt{(C1+C2)^2 + C2^2} + C4^{53} \tag{1.3}$$

This RBC is then compared to total adjusted capital (TAC), where TAC includes capital and policyholder surplus (reserves) as determined, in the United States, by each state's statutory accounting requirements. The ratio of TAC to RBC determines when regulatory action may be taken. For values of this ratio exceeding two, no regulatory action is taken.[54] If the ratio falls below 0.7, the regulator must take control of the insurance company. Values in between lead to different levels of regulatory intervention that are less severe than outright placement under regulatory control (e.g., rehabilitation, liquidation).

Market Risk Under NAIC's RBC

As noted earlier, the NAIC does not use terms such as "position" or "market" risk. Indeed, even the minor part of the investment book that is marked to market (equity positions) is done so only at the same frequency as the reporting cycle, which is at most quarterly and often only year's end. But both C1 (asset risk) and especially C3 (interest rate risk) contain elements of what would be regarded as position risk by regulators in the other two sectors of the financial services industry.[55] In spirit, C1 is closer to the Basel risk-adjusted assets for credit risk. For example, risk weights for C1 are

Table 1.4. NAIC Asset Risk (C1) Weights (%)

Assets	LIFE	P&C
U.S. govt. bonds	0	0
Cash	0.3	0.3
NAIC 1: AAA- to A-rated bonds, including GSE debt and most collateralized debt obligations	0.3	0.3
NAIC 2: BBB-rated bonds	1.0	1.0
NAIC 3: BB-rated bonds	4.0	2.0
NAIC 4: B-rated bonds	9.0	4.5
NAIC 5: CCC-rated bonds	20.0	10.0
NAIC 6: Bonds "near default"	30.0	30.0
Whole residential mortgages	0.5	5.0
Commercial mortgages	3.0	5.0
Common stock	30.0	15.0
Preferred stock (+)	2.0	2.0

Source: Kupiec and Nickerson (2001); Saunders (2000).

30 basis points (bp) for cash (for the possibility of bank failure)[56] and 0% for U.S. government bonds (which are effectively immune from credit risk but not from market risk factors such as interest rate fluctuation and inflation), 0.3% for AAA- to A-rated bonds; then increasing for lower rated bonds (there are six risk bands in total); 0.5% for residential mortgages; 3% for commercial mortgages, and 30% for common stock (see table 1.4).[57]

Risk weights for interest rate risk (C3) are based on analysis of U.S. treasury spot rates from 1977 to 1990. Over that period, the 95% confidence interval for interest rate volatility was reported to be 3.5%–4% (Webb and Lilly 1994, p. 40). The risk applies to the asset liability mismatch (ALM) and hence depends crucially on accurate estimates of liability exposures and outflows. For example, annuity reserves are divided into three risk categories (low, medium, and high), depending on callability of the contract. The capital charge for C3 risk is reduced by one-third if regulators judge that the insurance company is running a well-balanced ALM portfolio. Insurance companies are also permitted to net out most reinsurance.

Treatment of Derivatives and Options. Broadly speaking, derivative instruments are treated the same as bonds by the NAIC for life insurers and receive a flat 5% RBC weight for health and P&C companies (AAA 2002). No "credit" is given for hedging a position. Rather, the hedge is added as a separate exposure. Risk mitigation through reinsurance, which could be thought of as a credit derivative, is credited with capital reduction.

VaR in Insurance

VaR has not yet become a standard risk measurement tool in the insurance industry. In a survey for the Society of Actuaries, Britt et al. (2001) report that only about one-third of survey responders (8 of 24 large U.S. insurers) use value-at-risk (VaR). Of those who use VaR, 50% stated that they generate reports only quarterly, 25% do so monthly or more often. This longer horizon is also reflected in liquidity reporting.[58] Of the survey respondents, 42% filed liquidity reports at quarterly frequency; only 33% generated such reports once a month or more frequently. This study, consistent with the Joint Forum (2001) report, indicates that insurance companies are much less subject to sudden liquidity needs than either banks or securities firms might be. Both banks and securities firms are much more transaction intensive, and of course the average duration of both assets and liabilities are considerably longer for life insurance companies. Moreover, the liabilities of an insurer are typically not tradable financial assets, unlike those of the other two sectors, and, as such, can be very difficult to value.

THE TRADING EXPERIMENT—A MODEL PORTFOLIO

In order to quantify some of the differences in regulatory framework across the three sectors, we have constructed a model portfolio to compute the capital charges under each framework. The portfolio is broadly representative of the financial instruments that might be traded by an internationally active financial institution. The portfolio has been constructed to emphasize two of the most important challenges that face any attempt to model position risk: fat-tailed distributions of returns, in which extreme returns occur more frequently than one would expect under the normal distribution (leptokurtosis), and nonlinear returns, such as those from options. (See appendix 2 for an extensive discussion of key issues in modeling volatility.)

Table 1.5 displays the model portfolio (along with the associated risk factors). Leptokurtosis is introduced by including risk factors from an emerging market (Mexico) and nonlinearity through a series of simple combinations of European equity options. Straightforward hedging techniques are employed; for instance, option positions are delta hedged, exposures to foreign equities are hedged by foreign exchange (FX), and so forth.

This section may be viewed as an extension of the work of Dimson and Marsh (1995), who used an actual portfolio of equities to contrast the capital charges under an earlier version of the SEC Net Capital Rule, the E.U. building block approach, and a portfolio approach used by regulators in the United Kingdom. Our portfolio contains a much broader range of financial instruments, and we use the current SEC Net Capital Rule, the BCBS internal models approach—which was introduced after the Dimson and Marsh (1995) paper was written—and the RBC framework of the NAIC.

Risk Factors

We cover the range of typical risk factors: FX, interest rates, equity, and, for options, implied volatilities, as summarized in table 1.6 and table 1.7. For

Table 1.5. Positions in the Portfolio (Columns) and Exposure to Risk Factors (Rows)

Instruments	Long 5-yr., Short 1-yr. (U.S. Yield Curve Slope Exposure)	Long U.K. 5-yr. (U.K. Yield Curve + FX Exposure)	Flat	FX Swap (USD/GBP)	Long £, Short Peso, Long MX 6M	Long Mexican IPC, Short S&P, FX Hedged	Calendar Spread on S&P 500 (Δ & Rho Hedged)	FTSE 100 Protection Put Per SEC 5.4)	Straddle on S&P 500 (Δ Hedged)	Total Portfolio
US$ cash			10,000	(14,556)		120,000	10,313	(765,075)		(649,631)
1-yr. U.S. treasury	(50,000)		50,000 & (50,000)	14,556						(25,131)
5-yr. U.S. treasury	100,000						(431)			99,569
S&P 500 index						(100)	(3)		(2)	(105)
GBP cash		(77,925)		10,000	100,000					32,075
1-yr. U.K. treasury				(10,000)						(10,000)
5-yr. U.K. treasury		100,000								100,000
FTSE 100 index								100		100
MXP cash					(1,429,868)	(114,701)				(1,544,569)
6-month CETES					100,000					100,000
IPC (Bolsa) index						18				18
S&P 500 put[a]							1 and (1)		1	1
S&P 500 call									1	2 and (1)
FTSE put								1		1

[a]Options are denominated in 100 contracts. All options are European.
Source: Authors' compilation.

Table 1.6. Risk Factors and Financial Instruments

Geography	FX/Cash	Fixed Income	Equity	Options
U.S.	USD cash	1-yr. treasury	S&P 500	S&P 500 implied volatilities (put/call)
		5-yr. treasury		
U.K.	GBP cash	1-yr. treasury	FTSE 100	FTSE 100 implied volatilities (put/call)
	(USD/GBP exposure)	5-yr. treasury		
EM (Mexico)	MPX cash	6-m. treasury	IPC (bolsa)	
	(MXP/US$ exposure)	1-yr. treasury		

Source: Authors' compilation.

fixed income we chose treasuries representing two points on the yield curve, one-year and five-year, except for Mexico, where the yield curve beyond two years can be quite unreliable, which is characteristic of emerging markets. There we stick with the shorter end of the yield curve: six-month and one-year Mexican treasuries (Cetes). The sample range is January 1, 1997 to December 31, 2001 for a total of 1,304 trading days.

Trading Positions

The portfolio features a range of positions that an internationally active financial institution might trade. Our aim in constructing the portfolio is to explore a broad set of risk factors across geography and asset type. Naturally, such an exploration cannot be exhaustive. Nor is it engineered to maximize differences in regulatory capital. Indeed, as will become clear, the overall differences in capital charges are sometimes surprisingly small.

Table 1.7. Risk Factor Data Sources

Risk Factor	Data Source and Comments
U.S. 1-yr.	1-yr. constant maturity[a]
U.S. 5-yr.	5-yr. benchmark
S&P 500 implied volatility	Put and call implied volatilities
U.K. 1-yr.	1-yr. interbank middle rate
U.K. 5-yr.	5-yr. U.K. govt. bond
FTSE 100 implied volatility	Put and call implied volatilities
MX 6-m.	Mexico Cetes 182-day note (secondary market prices)
MX 1-yr.	Mexico Cetes 364-day note (secondary market prices)

[a]1-yr. constant maturity was chosen because the 1-yr. benchmark was discontinued on August 29, 2001.
Source: Data source for implied volatilities is Bloomberg; all others, Datastream.

Option Positions

The simplest option is the European call (put) equity option. This instrument gives the buyer the right, but not the obligation, to buy (sell) the underlying stock at some predetermined strike price at a fixed date in the future.[59] To gain a bit more richness in our simple portfolio, we combined a set of plain-vanilla European calls and puts to form a set of well-known complex options (see Hull 1993, chapter 8). We have the following option positions in our portfolio, all expiring within one month:

- *Straddle:* Buy call and put with same strike price and expiration date. The trader is betting on a large move but does not want to commit to a particular direction. Ostensibly, the trader is long volatility. This is a natural strategy for the stock of a company subject to a takeover bid.
- *Protective put:* Buy a put on stock and the stock itself. The put insures the buyer against downside movement.
- *Calendar spread:* Sell one call with a certain strike and buy a call with same strike but a later expiration date. The investor is betting on small movements; the loss is small if the movements are large. If the strike is close to the current price, it is called a neutral calendar spread. If the strike is above (below) the current spread, it is a bullish (bearish) calendar spread. Ours is relatively neutral.

Simulation Results

We collected data on 11 risk factors on a daily basis from the beginning of 1997 to the end of 2001. Given a set of positions laid out in table 1.5, we then asked, What is the risk assessment on December 31, 2001, using the different approaches to establishing capital charges for position risk? Specifically, we compute the capital charges under the following: (1) the three variants of VaR—the parametric, historical,[60] and Monte Carlo simulations;[61] for parametric VaR we follow the RiskMetrics approach; (2) the Basel Committee standardized approach; (3) the SEC Net Capital Rule; and (4) the NAIC RBC rules for a life insurance company. This exercise highlights some (but, certainly not all) of the differences among the different regulatory capital regimes.

Any comparative discussion of these capital charges, be it at the position or portfolio level, is easier if one has a benchmark against which to base any number. Certainly the internal models approach is the most sophisticated and comprehensive of the available methods, and of the three variants available, historical simulation is arguably best able to capture many of the salient features of market risk—volatility clustering, fat-tailed returns, and nonlinearity in options.[62]

Capital charges for individual positions are given in table 1.8, and portfolio-level results are given in the last column of table 1.8 (and in figure 1.2).

Table 1.8. Comparing Capital Charges ($)

Risk Measurement Approaches	Long 5-yr., Short 1-yr. (U.S. Yield Curve Slope Exposure)	Long U.K. 5-yr. (U.K. Yield Curve + FX Exposure)	Flat	FX Swap (USD/GBP)	Long £, Short Peso, Long MX 6M	Long Mexican Peso, IPC, Short S&P, FX Hedged	Calendar Spread on S&P 500 (Δ & rho Hedged)	FTSE 100 Protection Put Per Text	Straddle on S&P 500 (Δ Hedged)	Total Portfolio
New value	31,940	(0.07)	10,000	309	8	5,192	8,889	0.15	3,043	59,382
Contributory VaR[a] (parametric)	(87)	(158)	0	(0.46)	777	(703)	4	13,009	(1)	12,841
Basel capital (parametric VaR)	7,061	7,420	0	271	20,503	21,030	103	127,924	14	121,818
Basel capital (Monte Carlo VaR)	6,384	7,633	0	258	18,887	20,623	2,144	121,640	7	113,624
Basel capital (historical simulation VaR)	5,128	6,987	0	167	26,345	33,212	3,573	150,705	11,726	152,638
Basel standardized approach	3,250	4,412	0	1,362	1,098	11,481	31,225	263,332	17,885	334,044
SEC rule 15c3-1 haircut	2,500	8,734	0	29,112	2,348	17,221	1,716	119,391	509	181,531
NAIC RBC: C1	0	437	30	44	109	37,516	1,163	228,120	956	268,374

[a] Contributory VaR takes into account diversification benefits contributed by this position to the overall portfolio.
Source: Authors' compilation.

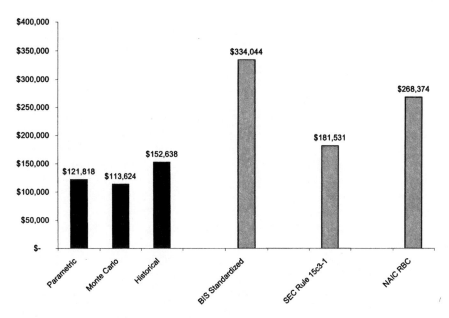

Figure 1.2. Regulatory Capital Compared. Source: Authors' compilation.

The differences are sometimes dramatic, although, to be sure, this result may just be an artifact of this particular portfolio. Leaving aside the most dominant position, the protection put on the FTSE 100, for the moment, consider first a comparison of the three variants of VaR (parametric, Monte Carlo, and historical simulation). At the individual position level, we see the expected result: historical VaR often yields a higher capital charge than parametric VaR, especially for emerging markets exposure. A good example is the long pound, short peso, and Mexican 6M position, where historical VaR ($26,345) is about 30% higher than parametric VaR ($20,503). For some of the options positions, this spread is even more dramatic. Both the calendar spread and the straddle on the S&P 500 have risk levels implied by historical simulation that far exceed parametric VaR. We discuss the option positions in greater detail later.

Historical VaR tends to be the most conservative of the three VaR variants in common use precisely because it takes into account the fat tails and whether returns are linear or nonlinear. They are particularly prevalent in emerging markets.[63]

Moving on to the rule-based approaches, capital charges for the simple bond positions differ only modestly, the outlier being the NAIC RBC capital, which gives very favorable treatment to government bonds. Note also that some of the interest rate risk captured by the other approaches may be captured separately by the NAIC rules under C3 interest rate risk. However, C3 calculations of RBC must be done in the context of a particular liability exposure, which is beyond the scope of our experiment.

The NAIC RBC approach is the only approach that assigned a capital charge to our long $10,000 (flat) position. Recall that the NAIC RBC assigns a 30 bp charge against cash (see table 1.4), resulting in a $30 charge here. The other case in which the NAIC capital charge is substantially higher than either the SEC or various Basel capital charges is for the long Mexican IPC, short S&P, FX-hedged position. This is largely driven by the high capital charge the NAIC has assigned to equities (30%) without allowing for netting.

The swap position receives a much higher capital charge under the SEC Net Capital Rule, 15c3-1 ($29,112) than under any other approach. As a basis for comparison, Basel capital under historical simulation VaR would be $167. The SEC haircuts are extremely unfavorable to swaps on the accounts of the broker/dealer. Indeed, leaving out the dominant protection put, nearly half of the total remaining SEC capital charge comes from the FX swap position.[64]

The Basel standardized approach was designed to be generally more conservative than the internal models approach, precisely to motivate banks to invest in the infrastructure necessary to be able to adopt the latter. At the portfolio level, this is obviously the case: under this approach, the portfolio receives the highest capital charge of any of the approaches There are exceptions, however, even on some simple positions. For example, the first two positions (long U.S. five-year; short U.S. one-year treasury; long U.K. five-year treasury) receive a lower capital charge than under any of the internal models approaches. This is likely due to higher than anticipated (under the standardized approach) risk factor volatilities. Fattailed returns are obviously not driving the results, since, in both cases, historical VaR-based capital is lower than the other two internal models approaches imply, suggesting that the risk factor volatilities are the likely cause.

A picture of the risk contribution of individual positions under the VaR approach can be obtained by looking at contributory VaR in table 1.9.[65] Contributory VaR may be negative, as is the case for the long-short equity position (long Mexican IPC, short S&P 500), if it provides diversification benefits at the portfolio level. This may be due to natural offsets—elsewhere in the portfolio we are long the S&P 500—or it may be due to negative correlations of the underlying risk factors. We can get a glimpse of this by looking at the correlations of the risk factors (except implied volatilities) at the end of the sample period in table 1.9. The exchange rate returns seem to be weakly negatively correlated with equity returns. Looking down (or across) the USD/MX peso column, we see negative correlations with the S&P 500, the FTSE 100, and the IPC itself, as well as with U.S. and U.K. treasury rates, all of which appear elsewhere in the portfolio.

Finally, it is worth dissecting the options positions. Note that for the options positions, implied instead of parametric volatilities were computed. The protection put on the FTSE 100 (long the FTSE 100, the underlying position, and long a put, essentially insurance against downward movements

Table 1.9. EWMA Correlation Matrix of Risk Factor Changes (absolute level changes), at sample end (12/21/2001); Lambda = 0.94

Holding	S&P 500	FTSE 100	IPC (Bolsa)	US$/GBP	US$/Peso	U.S. 1-year	U.S. 5-year	U.K. 1-year	U.K. 5-year	6-month Cetes	1-year Cetes
S&P 500	1.00	0.65	0.61	-0.25	-0.09	0.28	0.08	-0.02	0.17	0.05	-0.12
FTSE 100	0.65	1.00	0.54	-0.30	-0.14	0.32	0.18	0.18	0.32	-0.19	-0.18
IPC (Bolsa)	0.61	0.54	1.00	-0.08	-0.18	0.24	0.32	0.19	0.44	-0.08	-0.20
US$/GBP	-0.25	-0.30	-0.08	1.00	0.24	-0.17	-0.02	-0.20	-0.01	0.30	0.25
US$/Peso	-0.09	-0.14	-0.18	0.24	1.00	-0.19	-0.23	-0.18	0.18	-0.04	0.23
U.S. 1-yr.	0.28	0.32	0.24	-0.17	-0.19	1.00	0.80	0.12	0.14	-0.14	-0.13
U.S. 5-yr.	0.08	0.18	0.32	-0.02	-0.23	0.80	1.00	0.21	0.35	-0.12	-0.14
U.K. 1-yr.	-0.02	0.18	0.19	-0.20	-0.18	0.12	0.21	1.00	0.54	0.06	0.01
U.K. 5-yr.	0.17	0.32	0.44	-0.01	0.18	0.14	0.35	0.54	1.00	0.01	0.03
6-month Cetes	0.05	-0.19	-0.08	0.30	-0.04	-0.14	-0.12	0.06	0.01	1.00	0.48
1-year Cetes	-0.12	-0.18	-0.20	0.25	0.23	-0.13	-0.14	0.01	0.03	0.48	1.00

Source: Authors' compilation.

in the FTSE 100) is a large position. It cost $765,075 (which appears as a negative entry for US$ cash in table 1.9) and has a capital charge of $150,705 under the historical simulation VaR internal models approach. This is larger than either of the other VaR approaches, indicating that there are fat tails in the FTSE 100 as well as the USD/GBP exchange rate.[66] The SEC Net Capital Rule assigns a capital charge that is closest to the internal models approach. This is likely due to changes made in February 1997 in the method for the capital calculation for options positions, which are significantly more nuanced than the previous simple haircuts. The NAIC RBC approach falls between the internal models and BIS Standardized approach, the latter topping out at $263,332, a good example of appropriately providing banks an incentive to move to the more complex internal models approach.

An excellent example of capital charge differences is the calendar spread on the S&P 500, delta and rho (interest rate risk) hedged. The parametric VaR approach severely underestimates the risk of nonlinearity ($103 vs. $2,144 for the Monte Carlo approach), while incorporating fat tails and implied (instead of parametric) volatilities, as was done in the historical simulation VaR approach, provides a better picture of the risk in this position: $3,573.

Hedging is given only partial credit in the rules-based approaches. A major distinguishing feature of the internal models approach is that it is a portfolio approach by design. Hedges are meaningful only in the context of another position, the one that is being hedged, a feature that may not be captured in rules that focus on individual positions. In table 1.10, we explore the impact of hedging for the calendar spread on the S&P 500. First, we add a delta hedge to provide protection against changes in the underlying price, and then we add a rho hedge to protect against interest rate risk and show the resulting capital charges for the three variants of VaR and the SEC Net Capital Rule. For all approaches, the delta hedge is the most significant risk mitigant, but there is large disagreement between the methods around the amount of risk mitigation. Parametric VaR indicates a 77% reduction, from $829 to $187, while historical VaR suggests that the reduction is more like 3%, from $3,711 to $3,602. Adding a rho hedge results in a further drop of

Table 1.10. Impact of Hedging for Calendar Spread on S&P 500 ($)

Risk Measurement Approaches	Naked	Delta Hedged	Delta and rho Hedged
Parametric VaR	829	187	103
Monte Carlo VaR	2,828	2,148	2,144
Historical simulation VaR	3,711	3,602	3,573
Basel Standardized Approach	30,809	31,153	31,225
SEC Net Capital Rule	2,142	1,625	1,716

Source: Authors' compilation.

45%, according to parametric VaR, but only a 1% drop according to historical simulation VaR. Rather than reducing capital charges as hedges are added, the Basel standardized approach calls for increased capital because each hedge is treated as an additional position. The SEC Net Capital Rule gives credit for the delta hedge (a short on the underlying position), but not for the rho hedge, which is a net long position (a combination of long 1Y and short 5Y on the U.S. treasury).

Finally, consider the ninth position in our portfolio, a straddle on the S&P 500, which is delta hedged. For the internal models approaches, capital difference are surprisingly large: $14 for parametric VaR against $11,726 for historical simulation VaR. A straddle is a bet on large moves in the underlying position; a move in either direction results in a large value change of the option. These large moves can be driven by high volatilities or fat-tailed returns. The S&P 500 is only moderately fat-tailed (a kurtosis of around 5.5, where 3 is considered normal), but the parametric volatility, used by both the parametric and the Monte Carlo VaR methods, was 14.6% (annualized) at the end of the sample period (i.e., on the day this hypothetical risk exercise was undertaken), compared with 20.3% (call) or 20.1% (put) for the implied volatility. In combination, the slightly fatter tails and the higher volatility of the historical simulation lead to a much larger capital charge than is implied by the other two internal models approaches. The BCBS standardized approach is again the most conservative ($17,885), while capital charges under the other two rules-based approaches are both less than $1,000.

PITFALLS IN THE USE OF VAR

Regulatory approaches for setting capital charges for market risk seem to be converging across the three financial sectors to an internal models approach—some variant of VaR, supplemented by stress testing and scenario analysis. This approach is already widespread among internationally active banks and European securities houses. The SEC has experimented with an internal models approach for derivatives dealers, and a recent report to the European Commission has recommended adaptation of the Basel approach for insurance companies (KPMG 2002). But is VaR the optimal approach to risk measurement?

Evaluating VaR

Does VaR accurately measure market risk? We consider this question at a theoretical level later. At an empirical level, Kupiec (1995) and Jorion (1995) point out that VaR is itself an estimate of a true but unknown distribution quantile and thus suffers from estimation error just like any other parameter, an error that increases with the confidence level (99% VaR suffers greater error than 95% VaR). Kupiec (1995) shows that this error can be quite large.[67]

Several papers have examined the accuracy and information content of VaR model estimates with subsequent bank performance. Berkowitz and O'Brien (2002) compare daily VaR forecasts with next-day trading results using a sample of large U.S. banks and confidential supervisory data. While the VaR models provide a conservative estimate of the 99% tail on average, there is substantial variation across institutions. Moreover, they demonstrate that a simple Generalized Autoregressive Conditional Heteroskedasticity (GARCH) volatility model based on daily trading P&L outperforms the VaR models in forecasting next-day trading results. Jorion (2002) and Hirtle (2003) examine the information content of VaR reporting. Both studies suggest that such disclosures are indeed informative. Jorion (2002) finds that VaR disclosures predict variability in trading revenues. Similarly, Hirtle (2003) reports that data on reported market risk capital are useful for predicting changes in market risk exposure over time for individual banks; however, such disclosures provide little information about differences in market risk exposure across banks. In sum, VaR seems far from the last word in market risk measurement.

Horizons, Time Scaling, Liquidity, Extreme Events

What is the appropriate horizon over which to measure market risk? If volatility is measured at high frequency, how should it be scaled to a lower frequency? What is the impact of illiquidity on the market risk measure? Finally, since the risk manager is really interested in extreme events, why not model those directly?

The issues of horizon, time scaling, and liquidity are intimately related.[68] For very liquid instruments, a shorter horizon is certainly appropriate, while an instrument or position that is known to be relatively illiquid should be modeled with a longer horizon. The BCBS and CAD rules require that the market risk capital charge be sufficient to cover a 10-day holding period. For practical purposes, banks measure market risk, using VaR, for example, at a daily frequency, and the conversion from daily to 10-day (time scaling) is done using the root-t (or root-h) rule: multiply the daily standard deviation by the square root of the horizon. Thus, for a 10-day horizon, the daily VaR estimates are increased by $\sqrt{10} \approx 3.16$. Diebold et al. (1998) show that such scaling is inappropriate. They show it is strictly appropriate only for independently and identically distributed data and that it overestimates volatility at longer horizons.

Naturally, the horizon over which market risk is measured should also reflect the frequency of trading (Joint Forum 2001). This tends to be shortest for securities firms and longest for insurers. For example, the NAIC Life RBC for equities explicitly assumes a two-year holding period (AAA 2002), a period during which credit risk issues tend to dominate market risk. SEC haircuts are calibrated largely along lines of perceived liquidity, rendering U.S. treasuries the most liquid and nonlisted stocks relatively illiquid.

The purpose of the 10-day holding period in the BCBS and CAD regulations for banks is to build in an illiquidity premium. Jorion (2001) discusses various other approaches to dealing with liquidity risk, including the incorporation of information from the bid-ask spread and specific trading strategies. Bangia et al. (1999) distinguish between endogenous and exogenous liquidity risk depending on whether the position is large enough to influence the market price upon liquidation (endogenous) or whether the particular market, such as emerging markets equities (exogenous), is just inherently less liquid.

Finally, the direct modeling of extreme events using recent advances in the area of extreme value theory (EVT) has generated some new approaches to dealing with long-tail events. Originally developed for insurance questions (e.g., how high should the dykes be to prevent the one-in-500-year flood?), the toolkit of EVT is succinctly described for a broader technical audience in Embrechts, Klüppelberg, and Mikosch (1997). EVT holds the promise of providing a means of assessing probabilities of extreme events outside the range of historical experience. What, for example, is the probability of a 35% one-day drop in the S&P 500, and the consequent expected loss in a portfolio? Several papers are collected in a volume edited by Embrechts (2000) that includes an excellent introduction to the area for risk managers (McNeil), applications to value-at-risk (Danielsson and DeVries), multivariate EVT (Embrechts, de Haan, and Huang), and correlations (Embrechts, McNeil, and Straumann).[69] A more sobering assessment of EVT and its potential for risk management is provided in a contribution by Diebold, Schuermann, and Stroughair (1998) to *Decision Technologies for Computational Finance* edited by A. N. Burgess and J. D. Moody (1998).

Stress Testing and Scenario Analysis

It is industry best practice and a supervisory requirement in several countries to conduct stress testing and scenario analysis of one's portfolio. Stress testing serves two main objectives: it tests for capital adequacy/regulatory compliance, since it is required by the regulators; and it serves the market risk goal of control by informing management of potential losses/gains under extreme market conditions. The test should be performed regularly (quarterly or monthly firmwide, weekly or daily on a business level), and business lines should respond to stress testing results. While stress testing is supplemental to VaR for most firms, for some it has at least equal footing in their risk management process. Jorion (2000) points out that modest stress testing of one important correlation parameter would have exposed some significant risks to Long Term Capital Management in that firm's portfolio.

The extent to which supervisors should specify stress tests remains an open question. Supervisors in some countries resist specifying stress tests because they are concerned about an implicit implication that official support will be forthcoming in the event of shocks that exceed the levels specified in stress tests and because they believe that a supervisory requirement might subvert

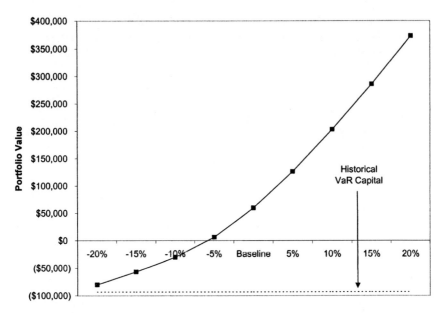

Figure 1.3. Impact of Stress Tests on Portfolio Value. Source: Authors'
compilation.

what should be a valuable management tool by making it a routine compliance task. Supervisors in other countries believe that they can gain valuable information about the vulnerability of the financial system to systemic
risk by reviewing the results of some standard stress tests for all regulated
market participants. Even supervisors who hold this view, however, believe
that firms should be encouraged to design their own stress tests, as well.

Stressing the Risk Factors. We conducted two sets of stress tests. The first
simply increased (decreased) each risk factor by 0 to 20% in steps of 5%.
The results are presented in figure 1.3, with the capital levels implied by the
historical simulation VaR indicated by a dotted line. Because the portfolio
has a combination of long and short positions as well as options, the relationship between risk factor changes is not linear (i.e., directly proportional to the changes in risk factors). A drop of a little more than 5% in all
of the risk factors is enough to render the portfolio to negative value. But
the option positions, designed largely to protect against adverse movements,
result in a less than proportional decline in portfolio values as the risk
factors drop by more and more. Even a drop of 20% in all the risk factors
does not cross the capital barrier implied by historical simulation VaR.

Scenario Tests. The second stress test was a series of three specific scenarios
as shown in table 1.11: (1) an E.U. crisis characterized by a flight from
equities to fixed income; (2) a Mexico crisis combining a drop in the peso
exchange rate with a dramatic increase in Mexican interest rates and a flight

Table 1.11. Stress Scenarios

Risk Factor	Scenarios: % Change of Risk Factor		
	E.U. crisis %	Mexican crisis %	Terrorism %
S&P 500	−10	−2	−10
FTSE 100	−20	−1	−10
Mexico IPC (Bolsa)	−10	−25	−10
U.S.$/UK£	−15	0	0
U.S.$/MX Peso	+10	−40	−5
U.S. treas. 1-yr.	+10	+10	−5
U.S. treas. 5-yr.	+10	+20	0
U.K. Interbank 1-yr.	+40	+10	−5
U.K. treas. 5-yr.	+30	+20	0
Mex. treas. 6-mo.	+10	+100	+5
Mex. treas. 1-yr.	+10	+100	0

Source: Authors' compilation.

to U.S. treasuries; and (3) a terrorism scenario that mimics broadly the market reactions following the September 11 attacks in New York and Washington, D.C. The percentage changes are judgmental and are designed to be a bit extreme for the purposes of the stress scenarios. The specific risk factor impacts are described in table 1.12.

The results are contained in table 1.12, with the last column summarizing the impact at the portfolio level. At the portfolio level it makes sense to ask the question, Does the scenario generate losses that exceed the required capital levels implied by the different capital regimes? Asking this question at the position level is not meaningful unless firms base their position limits on required capital. Still, it is interesting to track the impact of specific scenarios on individual position values. Only the E.U. crisis position results in a loss that exceeds the internal models capital levels, although it does not exceed any of the rules-based capital levels, Interestingly, the scenario we call "Mexico Crisis" results in a value gain of $44,148, from an initial value of $59,382 to $103,430.

Taking each crisis in turn for some position level outcomes, the E.U. crisis scenario has a significant adverse effect on the long U.K. bond, the long pound/short peso position, and the FTSE 100 protection put positions. It is worth dissecting the effect on the protection put, which, recall, is a long position in the FTSE 100 itself, protected with a put (strike just below the current FTSE 100 level), but valued in US$. The decline of 20% in the FTSE results in a large loss on the underlying position, partially offset by the put getting into the money. Once one factors in the change in the dollar/pound exchange rate, the net loss is about $150K. Some positions gain in value, namely the long IPC, the short S&P 500, and the FX hedged position (largely because U.S. and Mexican asset prices react positively in this scenario) as

Table 1.12. Impact of the Stress Test Scenarios ($)

Approaches	Long 5-yr., Short 1-yr. (U.S. Yield Curve Slope Exposure)	Long U.K. 5-yr. (U.K. Yield Curve + FX Exposure)	Flat	FX Swap (USD/GBP)	Long £, Short Peso, Long MX 6M	Long Mexican IPC, Short S&P, FX Hedged	Calendar Spread on S&P 500 (Δ & Rho Hedged)	Protection Put (FTSE)	Straddle on S&P 500 (Δ Hedged)	Total Portfolio
Net value	31,940	(0.07)	10,000	309	8	5,192	8,889	0.15	3,043	59,382
Basel capital (parametric VaR)	7,061	7,420	0	271	20,503	21,030	103	127,924	14	121,818
Basel capital (Monte Carlo VaR)	6,384	7,633	0	258	18,887	20,623	2,144	121,640	7	113,624
Basel capital (historical simulation VaR)	5,128	6,987	0	167	26,345	33,212	3,573	150,705	11,726	152,638
Basel standardized approach	3,250	4,412	0	1,362	1,098	11,481	31,225	263,332	17,885	334,044
SEC Rule 15c3-1 haircut	2,500	8,734	0	29,112	2,348	17,221	1,716	119,391	509	81,531
NAIC RBC: C1	0	437	30	44	109	37,516	1,163	228,120	956	268,374
E.U. crisis (net value)	30,384	(6,740)	10,000	384	(36,430)	15,296	7,080	(149,551)	9,607	(119,969)
Mexico crisis (net value)	28,765	(5,362)	10,000	338	57,983	5,611	8,687	(5,848)	3,356	103,530
Terrorism (net value)	31,888	0	10,000	295	7,265	15,484	7,099	(36,131)	9,634	45,534

Source: Authors' compilation.

well as the straddle on the S&P 500. The Mexico crisis generates a gain in the long pound/short peso position of nearly $58K, more than making up for losses in some of the other positions. Finally, the terrorism scenario yields large losses only on the protection put on the FTSE 100 (about $36K), while several of the other positions gain in value: the long pound, the short peso (up from $8 to $7,265), the long IPC, the short S&P (up from $5,192 to $15,484), and the straddle on the S&P 500 (up from $3,043 to $9,634).

Coherent Risk Measures and the Regulatory Framework

If regulators are to achieve their stated goal of making capital charges sensitive to the actual positions risks taken by regulated firms, how should their regulatory frameworks be designed? Christoffersen and Diebold (2000) and Berkowitz (2001) argue that, rather than focus on just one number such as VaR, risk managers and, implicitly, regulators should focus on the whole density function of returns, perhaps using techniques such as those laid out in Diebold, Gunther, and Tay (1998) and in Berkowitz (2001). Nonetheless, interest in a simpler, summary measure continues. What standards should such a summary measure meet, and how do the regulatory approaches currently in use measure up to these standards?

Artzner et al. (1997, 1999) lay out a set of criteria necessary for what they call a "coherent" measure of risk. Following roughly their notation, let X and Y be the returns k-periods from now for two subportfolios,[70] and let v be any real number, $\lambda \geq 0$, and r the risk-free interest rate. Then a coherent risk measure ρ must satisfy the following four conditions:[71]

(1) $\rho(X + Y) \leq \rho(X) + \rho(Y)$ [subadditivity]
(2) $\rho(\lambda \cdot X) = \lambda \cdot \rho(X)$ [homogeneity]
(3) $\rho(X) \geq \rho(Y)$ if $X \leq Y$ [monotonicity][72]
(4) $\rho(X + r \cdot v) = \rho(X) - v$ [risk-free condition]

Condition (1) is crucial in that it reflects basic portfolio effects: the risk of the sum cannot be greater than the sum of the risks. Condition (2), reflecting position scaling, raises the specter of large position sizes, since it states that breaking up the position/portfolio into λ pieces should be the same as λ times the risk of each piece. Indeed, a rather large position, especially if many market participants hold that same position, could be more than proportionately riskier than a small one due to impacts on prices upon liquidation. Ideally the liquidation impact should be reflected in the forecast of X (i.e., X_{t+k}). Conditions (1) and (2) together imply convexity of the risk measure corresponding to risk aversion by the regulator and/or the risk manager. Condition (3) simply means that if the value X (portfolio value k-periods ahead) is always less than (or equal to) Y, X must be riskier than Y. The last property (4) reflects risk treatments of risk-free investments: if an initial quantity v, invested at the risk-free rate r, is added to the portfolio of future value X, the firm enjoys capital relief of v.[73] If the entire portfolio is invested in the risk-free asset, it should be riskless.

A Returns   *B Returns*

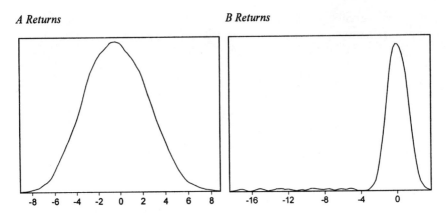

Figure 1.4. Two Portfolios: Bumps in the Tails. Source: Authors' compilation.

VaR satisfies all conditions except the first, subadditivity—that the risk of the sum is never greater than the sum of the risks.[74] Unfortunately, the subadditivity condition has important implications for the measurement and management of position risk. Specifically, it allows for decentralized measurement of risks, say for each position or product (an FX swap), to be added up to higher levels of aggregation—say to a desk (swaps), then to a group (trading) and a business unit (capital markets) in a coherent fashion. Financial institutions actually do manage their business in this drill-down/build-up fashion, so that violation of the subadditivity condition is a concern. One consequence is that VaR could be influenced by reorganizing the trading floor without changing the overall portfolio. Moreover, a firm could concentrate all of its tail risks in one desk in such a way that the risk borne by that desk appears just beyond the overall portfolio VaR threshold.[75]

How might this happen? One possibility is that the portfolio contains a position that might generate a loss only in extreme market conditions, effectively generating a bump or set of bumps in the tail of the portfolio return distribution. As an illustration, consider the following return distributions for two portfolios shown in figure 1.4. They have identical means and variances. Portfolio A is a Gaussian ($\mu = -0.5$, $\sigma = 2.6$), and portfolio B is a Gaussian mixture—95% N(0,1), 5% N(−10,25). Thus, portfolio B has some loss results that are large, albeit unlikely. The two portfolios may have identical VaRs at about the 5% level, but B is clearly more risky (which would show up at the 1% level in this case).

Crouhy, Galai, and Mark (2001, p. 253) point out that this situation is common in credit risk with concentrated portfolios that have large single exposures.[76] However, those same conditions may also occur in position risk, especially in the presence of options.

The other regulatory measures of position risk fare much worse. In addition to violating the subadditivity condition, they violate two more of the conditions for a coherent risk measure. While it is beyond the scope of this chapter to provide a formal evaluation of the coherency of each regulatory approach, we can make some simple observations. All of the regulatory approaches fail to satisfy the subadditivity condition because they fail to detect bumps in the tails (or "holes" on the way to the tails) in the portfolio return or value distribution. Artzner et al. (1999) point out that the SEC net capital rule also falls short of a coherent risk measure because it fails at least two additional conditions—(2) monotonicity and (3) homogeneity. The monotonicity condition is also violated by both the Basel Committee standardized approach and the NAIC RBC approach. A simple example is a calendar option with and without rho hedging (interest rate hedging). The hedge reduces risk while increasing required capital under both regulatory regimes. Similarly, the NAIC RBC approach violates the homogeneity condition because it penalizes concentrations of risk (i.e., position scaling). Specifically, the NAIC RBC provide a "concentration adjustment," or additional capital charge for lack of diversification (Webb and Lilly 1994, p. 139), to the 10 largest single-name exposures, since the baseline methodology does not sufficiently address concentration risk. To be sure, the ex post adjustment is appropriate in the context of the NAIC approach, but a coherent risk measure would not need such an ex post adjustment.

Expected Shortfall, Exceedence, Tail VaR

How could VaR be strengthened to meet the subadditivity condition? One potential solution is to include the expected shortfall or exceedence. It answers the simple question, How bad is bad? Borrowing from the insurance literature, authors such as Embrechts, Klüppelberg, and Mikosch (1997), Artzner et al. (1997, 1999), Neftci (2000), and Basak and Shapiro (2001), among others, suggest looking at the beyond-VaR region. Recall that we denoted $VaR(k,\alpha)$ as the VaR estimate at time t for a k-period ahead return. It is the critical value of the return distribution $f_{t+k}(\cdot)$ that corresponds to its lower α percent tail. More specifically, $VaR(k,\alpha)$ is the solution to

$$\alpha = \int_{VaR(k,\alpha)}^{\infty} f_{t+k}(x)dx \tag{1.4}$$

The BIS requirement for α and k are $\alpha = 1\%$ and $k = 10$ days. In the previous section, we saw that distributions with bumps in the tails are troublesome for standard VaR. One way to capture this tail effect is through the tail conditional expectation, called "Tail VaR" by Artzner et al. (1999) and EVaR by Crouhy, Galai, and Mark (2001). Very simply, it is the expected value of returns of the beyond-$VaR(k,\alpha)$ threshold:

$$E(x_t|x_t \le VaR(k,\alpha)) = \int_{-\infty}^{VaR(k,\alpha)} x \cdot f_{t+k}(x)dx \tag{1.5}$$

This measure describes the expected loss given that $VaR(k,\alpha)$ has been exceeded. Taking the mean is a very simple summary statistic of the beyond-VaR tail. However, the risk manager (and regulator) might care differently about the probability mass being piled up near the VaR threshold or further away (i.e., deeper into the tail), prompting one to consider estimating higher moments of the tail region (standard deviation, skewness, and so on). It becomes clear again that the information loss from attempting to summarize the portfolio risk in a single number from the whole density can be substantial.

Several researchers have already made use of this measure. Neftci (2000) applies the metric in combination with EVT to the tails of the distribution only. His portfolio contains fixed income and FX positions, and he finds that it performs surprisingly well in measuring the mean excess beyond some threshold (e.g., 1%), both in and out of sample. Basak and Shapiro (2001) show that risk managers who maximize their expected utility subject to a VaR constraint will optimally choose riskier portfolios than agents without the VaR constraint. While they ensure that their probability of loss is fixed (at α, their VaR constraint), as a consequence they suffer larger losses when a large loss does occur. Finally, Berkowitz (2001) provides a method for evaluating these tail-based metrics.

We can compute a tail VaR for our portfolio in the following fashion. The historical simulation VaR generates a distribution of portfolio returns for the current (12/31/2001) portfolio using all observed return values in the 1,300-day sample (see figure 1.5).

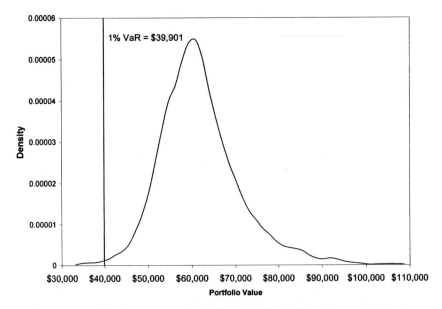

Figure 1.5. Portfolio Return Density—Historical Simulation. Source: Authors' compilation. Note: The distribution of values on the X axis is based on historical VaR.

The tail VaR at $\alpha = 1\%$ is the mean of all portfolio returns beyond the 1% tail. That value is $39,901, which exceeds the capital levels of all methods. That the tails are somewhat fat is confirmed by the portfolio kurtosis, 4.8, but it so happens that in our portfolio return distribution, the bumps are in the "good" tail.[77]

REGULATORY VERSUS MARKET CAPITAL REQUIREMENTS: CONCLUDING COMMENT

Leading firms in all three sectors customarily maintain levels of eligible regulatory capital far in excess of the regulatory minimums. The recent Joint Forum survey (2001, p. 53) found that banks typically operate with capital levels between 1.3 and 1.8 times required capital, securities firms maintain from 1.2 to 1.3 times the warning level,[78] and insurance companies have more than 5 times required capital. In part, this is due to regulatory inducements. In the United States, for example, banks must have a Tier 1 risk-based capital ratio of 6% or more (rather than the minimum of 4%) and a Tier 1 to total asset (leverage) capital ratio of 5% or more (rather than the 4% minimum) to be considered "well-capitalized" (USGAO 1998, p. 129). Well-capitalized banks have lower risk-based deposit insurance premiums and are more likely to receive regulatory permission for expansion of activities.

In addition, some regulatory sanctions cut in before the regulatory minimum. For example, broker-dealers undergo "heightened supervision" if their net capital falls below a warning level of 5% of their aggregate debit items relative to the regulatory minimum ratio of 2% (Joint Forum 2001, p. 95). Similarly, if an insurance company has total adjusted capital less than 200% of the regulatory minimum under which the supervisor may place the insurer under regulatory control, the insurance company is required to submit a plan to the supervisor for raising total adjusted capital above 200% (Joint Forum 2001, p. 98). But even allowing for a margin of safety to avoid regulatory sanctions, it appears that firms have significantly more capital than the regulators require. While some of the excess may represent an effort to stockpile capital to provide flexibility for strategic acquisitions, it appears that the binding constraint is not regulatory requirements but the market requirement.

Leading firms appear to target ratings for their long-term debt that exceed the degree of protection from insolvency that the regulators require. This decision is presumably driven by calculations of the debt rating and leverage ratio that will maximize shareholder returns. And so market discipline, not regulatory discipline, is the main constraint for most firms.

The rating agencies and financial analysts, which serve as delegated monitors for many investors, inform market assessments of position risk and capital adequacy for position risk. Their evaluations are based on qualitative and quantitative analysis of publicly available information, augmented sometimes in the case of rating agencies by private disclosures of information.[79] They are asked by investors and debtors to make comparative judgments across the three sectors—a challenge that the Joint Forum (2001, p. 5) concluded could not be met with confidence on the basis of regulatory data because "the frameworks and underlying accounting are different in so many respects." In response to market demands and regulatory pressure, the publicly available data for making such assessments are steadily improving.

Financial institutions are particularly opaque, however, making assessments by rating agencies and equity analysts more difficult. Morgan (2002) measures this opacity by showing that bond raters disagree more about banks and insurance companies than about any other kind of firm.

In the wake of a string of corporate losses from derivatives activity and in recognition of the increasing relevance of market risk in the assessment of corporate performance, the SEC (1997b) established disclosure standards for quantitative and qualitative information about market risk that took effect in June 1998. Virtually all publicly traded corporations in the United States must report quantitative information about their exposure to market risk in one of three formats: (1) a table of contract terms, including fair value of market-risk sensitive instruments and expected cash flows for each over the next five years and in the aggregate thereafter; (2) a sensitivity analysis of the potential loss in earnings due to possible near-term changes in interest rates, foreign exchange rates, commodity prices, and other market prices; or (3) VaR disclosures for market risk sensitive-instruments that might arise from market movements of a given likelihood over a specified interval.[80] The SEC's (1998) early evaluation of the new disclosures indicated that market participants find them useful, and the direct costs of disclosure have been relatively low.

In a study of oil and gas firms, Rajgopal (1999) found that the tabular and sensitivity analyses were, indeed, related to their exposure to energy prices. Trading portfolios at major financial institutions, however, are subject to a much broader range of risk factors in which VaR measures appear to be a more informative form of disclosure. Jorion (2002) has shown VaR disclosures by eight U.S. banks do indeed predict realized market risk.[81] It was not possible, however, to make meaningful direct comparisons of VaR disclosures across institutions. The sophisticated transformations that Jorion performed to extract useful comparative information indicate some of the limitations in current disclosure practices. VaR data were reported for different intervals—as period averages or as end-of-period levels or as graphs of daily levels—and with different underlying assumptions about the holding period and confidence level. Berkowitz and O'Brien (2002) compare daily VaR forecasts with next-day trading results using a sample of large U.S. banks containing confidential supervisory data. While the VaR models provide a conservative estimate of the 99% tail on average, there is substantial variation across institutions.

The recent BCBS (2002, p. 12) survey of public disclosures by 48 banks from 13 countries indicates that the challenge of making meaningful *international* comparisons across banks is even more difficult. Although almost all of the surveyed banks use VaR to assess their market risk, the details they disclosed about their VaR estimates varied considerably. While 96% of the banks disclosed the confidence level used for VaR estimates, only 89% disclosed the holding period assumption and 74% disclosed the observation period on which the VaR estimates were based. Only 47% provided a graph of daily profits and losses on trading activities combined with VaR, and 51% provided summary VaR data on a weekly or monthly basis. Nonetheless, this survey indicated an increased level of transparency of position risk exposures relative to a similar survey conducted two years earlier (BCBS/IOSCO 1999b, December).[82] In 1998, only two-thirds of the firms reported VaR measures, and only a quarter reported VaR results on a weekly or monthly basis.

The Technical Committee of IOSCO and the BCBS have agreed to a set of recommendations for public disclosure of trading activities of banks and securities firms (BCBS/IOSCO 1999a, February) that would enhance transparency and provide a sounder basis for market discipline by customers, creditors, counterparties, and investors.[83] The two committees agreed that information should be (1) provided with sufficient frequency and timeliness to give a meaningful picture of the institution's financial position and prospects; (2) comparable across institutions and countries and over time; and (3) consistent with approaches that institutions use internally to measure and manage risk, thus capturing enhancements in risk management practices over time. Their specific recommendations with regard to market risk disclosure include:

- Description of the major assumptions used to estimate VaR, including the type of model, holding period, confidence level, observation period, and portfolios covered
- Daily information on profits and losses on trading activities, combined with daily VaR
- Summary VaR results on a weekly or monthly basis
- Average and high/low VaR for the period
- Results of scenario analysis
- Discussion of the number of days actual portfolio loss exceeded VaR

The Basel Committee has made a renewed commitment to strengthening market discipline in the New Basel Capital Accord, although the recent working paper on Pillar 3 (BCBS 2001b) appears not to go quite as far as the earlier set of joint principles agreed to with IOSCO. Quantitative disclosures include only (1) the aggregate VaR; (2) the high, median, and low VaR values over the reporting period and the period end; and (3) a comparison of VaR estimates with actual outcomes, with analysis of important "outliers" in backtest results (BCBS 2001b, p. 13).

In view of the more limited use of mark-to-market accounting conventions and VaR in insurance companies, it is understandable that the insurance regulators did not join the Basel Committee and IOSCO in this statement of principles. But, until insurance companies make comparable disclosures, it will be difficult to compare position risk across the three sectors. Nonetheless, market discipline holds out greater hope for consistent treatment of position risk in the three sectors than harmonization of regulatory requirements. Once market participants gain a consistent picture of position risk exposures, they are likely to impose consistent capital standards in terms of economic capital, not the idiosyncratic kinds of regulatory capital recognized across the three sectors. So long as market demands, not regulatory capital requirements, remain the binding constraint on the largest firms, that should be sufficient to remove concerns about inconsistencies in the regulatory treatment of position risk.

APPENDIX 1: VALUE-AT-RISK

Value-at-risk has become the method of choice among financial institutions for measuring market risk and thus deserves perhaps more detailed treatment in this chapter. It is embedded in banking regulation in the form of the internal models approach implemented by the Basel Committee in 1996. Even insurance companies, the sector least focused on position risk, are beginning to make use of this approach.

DEFINITION OF VAR

VaR is used to answer the question, "On a daily basis, what is the value which is at risk during severe market fluctuations?" It is the potential loss of market value of a given portfolio of traded securities that is expected to be exceeded only according to a fixed probability (*tail probability* = 1 - *confidence level*) if the securities are held for a particular *holding period*. Hence, VaR is a specified quantile of the forecast portfolio return distribution over the holding period.

Suppose we have N risk factors, y_i, $i = 1, \ldots, N$. The return on risk factor y_i at time t is defined at $r_{i,t} = \ln(y_{i,t+1}/y_{i,t})$. Then the portfolio return is simply $r_{p,t} = \sum_{i=1}^{N} w_t r_{i,t}$ where the weights w_i sum to unity by scaling the dollar positions in each asset $y_{i,t}$ by the portfolio total market value Y_t. We may conveniently define portfolio mean return and portfolio volatility as:

$$E(r_{p,t}) = \mu_{p,t} = \sum_{i=1}^{N} w_{i,t}\mu_{i,t}$$

$$V(r_{p,t}) = \sigma_{p,t}^2 = \sum_{i=1}^{N} w_{i,t}^2 \sigma_{i,t}^2 + \sum_{i=1}^{N} \sum_{j=1, j\neq i}^{N} w_{i,t} w_{j,t} \sigma_{ij,t} = \mathbf{w}_t^T \Sigma_t \mathbf{w}_t$$

where Σ_t is the portfolio covariance matrix at time t.[84]

Let Y_t be the portfolio value at time t, and define the k-period ahead portfolio return as $r_{p,t+k} = \ln(Y_{t+k}/Y_t)$. Conditional on the information at time t, Ω_t, $r_{p,t+k}$ is a random variable with distribution $f_{t+k}(\cdot)$: $r_{p,t+k}|\Omega_t \sim f_{t+k}(\cdot)$. We denote the VaR estimate at time t for a k-period ahead return as VaR(k,α). It is the critical value of $f_{t+k}(\cdot)$ that corresponds to its lower α percent tail. More specifically, VaR(k,α) is the solution to

$$\alpha = \int_{\text{VaR}(k,\alpha)}^{\infty} f_{t+k}(x)dx \qquad (1.5)$$

As an example, the BIS requirement for α and k are $\alpha = 1\%$ and $k = 10$ days (see figure 1.6). The resulting capital charge from the internal model is the max of yesterday's 99% 10-day adjusted ($\sqrt{10}$) daily VaR or the average of the daily VaR over the preceding 60 trading days multiplied by the regulatory capital multiplier $\kappa \in [3,4]$, plus an additional capital charge for specific risk: $C_t^{BIS} = \max[VaR_{t-1}, \kappa \times \frac{1}{60}\sum_{i=1}^{60} VaR_{t-i}] + SR_t$. The calculations are to be based on data from at least one year (about 250 trading days).

Broadly, there are three approaches to computing VaR: two use parametric methods that make particular assumptions about the asset return distribution—specifically, that $f_{t+k}(\cdot)$ is multivariate Gaussian—and one is a nonparametric method that makes much weaker assumptions about the underlying return process. The first is called *parametric VaR*, a version of which has been popularized under the RiskMetrics moniker. This method is popular because it is so easy to compute. If the portfolio contains many nonlinear instruments such as options, VaR is best computed by parametric simulation, or *Monte Carlo*. The nonparametric approach, called *historical simulation*, lets the data speak more for themselves by simply resampling from the available sample path of risk factor returns. There is a price one pays, however; in addition to a significant computational burden, one is literally condemned to repeating history.

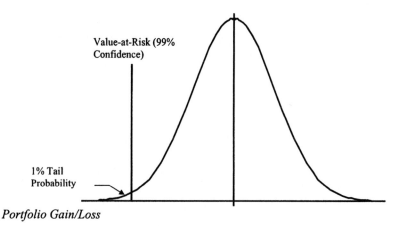

Figure 1.6. Stylized Value-at-Risk. Source: Authors' compilation.

A SHORT DIVERSION: OPTIONS

Because options play such a central role in risk management, it may be useful to briefly pin down their notation. Consider the value of an option $V = V(S, X, t, T, r, \sigma)$ where S = price of underlying position, X = strike price, t is a time indicator, T is the strike time (i.e., $T-t$ is the maturity), r = risk-free rate, and σ = volatility (annual) of the underlying position. We're interested in obtaining the change in value of the option as these factors change. This is easily obtained using a Taylor Series expansion ("the Greeks"):

$$dV = \frac{\partial V}{\partial S} dS + \frac{1}{2}\frac{\partial^2 V}{\partial S^2} dS^2 + \frac{\partial V}{\partial t} dt + \frac{\partial V}{\partial \sigma} d\sigma + \frac{\partial V}{\partial r} dr + \cdots \qquad (1.6)$$

where $\frac{\partial V}{\partial S}$ is called *delta*, $\frac{\partial^2 V}{\partial S^2}$ is called *gamma* (an option's convexity), $\frac{\partial V}{\partial t}$ is called *theta* (sometimes also called the time decay rate of the option), $\frac{\partial V}{\partial ma}$ is called *vega*, and $\frac{\partial V}{\partial r}$ is called *rho*. By definition, these changes are local, as they describe the effect of small changes of the arguments to the value of the option. Risk managers, however, are interested in more global characteristics. Hence, the Greeks are often of limited usefulness for risk management, if not for short-term (dynamic) hedging.

The simplest options are European equity options, either puts or calls. These can be valued using the well-known Black-Scholes pricing formulae. While these plain-vanilla options remain common and are even traded, there seems to be a nearly infinite variety of so-called exotic options (see, for instance, Zhang 1998). One can already achieve a modest degree of complexity by simply combining a set of simple European puts and calls, as we do in our simulation exercise.

VaR ESTIMATION

Parametric/Linear VaR

There are three fundamental elements in the basic approach. The first is the choice of *risk factors* to assess the risk of the portfolio, the second is the *covariance matrix,* and the third is the *sensitivity vector* that encapsulates the response of the portfolio.

There are two important assumptions on which the statistical structure of VaR rests:

1. Asset or security returns are linear functions of the underlying risk factors.
2. These returns follow a normal distribution and are linearly correlated.

The covariance matrix encapsulates all of the information concerning the volatility and the correlation of the risk factors. The sensitivity of each instrument to the risk factors is captured by the sensitivity vector, which is essentially the derivative of the price of each instrument with respect to each individual risk factor (also called Delta).[85]

Ultimately, the final expression for the value-at-risk of a portfolio results from combining the sensitivity vector for the portfolio with the covariance matrix:

$$\text{VaR}_t = \theta \cdot \sqrt{\mathbf{w}_t' \Sigma_{t+1} \mathbf{w}_t} \qquad (1.7)$$

The parameter θ depends on the desired confidence level; if, for example, this is 99%, then θ will be 2.33 for the Gaussian distribution.

It is common practice to determine parametric VaR by augmenting linear sensitivities (deltas, Δ) with quadratic changes of portfolio value with accompanying changes in underlying risk factors (gamma, Γ). Furthermore, BIS guidelines recommend that the parametric calculation be supplemented by including the effect of Γ.[86] This is straightforward, and any good commercial VaR system should be able to incorporate Γ effects.[87] The problem with relying on the Greeks for risk management is that these parameters are reliable only for small changes in the inputs to pricing models. They provide "local" answers and are essentially trader's tools, providing a useful guide for the continual rebalancing of the portfolio. But, for risk management, the interest usually lies in the large movements of the input variables— "global" answers across broad changes of the underlying positions—and for large movements, the Greeks are a very poor guide, since they themselves change rapidly.

We know that the linearity assumption is violated by having derivative products like options in one's portfolio. However, VaR is often a reasonable approximation of a firm's risk profile. For example, Nick Leeson's portfolio shortly before his downfall was dominated by positions in Japanese government bond futures and Nikkei futures (Jorion 2001). Not only is this portfolio highly concentrated (there are only two instruments), but it contains derivative products (a short straddle in Nikkei futures).[88] Nevertheless, basic VaR would have revealed that Leeson had almost $1 billion at risk! His final loss amounted to approximately $1.3 billion. Given the unusually large drop in the Nikkei following the Kobe earthquake, the highly concentrated nature of the portfolio, and its high proportion of derivatives, this loss is still remarkably close to the VaR forecast.[89]

The second assumption, multivariate normality, simplifies the VaR computation dramatically. Specifically, all we need to measure and model VaR are the variance and the correlation between assets or instruments, since the normal distribution is fully described by its first two moments. Then we should be able to predict well the likelihood of severe market fluctuations and their impact on loss, if not their exact timing.

VaR with Simulation: Parametric Monte Carlo and Historical

It turns out that it is easier to accommodate violations of the first assumption (nonlinearity) than of the second (fat tails). Fixes run the gamut

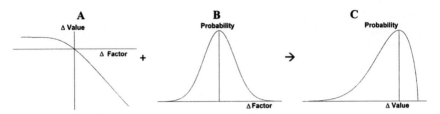

Figure 1.7. Option Payoffs and Value Distributions. Source: Authors' compilation.

from approximations via "the Greeks" to full valuation using extensive Monte Carlo simulation. Simulation-based approaches are the only way to adequately characterize the risk of even moderately complex options. To understand the distribution of value changes for the derivative instrument, consider the following diagram in figure 1.7.

Panel A describes the payoff function of the option as the underlying changes; here it is nonlinear. The next panel is the familiar distribution of the risk factor or the underlying, while panel C combines the two; it describes the distribution of value changes of the derivative product. In simulation, we generate artificially the data for B and recompute the value of the derivative product using A to obtain C. Note that C looks rather nonnormal, even though B looks quite normal. The reason is simple: the nonlinearity we see in A results in a nonnormal derivative value change distribution. Only a simulation-based approach will capture this.

Finally, even the distribution of the market factors themselves, panel B, might be nonnormal. One solution to this problem is to use the actual history, instead of a synthetically generated one, of the underlying risk factor to repeatedly revalue the derivative product. By using parametric Monte Carlo to understand the impact of nonlinearity and historical simulation to see the impact of nonnormality, one can achieve a reasonably satisfactory approximation of the risk profile of any instrument.

An example using two options from our mock portfolio is instructive. Consider a European calendar spread option on the S&P 500 index, delta and rho hedged, as well as a protection put on the FTSE 100 equity index, FX hedged.[90] [91] We compare VaR estimates obtained from a Monte Carlo simulation with similar estimates obtained from a historical simulation and the linear parametric variance-covariance approach in table 1.13. For the calendar spread option, the result of the linear parametric approach is significantly below the other two methods. Interestingly, the nonlinearity of options does not necessarily mean that this linear approach always underestimates risk. This becomes evident in the second example, the protection put, where the Monte Carlo approach actually indicates a lower risk value than the linear parametric. Fat tails, however, are ubiquitous. The historical simulation method yields the highest risk value in both examples.

Table 1.13. Comparison of VaR Techniques for Two Positions

	VaR Estimates	
Technique	S&P 500 Calendar Spread, Δ and ρ Hedged $	Protection Put on FTSE 100, FX Hedged $
Linear parametric	11	13,484
Monte Carlo simulation	226	12,822
Historical simulation	377	15,886

Source: Authors' compilation.

COMPARISON OF STATISTICAL VaR TECHNIQUES

Here we briefly summarize the strengths and weaknesses of the three VaR techniques described (see table 1.14).

- *Parametric delta-plus approach.* In the parametric technique, changes in value of a position are related to changes in underlying risk factors through linear sensitivities of the position to the risk factors. Changes in portfolio value result from an aggregation of such changes corresponding to all positions in the portfolio. Furthermore, risk factor returns are assumed to be joint normally distributed. With the knowledge of the covariance matrix and linear sensitivities of the portfolio value to changes in underlying risk factors, we can calculate the standard deviation of portfolio value through a simple matrix multiplication. VaR is proportional to this standard deviation, the proportionality constant being the inverse of a standard normal distribution corresponding to a desired level of confidence.

Table 1.14. Comparison of VaR Approaches

Attribute	Parametric Technique	Monte Carlo Simulation	Historical Simulation
Risk calculation			
Ease of computation	✓✓✓	✓	✓✓
Ability to capture nonlinearity	✓	✓✓✓	✓✓✓
Risk factor dynamics			
Ability to model nonnormality	✓	✓	✓✓✓
Independence from historical data	✓✓	✓✓✓	✓
Stress testing and risk decomposition			
Ability to model significant disturbance	✓	✓✓	✓✓
Ability to stress parameter assumptions	✓✓✓	✓✓✓	—
Ability to perform contributory risk analysis or to breakout risk sources	✓✓✓	✓✓	✓✓

Source: Authors' compilation.

The main advantage of the parametric approach is that it does not require large amounts of data and is computationally easy. The two underlying assumptions are the joint normally distributed risk factors and the linear response to changes in risk factors.

- *Monte Carlo approach.* This approach involves generating synthetic draws from a multivariate distribution with estimated parameters from the sample path of risk factor movements. Typically, that distribution is multivariate normal. The portfolio is revalued at the generated risk factor movements, and VaR is determined from the resulting distribution of portfolio value changes for a given level of confidence.

The Monte Carlo approach relaxes the assumption of linear response to changes in risk factors and therefore provides significantly better results for portfolios with a large number of options, albeit at the cost of computational intensity. This can become a binding constraint if the portfolio contains many options and/or those options are quite complex, sometimes known as exotic options.

- *Historical simulation approach.* Historical simulation entails generating the joint variation of risk factor returns from historical time series information. The daily returns obtained from historical data are used to determine potential movements in the value of today's risk factors, and these represent historical "trials." The current portfolio is revalued for each historical trial, and resulting changes in value are used to determine the distribution of portfolio value change. VaR is defined as the distance from the mean of this empirical distribution to a point corresponding to the desired confidence level.

The historical simulation approach relaxes both assumptions of joint normality and linear response, but it is the hardest to implement: it is computationally very intensive and requires a large amount of data to be effective.

APPENDIX 2: MODELING VOLATILITY OF ASSET RETURNS

We commonly observe asset or security prices P_t, but we are interested in modeling daily returns, which are a function of the price changes. The return is defined as the natural log of the ratio of today's price to yesterday's price:

$$r_t = \ln(P_t/P_{t-1}) \tag{1.8}$$

Daily return processes are usually assumed to have a zero mean and no serial correlation. These conditions are typically met. Note, however, that simply because we find no serial correlation (i.e., dependence over time) for the returns does not necessarily mean that no temporal dependence exists. This subtle but important distinction is a result of the first of two stylized

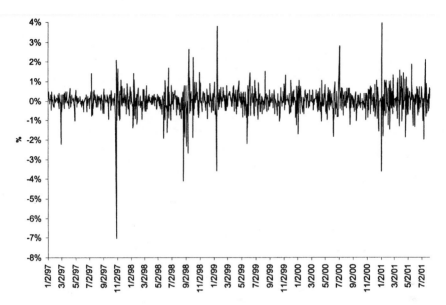

Figure 1.8. Time Series of Daily Returns, MXP/US$, 1/1/1997–12/31/2001.
Source: Authors' compilation.

facts about asset returns:

- They exhibit volatility clustering; low volatility periods tend to cluster together as do periods of high volatility.
- The distribution has fat tails relative to the normal; it is said to be leptokurtic (have excess kurtosis).

We illustrate these points using a time series of daily returns for the U.S. dollar price of the Mexican peso, a currency we will use in the risk illustrations later. Volatility clustering is illustrated in figure 1.8, while leptokurtosis is illustrated in figure 1.9.

Fat-tailed returns are particularly prevalent in emerging markets. For example, for the range of our sample (January 1, 1997 to December 31, 2001), daily returns on the pound sterling price of the dollar has a kurtosis of 4.0, while for the U.S. dollar price of the Mexican peso the kurtosis is 22.6, Note that the kurtosis of a normally distributed random variable is always exactly 3.

In figure 1.9, we show in the left panel the entire density, and in the right we show only the left tail. Relative to the superimposed normal, the phenomenon of "too many large moves" becomes clear. This is a direct result of the leptokurtosis, or fat-tail phenomenon.

Volatility models for risk management should capture these two phenomena of volatility clustering and fat tails. In the next section, we illustrate some of the approaches commonly used in industry for risk management.

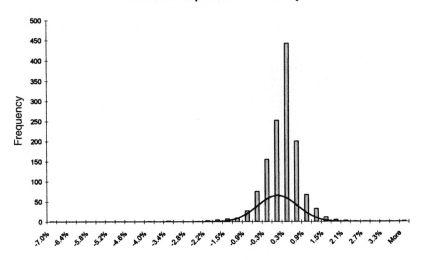

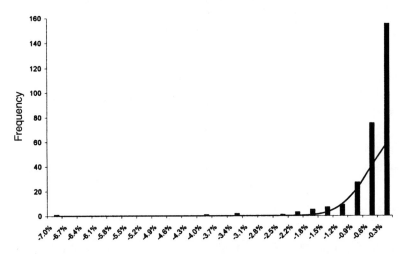

Figure 1.9. Density of Daily Returns: MXP/US$, 1/1/1997–12/31/2001.
Source: Authors' compilation.

MODELS OF VOLATILITY

There are two approaches to obtaining an estimate of volatility: historical, based on past returns, and implied, which is based on options.

Historical (Return-Based) Models of Volatility

Historical models of volatility involve a combination of the immediate past, usually yesterday, and the historical average. They differ in the weight they assign to these two factors. Putting too much weight on the historical average risks ignoring important recent events or structural changes. Conversely, placing too much weight on yesterday's activity produces very noisy estimates that perform quite poorly in forecasting.

At one extreme is the straight moving average (MA) model that weights the immediate past equally with all other observations. The estimate of today's variance is merely the estimate we have today of the historic average:

$$\sigma_T^2 = \frac{1}{T-1}\sum_{t=1}^{T} r_t^2.$$

For banking, the BIS requires the sample length T to be at least one trading year, or about 250 days, although institutions are encouraged to use longer periods.[92]

The workhorse of volatility models in finance is surely the GARCH (1,1) model.[93] This model was first developed by Engle (1982) as ARCH and then extended by Bollerslev (1986) to G(eneralized) ARCH. Its popularity stems largely from its ability to model well univariate asset returns and to capture the two important stylized facts of volatility clustering (serial correlation in the squared returns) and fat tails. The GARCH forecast of the variance is a linear combination of the historical variance, the previous day's squared return, and a constant term, ω:

$$\sigma_T^2 = \omega + \alpha r_T^2 + \beta \sigma_{T-1}^2 \qquad (1.10)$$

A special case of this three-parameter model is the one-parameter Exponentially Weighted Moving Average (EWMA) model implemented in a popular industry risk model, RiskMetrics:

$$\sigma_T^2 = (1-\lambda)r_T^2 + \lambda \sigma_{T-1}^2 \qquad (1.11)$$

where the weighting parameter λ is between 0 and 1. A comparison of the GARCH and EWMA model reveals that GARCH reduces to EWMA if $\alpha + \beta = 1$ and $\omega = 0$.

A simple interpretation of the EWMA model is as an information updating model: new information receives weight $(1 - \lambda)$; thus, the decay rate of information is λ^t. The smaller is λ, the more weight is placed on today's information set as described by r_T^2.[94] Several empirical studies have found that for modeling daily asset prices in general, values of $\lambda = 0.93$, 0.95, and 0.97 are appropriate. RiskMetrics uses $\lambda = 0.94$ for its daily forecast.

Implied Volatility

An alternative to the historical returns-based view of estimating volatility is simply to look at the prices of options in the market. The value of an option $V = V(S, Xt, T, r, \sigma)$ where S = price of the underlying position, X = strike price, t is a time indicator, T is the strike time (i.e., T-t is the maturity), r = risk-free rate, and σ = volatility (annual) of the value of the underlying position. Given a market price of an option denoted $\tilde{V}$, one can solve for the volatility *implied* by that option price, call it $\tilde{\sigma}$, using the relevant options pricing formula (e.g., Black-Scholes for European options). Implied volatilities are sometimes favored, since they are said to be forward looking and better able to reflect market sentiment, but they are available for only a limited set of assets.

PERFORMANCE OF VOLATILITY MODELS

Historical Models

If GARCH fits the data well and is a general case of the other two models, why would it not necessarily be the model of choice? The first and dominant reason is that GARCH does not extend easily to a multivariate environment. Second, GARCH has in fact not lived up to its promise in out-of-sample forecasting and prediction. Hendricks (1996) compares many different models, among them several EWMAs, GARCH, and MA, and finds that EWMA performs consistently as well or better than all others. His paper is important because the comparison is across a very broad class of assets and models. Diebold and Lopez (1995) point out that volatility model performance can differ greatly across asset classes and markets. One model may predict bonds in Europe very well but do quite poorly modeling stock return volatility in Japan.

Implied Volatility Models

Which broad class of models does better: historical returns-based or implied volatility models? Day and Lewis (1992) were among the first to examine this question. Using implied volatilities from S&P 100 options, they compare these to GARCH and to exponential GARCH volatility forecasts and find that the implied forecasts do contain some contain useful information in forecasting volatility but perform no better than the historical. Canina and Figlewski (1993), by contrast, find that implied volatility is almost always dominated by historical models. More recently, Fleming (1998) finds mixed evidence on which model yields a better forecast. He finds that implied volatilities systematically overpredict future volatilities but that the bias is not large enough to suggest trading opportunities.

What Is "True" Volatility?

Each of the model classes mentioned, historical and implied, is in no way model-free. In fact, one might argue that implied volatility is doubly model-dependent: one to price the option, (perhaps the same, perhaps not) to back out the volatility from the observed market price. A model-free approach based on squared returns over the relevant horizon is, unfortunately, a very noisy indicator of volatility.

With the availability of ultra-high frequency data for markets such as FX and equities, it has become possible to approximate the (unobservable) continuous time data generating process. One such approach is outlined in Andersen, Bollerslev, Diebold, and Labys (2001) for FX and in Andersen, Bollerslev, Diebold, and Ebens (2001) for equities. Here the authors lay out a method for constructing so-called expost realized daily volatilities from much higher frequency (e.g., two-minutely) squared returns. These authors find impressive improvements over GARCH type models in forecasting realized volatility. By contrast, Blair, Poon, and Taylor (2001) look at intraday returns and find that nearly all relevant information is contained in the implied volatilities. Moreover, in out-of-sample forecasting, the implied volatilities are tough to beat.

Acknowledgments We would like to thank the following people for sharing their insights with us: Terry Allen, David Andrews, Tanya Azarchs, George Benston, Richard Cantor, Jane Carlin, Shelley Cooper, Michel Crouhy, David Cummins, John Ehinger, Jr., David Fanger, Jerry Fons, Beverly Hirtle, Ugur Koyluoglu, Paul Kupiec, Elise Liebers, Richard Lindsey, Julian Manning, Geoffrey Mayne, Thomas McGowan, Basil Miller, Robert Mills, Lyndon Nelson, Peter Nerby, Evan Picoult, Stefan Walter, Kate Wormald, and George Zanjani, as well as the participants in the Conference on Risk-Based Capital at Harvard Law School. We are also grateful to Robert Jackson, Chris Metli, and David Muir for their excellent research assistance. All remaining errors are ours.

Notes

1. See Dimson and Marsh (1995, pp. 831–33) for a discussion of the abortive attempts to reach international agreement on capital requirements for securities firms. There were extensive negotiations to harmonize the capital regulation of position risk, not only for securities firms but also for internationally active banks.

2. Capital Adequacy Directive (93/6/EEC) and its amendments are virtually identical with the Basel Committee Amendment on Market Risk (BCBS 1996a) and applies to both banks and securities firms in the European Union.

3. Kuritzkes, Schuermann, and Weiner (2003) report the results of a benchmarking study conducted by Oliver, Wyman & Company that surveyed the internal economic capital allocations of nine leading international banks in Europe and North America, as well as summarizing other practitioner studies. In each case, the amount of economic capital allocated for credit risk far exceeded allocations to market/asset/liability management risk or operational risk.

4. The 10 financial institutions with the largest share of foreign-exchange market activity in 2001, which together accounted for 53.4% of total activity, included four U.S. banks, two U.S. securities firms, three European universal banks, and a British bank (Wilke 2002).

5. Technical provisions must take account not only of the expected payout but also of future premiums and investment income. For an excellent discussion of technical provisions see Annex 3 in Joint Forum (2001, pp. 85–90).

6. As pointed out in Joint Forum (2001, p. 29), capital plays a smaller role in absorbing volatility for insurance companies than for banks because of the importance of these technical provisions.

7. This may be subject to change. A recent report to the European Commission (KPMG 2002, p. 17) recommended that a new risk-based system include market risk as well as underwriting risk and credit risk.

8. Because the customers of reinsurers are other insurers, not unsophisticated retail clients, reinsurers are not subject to capital regulation in many countries (IMF 2002, p. 49).

9. Other regulatory tools include fit-and-proper tests, enforcement of conduct-of-business and conflict-of-interest rules, and customer suitability requirements. Insurance that would indemnify customers in the event that the firm cannot honor its obligations also serves this function. Examples include deposit insurance, pension benefit guarantee insurance, and insurance for customers of brokers and dealers. In the United States, the Securities Investor Protection Corporation insures customers of brokers and dealers against fraud.

10. Benston (2000) rejects the consumer protection rationale for regulating financial services, arguing that, in comparison with other consumer products, financial products are less difficult to understand, less difficult to identify as defective, and, apart from life insurance, shorter in period of service, Moreover, he argues that consumers of financial services have readier access to redress against products that turn out to be "lemons."

11. Not all observers agree that the prevention of systemic risk should be an important objective of bank capital regulation. See, for example, Benston and Kaufman (1995).

12. In many countries, banks control 70% or more of the assets in the financial system. In the United States, however, the bank share of total assets has fallen to little more than 20% (BIS 1996, p. 126).

13. Allen and Gale (1998) develop a model in this spirit that is based on the empirical work of Gorton (1988) and Calomiris and Gorton (1991). It shows that nineteenth-century banking panics were preceded by a downturn in leading economic indicators.

14. In contrast, the Shadow Financial Regulatory Committee has argued that regulation should focus on the insured depository institution and need not be concerned with other entities in the group so long as their liabilities vis-à-vis the bank are strictly limited (U.S. Shadow Financial Regulatory Committee 2000).

15. In the United States, the Securities Investor Protection Corporation protects the assets of clients in case the separation of client funds from the firm's own funds has been compromised through incompetence or fraud.

16. The solvent, regulated subsidiaries were not included in the filing. Indeed, broker/dealers are prohibited from entering reorganization proceedings.

17. Because of concern over settlement risks, some difficulties were experienced in winding down DBLG's positions in markets that did not clear and settle through simultaneous delivery of instruments against payment. To allay fears that that the settlement process might be aborted after delivery of payment to the trustee for DBLG but before delivery of the securities to the counterparty, the Bank of England intervened to assure market participants that transactions with the trustee of DBLG would be completed.

18. This is based on data provided by the national authorities in France, Germany, Italy, Japan, Switzerland, the United Kingdom, and the United States and reported in table I.6 of Group of Ten (2001). Unfortunately, data are not available for the entire decade, but concentration increased markedly between December 1998 and December 1999.

19. A recent Group of Thirty (1997, p. 7) study on systemic risk includes large securities among "core institutions" that may be a source of systemic risk. Core institutions include "large, internationally-active commercial banks, which are major participants in large-value payments systems, along with the largest investment banks which are key participants in the clearing and settlement systems for globally-traded securities."

20. The IOSCO (1989) paper "Capital Adequacy for Securities Firms" elaborates on this point, asserting that capital adequacy standards should be designed "to achieve an environment in which a securities firm could wind down its business without loss to its customers or the customers of other broker-dealers and without disruption to the orderly functioning of financial markets."

21. Section 3, Article 14 (Commission of the European Communities 2001, p. 24), states, "Competent authorities may in particular require the establishment of a mixed financial holding company that has its head office in the Community, and apply to the regulated entities in the financial conglomerate headed by the holding the provisions of this Directive."

22. These firms include Credit Suisse First Boston (CSFB), Goldman Sachs, Lehman Brothers, Merrill Lynch, Morgan Stanley, and Salomon Brothers (Derivatives Policy Group 1995).

23. To date, only two large nonbanks have formed Financial Services Holding Companies—Charles Schwab and MetLife. Of the DPG, both CSFB and Salomon Brothers are affiliated with banks and are therefore subject to consolidated supervision.

24. Nor does it play a prominent role in academic analysis. Cummins, Harrington, and Niehaus (1993), for example, make no mention of systemic risk in their analysis of the objectives of solvency regulation.

25. The Group of Thirty (1997, p. 7) study on systemic risk concluded that the insurance companies were not among the core institutions that could be sources of systemic risk: "Core institutions do not include large insurance companies or large finance companies, even those that are very active in international markets. Although these institutions are important by virtue of their size, they present substantially less risk to the system than failure of the core institutions of which they are customers."

26. A possible exception to this generalization is provided by the failure of HIH, an Australian insurance company with operations in Europe, Asia, North America, and South America and a large number of creditors that included several globally active banks. This was the largest failure in Australian history, with losses totaling between \$3.6 and \$5.3 billion. Nonetheless, the event did not cause significant volatility in Australian or global capital markets (IMF 2002, p. 54). It did, however, cause substantial dislocations in the construction market, although this appears to have been attributable more to its monopoly position in this market than to its status as an insurance company. The commission charged with investigating the collapse of HIH (HIH Royal Commission 2003, chapter 8.2.1) concluded, in its analysis of the rationale for prudential regulation, that "Contagion is less relevant in the insurance industry. The failure of HIH did, however, impose significant costs on other sectors, For example, the building industry was seriously affected when HIH collapsed as builders found it difficult to find warranty insurance cover to projects in some states. This was at least partly the result of the dominance of parts of the builders warranty market by HIH. A market with a larger number of providers may be better able to cope with the failure of one provider than a market dominated by one company."

27. Since ING is a financial conglomerate that contains a bank as well as insurance companies, the incident also raises a question about the extent of contagion from a nonbank affiliate to the bank within the group.

28. Of course, an insurance company can adopt a liability structure that makes it vulnerable to a liquidity crisis. For example, General America Life issued $6.8 billion in short-term debt containing an option that permitted investors to redeem their claims with only seven days' notice. After a downgrade by Moody's, investors tried to redeem more than $4 billion, forcing the regulator to intervene (Swiss Re 2000).

29. A recent IMF report (2002, p. 55) concludes that "many observers—including many involved with the insurance industry in some meaningful ways—have reached a comfort level with the judgment that the international systemic risks associated with the financial market activities of insurance companies are relatively limited." The report cautions, however, that the collapse of an insurance company could affect financial stability by inflicting losses on counterparties that do play a central role in the payment and securities settlement systems. But this concern applies equally to any large counterparty of a core financial institution.

30. The Basel Committee (BCBS 1988, p. 20) justified limitations on the use of subordinated term debt by noting that such instruments are "not normally available to participate in the losses of a bank which continues trading." Nonetheless, the authorities in several countries have the authority to permit a bank to continue trading under supervisory control after its capital is depleted. For example, in the United States the FDIC is authorized to create a bridge bank that enables it to impose losses on holders of subordinated debt even though the bank continues operation.

31. Nonetheless, as Scott and Iwahara (1994) have shown in their careful comparison of the implementation of the Basel Accord in Japan and the United States, cross-country differences are also highly significant.

32. For a more detailed comparison of balance sheets, see Joint Forum (2001, Annex 2).

33. Brick (2002, p. 1) asserts that traders made optimistic estimates of long-run energy prices and booked the resulting (unrealized) capital gains in current income.

34. Reserving practices vary markedly across countries for tax, regulatory, and accounting reasons. Scott and Iwahara (1994) highlight differences between practices in Japan and the United States. See Carey (2002, appendix A) for a discussion of accounting conventions with regard to credit losses.

35. This treatment applies only to bonds "in good standing." A bond is considered "in good standing" if (Troxel and Bouchie 1995, p. 9) "it is not in default, has a maturity date, is amply secured, and is among the classes of bonds approved by the NAIC. Other bonds are shown at market value unless there is a reason to believe a lower value would be realized for their sale."

36. Appendix D to the U.S. Net Capital Rule, 15c3-1 (SEC 1997a), sets out the conditions for satisfactory subordination agreements.

37. National regulators are free to decide whether to allow banks to employ Tier 3 capital at all. Several have chosen not to authorize Tier 3 capital. Linnel, Andrews, and Moss (2000, p. 4) conclude that banks have been deterred from issuing Tier 3 capital because the lock-in clause gives it a higher risk profile compared to Tier 2 subordinated debt, so that "spreads on such instruments must exceed the spread of lower Tier 2 to compensate investors for the additional risk. As a result, not only is Tier 2 term subordinated debt cheaper, but it is also a more flexible capital instrument because it can be used against both trading and banking book exposure."

38. Applying market risk capital to interest rate instruments in the trading book only may discourage the taking of positions in the trading book to hedge interest rate risk exposure in the banking book.

39. "Specific risk means the changes in the market value of specific positions due to factors other than broad market movements, including idiosyncratic variations as well as event and default risk." (USGAO 1998, p. 125).

40. Hendricks and Hirtle (1997) point out that "[t]he actual number of institutions that are ultimately subject to the market risk capital requirements may differ from these figures for two reasons: supervisors can, at their own discretion, include or exclude particular institutions, and institutions have the option to become subject to the capital requirements with supervisory approval."

41. EU (93/6/EEC).

42. See Hendricks and Hirtle (1997) for an excellent overview.

43. Stahl (1997) shows that there is probabilistic rationale for the range of the multiplier, albeit post hoc. VaR estimates are just that—estimates—and hence suffer from noise. Stahl shows that the relevant scaling factor should be between 2.5 and 4, making the choice of 3 quite reasonable.

44. I.e., $6\frac{2}{3}$ % of L^{sec}.

45. Often the major U.S. securities firms maintain two unregistered affiliates to deal in OTC derivatives: one that is AAA-rated and bankruptcy remote for ultra-credit-sensitive counterparties and an unrated affiliate.

46. SEC 1998 (Release No. 34-40594, OTC Derivatives Dealers).

47. Section (c)(2)(vi) of Rule 15c3-1.

48. See the December 1997 Commentary SEC Release No. 34–39456; File No. S7-32-97, especially pp. 9–10.

49. SEC 1998 (Release No. 34–38248; File No. S7-7-94, pp. 9–11).

50. The major market currencies are Deutschemark, British pound, Swiss franc, French franc, Canadian dollar, Japanese yen, and European currency unit.

51. For more detail on the P&C RBC formulation, see Feldblum (1996). For a comparison of life, health, and P&C, see AAA (2002).

52. Capital for business risk is typically assessed in the United States by the state insurance guaranty fund.

53. In 1991, the average diversification benefit via this formula was 11.4% for U.S. insurers.

54. Actually, if the ratio is between 2 and 2.5 and declining, the insurer may drop into the first category ("Company Action Level") at the discretion of the supervisor (Webb and Lilly (1994, p. 4).

55. Interest rate risk appears only in the life, not in the P&CRBC, formula.

56. A 30bp probability of failure over a one-year horizon corresponds roughly to a BBB rating, about the average for the U.S banking system, Interestingly, the average annual default rate of U.S. banks from 1934 through 2000 has been 26 bp.

57. Webb and Lilly (1994) contains full detail, including adjustments for differing loss given default (LGD) assumptions.

58. Examples of liquidity reports include lists of highly liquid securities that can be sold without triggering a capital loss, maximum cash that can be raised in 30 days, and ratio of liquid assets to projected surrender under three scenarios (base, stressed, and panic).

59. The Black-Scholes pricing formula applies strictly only to these simple options. Even the simple extension to the American option, which can be exercised at

any time between the purchase and expiry date, cannot be accurately priced using the Black-Scholes formula.

60. The historical simulation approach requires repricing the position at time t for $t = 1, \ldots, T$ total trading days (we have 1,304 days) at the prevailing price. For options positions this requires using the prevailing implied volatility to reprice the option at that date. Our simplified approach ignores smile features of the implied volatility.

61. For additional discussion of these approaches to modeling VaR, see appendix 1.

62. See appendix 2 for a more detailed discussion of modeling the volatility of asset returns. See also Hendricks (1996).

63. Pritsker (2001) reminds us that historical VaR is not a panacea by showing that even this method misses significant tail events.

64. Consequently, broker/dealers book most swap activity in affiliates.

65. For computational convenience, we calculate contributory VaR for the linear approach only, which does not take account of the nonlinearities in returns introduced by the option positions.

66. Recall that this portfolio is valued from the perspective of a \$-denominated institution.

67. Lopez (1999) compares alternative methods for evaluating VaR models and develops his own superior method based on proper scoring rules of probability forecasts.

68. See Christofferson, Diebold, and Schuermann (1998).

69. See also Neftci (2000).

70. We suppress subscripts k (periods into the future) and α (confidence level or critical value) here.

71. Ugur Koyluoglu's comments were very helpful in this section.

72. There is some confusion about the inequalities in this expression. In their more technical paper—Arztner et. al. (1999)—the inequality is reversed because of a slight difference in definition of X and Y. Their 1997 paper, as well as Jorion's (2001) treatment of coherent risk measures, reflects our notation.

73. Arztner et al. (1999) call this condition "translation invariance," with the implication that for each X, $\rho(X + \rho(X) \cdot r) = 0$.

74. Note that if the underlying distributions of all the risk factors are normal, then subadditivity is not violated.

75. For a fascinating discussion about the difficulty of risk capital attribution, see Koyluoglu and Stoker (2002).

76. One need not have a large position to violate subadditivity, Consider the example of two uncorrelated \$1 loans, each with a probability of default equal to 0.9%. Their individual 99% VaRs would both be zero. However, their combined VaR will be \$1 because the probability that one of the loans will default in this two-loan portfolio is 1.784%. (Ugur Koyluoglu kindly provided us with this example.)

77. These and other approaches are discussed in a special issue of the *Journal of Banking and Finance* 26 (7) (July 2002), which is devoted to the topic of VaR and beyond VaR.

78. Defined below as 5% of aggregate debit items.

79. The SEC's recent Fair Disclosure regulation (Regulation FD) requires that material disclosures to security analysts be made available at the same time to the public at large.

80. Linsmeier and Pearson (1997) describe the rationale for the SEC's approach.

81. Hirtle (2003) finds that reported market risk capital is useful for predicting changes in market risk exposure over time for individual banks; however, such disclosures provide little information about differences in market risk exposure across banks.

82. The results are not directly comparable because the sample included 40 banks and investment banks from 12 different countries.

83. One channel of market discipline has received considerable attention—subordinated debt. At least eight recent studies—Board of Governors (2000), DeYoung et al. (2001), Flannery and Sorescu (1996), Hassan (1993), Hassan, Karels, and Peterson (1993), Jagtiani and Lemieux (2001), Jagtiani, Kaufman, and Lemieux (2002), and Morgan and Stiroh (1999)—have found that secondary market debt spreads consistently reflect risk differences across banking organizations. Unfortunately, several factors in addition to the probability of default affect yields and spread. Hancock and Kwast (2001) have emphasized the lack of liquidity in many secondary markets. Elton et al. (2001) found that, while default risk is significant in spreads between (nonfinancial) corporate and government bonds, it accounts for a smaller proportion of the spread than the tax premium and risk premium. Similarly, Collin-Dufresne, Goldstein, and Martin (2001) find that default risk explains only about one-quarter of the variation in the changes in spreads. Although liquidity factors explain a bit more of the remaining variation, most of it is explained by a component that is unrelated to firm-specific or macroeconomic factors. Partly because variations in the price of subordinated debt are not related solely to credit risk, the U.S. Shadow Financial Regulatory Committee (2000) has suggested that regulatory sanctions be linked to a sustained rise in a bank's spread above the investment grade spread. Further, the Committee suggested that, if secondary markets are thin, greater emphasis be placed on regular issuance of subordinated debt at spreads no greater than the spreads on investment-grade securities on the assumption that in order to place an issue of subordinated debt on reasonable terms, the bank will be obliged to make appropriate disclosures to potential investors.

84. Since VaR is the value at risk at the end of the day t over the day $t+1$, Σ_t is then used as a forecast for $t+1$ and hence sometimes assumes that subscript, Σ_{t+1}.

85. Note that we do not describe the important and nontrivial process of mapping position cash flows into risk factors. Typically, a financial institution will have a very large number of positions (50,000 or more is not rare) but a smaller number of risk factors (N). For instance, the RiskMetrics dataset comprises fewer than 500 risk factors. See Jorion (2001, chapter 7) and J. P. Morgan (1995, part III).

86. In fact, even the Basel standardized approach requires the use of Γ and vega for the calculation of capital if options are both bought and sold by the bank.

87. An exercise conducted by Marshall and Siegel (1997) is revealing. They gave portfolios of varying degrees of complexity to 11 different vendors and found the discrepancy in risk outputs to be distressingly wide.

88. Our mock portfolio contains a straddle, as well.

89. Leeson's portfolio risk is still underestimated by 25%, a large portion of which would have been captured using a simulation-based method as described in the next section. If, in addition, the derivative instrument has a discontinuous payoff function such as with a barrier option, the limitations of the parametric linear method become even more apparent. Only a simulation-based approach reveals the value impact of these trigger points.

90. A calendar spread option is composed of two calls with the same strike but different maturity dates.

91. A protection put is a put option with a strike at or below the current level and a long position in the underlying security.

92. Sometimes the variance is normalized by T instead of $T-1$. Clearly, for large T, this makes very little difference. Technically, this will still produce a consistent if biased (for finite samples) result.

93. For an extensive discussion of ARCH modeling in finance, see Bollerslev, Chou, and Kroner (1992).

94. There is sometimes confusion about the subscripts in (11), specifically that the right side is not contemporaneous. Strictly speaking it is; (11) should be interpreted as an updating equation. Given σ^2_{T-1} that is known by time $=T$, the analyst takes the observation realized at T, squares it, and updates the volatility, as in (11).

References

Allen, Franklin, and Douglas Gale. 1998. Optimal Financial Crises. *Journal of Finance* 53 (4): 1245–84.

American Academy of Actuaries (AAA). 2002. Comparison of the NAIC Life, P&C, and Health RBC Formulas. *Report from the Academy Joint RBC Taskforce* (February).

Andersen, Torben G., Tim Bollerslev, Francis X. Diebold, and Heiko Ebens. 2001. The Distribution of Realized Stock Return Volatility. *Journal of Financial Economics* 61 (1): 43–76.

Andersen, Torben G., Tim Bollerslev, Francis X. Diebold, and Paul Labys. 2001. The Distribution of Realized Exchange Rate Volatility. *Journal of the American Statistical Association* 96 (453): 42–55.

Artzner, Philippe, Freddy Delbaen, Jean-Marc Eber, and David Heath. 1997. Thinking Coherently. *Risk* 10 (11): 68–71.

———. 1999. Coherent Measures of Risk. *Mathematical Finance* 9 (3): 203–28.

Ball, Clifford A., and Hans R. Stoll. 1998. Regulatory Capital of Financial Institutions: A Comparative Analysis. *Financial Markets, Institutions, and Instruments* 7 (3): 1–57.

Bangia, Anil, Francis X. Diebold, Til Schuermann, and John D. Stroughair. 1999. Liquidity on the Outside. *Risk* 12 (June): 68–73. Reprinted in expanded form as: Modeling Liquidity Risk, with Implications for Traditional Market Risk Measurement and Management. In *Risk Management: The State of the Art*, ed. S. Figlewski and R. Levich. Amsterdam: Kluwer Academic Publishers, 2001.

Bank for International Settlements (BIS). 1996. *66th Annual Report*. Basel, Switzerland.

Basak, Suleyman, and Alexander Shapiro. 2001. Value-at-Risk Based Risk Management: Optimal Policies and Asset Prices. *Review of Financial Studies* 14 (2): 371–405.

Basel Committee on Banking Supervision (BCBS). 1979. Consolidated Supervision of Bank's International Activities. Available at: www.bis.org/publ/bcbsc112.pdf.

———. 1988. International Convergence of Capital Measurement and Capital Standards. Basel Committee Publication No. 4. Available at: www.bis.org/publ/bcbs04A.pdf.

———. 1996a. Amendment to the Capital Accord to Incorporate Market Risks. Basel Committee Publication No. 24. Available at: www.bis.org/publ/bcbs24.pdf.

————. 1996b. Supervisory Framework for the Use of "Backtesting" in Conjunction with the Internal Models Approach to Market Risk Capital Requirements. Basel Committee Publication No. 22. Available at: www.bis.org/publ/bcbs22.pdf.

————. 2001a. Overview of the New Basel Capital Accord. Second Consultative Paper on the New Basel Capital Accord. Available at: www.bis.org/publ/bcbsca02.pdf

————. 2001b. Pillar 3—Market Discipline. Basel Committee Working Paper No. 7. Available at: www.bis.org/publ/bcbs_wp7.pdf.

————. 2002. Public Disclosures by Banks: Results of the 2000 Disclosure Survey. Basel Committee Publication No. 90. Available at: www.bis.org/publ/bcbs90.pdf.

Basel Committee on Banking Supervision and the Technical Committee of IOSCO (BCBS/IOSCO). 1999a. Recommendations for Public Disclosure of Trading and Derivatives Activities of Banks and Securities Firms. Basel Committee Publication No. 48. Available at: www.bis.org/publ/bcbs48.pdf

————. 1999b. Trading and Derivatives Disclosures of Banks and Securities Firms. Basel Committee Publication No. 64. Available at: www.bis.org/publ/bcbs64.pdf.

Benston, George J. 1999. *Regulating Financial Markets: A Critique and Some Proposals*. Washington, D.C.: AEI Press.

————. 2000. Consumer Protection as a Justification for Regulating Financial-Services Firms and Products. *Journal of Financial Services Research* 17 (3): 277–301.

Benston, George J., and George Kaufman. 1995. Is the Banking and Payment System Fragile? *Journal of Financial Services Research* 9: 209–40.

Berger, Allen N., Richard J. Herring, and Giorgio P. Szegö. 1995. The Role of Capital in Financial Institutions. *Journal of Banking and Finance* 19 (3/4): 393–430.

Berkowitz, Jeremy. 2001. Testing the Accuracy of Density Forecasts, Applications to Risk Management. *Journal of Business and Economic Statistics* 19: 465–74.

Berkowitz, Jeremy, and James O'Brien. 2002. How Accurate Are Value-at-Risk Models at Commercial Banks? *Journal of Finance* 57 (3): 1093–1111.

Blair, Bevan J., Ser-Huang Poon, and Stephen J. Taylor, 2001. Forecasting S&P 100 Volatility: The Incremental Information Content of Implied Volatilities and High Frequency Index Returns. *Journal of Econometrics* 105 (1): 5–26.

Board of Governors of the Federal Reserve System and U. S. Department of the Treasury. 2000. The Feasibility and Desirability of Mandatory Subordinated Debt. Report submitted to the Congress pursuant to Section 108 of the Gramm-Leach-Bliley Act of 1999 (December). Available at: www.federalreserve.gov/boarddocs/rptcongress/debt/subord_debt_2000.pdf.

Bollerslev, Tim. 1986. Generalized Autoregressive Conditional Heteroskedasticity. *Journal of Econometrics* 31 (3): 307–27.

Bollerslev, Tim, Ray Y. Chou, and Kenneth F. Kroner. 1992. ARCH Modeling in Finance: A Review of the Theory and Empirical Evidence. *Journal of Econometrics* 52 (1/2): 5–59.

Brick, Michael. 2002. What Was the Heart of Enron Keeps Shrinking. *New York Times*, April 6, Section C.

Britt, Stephen, Anthony Dardis, Mary Gilkison, François Morin, and Mary M. Wilson. 2001. Risk Position Reporting. Society of Actuaries Research Report. Available at: www.soa.org/research/risk_position.pdf.

Calomiris, Charles, and Gary Gorton. 1991. The Origins of Banking Panics, Models, Facts, and Bank Regulation. In *Financial Markets and Financial Crises*, ed. R. Glenn Hubbard, 109–73. Chicago: University of Chicago Press.

Canina, Linda, and Stephen Figlewski. 1993. The Informational Content of Implied Volatility. *Review of Financial Studies* 6 (3): 659–81.

Carey, Mark S. 1993. Snacking and Smoothing: Gains Trading of Investment Account Securities by Commercial Banks. Board of Governors of the Federal Reserve Working Paper.

———. 2002. A Guide to Choosing Absolute Capital Requirements. *Journal of Banking and Finance* 26 (5): 929–51.

Christoffersen, Peter F., and Francis X. Diebold. 2000. How Relevant Is Volatility Forecasting for Financial Risk Management? *Review of Economics and Statistics* 82 (1): 12–22.

Christoffersen, Peter F., Francis X. Diebold, and Til Schuermann. 1998. Horizon Problems and Extreme Events in Financial Risk Management. *Federal Reserve Bank of New York Economic Policy Review* 4 (3): 109–18. Available at: www .newyorkfed.org/rmaghome/econ_pol/1098pchr.pdf.

Collin-Dufresne, Pierre, Robert S. Goldstein, and J. Spencer Martin. 2001. The Determinants of Credit Spread Changes. *Journal of Finance* 56 (6): 2177–2207.

Commission of the European Communities. 2001. Proposal for a Directive of the European Parliament and of the Council on the Supplementary Supervision of Credit Institutions, Insurance Undertakings, and Investment Firms in a Financial Conglomerate. Brussels: CEC (April).

Committee on Payment and Settlement Systems. 1996. Settlement Risk in Foreign Exchange Transactions. Report prepared by the Committee on Payment and Settlement Systems of the Central Banks of the Group of Ten Countries. Committee on Payment and Settlement Systems Publication No. 17. Available at: www.bis.org/publ/cpss17.pdf.

Crouhy, Michel, Dan Galai, and Robert Mark. 2001. *Risk Management.* New York: McGraw-Hill.

Cummins, J. David, Scott E. Harrington, and Greg Niehaus. 1993. An Economic Overview of Risk-Based Capital Requirements for the Property-Liability Insurance Industry. *Journal of Insurance Regulation* 11: 427–47.

Day, Theodore E., and Craig M. Lewis. 1992. Stock Market Volatility and the Informational Content of Stock Index Options. *Journal of Econometrics* 52 (1/2): 267–87.

Derivatives Policy Group. 1995. Framework for Voluntary Oversight: The OTC Activities of Securities Firm Affiliates to Promote Confidence and Stability in Financial Markets (March). Available at: http://riskinstitute.ch/137790.htm.

DeYoung, Robert, Mark J. Flannery, William W. Lang, and Sorin M. Sorescu. 2001. The Informational Content of Bank Exam Ratings and Subordinated Debt Prices. *Journal of Money, Credit and Banking* 33 (4): 900–25.

Diamond, Douglas W., and Philip H. Dybvig. 1983. Bank Runs, Deposit Insurance, and Liquidity. *Journal of Political Economy* 91 (3): 401–19.

Diebold, Francis X., and Jose A. Lopez. 1995. Modeling Volatility Dynamics. In *Macroeconometrics: Developments, Tensions and Prospects*, ed. Kevin D. Hoover, 427–72. Boston: Kluwer Academic Press. Available at: www.ssc.upenn.edu/ ~fdiebold/papers/paper38/dl1995.pdf.

Diebold, Francis X., Todd A. Gunther, and Anthony S. Tay. 1998. Evaluating Density Forecasts with Applications to Financial Risk Management. *International Economic Review* 39: 863–83.

Diebold, Francis X., Til Schuermann, and John D. Stroughair. 1998. Pitfalls and Opportunities in the Use of Extreme Value Theory in Risk Management. In

Decision Technologies for Computational Finance, ed. Andrew N. Burgess, John Moody, and Apostolos-Paul N. Refenes, 3–12. Amsterdam: Kluwer Academic Publishers.

Diebold, Francis X., Andrew Hickman, Atsushi Inoue, and Til Schuermann. 1998. Scale Models. *Risk* 11: 104–7.

Dimson, Elroy, and Paul R. Marsh. 1995. Capital Requirements for Securities Firms. *Journal of Finance* 50 (3): 821–51.

Economist. 2003. *Poor Cover for a Rainy Day.* March 8, pp. 63–65.

Elton, Edwin J., Martin J. Gruber, Deepak Agrawal, and Christopher Mann. 2001. Explaining the Rate Spread on Corporate Bonds. *Journal of Finance* 56 (1): 247–77. Available at: pages.stern.nyu.edu/∼cmann/corpbond.pdf.

Embrechts, Paul, ed. 2000. *Extremes and Integrated Risk Management*. London: Risk Books.

Embrechts, Paul, Claudia Klüppelberg, and Thomas Mikosch. 1997. *Modelling Extremal Events for Insurance and Finance*. Berlin: Springer Verlag.

Engle, Robert F. 1982. Autoregressive Conditional Heteroskedasticity with Estimates of the Variance of United Kingdom Inflation. *Econometrica* 50: 987–1008.

European Union (EU). 1993. Council Directive 93/6/EEC of 15 March 1993 on the Capital Adequacy of Investments Firms and Credit Institutions.

Everett, James, Barbara Bouchard, Larry Gorski, Diane Fraser, Robert Loo, Anna Lee Hewko, Ray Spudeck, Richard Kopcke, and Elise Liebers. 2002. Report of the National Association of Insurance Commissioners (NAIC) and the Federal Reserve System Joint Subgroup on Risk-Based Capital and Regulatory Arbitrage. Federal Reserve System Working Paper (May).

Feldblum, Sholom. 1996. NAIC Property/Casualty Insurance Company Risk-Based Capital Requirements. *Proceeding of the Casualty Actuarial Society* 83 (158/159): 297–435. Available at: www.casact.org/pubs/proceed/proceed96/96297.pdf.

Flannery, Mark J., and Sorin M. Sorescu. 1996. Evidence of Bank Market Discipline in Subordinated Debenture Yields 1983–91. *Journal of Finance* 51: 1347–77.

Fleming, Jeff. 1998. The Quality of Market Volatility Forecasts Implied by S&P 100 Index Option Prices. *Journal of Empirical Finance* 5 (4): 317–45.

Gorton, Gary. 1988. Banking Panics and Business Cycles. *Oxford Economic Papers* 40 (4): 751–81.

Group of Ten. 2001. Report on Consolidation in the Financial Sector. Available on the OECD website as well as at: www.imf.org/external/np/g10/2001/01/Eng/ and at www.bis.org/publ/gten05.pdf.

Group of Thirty. 1997. Global Institutions, National Supervision, and Systemic Risk. A Study Group Report. Washington, D.C.: Group of Thirty.

Haberman, Gary. 1987. Capital Requirements of Commercial and Investment Banks: Contrasts in Regulation. *Federal Reserve Bank of New York Quarterly Review* (Fall): 1–10.

Hancock, Diana, and Myron L. Kwast. 2001. Using Subordinated Debt to Monitor Bank Holding Companies: Is It Feasible? *Journal of Financial Services Research* 20 (2/3): 147–87.

Hassan, M. Kabir. 1993. Capital Market Tests of Risk Exposure of Loan Sales Activities of Large U.S. Commercial Banks. *Quarterly Journal of Business and Economics* 32 (1): 27–49.

Hassan, M. Kabir, Gordon V. Karels, and Manfred O. Peterson. 1993. Off-Balance Sheet Activities and Bank Default-Risk Premia: A Comparison of Risk Measures. *Journal of Economics and Finance* 17 (3): 69–83.

Hendricks, Darryll. 1996. Evaluation of Value-at-Risk Models Using Historical Data. *Federal Reserve Bank of New York Economic Policy Review* 2 (1): 39–69. Available at: www.newyorkfed.org/rmaghome/econ_pol/496end.pdf.

Hendricks, Darryll, and Beverly J. Hirtle. 1997. Bank Capital Requirements for Market Risk: The Internal Models Approach. *Federal Reserve Bank of New York Economic Policy Review* 3 (4): 1–12. Available at: www.newyorkfed.org/rmaghome/econ_pol/1297dhen.pdf.

Herring, Richard J., and Prashant Vankudre. 1987. Growth Opportunities and Risk-Taking by Financial Intermediaries. *Journal of Finance* 42 (July): 583–99.

HIH Royal Commission of the Commonwealth of Australia. 2003. The Failure of HIH: A Corporate Collapse and Its Lessons. Report of the HIH Royal Commission, Vol. 1. Available at: www.hihroyalcom.gov.au/finalreport/.

Hirtle, Beverly J. 2003. What Market Risk Capital Reporting Tells Us About Bank Risk. *Federal Reserve Bank of New York Economic Policy Review* 9 (3): 37–54. Available at: www.newyorkfed.org/rmaghome/econ_pol/2003/0309hirt.pdf.

Hull, John C. 1993. *Options, Futures, and other Derivative Securities*, 2nd ed. Englewood Cliffs, N.J.: Prentice Hall.

Hulverscheidt, Claus, and Herbert Fromme. 2003. No State Help for German Insurers. *Financial Times*, April 4, 1.

International Monetary Fund (IMF). 2002. Global Financial Stability Report: A Quarterly Report on Market Developments and Issues. A Report by the International Capital Markets Department on Market Developments and Issues.

IOSCO. 1989. Capital Adequacy Standards for Securities Firms. A Report by the Technical Committee of the International Organization of Securities Commissions. Available at: http://riskinstitute.ch/138200.htm.

———. 1998. Methodologies for Determining Minimum Capital Standards for Internationally Active Securities Firms Which Permit the Use of Models Under Prescribed Conditions. A Report by the Technical Committee of the International Organization of Securities Commissions. Available at: www.iosco.org/pubdocs/pdf/IOSCOPD77.pdf.

Jagtiani, Julapa, and Catharine Lemieux. 2001. Market Discipline Prior to Bank Failure. *Journal of Economics and Business* 53 (2/3): 313–24.

Jagtiani, Julapa, George G. Kaufman, and Catharine Lemieux. 2002. The Effect of Credit Risk on Bank and Bank Holding Company Bond Yields: Evidence from the Post-FDICIA Period. *Journal of Financial Research* 25 (4): 559–75.

Joint Forum. 2001. Risk Management Practices and Regulatory Capital, Cross-Sectoral Comparison. Basel Committee Joint Publication No. 4. Available at: www.bis.org/publ/joint04.pdf.

Jorion, Philippe. 1995. Risk^2: Measuring the Risk in Value-at-Risk. *Financial Analysts Journal* 52 (November): 47–56.

———. 2000. Risk Management Lessons from Long-Term Capital Management. *European Financial Management* 6: 277–300.

———. 2001. *Value at Risk: The Benchmark for Managing Financial Risk*, 2nd ed. New York: McGraw-Hill.

———. 2002. How Informative Are Value-at-Risk Disclosures? *Accounting Review* 77 (October): 911–31.

J.P. Morgan. 1995. RiskMetrics Technical Manual. Available at: http://www.riskmetrics.com/pdf/td4c.pdf.

Koyluoglu, Ugur, and Jim Stoker. 2002. Honour Your Contribution. *Risk* 15 (4): 90–94.

KPMG. 2002. Study in the Methodologies to Assess the Overall Financial Position of an Insurance Undertaking from the Perspective of Prudential Supervision. Report to European Commission Contract No. ETD/2000/BS-3001/C/45. Available at: http://europa.eu.int/comm/internal_market/insurance/docs/solvency/solvency2-study-kpmg_en.pdf.

Kupiec, Paul. 1995. Techniques for Verifying the Accuracy of Risk Measurement Models. *Journal of Derivatives* 3: 73–84.

Kupiec, Paul, and David Nickerson. 2001. Assessing Systemic Risk Exposure under Alternative Approaches for Capital Adequacy. Presented at the Bank of England Conference on Banks and Systemic Risk. Available at: www.bankofengland.co.uk/financialstability/paper16may01.pdf.

Kuritzkes, Andrew P., and Hal S. Scott. 2004. Sizing Operational Risk and the Effect of Insurance: Implications for the Basel II Capital Accord. In *Capital Adequacy Beyond Basel: Banking, Securities, and Insurance*, ed. Hal S. Scott. New York: Oxford University Press.

Kuritzkes, Andrew P., Til Schuermann, and Scott M. Weiner. 2003. Risk Measurement, Risk Management, and Capital Adequacy in Financial Conglomerates. In *Brookings-Wharton Papers on Financial Services*, ed. Richard Herring and Robert E. Litan. Washington, D.C.: Brookings Institution Press.

Ladbury, Adrian. 1995. ING Deal Draws Insurers' Ire, ING's Write-Off of Insurance Units Cited. *Business Insurance*, Crains Communications, March 20, p. 69.

Linnell, Ian, David Andrews, and Jim Moss. 2000. Tier 3 Capital—Well Named and Unloved. *Fitch Financial Institutions Special Report* (July).

Linsmeier, Thomas J., and Neil D. Pearson. 1997. Quantitative Disclosures of Market Risk in the SEC Release. *Accounting Horizons* 11 (1): 107–35.

Lopez, Jose A. 1999. Regulatory Evaluation of Value-at-Risk Models. *Journal of Risk* 1 (2): 37–63.

Marshall, Christopher, and Michael Siegel. 1996. Value at Risk: Implementing a Risk Measurement Standard. *Journal of Derivatives* 4: 91–111.

Morgan, Donald P. 2002. Rating Banks: Risk and Uncertainty in an Opaque Industry. *American Economic Review* 92 (4): 874–88.

Morgan, Donald P., and Kevin J. Stiroh. 1999. Bond Market Discipline of Banks: Is the Market Tough Enough? Federal Reserve Bank of New York Staff Report 95 (December). Available at: www.newyorkfed.org/rmaghome/staff_rp/sr95.pdf.

Neftci, Salih N. 2000. Value-at-Risk Calculations, Extreme Events, and Tail Estimation. *Journal of Derivatives* 7 (3): 23–38.

Pritsker, Matthew G. 2001. The Hidden Dangers of Historical Simulation. Board of Governors of the Federal Reserve System FEDS Working Paper No. 2001-27. Available at: www.federalreserve.gov/pubs/feds/2001/200127/200127pap.pdf.

Rajgopal, Shivaram. 1999. Early Evidence on the Informativeness of the SEC's Market Risk Disclosures: The Case of Commodity Price Risk Exposure of Oil and Gas Products. *Accounting Review* 74 (3): 251–80.

Saunders, Anthony. 2000. *Financial Institutions Management, A Modern Perspective*, 3rd ed. Boston: Irwin McGraw-Hill.

Scott, Hal S., and Shinsaku Iwahara. 1994. In Search of a Level Playing Field: The Implementation of the Basel Accord in Japan and the United States. Washington, D.C.: Group of Thirty Occasional Paper No. 46.

Scott, Hal S., and Philip A. Wellons. 1999. *International Finance: Transactions, Policy and Regulation*, 6th ed. New York: Foundation Press.

86 Capital Adequacy Beyond Basel

Securities and Exchange Commission (SEC). 1997a. *Net Capital Rule.* SEC Release No. 34-39456, File No. S7-32-97. Available at: www.sec.gov/rules/concept/34-39456.txt.

————. 1997b. Disclosure of Accounting Policies for Derivative Financial Instruments and Derivative Commodity Instruments and Disclosure of Quantitative and Qualitative Information about Market Risk Inherent in Derivative Financial Instruments, Other Financial Instruments, and Derivative Commodity Instruments. Release 33-7386, FFR-48. Available at: www.sec.gov/rules/final/33-7386.txt.

————. 1998. OTC Derivatives Dealers. SEC Release No. 34-40594, File No. S7-30-97. Available at: www.sec.gov/rules/final/34-40594.htm.

————. 2002. Regulation FD—Fair Disclosure, Reg. §243.

Stahl, Gerhard. 1997. Three Cheers. *Risk* 10 (5): 67–9.

Swiss Re. 2000. Asset Liability Management for Insurers. *Sigma* 6.

Troxel, Terrie E., and George E. Bouchie. 1995. *Property-Liability Insurance Accounting and Finance,* 4th ed. Malvern, PA: American Institute for CPCU.

U. S. General Accounting Office (USGAO). 1998. Risk-Based Capital: Regulatory and Industry Approaches to Capital and Risk. Report to the Chairman, Committee on Banking, Housing, and Urban Affairs, U.S. Senate, and the Chairman, Committee on Banking and Financial Services, House of Representatives, GAO/GGD-98-153. Available at: www.gao.gov/archive/1998/gg98153.pdf.

U.S. Shadow Financial Regulatory Committee. 2000. *Reforming Bank Capital Regulation.* Washington, D.C.: American Enterprise Institute. Available at: www.aei.org/research/shadow/publications/pubID.16542,projectID.15/pub_detail.asp.

Webb, Bernard L., and Claude C. Lilly III. 1994. *Raising the Safety Net: Risk-Based Capital for Life Insurance Companies.* Kansas City: NAIC Publications.

Wilke, John R. 2002. U.S. Probes Whether Big Banks Stifled Rival in Currency Trading. *The Wall Street Journal,* May 15, A1.

Zhang, Peter G. 1998. *Exotic Options: A Guide to Second Generation Options,* 2nd ed. Singapore: World Scientific.

2

Capital Adequacy in Insurance and Reinsurance

SCOTT E. HARRINGTON

This chapter considers capital adequacy and capital regulation of insurers and reinsurers. A basic theme is that capital standards should be less stringent for financial sectors characterized by greater market discipline and less systemic risk. Because market discipline is greater and systemic risk is lower for insurance than in banking, capital requirements should be less stringent for insurers than for banks. Similarly, because market discipline is generally greater in reinsurance (wholesale) markets than in direct insurance (retail) markets, capital requirements and related regulation plausibly need not be as stringent for reinsurers as for direct insurers. Current capital requirements and related solvency regulation for U.S. and E.U. insurers and reinsurers are largely consistent with significant market discipline in the insurance and reinsurance sectors. Any federal regulation of U.S. insurers/ reinsurers, harmonized regulation of E.U. reinsurers, consolidated oversight of financial conglomerates, and increased centralization of regulatory authority to supervise insurance and other financial activities should be designed with full recognition of the limited systemic risk and strong market discipline in insurance/reinsurance and avoid undermining that discipline.

This chapter elaborates on the need indicated in the previous chapter to set capital for insurance firms and for banks differently, given the different businesses and risks the two different firms run. The chapter also shows that insurance firms are subject to sufficient market discipline, in large part, because of the absence of systemic risk and public subsidies. Thus, the approach to insurance firm capital may be a model for banks in the future, once increased market discipline and effective use of prompt corrective action allow considerations of systemic risk to subside.

INTRODUCTION

Increased cross-sector and cross-border competition among financial institutions has led to considerable discussion of possible revisions in traditional insurance/reinsurance solvency regulation, including possibly greater regulatory centralization and harmonization within the United States and the European Union. Important issues include a possible extension to insurance of the Basel approach to bank capital regulation, possible expansion of direct regulatory supervision and capital requirements for international re-insurers, possible development of mutual recognition systems across na-tional borders, and possible expansion of consolidated or more centralized regulatory oversight.

This chapter deals with capital adequacy and capital regulation of insurers and reinsurers. I first review the main risks, degree of market discipline, and scope of solvency regulation in insurance and reinsurance markets, with an emphasis on the United States. Given that background, I next consider key principles of efficient capital regulation, focusing on the relation between op-timal capital requirement stringency and market discipline. I then briefly de-scribe and evaluate, in relation to those principles, capital requirements and related supervision of U.S. and E.U. insurers and reinsurers. Here I compare the U.S. and E.U. systems, consider the implications of possible federal insurance/reinsurance regulation in the United States, and discuss whether regulation of reinsurers should be expanded abroad. I also briefly discuss pres-sure for consolidated regulation of financial conglomerates that include insur-ance and for greater centralization of regulatory authority over financial firms.

My main conclusions are as follows:

- Capital standards (and, more generally, regulatory solvency super-vision) should be less stringent for sectors characterized by greater market discipline and less systemic risk.
- Market discipline is greater and systemic risk is lower for insurance than in banking. Capital requirements therefore should be less stringent for insurers than for banks.
- Market discipline is generally greater in reinsurance (wholesale) markets than in direct insurance (retail) markets. Capital require-ments and related regulation need not be as stringent for reinsurers as for direct insurers.
- Current capital requirements and related solvency regulation for U.S. and E.U. insurers and reinsurers are largely consistent with significant market discipline in the insurance and reinsurance sectors.
- Any federal regulation of U.S. insurers/reinsurers, harmonized regu-lation of E.U. reinsurers, consolidated oversight of financial conglom-erates, and increased centralization of regulatory authority to supervise insurance and other financial activities should be designed with full recognition of the limited systemic risk and strong market discipline in insurance/reinsurance and should avoid undermining that discipline.

RISK, MARKET DISCIPLINE, AND SOLVENCY REGULATION IN INSURANCE AND REINSURANCE

Insurance Risk

Nonlife (property-casualty) insurers face a variety of risks including un-derwriting risk, which encompasses premium and reserve risks, credit risk, asset (market) risk, and interest rate risk.[1] Asset risk is generally modest, reflecting heavy investments in government or highly rated bonds. Although many U.S. nonlife insurers have greater asset than liability durations, interest rate risk is relatively modest, in part because payments to policyholders are not highly correlated with interest rate increases. Credit (counterparty) risk is largely related to reinsurance transactions, which are widely employed to manage underwriting and reserve risks.

Underwriting risk is paramount for nonlife insurers. Both premium and reserve risks reflect the possibility of large errors in predicting ultimate claim costs. When insurers write coverage, there is always some risk that claim costs will exceed those predicted. Similarly, once claims have occurred, the provisions for unpaid claim liabilities (loss reserves) may prove deficient. Premium risk and reserve risk differ in timing. Premium risk involves possible divergence between ultimate costs and conditional forecasts of costs at the time policies are priced. Reserve risk involves possible divergence between ultimate costs and conditional forecasts of costs after claims have occurred (or are assumed to have occurred in provisions for incurred but not reported claims).

In either case, ultimate claim costs may substantially exceed those predicted when policies are priced and written. Natural or manmade catastrophes (e.g., Hurricane Andrew and the World Trade Center attack in the United States) can create large, sudden increases in costs for property and related coverages. More benign changes in the weather and unexpected changes in property repair costs also create risk. For long-tail coverages, such as general liability, ultimate claims may not be known for many years after policies are priced and written, giving rise in some cases to enormous reserve risk long after policies have been sold. This has been vividly documented in the asbestos and environmental arenas. Both forms of underwriting risk are aggravated by relentless price competition in many nonlife insurance markets, which may encourage prices to become arguably too low during "soft market" episodes of the insurance cycle (see Danzon and Harrington 1994). Subsequent negative shocks to capital have occasionally led to very hard markets characterized by scarce capital, large rate increases, and less favorable coverage terms, often with material effects on real (nonfinancial) activity.[2]

Compared to their life insurer brethren and to commercial banks, nonlife insurers hold relatively large amounts of capital (i.e., assets in excess of their liabilities) as a cushion against unexpected increases in claim costs or reductions in asset values.[3] Holding that capital involves material tax and agency costs.[4] Depending on the jurisdiction, double taxation of returns from investing capital to support the sale of policies significantly increases the cost of capital and the prices needed to offer coverage, especially for low-probability events with large potential claim severities (see Harrington and Niehaus 2003). Nonlife insurers manage their underwriting risk and thus economize on costly capital by diversifying underwriting risk across policies of a given type and region, across types of coverage, and geographically.

They also transfer significant amounts of underwriting risk to reinsurers, which achieves additional risk spreading, including across national borders, thus reducing both the amount of capital held by ceding insurers and the aggregate amount of capital held by insurers and reinsurers to support aggregate writings.

Life insurers' primary risks arise from the asset side of the balance sheet, as was clearly illustrated by asset quality problems in real estate and high yield bonds in the United States during the late 1980s and early 1990s and by large drops in the value of equity portfolios of E.U. life insurers during 1999–2001. Significant reductions in asset values and changes in interest rates can cause policyholders to withdraw funds and/or reduce sales and conceivably force some assets to be sold at temporarily depressed prices. Although life insurers also face some mortality/morbidity risk, volatility on these dimensions is relatively modest and frequently managed effectively by transferring the risk to specialized reinsurers. U.S. life insurer capital levels in relation to assets are much smaller than those for nonlife insurers and more comparable to those for banks.

Private Incentives for Safety and Soundness

The United States and a number of E.U. countries guarantee certain obligations of insolvent insurers, thus protecting some policyholders from the full consequences of insurer default (see additional discussion later). Holding the specific arrangements and general solvency regulation aside for moment, it is useful to highlight first private incentives for safety and soundness in insurance markets. Those incentives ultimately determine the degree of safety and soundness, including insurers' ability to withstand large shocks that reduce asset values or increase liabilities.[5] Three main influences encourage safety and soundness:

- Many, if not most, policyholders prefer to deal with safe and sound insurers and, up to some point, are willing to pay the higher costs that greater safety requires. A variety of institutions help match policyholders with safe insurers. They include widely used insurance intermediaries (agents, brokers, advisers), a highly developed system of private ratings of insurers' claims-paying abilities, and, for business coverages, knowledgeable corporate staff who oversee risk management and insurance programs.
- Insurance production and distribution often involve the creation of sizable firm-specific assets, commonly known as franchise value, which can diminish or evaporate if the insurer experiences severe financial difficulty. Protection of those assets from loss due to financial difficulty therefore provides a significant incentive for adequate capitalization and other forms of risk management.[6] Firm-specific assets arise in two main ways. First, attracting and providing coverage to a new customer typically requires relatively high upfront costs, which insurers expect to recover from higher margins on

renewal business. Thus, renewal premiums often include quasi rents as a return for the initial investment in creating the customer relationship. Those quasi rents would be jeopardized in the event of financial difficulty. Second, insurers often make substantial investments in developing a brand name or reputation for quality service (especially nonlife insurers). Those investments also produce quasi rents, all or part of which would be lost in the event of insolvency. Both factors reduce the problem of time inconsistent incentives and associated excessive risk taking (e.g., asset substitution).

- Many insurers in the United States and abroad issue debt, primarily at the holding company level. That debt is effectively subordinated to policyholder claims. It creates an additional category of stakeholders that presses for efficient risk management, which in turn allows insurers to lower their cost of capital, including tax and agency costs.[7]

In view of these influences, efficient management of risk by insurers involves balancing the benefits of holding more capital and more effectively managing risk (e.g., higher premiums, preservation of franchise value, lower debt funding costs) against the tax and agency costs of capital and frictional costs associated with other risk management methods. Given those costs, the optimal level of safety and soundness generally will achieve low default risk, but it is too costly to eliminate insolvency risk. The optimal insolvency rate for insurers is not zero.

Market Imperfections and Efficiency Rationales for Regulation

The traditional rationale for economic regulation is to protect the public interest by efficiently mitigating market failures. The test for whether government intervention into market activity will likely be efficient is two pronged (Breyer 1982). First, there should be a demonstrable market failure compared to the standard of a reasonably competitive market characterized by (1) large numbers of sellers with relatively low market shares and low-cost entry by new firms, (2) low-cost information to firms concerning the cost of production and to consumers concerning prices and quality, and (3) an absence of material spillovers (i.e., all costs are internalized to sellers or buyers). Second, there should be substantial evidence that regulation can efficiently address any market failure; that is, that regulation's benefits will exceed its direct and indirect costs. Regulatory tools are necessarily imperfect. Regulation always involves direct and indirect costs, and it risks unintended consequences. If both tests are met, efficient intervention then requires matching appropriate regulatory tools to specific market failures.

Market structure and ease of entry are highly conducive to competition in most insurance markets. Modern insurance markets that are relatively free from regulatory constraints on prices and risk classification exhibit pervasive evidence of competitive conduct and performance. The principal imperfections that plausibly justify some degree of government regulation take the form of costly and imperfect information and spillovers. The primary rationale for insurance regulation is to improve efficiency by promoting safety and soundness and healthy competition in view of those problems.

Costly/Imperfect Information and Potential Spillovers

Some form of solvency regulation is efficient because of costly/imperfect information and potential spillovers. As noted, for example, nonlife insurers bear enormous risk of loss from natural catastrophes and unexpected events. Liability insurers have paid hundreds of billions of dollars for claims brought many years after policies were sold, when legal liability standards and legal interpretations of policy provisions had changed substantially. The risk of many nonlife losses is very difficult to evaluate and price accurately. Insurers must hold large amounts of capital to maintain reasonably low probabilities of insolvency. Competition creates relentless pressure for low premiums, which in some cases may contribute to inadequate rates and increase insolvency risk, especially for difficult-to-price coverages subject to large but slow developing losses.

With solvency regulation, policyholders that would find assessing and monitoring insurer insolvency risk very difficult (or who might have little incentive to do so on their own or using brokers or advisers) in effect delegate significant responsibility for monitoring to regulators. This rationale for solvency regulation is considerably stronger for direct (retail) insurance for personal lines than for larger commercial policyholders and reinsurance (wholesale) transactions.[8]

Regulatory monitoring might detect insurer financial problems early enough to prevent insolvency. In other cases, monitoring can help regulators intervene before the deficit between an insolvent insurer's assets and liabilities gets any larger. Some degree of regulatory restrictions on insurer risk taking (e.g., investment limitations and capital requirements) also is plausibly efficient.

Protecting Risk-Averse Policyholders from Loss

Limited, government-mandated protection of policyholders' claims against insolvent insurers is likely to be efficient, at least arguably, in view of costly or imperfect information and possible spillovers on other parties (such as those with legally valid workers' compensation or liability claims against policyholders of insolvent insurers). The insurance industry also has a collective interest in bonding its promises to pay claims. Given costly and imperfect information, in the absence of any guarantees insolvencies might damage the reputations of many insurers, including perhaps some financially strong ones, therefore motivating many or most insurers to participate in a joint guaranty system. Joint guarantees help maintain collective pressure for efficient solvency regulation by giving member insurers a direct stake in the outcomes of such regulation. Government-mandated systems reduce free-rider problems and obviate antitrust concerns that might otherwise arise with privately initiated and managed joint guarantees.

Systemic Risk

It generally is agreed that systemic risk is relatively low in insurance markets compared with banking, especially for nonlife insurance.[9] Low-probability events with large losses can simultaneously damage many nonlife insurers, and the impact is spread broadly through product line and geographic diversification and especially through reinsurance, which creates material contractual interdependence among insurers. As noted earlier, large shocks can temporarily disrupt nonlife insurance markets, with attendant adverse effects on real activity. However, there is little likelihood and no evidence of "pure" contagion associated with major events, as opposed to rational, information-based flights to quality. Systemic risk is plausibly larger for life insurers (e.g., as a result of a collapse in major real estate markets), especially when some policyholders may seek to withdraw funds following large negative shocks, thus causing some insurers to unload assets at temporarily depressed prices. But such shocks do not threaten the payment system, as might be true for commercial banks, and pure contagion is less problematic than with banking.[10]

Main Features of Insurance Solvency Regulation

While the details vary significantly and frequently change across jurisdictions, insurance/reinsurance solvency regulation in the United States, the European Union, and other developed countries generally has most or all of the following features:

- Regulatory establishment and monitoring of compliance with asset/ liability rules
- Regulatory rules that restrict certain types of risk taking (such as restrictions on permissible investments)
- Regulatory capital requirements
- Solvency monitoring (early warning) systems to identify troubled companies
- Monitoring of primary insurers' reinsurance ceded, rules for allowing primary insurers to receive balance sheet credit for such reinsurance, and/or direct supervision of reinsurers
- Guaranty systems to pay a portion of claims against insolvent insurers, usually funded by postinsolvency assessments on solvent insurers
- Procedures for receivership, rehabilitation, and liquidation of troubled companies.

MARKET AND REGULATORY DISCIPLINE: INSURANCE, REINSURANCE, AND BANKING

Regardless of whether different financial services are regulated on a consolidated basis or are regulated functionally with distinct regulatory regimes for different services, the design of efficient solvency regulation necessarily confronts difficult tradeoffs. Beyond some point, lowering insolvency risk through tighter regulatory constraints, such as higher capital requirements, inefficiently increases the total costs of financial services. Regulatory monitoring and controls to reduce insolvency risk involve direct costs, such as salaries paid to regulators and data collection, processing, and analysis costs. They also produce indirect costs, for example, by distorting the decisions of some financially sound institutions in ways that increase their costs (or seek to undermine regulatory requirements).

A tradeoff also exists between protecting customers against loss when financial institutions fail and providing incentives for financial institutions to be safe. For example, protection against loss reduces bank depositors' or insurance policyholders' demand for lower insolvency risk and their incentives to seek safe institutions, thus in turn dulling those institutions' incentives to hold more capital and manage risk effectively. Even well-designed government (or government-mandated) guarantees may increase insolvency risk. Accurate risk-based premiums for guaranty protection, which could mitigate the dulling effects of guarantees on incentives for safety and soundness, are infeasible in practice. Government guarantees therefore are very well known to involve moral hazard: depositors or policyholders have less incentive to deal with safe institutions, and some institutions have less incentive to be safe.

In the United States, a modest increase in insolvency risk and insolvencies following the breakdown of adherence to collective pricing systems, greater reliance on competition to determine rates in many states, and regulatory pressure toward rate inadequacy in others made limited guarantees of insolvent insurers' obligations more advantageous beginning in the late 1960s. State guarantees developed with substantial input from insurers (and in conjunction with proposed federal guarantees). The vast majority rely on ex post assessment funding mechanisms, which enhance incentives for financially strong insurers to press for effective solvency surveillance and efficient liquidation of insolvent insurers. Such incentives are generated because unexpected increases in the costs of assessments are likely to be borne in large part by insurers, as opposed to being fully shifted to customers or taxpayers.[11]

Because systemic risk is materially lower for insurance, especially nonlife insurance, than for the banking system, the efficient level of guaranty fund protection is correspondingly lower. Contrary to some complaints that state guaranty fund protection is inadequate in the United States, limited coverage is advantageous. Reinsurance is not covered. Coverage for large business policyholders is limited in part by maximums (e.g., $300,000) per occurrence of a covered claim. About a third of the states further reduce protection or exclude large business policyholders from coverage, which encourages them to trade with safe insurers and discourages them from buying coverage that they believe may be underpriced.[12] Those arrangements are very likely more efficient than state systems without such restrictions.[13] Several E.U. guaranty

Table 2.1. Safety and Soundness Incentives for Banks and Insurers

Issue	Banking	Nonlife Insurance	Life Insurance	Reinsurance
Risk-insensitive demand				
Explicit insurance/ guarantees	High	Moderate	Moderate	Negligible
Implicit insurance/ guarantees	High	Low	Low– moderate	Low
Imperfect information/ costly search				
Buyer sophistication	Moderate	Moderate–high	Moderate	High
Entity transparency	Low	Low	Low	Low
Firm-specific assets (franchise value)				
Production (front-end costs)	Moderate	Moderate– high	High	Moderate
Reputation (service quality)	Moderate	Moderate– high	Low- moderate	Moderate
Overall Market Discipline	Low	Moderate– high	Moderate– high	High
Systemic risk				
Risk of large, common shocks	High	Moderate– high	Moderate– high	Moderate– high
Contractual interdependence	High	High	Moderate	High
Risk of pure contagion	High	Low	Moderate	Low
Need for Regulatory Discipline	High	Low	Low– moderate	Lowest

Source: Author's assessment of factors that affect market discipline.

systems have even stronger limitations, and a few E.U. countries have no guarantees.[14]

Table 2.1 summarizes incentives for safety and soundness and the associated need (or lack thereof) for regulatory discipline for banks, nonlife insurers, life insurers, and reinsurers. Although it reflects subjective assessments of the magnitude of each influence in each sector, the key point is that market discipline is stronger in insurance (and especially reinsurance) than in banking. In the United States, this difference in large part reflects that insurance guarantees have much smaller effects on market discipline than federal deposit insurance, with its broad explicit protection and the history of implicit federal guarantees (e.g., the "too big to fail" doctrine, which protected nominally uninsured deposits at very large banks). In addition (and related), private incentives for safety and soundness will also be stronger in insurance if franchise value tends to be greater for insurers than banks as a by-product of insurance production.

A conclusion that market discipline is stronger in insurance than banking and strongest in reinsurance does not imply that insurance guarantees are free from moral hazard. Instead, a number of empirical studies provide evidence that the adoption of guarantees in the United States increased insurer risk taking (Lee, Mayers, and Smith 1997; Brewer, Mondschean, and Strahan 1997; Downs and Sommer 1999; also see Bohn and Hall 1999). But the conclusion that market discipline is stronger in insurance is hardly controversial in view of the large literature on moral hazard and excessive risk taking in banking. As one example, Billet, Garfinkel, and O'Neal (1998) provide evidence that banks downgraded by rating agencies increase their insured deposits following the downgrade. In insurance, on the other hand, my own work with Karen Epermanis documents that U.S. nonlife insurers that received rating downgrades experienced economically and statistically significant revenue declines compared to insurers that experienced no rating change (Epermanis and Harrington 2001; also see Zanjani 2002 for related analysis of ordinary life insurance policy terminations). Fenn and Cole (1994) provide evidence that policyholders' reactions to asset quality problems at life insurers in the late 1980s and early 1990s targeted weak institutions and thus were consistent with a rational flight to quality as opposed to pure contagion. As noted earlier, Brewer and Jackson (2002) provide evidence that pure contagion is much greater in banking than in life insurance.

In summary, economically efficient regulation implies a tradeoff between the types and intensities of regulation and the degree of market discipline that is closely linked with the magnitude of systemic risk and government guarantees of financial institutions' obligations. *Greater market discipline in insurance implies that insurance/reinsurance solvency regulation and capital requirements should be less restrictive than in banking.* The next section elaborates this issue conceptually in the specific context of capital requirements.

CAPITAL REGULATION WITH IMPERFECT RISK ASSESSMENT

Risk-based capital standards may provide regulators and other parties with valuable information about institutions' capital adequacy. They also can provide regulators with greater authority and motivation to take specific actions against insurers that violate the standards. Perhaps more important, capital standards can induce some financially weak institutions to hold more capital (or limit their risk in relation to existing capital). This section focuses on such inducement. I ignore a variety of complicating factors, such as possible gaming of capital requirements by banks or insurers.

Market discipline will generally be inadequate for some firms. They will hold too little capital in relation to risk, thus making the values of their default put options ("default puts") socially excessive. Ignoring specific details about government insurance/guarantees and the incidence of excessive put costs, and assuming crude or risk-insensitive charges for guarantees, the essence of the problem is that some firms' put values will be inefficiently high compared with the costs of holding additional capital (or reducing risk) to reduce those values. Holding more capital (or reducing risk) would lower total costs (the sum of the firm's default put and capital costs). But because some default costs are not internalized to the firm, it rationally foregoes minimization of social costs.

By requiring some firms to hold more capital in relation to their observed risk, risk-based capital rules may reduce their put values. With perfect information and costless enforcement, capital standards could correspond exactly with a firm's risk. Each firm could be forced to hold the efficient level of capital. But risk assessment is costly, inherently imperfect, and perhaps even relatively crude in the best of circumstances. Two types of errors are therefore inevitable with risk-based capital. First, borrowing from the language of basic statistics, capital standards involve Type 1 errors: they incorrectly identify some otherwise adequately capitalized ("sound") firms (i.e., those with efficient put values) as holding insufficient capital and thereby force them to hold too much capital (or to reduce their risk inefficiently). Second, capital standards involve a form of Type 2 errors: they fail to identify some firms with excessive put values and thereby fail to force them to hold enough capital in relation to risk.

The cost of Type 1 errors reflects capital costs in excess of any marginal reduction in sound firms' put values. Those costs are in large part borne by customers (insurance policyholders, bank depositors, and borrowers) through higher prices or less favorable terms. The benefit from inducing some weak firms (those that otherwise would have excessive put values) to hold more capital is the reduction in their put values above the marginal increase in their capital costs. The costs and benefits of capital standards depend on their ability to target weak firms.

The design of capital standards therefore confronts a difficult tradeoff. Up to some point, increases in capital requirement stringency cause a greater number of weak firms to hold more efficient levels of capital (or reduce their risk), but they also cause a greater number of sound firms to hold too much capital (or inefficiently shed risk). For a given degree of accuracy, efficient capital standards balance the net benefits from getting some weaker firms to hold more capital with the net costs imposed on some sound firms.

It is useful to distinguish conceptually two dimensions of the accuracy of risk-based capital systems, even though those dimensions are implicit or blurred in practice. In effect, risk-based capital systems classify some firms as having too little capital and others as having adequate capital. One dimension of accuracy relates to the additional capital amounts that firms classified as having too little capital must hold. The second dimension of accuracy relates to classification precision. The distinction highlights two closely related issues: (1) the optimal stringency of capital requirements for firms explicitly or implicitly classified as having too little capital, and (2) the optimal degree of classification accuracy. Most of my brief comments deal with the first issue. The appendix outlines a simple model that supports the main points.

Tempering Capital Requirements to Reflect Market Discipline

Any specific capital standard will (1) encourage some weak firms to hold more capital, (2) require some sound firms to hold too much capital (Type 1 errors), and (3) fail to mitigate capital inadequacy for some weak firms (Type 2 errors). Up to some point, increasing the rule's stringency generally causes more weak firms to be constrained, reducing the Type 2 error rate and associated costs. But increased stringency also increases the Type 1 error rate (the proportion of sound firms whose decisions are inefficiently distorted), which again increases costs. The key question is how to set stringency in order to minimize total costs.[15]

The qualitative answer is that the optimal capital rule(s) should satisfy two general principles. First, *the additional capital required for firms believed to be inadequately capitalized should be less than the amount that would be required if they were known with certainty to be inadequately capitalized.* With imperfect risk assessment (classification), capital requirements for firms that *appear* weak should be tempered: they should be lower than the optimal amounts with perfect risk assessment. The intuition is straightforward. Because higher capital requirements distort some sound firms' decisions (and fail to constrain some weak firms), tempering of the requirements reduces those costs and minimizes total costs. While tempering sacrifices benefits for correctly classified weak firms, it reduces costs for sound firms that are mistakenly constrained by the rule.

The second general principle deals with the relationship between capital requirement stringency (the efficient level of tempering) and the extent of market discipline. As market discipline increases, fewer firms will hold too little capital in relation to risk without capital regulation. For a given Type 1 error rate (proportion of sound firms forced to hold more capital), higher market discipline therefore implies that decisions of a greater number of sound firms will be inefficiently distorted. Moreover, for a given level of power to identify weak firms correctly, greater market discipline implies a smaller number of weak firms and thus fewer total benefits from requiring firms classified as weak to hold more capital. Both factors imply that tempering should increase—capital standards should be less stringent—as market discipline and the proportion of sound firms increases (see appendix for more details).

The implications of this discussion are that as long as market discipline motivates some firms to be adequately capitalized without capital requirements, (1) imperfect risk assessment will favor less stringent capital standards for firms that appear inadequately capitalized, and (2) the stringency of capital standards should decline as market discipline increases.

Optimal Risk Assessment and Market Discipline

Up to some point, additional expenditures on risk analysis and assessment (for data, model development and validation, expert evaluation, and so on) should increase accuracy; that is, they should reduce explicit or implicit Type 1 and Type 2 error rates for a risk-based capital system. Risk assessment is costly, however, and will remain inherently imperfect even if much higher costs are incurred. The optimal degree of accuracy (crudity) will (1) reflect those costs and inherent inaccuracy, and (2) will be lower the greater are the costs of improving accuracy.

Intuitively, accuracy becomes more important as the stringency of capital standards increases. For a given Type 1 error rate, for example, more stringent capital requirements increase the costs of Type 1 errors. Greater stringency therefore increases the potential benefits of lowering the Type 1 error rate (and of lowering the Type 2 error rate, as well). Because optimal stringency is inversely related to the degree of market discipline, the optimal degree of accuracy (error rate) should likewise be inversely related to market discipline. When market discipline is strong, capital requirements should constrain relatively few firms, and classification accuracy is less important. When market discipline is weak, capital requirements should be more stringent and accuracy is more important. Of course, an alternative to more stringent capital requirements and a continued search for greater refinement of those requirements is to encourage market discipline (see U.S. Shadow Financial Regulatory Committee 2000, for extended discussion).

The overall implications of this discussion are these:

- The stringency of capital requirements should be inversely related to the degree of market discipline (positively related to the degree of market failure).
- The accuracy of capital requirements in relation to risk is more important when standards are stringent, which ideally will not be the case unless market discipline is weak.
- A conceptual and, in some instances, practical alternative to more stringent capital requirements would be to increase market discipline (e.g., by encouraging more stakeholders to care about default risk).

CAPITAL REGULATION IN PRACTICE

This section describes insurance capital regulation in practice and how it compares with the preceding analysis, focusing on the United States and the European Union. I briefly describe bank capital regulation as a point of departure. I then turn to regulation of direct insurance, first in the United States and then in the European Union. I then discuss supervision and capital regulation for reinsurers and conclude with brief comments on the regulation of financial conglomerates and cross-sector risk transfers.

Lessons from Banking

The 1988 Basel Accord was designed to harmonize capital standards and to increase capital adequacy for international banks. The original system defining Tier 1 and Tier 2 capital standards in relation to risk-weighted assets focused on credit risk. Market risk was added later, along with provisions that allowed banks to use internal models to determine their required capital for market risk under certain conditions. Basel II establishes a three-pillar approach: (1) risk-based capital standards, (2) supervision, and (3) market discipline (i.e., disclosure requirements). Formula-based capital standards are the default under Pillar 1, with basic and advanced internal model provisions for banks that qualify. A major emphasis is placed on achieving more accurate standards, thus continuing the search for the Holy Grail of highly accurate requirements.

The evolution of the Basel framework illustrates the underlying dilemma of bank solvency regulation. Systemic risk is significant; deposit insurance mitigates systemic risk but materially undermines market discipline. The Basel view is that stringent capital standards are therefore necessary. That stringency in turn stimulates the search for greater accuracy in relation to risk. Inherent limitations on the accuracy of fixed-weight approaches create pressure for more sophisticated modeling to capture the risk of different institutions. Regulation evolves from standard setting and compliance monitoring to active encouragement and supervision or even regulatory micromanagement of risk modeling by banks. These regulatory responses involve direct and indirect costs.

An alternative approach to addressing the deposit insurance/moral hazard conundrum would be to promote stronger market discipline. The market discipline feature (Pillar 3) of Basel II stresses disclosure of risk and risk management by banks to provide outsiders with better information. But that approach by itself does not increase stakeholders' sensitivities to insolvency risk. A significant increase in market discipline instead might be achieved by (1) requiring banks to issue and maintain highly rated subordinated debt (see U.S. Shadow Committee 2000 for detailed discussion and a specific proposal; also see Benston 1998 and Evanoff and Wall 2003), and/or (2) by reducing—or at least not increasing—the scope of deposit insurance and implicit government guarantees of banks' obligations.

Capital Requirements for U.S. Insurers and Reinsurers

Until the early 1990s, U.S. insurers were required to meet only absolute minimum capital standards to establish and continue operations in a state. These requirements still serve as absolute minimums and usually vary depending on the type of insurer (stock or mutual) and the broad type of business written (e.g., nonlife versus life insurance); they average around $2 million, varying from several hundred thousand dollars in a few states up to $5 million or more in a few others. During 1991–1994, the National Association of Insurance Commissioners (NAIC) developed risk-based capital (RBC) standards for adoption by the states to supplement the absolute minimums. Those standards became effective in 1993 for nonlife insurers and in 1994 for life insurers. The capital charges vary in relation to the specific amounts and types of an insurer's assets, liabilities, and premiums. The development of insurance RBC standards followed (1) a significant deterioration in insolvency experience and increase in state guaranty fund assessments from the mid-1980s to the early 1990s (see figures 2.1 and 2.2), (2) associated congressional hearings and proposed legislation to establish federal insurance and reinsurance solvency regulation, and (3) promulgation of the 1988 Basel capital standards for banks.[16]

Description of RBC Standards

There currently are separate RBC standards for nonlife insurers, life insurers, and health insurance/HMO organizations. Table 2.2 provides a simplified summary of the NAIC nonlife and life RBC systems.[17] The NAIC's RBC formula for nonlife insurers encompasses four major risk categories (buckets): (1) asset (investment) risk, (2) credit risk, (3) underwriting risk, and (4) miscellaneous off-balance-sheet risks, such as the risk associated with rapid premium growth. The life insurer formula includes components for (1) asset risk, (2) insurance risk (underwriting risk associated with sickness and mortality), (3) interest rate risk (which focuses on the risk that policyholders will withdraw funds to invest elsewhere if market yields increase), and (4) miscellaneous business risks, such as the risk of

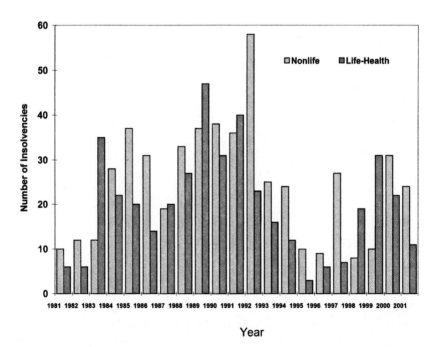

Year

Figure 2.1. Insurer Insolvency Frequency in the U.S., 1981–2001. Source: Standard & Poor's (2002) and author's compilations of unpublished NAIC data.

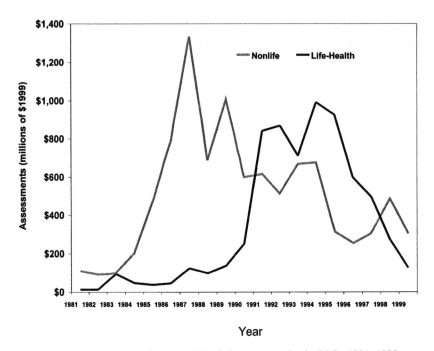

Figure 2.2. State Insurance Guaranty Fund Assessments in the U.S., 1981–1999.
Source: Author's compilations using National Organization of Life-Health
Guaranty Association and National Conference of Insurance Guaranty Fund data.

guaranty fund assessments. The specific RBC risk weights for the items
in each bucket and the formulas for aggregating the buckets' charges are
complex, and include nonlinear combination of various factors to allow
crudely for diversification (covariance risk). In the vast majority of states
that have adopted the NAIC's RBC standards, regulators can and/or must
take specific actions if the insurer's actual capital falls below specified percentages of its RBC (see table 2.2).

Most insurers and reinsurers easily exceeded the RBC thresholds when the
systems were adopted. The RBC standards nevertheless were purported to (1)
encourage weak insurers to limit their risk or increase their capital, (2) encourage faster corrective action by regulators and thus discourage unjustified
forbearance, and (3) help regulators identify insurers with too little capital.

RBC Ratios for Nonlife and Life Insurers

Figure 2.3 summarizes the distribution of ratios of total adjusted capital
to company action level RBC for nonlife and life insurers in 1999. For an
admittedly crude comparison, figure 2.3 also includes information on bank
RBC ratios (total capital/risk-weighted assets) as a percentage of the
required minimum (8%) for "adequate" capitalization.[18] The median nonlife insurer had capital equal to 327% of its company action level RBC; the

Table 2.2. Summary of U.S. Risk-Based Capital System

Nonlife Insurer RBC (Effective 1993)

Risk Category	Description
R0	Investment in insurance affiliates
R1	Fixed-income investment
R2	Equity investment
R3	Credit risk
R4	Loss reserve risk
R5	Premium and growth risk

Authorized control level

$$RBC^a = \tfrac{1}{2}[R0 + (R1^2 + R2^2 + R3^2 + R4^2 + R5^2)^{1/2}]$$

Ratio of Total Adjusted Capital to Authorized Control Level RBC (%)	Action
$\geq 200^a$	None
150–200	Insurer must submit plan to remedy deficiency.
100–150	Insurer plan; regulator can issue corrective orders.
70–100	Regulator is authorized to take control of insurer.
<70	Regulatory control is mandatory.

Life Insurer RBC (Effective 1994)

Risk Category	Description
C0	Investment in insurance affiliates
$C1_f$	Fixed-income investment
$C1_e$	Equity investment
C2	Insurance (underwriting) risk
C3	Interest rate risk
C4	Business risk

Authorized control level

$$RBC^a = \tfrac{1}{2}[C0 + ((C1_f + C3)^2 + C1_e^2 + C2^2)^{1/2} + C4]$$

[a]200% of authorized control level RBC is known as company action level RBC.

Note: The life formula also includes miscellaneous items related to health provider credit risk and health administration expense. A separate RBC system applies to specialty health insurers.

Source: American Academy of Actuaries (2002).

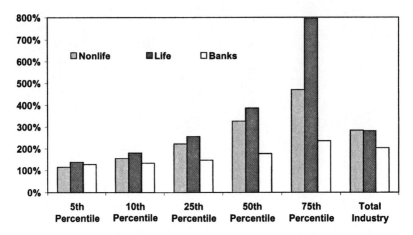

Figure 2.3. Selected Percentiles and Total Industry Values of RBC Ratios for Nonlife Insurers, Life Insurers, and Banks. Source: FDIC (2002) and author's compilations using NAIC data. Note: Insurer ratios = total adjusted capital/company action level RBC; Bank ratios = (total capital/risk-weighted assets)/0.08. Bank percentile values for 2001; all other values for 1999.

median life insurer had capital equal to 387% of its company action level RBC. The median bank had a total-capital-to-risk-weighted-assets ratio of 14.24%, which equaled 178% of the 8% threshold. Figure 2.4 plots nonlife insurer RBC ratios (total adjusted capital/company action level RBC) against net premium volume. There is some tendency for capital ratios to decline with premium volume, but most of the larger insurers have ratios well above 100%. The comparisons clearly indicate that insurer RBC requirements bind for relatively few insurers and suggest that bank RBC standards are more stringent than those for insurers.[19]

Available research indicates that relatively few nonlife insurers that failed in the late 1980s and early 1990s would have violated the RBC thresholds for regulatory action one to three years prior to insolvency (Cummins, Harrington, and Klein 1995; Grace, Harrington, and Klein 1998). Adding the ratio of actual capital to RBC also does not appear to increase the forecast accuracy of financial ratio based monitoring systems used by regulators, or to improve accuracy very much compared to using simple ratios, such as the ratio of surplus to premiums (see figure 2.5, which summarizes some results from Grace, Harrington, and Klein 1998). The extent to which RBC standards have increased capital levels or reduced risk taking is unknown.[20] Capital positions of nonlife and life insurers generally increased during the 1990s, and many life insurers curtailed asset risk following asset quality problems in the late 1980s and early 1990s. Those changes largely reflect market discipline, given limited guaranty fund protection and insurer incentives to preserve franchise value that could be eroded by financial difficulty.

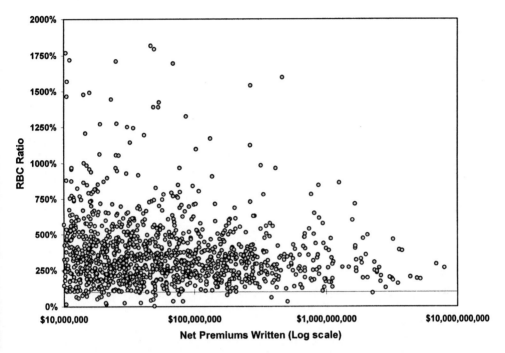

Figure 2.4. Total Adjusted Capital/Company Action Level RBC vs. Premium Volume for U.S. NonLife Insurers, 1999. Source: Author's compilations using NAIC data.

Criticisms of RBC

Like the Basel standards, the NAIC RBC standards have been criticized on a variety of dimensions.[21] One line of attack is that the types of risk reflected, the risk weights, and the aggregation methods are ad hoc and unnecessarily crude. As suggested earlier, however, it almost always can be argued that capital standards, although complex, are not complex enough to mimic market discipline (or sophisticated financial models) and that additional refinements could improve accuracy. A few observers suggest that the relatively low levels of total RBC compared to total insurance industry capital indicate that the formulas do not require enough capital.

Given substantial market discipline in the insurance industry, however, relatively low levels of RBC in relation to actual capital for the bulk of insurers represent a virtue of the system.[22] The levels suggest that RBC standards distort the decisions of relatively few sound insurers. Although the standards are complex, that complexity is probably relatively harmless given the modest levels of required capital. Attempting to achieve additional refinements in insurer capital standards and to increase the overall level of RBC materially would inevitably lead to undesirable distortions in decisions of many sound insurers. The effects could include reduced willingness of these

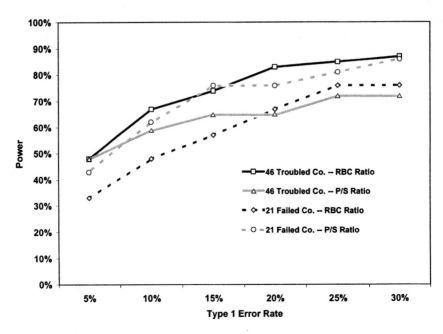

Figure 2.5. Power of Back-tested, Risk-based Capital Ratios and Surplus to Premium Ratios in 1991 to Identify Insolvent and Troubled Nonlife Insurers during 1992–1994. Note: Type 1 error rate is the proportion of solvent/nontroubled firms incorrectly categorized. Source: Grace, Harrington, and Klein (1998) and unpublished NAIC reports identifying troubled companies.

insurers to provide coverage, less efficient investment strategies, and/or higher prices, especially following any large negative shocks to insurer capital.

The preferred approach to enhancing efficiency is to consider possible methods of increasing market discipline where such discipline remains inadequate. The case for mandatory subordinated debt for large insurers is less forceful than that for banks, because of greater market discipline in the insurance sector that is associated with less comprehensive guarantees for insurer obligations. While evidently not politically viable, a strong case can be made for simpler capital requirements based on leverage, perhaps along the lines of the E.U. solvency margin requirements described later, in conjunction with possible targeted changes to promote market discipline (such as further reductions in guaranty fund protection for commercial policyholders).

Federal Insurance Regulation and Extension of the Basel Approach to U.S. Insurers

There is a risk that pressure will increase to further extend the Basel approach to insurers in the United States (and abroad; see discussion later in this chapter). The result of that extension might be further pressure to extend other measures parallel to those of bank regulation. U.S. state regulators often face pressure from some insurers and the U.S. Congress to mimic developments in bank regulation as a way to stave off federal insurance regulation. The enactment of the Gramm-Leach-Bliley (GLB) Act in 1999 increased debate over the direct and indirect costs of state regulation of rates, forms, and producer licensing in an environment of financial modernization, growing electronic commerce, and global competition. Representatives of many large U.S. nonlife insurers that specialize in business insurance and their main trade association, the American Insurance Association (AIA), advocate optional federal chartering and regulation as a means of regulatory modernization (i.e., of escaping inefficient state regulation of rates and certain policy forms). Representatives of many U.S. life insurers and the American Council of Life Insurance (ACLI) also favor optional federal regulation as a means of escaping inefficient regulation of policy forms and competing more effectively with banks.

State responses to the GLB Act, to increased concern about antiquated regulatory practices, and to the threat of federal chartering include the elimination, in many states, of prior approval regulation of rates and policy forms for "large" commercial policyholders. A large majority of states passed laws to meet GLB provisions dealing with reciprocity for nonresident producer licensing and to prevent federal licensing of producers. Various NAIC working groups are attempting the following: (1) to develop uniform state standards and centralized approval for policy form filings for "appropriate" life-health-annuity products, (2) to streamline and homogenize nonlife insurance rates and form filing and review processes, and (3) to promote regulation that recognizes competition. Those state actions have not prevented numerous proposals for dual chartering in the U.S. House and Senate and by the AIA, the ACLI, and the American Bankers Insurance Association (see, e.g., American Bankers Insurance Association 2002).

Optional federal chartering and regulation of U.S. insurers could ultimately undermine market discipline and create a demand for more stringent solvency regulation and capital requirements.[23] A federal guaranty covering the obligations of all insurers could be a precondition for an effective optional chartering system. It is highly probable that federal guarantees of both federally and state chartered insurers would result, leading to dual chartering, even if initial legislation eschewed federal guarantees and required federally chartered insurers to participate in state guaranty funds or established a federal guaranty system for federal insurers. A dual chartering system that required federally chartered insurers to participate in the state guaranty system without a federal guarantee would be unstable. Insolvency of a federally chartered insurer or a number of state chartered insurers would create strong pressure for a federal guarantee patterned after deposit insurance. The state guaranty system would likely be seriously weakened without participation of federally chartered insurers. A federal guaranty system would likely expand to cover both federally and state chartered insurers.

The danger is that federal guarantees would repeat some of the mistakes of deposit insurance. Specifically, they might inefficiently expand protection of insurance buyers against loss from insurer insolvency (e.g., by reflecting a policy, de facto or de jure, of "too big to fail"). Such expansion would materially undermine incentives for safety and soundness. More regulatory constraints on insurer operations, such as more stringent capital requirements and the extension of the Basel II approach to insurance and reinsurance, would eventually ensue. The ultimate result of dual chartering could therefore be less market discipline and more reliance on regulation.

Solvency Margin Requirements for E.U. Insurers

Compared to U.S. risk-based capital standards, "solvency margin" requirements for E.U. direct insurers generally are much simpler, at least at present. Although there exist cross-country differences in accounting procedures and other details, the main form of solvency requirements has been harmonized for direct E.U. insurers for many years. Table 2.3 summarizes some of the main features of the E.U. requirements for nonlife and life insurers as amended by the European Commission and Parliament in March 2002.[24] In contrast to the U.S. system, the E.U. solvency margin requirements are expressed as relatively simple proportions of relevant premiums, claims, or claim-related liabilities. There is no explicit provision for asset risk. Until the 2002 changes, the nonlife requirements did not distinguish types of coverage. The 2002 changes increase the required margin for aviation, marine, and general liability insurance compared with other coverages.[25]

Figure 2.6 illustrates the required solvency margin for nonlife insurers as a ratio of net (after reinsurance cessions) premiums under four different scenarios (and assuming factor A in table 2.3 produces the higher required margin). The figure illustrates the increased margin that can result from

Table 2.3. Highlights of E.U. Solvency Margin Requirements

Required Solvency Margin for Nonlife Insurance is the Greater of A or B:

A. [0.18 of Max (gross premiums,[a] EUR 50 m) + 0.16 of Max (gross premiums[a]– EUR 50 m, 0)] × Max [(net claims[a]/gross claims[*]), 0.5]
B. [0.26 of Max (gross claims,[a] EUR 35 m) + 0.23 of Max (gross claims[a]– EUR 35 m, 0)] × Max [(net claims[a]/gross claims[a]), 0.5]

Required Solvency Margin for Basic Life Insurance is the Sum of C and D:

C. [0.04 of mathematical provisions[b]] × Max [(net provisions/gross provisions), 0.85]
D. [0.03 of gross capital at risk[c]] × Max [(net capital at risk/gross capital at risk), 0.5]

[a]Gross premiums and claims for aviation, general liability, and marine insurance increased by 50%. Claim amounts are three-year averages.
[b]"Mathematical provisions" known as "policy reserves" in the United States.
[c]"Capital at risk" known as "net amount of risk" in the United States.
Note: Max (x, y) denotes the maximum of x or y; "gross" indicates before deduction for reinsurance ceded; "net" indicates after deduction for reinsurance ceded.
Source: Author's summary based on EU Directives 2002/12/EC and 2002/13/EC.

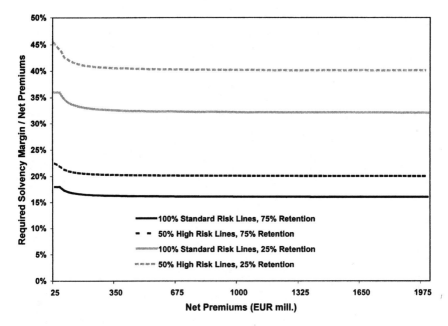

Figure 2.6. E.U. Required Solvency Margins as a Percentage of Net Premiums. Note: Calculations assume premium rule (item A in table 2). Sources: European Union (2002a, 2002b); author's calculations.

giving greater weight to higher risk coverages. It also shows the effects of the treatment of reinsurance ceded. Because the required margins limit the maximum reduction in the margin from ceding reinsurance to 50%, materially higher requirements result when an insurer retains less than 50% of claim liabilities (25% in two of the scenarios). The 50% limit has been a point of some contention.[26]

As is true in the United States, evidence indicates that most E.U. insurers generally have held considerably more capital than the required solvency margin (Swiss Re 2000).[26] Studies of European insolvencies have concluded that the system has performed reasonably well (Muller Group Report 1997). The relative simplicity of the requirements and their lack of stringency compared to actual capital levels are virtues in view of the degree of market discipline in insurance. Pressure is nonetheless mounting from some institutions and regulatory authorities for refinements in the solvency margin requirements that would consider other types of risks and possibly adopt the internal modeling, supervision, and market disclosure features of the Basel proposals. A study by KPMG for the European Commission (KPMG 2000a), as part of its Solvency II project, endorses the application of a Basel-like three-pillar approach to insurers (also see European Commission 2001). The European Commission describes that project as follows (European Commission 2002a):

The basic objective will be to try to better match solvency requirements to the true risk encountered by an insurance undertaking and also to encourage insurers to improve their measurement and monitoring of risks they incur. In this way, the objectives of the Solvency II project parallel those of the revision of the Basel Capital Accord for banks.[27]

The Financial Services Authority is developing a three-pillar approach for U.K. insurers and is working for such application throughout the European Union (Tiner 2002; Davies 2003).

Reinsurance Supervision and Capital Requirements

U.S. Regulation and Credit Requirements

Although the details are complex, the U.S. system of reinsurance regulation is relatively straightforward. State regulators review direct insurers' reinsurance arrangements. State-licensed reinsurers are subject to the same sorts of solvency regulation and are governed by the same RBC systems as direct insurers. U.S. direct insurers can take credit on their balance sheets for premiums and liabilities ceded to reinsurers only on the following conditions: (1) the reinsurer is licensed in the state, (2) the reinsurer is accredited in the state (which requires inter alia that it be licensed in at least one state), and (3) the reinsurer either collateralizes its obligations by deposits in an individual or multiple beneficiary trust, including a contingency reserve (surplus amount), or provides a letter of credit from a financial institution guaranteeing its obligations to each of its ceding insurers (see, for example, Hall 2001; Hall and Hall 1995).[28] Many non-U.S. entities satisfy the U.S. requirements by establishing a U.S. subsidiary (or U.S. branch) that is licensed or accredited in the states where it conducts business.

The rationale for the U.S. system, as expressed by state regulators and the Reinsurance Association of America (RAA), the leading trade association for U.S. reinsurers (see Hall 2001), is that credit for reinsurance rules are necessary to protect U.S. policyholders. However, representatives of non-U.S. reinsurers criticize the U.S. system as being overly burdensome and creating unnecessary barriers to free cross-border trade.[29] U.S. regulators and reinsurer representatives retort that U.S. reinsurers face the same state licensing and accreditation rules in the United States as non-U.S. reinsurers and that those rules have not prevented a large amount of coverage on U.S. risks from being ceded abroad (about 40% of U.S. nonaffiliated ceded premium; see Hall 2001). They note that U.S. regulators cannot be expected to have detailed familiarity or knowledge of hundreds of non-U.S. reinsurers.

Reinsurance Regulation in the European Union

Reinsurance in the European Union is not yet subject to any directives related to solvency regulation (see KPMG 2000b). The supervision of reinsurers is based on the laws of different E.U. countries. There is considerable diversity in those laws and procedures, ranging from virtually no regulation of domestic reinsurers in Belgium, Greece, and Ireland to regulation that largely mimics that for direct insurers in the United Kingdom and Italy. Some countries directly supervise reinsurers; some focus more on indirect supervision by reviewing direct insurers' reinsurance programs; some practice both direct and indirect supervision.[30] Table 2.4 summarizes some of the main differences across countries within the European Union.[31] Several countries do not require reinsurers to be licensed; many do not require nondomestic reinsurers to submit financial statements to regulators. Relatively few E.U. countries have required solvency margins for reinsurers.

Pressure is mounting for harmonization of direct supervision of reinsurer solvency and application of uniform solvency margin requirements to E.U. reinsurers. The leading trade association of European insurers has proposed harmonization around a set of core principles and a single passport system to the European Commission (CEA 2000). In October 2002, the International Association of Insurance Supervisors adopted a statement of principles calling for direct regulation of reinsurers (IAIS 2002). The KPMG study prepared for the European Commission on the question of reinsurance supervision has recommended harmonization and direct supervision, including solvency margin requirements and possible extension of the Basel approach to reinsurance (KPMG 2000b).[32] However, extensive market discipline in reinsurance—a wholesale market—suggests considerable caution in increasing the scope and intensity of reinsurance regulation.

Proposals for harmonization and more stringent supervision are partly motivated by the hope that they would eventually produce mutual recognition between United States and European Union regulators, which would allow E.U. reinsurers to operate in the United States (and vice versa) without having to be licensed (or accredited) in numerous jurisdictions. But

Table 2.4. Reinsurer Regulation in the European Union

Supervision	Germ.	France	U.K.	Neth.	Italy	Denmark	Sweden	Spain	Lux.
License required: domestic			•		•	•	•		•
License required: nondomestic			•		•	•			
Direct supervision	•		•		•	•	•	•	•
Indirect supervision	•	•	•	•		•		•	•
Financials required: domestic	•	•	•	•	•	•	•	•	•
Financials required: nondomestic			•		•				
Solvency margin requirement		pending	•		•				

Note: Domestic professional reinsurers are subject to no supervision in Belgium, Greece, and Ireland.

Source: KPMG (2000b).

there are several impediments to that development, and it would entail considerable risk. U.S. reinsurer representatives generally are strongly opposed to mutual recognition unless their companies can also obtain a single passport for operating in the United States (i.e., unless they can obtain a federal charter). At least for the moment, optional federal chartering of U.S. insurers and reinsurers does not appear imminent. Those representatives also have expressed concern that core regulatory requirements for reinsurers suggested in European Commission documents could be "far weaker" than regulation in some countries, such as the United States (Hall 2001, p. 15), and that promulgation of international accounting standards is another prerequisite for meaningful discussion of mutual recognition.[33]

Cross-border differences in the tax treatment of insurers/reinsurers also may substantially impede harmonization and mutual recognition, apart from state insurance regulation in the United States. As noted earlier, double taxation of investment earnings on insurers' capital can constitute a major cost of holding such capital. Some E.U. countries mitigate those tax costs by integrating corporate and personal taxation or through other mechanisms. Reinsurers in Bermuda and a number of other tax havens have attracted substantial reinsurance volume (including about $20 billion in new capital since September 11, 2001), in large part because they face lower capital costs. U.S. rules governing credit for reinsurance increase the costs to non-U.S. reinsurers of assuming U.S. business. As such, those rules probably lessen the amount of reinsurance that is ceded to reinsurers that operate in more tax-favored regimes. A certain degree of tax harmonization may be a prerequisite for substantial regulatory harmonization and mutual recognition, even if the United States permits federal chartering of insurers and reinsurers.

Financial Conglomerates and Cross-Sector Risk Transfers

The GLB Act subjects U.S. "financial service holding companies" to consolidated oversight by the Federal Reserve Board. Financial holding companies that do not include a commercial bank are not considered financial service holding companies and therefore are not subject to consolidated oversight by the Federal Reserve. The European Union's financial conglomerate directive (EU 2002c) requires financial companies with at least one entity in the insurance sector and at least one entity in the banking *or* the investment services sector to be subject to consolidated oversight. Entities based outside the European Union that are not subject to "equivalent" consolidated oversight would have to establish an E.U. holding company to conduct business in the European Union.

The emphasis on consolidated oversight in the European Union reflects concern with the effects on financial stability of combining cross-sector activities under common ownership. Debate also has arisen over the effects on financial stability of cross-sector risk transfers, largely as a result of insurers' (mainly global reinsurers and specialist monoline insurers) increased participation in markets for credit risk transfer. Concern has been expressed about possible arbitrage of regulatory capital requirements across sectors. Studies of credit risk and other cross-sector risk transfers by the Financial Services Authority (2002), the International Association of Insurance Supervisors (IAIS 2003), and the Committee on the Global Financial System (2003) suggest no cause for alarm, but the general issues suggest possible advantages of centralized regulatory authority over different types of financial firms.[34]

It is unclear how any of these issues will be resolved in the near term and whether they will ultimately give rise to substantially different regulatory structures in the United States and abroad. Prudent resolution of the appropriate degree of regulatory harmonization, centralization, and scope of regulatory authority would pay close attention to differences in market discipline across sectors. It would not undermine market discipline by applying banking-type guarantees and regulation to sectors with less systemic risk and greater market discipline. It would recognize the basic tradeoff between market discipline and the optimal degree of regulatory stringency.

CONCLUSIONS

If economically efficient regulation is the goal, capital standards and regulatory supervision should be less stringent for sectors characterized by greater market discipline and less systemic risk. Market discipline is greater and systemic risk is lower for insurance than for banking; therefore, capital requirements should be less stringent for insurers. Because market discipline is greater for reinsurance than for direct insurance, capital requirements and related regulation need not be as stringent for reinsurers as for direct insurers. The relative stringency of capital requirements for insurers and reinsurers in the United States and the European Union at the present time is by and large consistent with significant market discipline.

Any federal regulation of insurers in the United States, harmonization of reinsurance regulation in the European Union and internationally, and changes in the centralization and scope of regulatory authority over different financial activities should evolve under full appreciation of limited systemic risk and significant market discipline in insurance and avoid undermining that discipline. Even if appropriate in banking, extension of the Basel framework to insurance and reinsurance would be ill advised. Relatively simple capital requirements for insurers and reinsurers are a virtue; stringency is a vice. Complexity with little stringency is costly but relatively benign. Wise prudential policy would maintain and further promote insurance/reinsurance market discipline, thus obviating the need for intrusive, stringent, and complex capital rules and associated regulatory intervention in private decisionmaking.

APPENDIX: OPTIMAL CAPITAL STANDARDS WITH IMPERFECT RISK ASSESSMENT

This appendix sketches a simple model of the relation between optimal capital standards and the proportion of firms for which incentives would otherwise produce insufficient capital when risk assessment is imperfect. The focus is on the role of capital standards in encouraging some firms to hold more capital than would be held without such standards.

Assume that, without capital regulation, there would be two types of firms, low risk (L) and high risk (H). The proportion of high-risk firms is α. Each low-risk firm holds the efficient level of capital, defined as the amount of capital that minimizes the sum of the firm's default put value, P_L, and its capital costs, kK_L, where K_L is the amount of capital held and k is the per unit capital cost (due to tax and/or agency costs).[35] Thus, $K_L = K_{Le}$ and $P_L = P_{Le}$, where K_{Le} is the efficient (cost-minimizing) level of capital and P_{Le} is the efficient put value for low-risk firms. Also assume for simplicity that each high-risk firm would hold the same amount of capital as low-risk firms, which, given its greater risk, would produce an excessive value for its default put; that is, $K_H = K_L < K_{He} => P_H > P_{He}$, where K_{He} and P_{He} denote the efficient values of K and P for high-risk firms.

The efficient capital level for firm type i ($i = L, H$) minimizes the sum of the default put and capital costs:

$$P_i(K_i) + kK_i, \text{which requires:}$$
$$P_{ik} + \kappa = 0, \tag{2.1}$$

where P_{iK} is the derivative of P_i with respect to K_i. K_{ei} equates the marginal benefit from reducing the firm's default put with the marginal cost of holding more capital.

For high-risk firms, total costs are not minimized (the default put is too large), and $P_{HK} + k < 0$, that is, high-risk firms could lower costs by holding more capital. If high-risk firms could be identified with perfect accuracy (and with costless enforcement), optimal capital regulation would be trivial: each high-risk firm would be forced to hold $K_{He} > K_L$. Assume instead that (1) high-risk firms can be identified only imperfectly, and that (2) all firms classified as high-risk are forced to increase capital to $K > K_L$.

Define the Type 1 error rate, π_1, as the probability that a low-risk firm is classified as high risk and the Type 2 error rate, π_2, as the probability that a high-risk firm is classified as low risk. Then the power to classify a high-risk firm correctly is $1 - \pi_2$. To focus on the issue at hand, π_1 and π_2 are treated as exogenous. A fuller treatment would relax that assumption and incorporate assumptions about the technology and costs of influencing π_1 and π_2.

The benefit from requiring a high-risk firm to hold more capital equals the reduction in its put value less the additional capital cost: $P_H(K_L) - P_H(K) - (K - K_L)k > 0$.

The cost of incorrectly classifying a low-risk firm is the excess of the additional capital cost over the reduction in its put value: $(K - K_L)k + P_L(K) - P_L(K_L) > 0$.

Given this setup, the efficient capital requirement for firms classified as high-risk maximizes the expected net benefit, B (the proportion of high-risk firms classified correctly times the associated benefit less the proportion of low-risk firms classified incorrectly times the associated cost):

$$B = \alpha(1 - \pi_2)[P_H(K_L) - P_H(K) - (K - K_L)k]$$
$$- (1 - \alpha)\pi_1[(K - K_L)_k + P_L(K) - P_L(K_L)]$$

Differentiating B with respect to K gives the first-order condition:

$$B_K = -\alpha(1 - \pi_2)[P_{HK} + k] - (1 - \alpha)\pi_1[P_{LK} + k] = 0 \qquad (2.2)$$

This condition equates the marginal expected benefits of reducing put values for correctly classified high-risk firms with the marginal expected costs of requiring incorrectly classified low-risk firms to hold excess capital.

If K is set equal to the amount of capital that minimizes costs for a given high-risk firm, K_{He}, then $P_{HK} + k = 0$ (see expression [2.1]) and $B_K = -(1 - \alpha)\pi_1[P_{LK} + k]$. Because $P_{LK} + k > 0$ for $K > K_L = K_{Le}$, $B_K < 0$ if $\alpha < 1$, which then implies that K^*, the optimal value of K, is less than K_{He}, the cost minimizing level of K for high-risk firms. Thus, *the optimal value of K is less than the value that minimizes costs for a given high-risk firm unless all firms would hold too little capital absent regulation.* Intuitively, errors in classifying firms require a lower capital requirement for firms classified as high risk in order to reduce costs associated with requiring incorrectly classified low-risk firms to hold excess capital.

Equation (2.2) implicitly defines K^* (the optimal capital requirement for firms classified as high risk). Implicitly differentiating $B_K(K^*)$ with respect to α, π_1, π_2, $P_H(K_L)$, and k (and assuming $B_{KK} < 0$, the sufficient condition for a maximum), it is easy to show that:

1. K^* increases as α (the proportion of high-risk firms) increases,
2. K^* decreases as π_1 (the probability of misclassifying a low-risk firm) increases,
3. K^* increases as $1-\pi_2$ (the power to identify high-risk firms) increases,
4. K^* increases with $P_H(K_L)$ (the default put for high-risk firms that hold K_L) if P_{HK} declines for higher $P_H(K_L)$,
5. K^* declines as k increases (the per unit cost of holding capital becomes more expensive).

Given (1) and (4), less market discipline (a higher proportion of high-risk firms and higher put values for those firms) implies higher optimal capital requirements.

Acknowledgments I'd like to acknowledge Rolf Nebel of Swiss Re for helpful comments and input.

Notes

1. Using U.S. terminology, the two principal balance sheet liabilities are (1) the "loss reserve," which is the liability for unpaid claims for accidents that have

occurred to date, and (2) the "unearned premium 'reserve,'" which is the liability for premiums that have been paid by policyholders and are attributable to the unexpired portion of coverage. The term "reserve risk" generally refers to the risk that ultimate claim costs will exceed the reported loss reserve (reported liability for unpaid claims, discussed below).

2. Effects on real activity were widely reported during the mid-1980s crisis in U.S. liability insurance and more recently in the U.S. medical care sector. Odell and Weidenmier (2002) document real and monetary linkage following the San Francisco earthquake and associated insurance payments during 1906–1907.

3. Capital-to-asset ratios for U.S. nonlife insurers in the late 1990s averaged about 40%, compared with 10%–11% for life insurers and commercial banks.

4. See Jaffee and Russell (1997) for discussion of tax and agency costs of capital and Harrington and Niehaus (2001 and 2003) for detailed analysis of tax costs of capital in the United States.

5. As a recent, practical example, regulators' postmortems of E.U. insurer insolvencies since 1996 conclude that underlying internal problems related to management and incentives appear to be the root cause of most insolvencies (see Sharma 2002; also see McDonnell 2002).

6. The seminal theoretical treatment of this issue in the insurance literature is Finsinger and Pauly (1984). I have emphasized the role of franchise value in promoting market discipline in my work with Patricia Danzon (Danzon and Harrington 1994). Keeley (1990) and many others have considered the role of bank franchise value in bank capital decisions. See Santos (2000) for a review.

7. Swiss Re (2000) and Hancock, Huber, and Koch (2001) emphasize the tradeoff between capital (safety and soundness) and capital costs.

8. See Santos (2000) for general discussion of the wholesale/resale distinction in the rationale for financial services regulation.

9. Systemic risk is lower for all nonbank financial institutions (Santos 2000). Nebel (2001) provides a useful discussion of why systemic risk is low for insurance.

10. Brewer and Jackson (2002) analyze U.S. bank and life insurer stock price reactions to "financial distress" announcements and provide evidence that pure contagion is much lower for life insurance than for banks. Also see Malkiel (1991) and Fenn and Cole (1994).

11. See Lee, Mayers, and Smith (1997) and Downs and Sommer (1999) for further discussion. A poorly designed guaranty system that spread the cost of insurer insolvencies broadly among taxpayers could reduce pressure by insurers and policyholders for the government to commit resources and to adopt internal controls that are necessary for efficient monitoring. Although the desire to avoid loss of premium tax revenue in states that allow offset of guaranty fund assessments against premium taxes might produce legislative pressure for controlling the cost of assessments, Brewer, Mondschean, and Strahan (1997) argue and provide evidence that suggests that tax offsets of life guaranty association assessments reduce incentives for monitoring.

12. Life guaranty funds exclude coverage for large amounts of unallocated annuities and generally include haircut provisions on policyholder accounts.

13. The recent insolvency of Reliance Insurance Group, with an estimated $1.1 billion excess of liabilities over assets, is expected to cause guaranty fund annual assessment caps to be reached in a number of states, perhaps for several years, and especially in the states' separate workers' compensation insurance guaranty funds. Although existing procedures that permit or facilitate borrowing by guaranty funds should allow America's largest property-casualty insurer insolvency to be handled in

a relatively smooth fashion, the possible insolvencies of one or more other sizable insurers with relatively large workers' compensation portfolios would stress the system. Proposals are being discussed for new funding arrangements where solvent insurers would advance funding above the caps to be credited against future assessments. The Reliance insolvency and the recent financial difficulties of a number of other insurers in large part reflect intense price competition during the prolonged "soft" market for commercial property-casualty insurance in the 1990s and unexpected growth in claim costs for business written at relatively low rates. Thus, in many respects these problems illustrate the inherent risks of insuring property-casualty risk.

14. The U.K. guaranty system covers personal lines, financed by ex post assessments. France covers motor liability, financed ex ante by premium taxes. Germany covers motor liability with ex post assessments for covered claims. See Swiss Re (2000). Norway has a guaranty system; Ireland and the Netherlands have recently introduced such systems (IAIS 2000).

15. This problem is a straightforward application of standard analyses of loss functions in statistical testing.

16. During 1979–1997, nonlife insurance guaranty assessments in the United States averaged 0.15% of net premiums with a maximum of 0.47% (Swiss Re 2000).

17. See American Academy of Actuaries (2002) for comprehensive details. KPMG (2000a) and Swiss Re (2000) provide basic details and examples.

18. The bank ratio percentiles are for 2001 (which I could readily obtain) and probably are slightly lower than would be true in 1999. The result for the total banking industry uses data for 1999 (the same year as for the insurers).

19. This point is noted in IAIS (2001, p. 5); also see p. 53 of that study, which discusses ratios of capital to company action level RBC for life and nonlife insurers.

20. In contrast to extensive research on the effects of the Basel Accord on banks, much of which is inconclusive (see Jackson 1999 for an excellent survey), there has been relatively little work on the effects of U.S. RBC standards on behavior, perhaps because the required capital amounts are relatively low and a variety of nonregulatory factors led to larger capital ratios in the 1990s.

21. Cummins, Harrington, and Niehaus (1993, 1995) review some of the arguments. Also see chapter 10 of KPMG (2000a). A 1997 report (European Commission 1997) by the European Commission noted, "[T]he superiority of [the U.S. RBC approach] over the Community regulatory [solvency margin] approach has not been demonstrated. Such models are characterized in particular by their complexity and comparatively greater arbitrariness."

22. Dave Cummins, Greg Niehaus, and I argued this in our 1993 paper.

23. I have discussed this issue in detail in several earlier papers (e.g., Harrington 1991, 1992, 2002). Also see Wallison (2000).

24. The current rules date back to 1973 (nonlife) and 1979 (life). Appendix 10.1 of KPMG (2000a) provides a useful introduction to current solvency margin requirements. Also see Swiss Re (2000). The rules also define absolute minimum amounts of capital (the "minimum guarantee fund"), which will be indexed with inflation under the new amendments.

25. That change reflected concerns expressed in the Muller Group Report (1997). The 2002 amendments also strengthened provisions for regulatory intervention.

26. The CEA supports a maximum deduction higher than 50% (CEA 2000, p. 9). The Swiss Re study also provides evidence that the U.S. nonlife RBC

rules produce higher required capital on average than the E.U. solvency margin requirements.

27. A news story (see Bolger 2002) based on the press release for the KPMG report (2000a) quoted a KPMG executive who noted that insurers' "risk management systems—with some exceptions—have not evolved in line with advances made in the banking sector.... The existing solvency rules ... do not adequately reflect the full range of risks to which insurers are exposed." A coauthor of the report was quoted as stating: "While the solvency requirements for insurance undertakings in the European Union have generally worked well in protecting policyholders, they have been in place for many years and the need for reform has become pressing." One outcome of applying a three-pillar approach with emphasis on internal modeling would be significant expansion in the demand by insurers for risk modeling consulting services.

28. A few states' regulators have been reluctant to accept domiciliary state recommendations that a particular reinsurer qualifies for accreditation (Hall and Hall 1995).

29. Representatives of non-U.S. reinsurers have pressed for reductions in funding requirements for multiple beneficiary trusts. The United States also imposes a 1% excess tax on reinsurance ceded to non-U.S. reinsurers (4% for direct insurance), absent any reciprocity arrangement with the tax authorities in the reinsurer's home country.

30. Section 6.4 of KPMG (2000a) contains detailed discussion of procedures used to assess ceding insurers' reinsurance programs in different countries. France has a particularly stringent system; it requires collateralization of all ceded reserves.

31. See KPMG (2000b) for detailed discussion. According to KPMG, the two largest European reinsurers, Munich Re and Swiss Re, are regulated only to a "limited extent."

32. Nebel (2001) provides a counterview supporting liberal regulation of reinsurance.

33. Insurance liability and asset reporting procedures currently vary significantly across countries both within and outside the European Union. See chapters 4 and 5 of KPMG (2000a) for detailed discussion. Chapter 8 of that report considers possible changes in international accounting standards.

34. Borio (2003) discusses possible advantages of a macro approach to prudential regulation compared to the traditional micro (sector specific) approach.

35. I assume for simplicity that k is constant and the same for high- and low-risk firms.

References

American Academy of Actuaries Joint RBC Task Force. 2002. Comparison of the NAIC Life, P&C and Health RBC Formulas. Joint RBC Task Force Report (February). Available at: www.actuary.org/pdf/finreport/jrbc_12feb02.pdf.

American Bankers Insurance Association. 2002. Comparison of Optional Federal Insurance Charter Bills. Available at: www.aba.com/ABIA/ABIA_Reg_Mod_Page.htm.

Basel Committee on Banking Supervision Joint Forum. 2001. Risk Management Practices and Regulatory Capital: Cross-Sectoral Comparison. Available at: www.bis.org/publ/joint04.pdf.

Benston, George J. 1998. *Regulating Financial Markets: A Critique and Some Proposals.* London: Institute of Economic Affairs.

Billet, Matthew T., Jon A. Garfinkel, and Edward S. O'Neal. 1998. The Cost of Market vs. Regulatory Discipline in Banking. *Journal of Financial Economics* 48 (3): 333–58.

Bohn, James G., and Brian J. Hall. 1999. The Moral Hazard of Insuring the Insurers. In *The Financing of Catastrophe Risk,* ed. Kenneth Froot, 363–390. Chicago: University of Chicago Press.

Bolger, Andrew. 2002. Insurers Must Upgrade Means of Assessing Risk. *Financial Times,* May 2.

Borio, Claude. 2003. Towards a Macroprudential Framework for Financial Supervision and Regulation? BIS Working Paper No. 128. Available at: www.bis.org/publ/work128.pdf.

Brewer, Elijah, III, and William E. Jackson III. 2002. Inter-Industry Contagion and the Competitive Effects of Financial Distress Announcements: Evidence from Commercial Banks and Life Insurance Companies. Federal Reserve Bank of Chicago Working Paper 2002–23. Available at: www.chicagofed.org/publications/workingpapers/papers/wp2002-23.pdf.

Brewer, Elijah, III, Thomas H. Mondschean, and Philip E. Strahan. 1997. The Role of Monitoring in Reducing the Moral Hazard Problem Associated with Government Guarantees: Evidence from the Life Insurance Industry. *Journal of Risk and Insurance* 64 (2): 301–22.

Breyer, Stephen. 1982. *Regulation and Its Reform.* Cambridge, Mass.: Harvard University Press.

Comité Européen des Assurances (CEA). 2000. Framework for a European Regime for the Supervision of Cross-Border Reinsurance. Working Paper. Brussels.

Committee on the Global Financial System (CGFS). 2003. Credit Risk Transfer. CGFS Working Group Report No. 20. Available at: www.bis.org/publ/cgfs20.pdf.

Cummins, J. David, Scott E. Harrington, and Robert W. Klein. 1995. Insolvency Experience, Risk-Based Capital, and Prompt Corrective Action in Property-Liability Insurance. *Journal of Banking and Finance* 19 (3/4): 511–28.

Cummins, J. David, Scott E. Harrington, and Greg Niehaus. 1993. An Economic Overview of Risk-Based Capital Requirements for the Property-Liability Insurance Industry. *Journal of Insurance Regulation* 11: 427–47.

———. 1995. Risk-Based Capital Requirements for Property-Liability Insurers: A Financial Analysis. In *The Financial Dynamics of the Insurance Industry,* ed. Edward I. Altman and Irwin T. Vanderhoof, 111–152. New York: New York University Salomon Center.

Davies, Howard. 2003. FSA's Approach to Insurance Regulation. Speech before the Association of British Insurers Annual Conference (April 10). Available at: www.fsa.gov.uk/pubs/speeches/sp123.html.

Danzon, Patricia M., and Scott E. Harrington. 1994. Price-Cutting in Liability Insurance Markets. *Journal of Business* 67: 511–38.

Downs, David, and David Sommer. 1999. Monitoring, Ownership, and Risk-Taking: The Impact of Guaranty Funds. *Journal of Risk and Insurance* 66 (3): 477–97.

Epermanis, Karen, and Scott E. Harrington. 2001. Financial Rating Changes and Market Discipline in U.S. Property-Liability Insurance. Paper presented at 2001 Risk Theory Society Meeting and 2001 International Insurance Society Meeting.

European Commission (EC). 1997. Report to the Insurance Committee on the Need
for Further Harmonization of the Solvency Margin. Brussels.

———. 2001. Banking Rules: Relevance for the Insurance Sector? Note to the
Solvency Subcommittee MARKT/2056/01-EN (12 June).

———. 2002a. Insurance: Commission Welcomes Rapid Adoption of Directives to
Strengthen Protection of Policyholders. IP/02/252 (14 February).

———. 2002b. Insurance Solvency Margin Rules—Frequently Asked Questions.
MEMO/02/26 (14 February).

European Union (E.U.). 2002a. Directive 2002/12/EC of the European Parliament
and of the Council of 5 March 2002 Amending Council Directive 79/267/EEC as
Regards the Solvency Margin Requirements for Life Assurance Undertakings.

———. 2002b. Directive 2002/13/EC of the European Parliament and of the Council
of 5 March 2002 Amending Council Directive 73/239/EEC as Regards the Solvency Margin Requirements for Non-Life Insurance Undertakings.

———. 2002c. Directive 2002/87/EC of the European Parliament and of the Council
of 16 December 2002 on the Supplementary Supervision of Credit Institutions,
Insurance Undertakings, and Investment Firms in a Financial Conglomerate and
Amending Council Directives 73/239/EEC, 79/267/EEC, 92/49/EEC, 92/96/EEC,
93/6/EEC and 93/22/EEC, and Directives 98/78/EC and 2000/12/EC of the
European Parliament and of the Council.

Evanoff, Douglas D., and Larry D. Wall. 2003. Subordinated Debt and Prompt Corrective Regulatory Action. Federal Reserve Bank of Chicago Working Paper 2003-
03. Available at: http://www.chicagofed.org/publications/workingpapers/papers/
wp2003-03.pdf.

Federal Deposit Insurance Corporation Federal Financial Institutions Examination
Council (FDIC FFIEC). 2001. UBPR Peer Group Ratio Distribution Report for
12/31/2001 for All Insured Commercial Banks. Available at: www2.fdic.gov/
ubpr/PeerDistribution.

Fenn, George W., and Rebel A. Cole. 1994. Announcements of Asset Quality Problems and Contagion Effects in the Life Insurance Industry. *Journal of Financial
Economics* 35 (2): 181–98.

Financial Services Authority. 2002. *Cross Sector Risk Transfers*. Available at:
www.fsa.gov.uk/pubs/discussion/dp11.pdf.

Finsinger, Jorg, and Mark V. Pauly. 1991. Reserve Levels and Reserve Requirements
for Profit-Maximizing Insurance Firms. In *Foundations of Insurance Economics:
Readings in Economics and Finance*, ed. Georges Dionne and Scott E. Harrington.
Boston: Kluwer Academic Publishers.

Grace, Martin F., Scott E. Harrington, and Robert W. Klein. 1998. Risk-Based
Capital and Solvency Screening in Property-Liability Insurance: Hypotheses and
Empirical Tests. *Journal of Risk and Insurance* 65: 213–43.

Hall, Debra J. 2001. Reinsurance Regulation in a Global Marketplace: A View from
the United States. Available at: http://community.reinsurance.org/StaticContent/
Policy/hall_marketplace.pdf.

Hall, Robert M., and Debra J. Hall. 1995. Changes in U.S. Credit for Reinsurance
Laws. Available at: www.robertmhall.com/articles/a.htm.

Hancock, John, Paul Huber, and Pablo Koch. 2001. *The Economics of Insurance: How
Insurers Create Value for Shareholders*. Zurich: Swiss Re Technical Publishing.

Harrington, Scott E. 1991. Should the Feds Regulate Insurance Company Solvency?
Regulation 14 (2): 53–61. Available at: www.cato.org/pubs/regulation/reg14n2d
.html.

————. 1992. Policyholder Runs, Life Insurance Company Failures, and Insurance Solvency Regulation. *Regulation* 15 (2): 27–37. Available at: www.cato.org/pubs/regulation/reg15n2a.html.

————. 2002. *Optional Federal Chartering of Property/Casualty Insurance Companies.* Downers Grove, IL: Alliance of American Insurers.

Harrington, Scott E., and Greg Niehaus. 2001. Government Insurance, Tax Policy, and the Availability and Affordability of Catastrophe Insurance. *Journal of Insurance Regulation* 19 (Summer): 591–612. 2003.

————. Capital, Corporate Income Taxes, and Catastrophe Insurance. *Journal of Financial Intermediation* 12: 365–89.

International Association of Insurance Supervisors (IAIS). 2000. On Solvency, Solvency Assessments, and Actuarial Issues. An IAIS Issues Paper (March). Available at: http://www.iaisweb.org/08151istansolv.pdf.

————. 2002. Supervisory Standard on the Evaluation of the Reinsurance Cover of Primary Insurers and the Security of Their Reinsurers. Supervisory Standard No. 7 (January). Available at: http://www.iaisweb.org/02reinsurance.pdf.

————. 2003. Credit Risk Transfer Between Insurance, Banking, and Other Financial Sectors. IAIS paper presented to the Financial Stability Forum (March). Available at: http://www.iaisweb.org/03fsfcrt.pdf.

Jackson, Patricia. 1999. Capital Requirements and Bank Behavior: The Impact of the Basel Accord. Basel Committee on Bank Supervision Working Paper No. 1. Available at: www.bis.org/publ/bcbs_wp1.pdf.

Jaffee, Dwight M., and Thomas Russell. 1997. Catastrophe Insurance, Capital Markets, and Uninsurable Risk. *Journal of Risk and Insurance* 64 (2): 205–30.

Keeley, Michael C. 1990. Deposit Insurance, Risk, and Market Power in Banking. *American Economic Review* 80 (5): 1183–1200.

KPMG. 2000a. Study in the Methodologies to Assess the Overall Financial Position of an Insurance Undertaking from the Perspective of Prudential Supervision. Report to European Commission Contract No: ETD/2000/BS-3001/C/45. Available at: http://europa.eu.int/comm/internal_market/insurance/docs/solvency/solvency2-study-kpmg_en.pdf.

————. 2000b. Study into the Methodologies for Prudential Supervision of Reinsurance with a View to the Possible Establishment of an EU Framework. Report to European Commission Contract No: ETD/2000/BS-3001/C/44. Available at: http://europa.eu.int/comm/internal_market/insurance/docs/reinsurance/reinssup_en.pdf.

Lee, Soon-Jae, David Mayers, and Clifford W. Smith Jr. 1997. Guaranty Funds and Risk-Taking: Evidence from the Insurance Industry. *Journal of Financial Economics* 44: 3–24.

Malkiel, Burton G. 1991. Assessing the Solvency of the Insurance Industry. *Journal of Financial Services Research* 5: 167–80.

McDonnell, William. 2002. Managing Risk: Practical Lessons from Recent "Failures'" of E.U. Insurers. Financial Services Authority Occasional Paper Series 20. Available at: www.fsa.gov.uk/pubs/occpapers/op20.pdf.

Muller Group Report. 1997. Conference of Insurance Supervisory Departments of European Member States (April).

Nebel, Rolf. 2001. The Case for Liberal Reinsurance Regulation.

Odell, Kerry A., and Marc D. Weidenmier. 2002. Real Shock, Monetary Aftershock: The San Francisco Earthquake and the Panic of 1907. NBER Working Paper 9176. Available at: http://papers.nber.org/papers/w9176.pdf.

Santos, João A. C. 2000. Bank Capital Regulation in Contemporary Banking Theory: A Review of the Literature. BIS Working Paper No. 90. Available at: www.bis.org/publ/work90.pdf.

Sharma, Paul. 2002. *Prudential Supervision of Insurance Undertakings*. Conference of Insurance Supervisory Services of the Member States of the European Union. Available at: http://europa.eu.int/comm/internal_market/insurance/docs/solvency/solvency2-conference-report_en.pdf.

Standard & Poor's. 2002. U.S. Insurer Failures Decline by Almost 40% in 2001 Despite Adverse Economic Conditions. March 27.

Swiss Re. 2000. Solvency of Non-Life Insurers: Balancing Security and Profitability Expectations. *Sigma* 1: 1–38.

Tiner, John. 2002. The Future Regulation of Insurance—A Progress Report. Financial Services Authority. Available at: www.fsa.gov.uk/pubs/policy/bnr_progress3.pdf.

U.S. Shadow Financial Regulatory Committee. 2000. Reforming Bank Capital Regulation. Washington, D.C.: American Enterprise Institute. Available at: www.aei.org/research/shadow/publications/pubID.16542,projectID.15/pub_detail.asp.

Wallison, Peter, ed. 2000. Optional Federal Chartering and Regulation of Insurance Companies. Washington, D.C.: American Enterprise Institute.

Zanjani, George. 2002. Market Discipline and Government Guarantees in Life Insurance. Federal Reserve Bank of New York Working Paper.

3

Consolidated Capital Regulation for Financial Conglomerates

HOWELL E. JACKSON

Over the past few years, financial regulators have devoted considerable attention to the development of consolidated capital rules for financial conglomerates. In this chapter, the author explores the theoretical justifications for these new requirements and explains that the case for consolidated capital oversight consists of four separate lines of argument: technical weaknesses inherent in traditional entity-level capital requirements; unique risks associated with financial conglomerates; additional diversification benefits that financial conglomerates enjoy; and recognition that financial firms increasingly employ modern risk management techniques that work on a group-wide basis. The author then reviews the specific rules for consolidated capital requirements that the Basel Committee proposed in April 2003, and argues that the Basel proposals constitute a relatively rudimentary system of consolidated capital requirements, dealing primarily with the technical weaknesses of entity level capital and making little effort to deal with more subtle issues such as unique risks of financial conglomerates, diversification benefits, and modern risk-management techniques. As the author explains, a number of significant practical considerations contribute to the relatively limited scope of the Basel Committee's proposal, considerations that will likely prevent the development of a more comprehensive system of consolidated capital oversight for financial conglomerates in the foreseeable future.

This chapter discusses the difficulties of applying bank-focused regulation at the consolidated bank holding company level. This follows from the findings of other chapters that the approach to capital should be different for insurance, securities, and banking firms. Jackson explains how the accommodation to this reality leads Basel II to make significant exceptions to consolidation, such as requiring holding companies to deduct any investment in an insurance company. For firms with an 8% capital requirement, this would be equivalent to risk-weighting the investment at 1250%. This, in turn, may penalize financial conglomerates with banking subsidiaries.

INTRODUCTION

Over the past decade, supervision of financial conglomerates has been the focus of numerous multilateral reports and academic investigation. From this ongoing study has emerged widespread acceptance of the notions that regulatory authorities should oversee financial conglomerates on a consolidated basis and that this oversight should include consolidated capital supervision. However, no similar consensus has emerged as to how exactly this supervision should be imposed. Indeed, there exists substantial variation in existing consolidated capital regulation of financial conglomerates across national boundaries, and internal risk management procedures at financial conglomerates themselves differ radically from evolving legal standards.

My goal in this chapter is to review the regulatory justifications for imposing capital regulation on a consolidated basis and then to explore the approach that would implement a system of consolidated capital supervision under the proposed Basel Capital Accord of April 2003 (Basel II). As explained later, the Basel II proposals for consolidated capital requirements are fairly rudimentary, avoiding the more subtle aspects of conglomerate supervision and establishing only a crude system of consolidated capital oversight. In addition, the Basel II proposals grant considerable latitude to national authorities to determine how the new consolidated capital provisions are to be implemented, suggesting that variation in national rules may persist even if the new Accords are widely adopted. Nevertheless, viewed as part of broader efforts to oversee financial conglomerates, the Basel II proposals on consolidated capital supervision should, in my view, count as a modest improvement over past practices and a credible attempt to address a complex subject. The technical barriers to imposing a comprehensive and sophisticated system of consolidated capital supervision are too great to expect the framers of the Basel II revisions to have attempted much more.

JUSTIFICATIONS FOR IMPOSING CAPITAL REQUIREMENTS ON A CONSOLIDATED BASIS

Before turning to the Basel II requirements themselves, I begin with a brief discussion of a critical predicate question: Why does nearly everyone agree that capital requirements should be imposed on a consolidated basis, as opposed to traditional entity-based capital requirements? Consider the capital requirements of a U.S.-style financial conglomerate, such as Citigroup. As illustrated in figure 3.1, such a conglomerate has a number of regulated subsidiaries: depository institutions, insurance companies, and securities firms. Traditionally—and under the original Basel Accord—capital requirements were imposed solely on the regulated subsidiaries, with each sector of the financial services industry being subject to its own unique set of capital requirements.[1] Why is this regulatory approach to capital oversight—sometimes called entity-level capital requirements—not sufficient? The

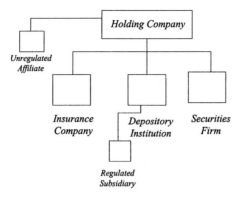

Figure 3.1. U.S.-Style Financial Conglomerate.
Source: Author's compilation.

received wisdom in the literature offers numerous, not entirely consistent responses.[2]

Weaknesses Inherent in Entity-Level Capital Requirements for Financial Conglomerates

Prior analyses of financial conglomerates suggest that there are three basic weaknesses in entity-level capital requirements for financial conglomerates.

First, there is the problem of "excessive leverage"—that is, the possibility that an unregulated holding company will finance the capital of its regulated subsidiaries through the issuance of debt instruments. (Joint Forum 1999; Meyers and Ballegeer 2003). With such holding-company financing, the consolidated capital of the conglomerate can be less than the sum of the capital positions of the regulated subsidiaries. The problem of excessive leverage is inherent in entity-level capital requirements because this system of capital oversight never measures the capital adequacy of holding companies. This potential for excessive leverage at the holding company level is thought to make the parent corporation likely to exploit regulated subsidiaries in times of financial stress, either by withdrawing capital from the regulated subsidiary or by forcing the subsidiary to make uneconomical transactions with related parties.[3]

An analogous problem occurs if a bank or other regulated entity uses its own assets to capitalize a regulated subsidiary that is subject to its own capital requirements (see Joint Forum 1999; Jackson and Half 2002, pp. 16–7; Meyers and Ballegeer 2003). This practice, known as double gearing or, sometimes, multiple gearing, allows the regulatory capital from the upstream entity to support assets for both the upstream and the downstream entity. This problem can best be illustrated if one considers a depository institution that just meets its own capital requirements and then uses $8 million of cash to capitalize a new bank subsidiary. The bank subsidiary then leverages up this $8 million investment of capital to make $100 million of new loans. If one just looks at each entity, both may appear to be adequately capitalized. But, taken together, the two banks have increased their assets by nearly $100 million more than the parent bank would have been allowed to do on its own, even though no new capital has been raised. Entity-level capital requirements do not typically have a mechanism for preventing parent banks from taking on additional risk in this manner.[4]

Unregulated affiliates present a related problem (see Jackson and Half 2002, p. 16; Kuritzkes, Schuermann, and Weiner 2003). Typically, financial conglomerates engage in some activities that are not subject to direct regulation—for example, leasing activities or consumer finance in many jurisdictions. These conglomerate activities—whether undertaken directly through holding companies or indirectly through separately incorporated unregulated affiliates—escape capital regulation if capital requirements are imposed only on regulated entities. Since some of the activities conducted in unregulated affiliates and holding companies are quite similar to activities conducted in regulated entities, there is a certain logic to bringing these affiliates under the same capital requirements. In addition, since financial difficulties in unregulated affiliates could cause problems to other parts of a financial conglomerate, there is further justification for capital oversight on a consolidated basis. Moreover, if capital regulation is not extended to unregulated affiliates, financial conglomerates face strong incentives to engage in regulatory arbitrage, escaping capital regulation by moving activities from regulated entities to unregulated affiliates.[5]

A principal justification for imposing consolidated capital requirements is the assumption that these three shortcomings of entity-level capital requirements—excessive holding company leverage, double gearing, and unregulated affiliates—allow financial conglomerates to evade traditional capital requirements.[6] Applying capital standards on a consolidated basis would potentially solve all these problems. By extending them to holding companies, consolidated capital requirements address both excessive leverage and the problem of unregulated affiliates. In addition, double gearing cannot occur if downstream regulated entities are consolidated into upstream intermediaries for purposes of determining compliance with capital requirements.

Risks Unique to Financial Conglomerates

Another justification for consolidated capital requirements concerns a collection of risks that is thought to be unique to financial conglomerates. One example of these risks is the size and complexity of some financial conglomerates (see Herring and Santomero 1990; Jackson and Half 2002, pp. 18–9). Because these firms tend to be much larger and more complex than financial intermediaries with a single line of business, conglomerates are said to pose greater amounts of systemic risk to the economy and thus require higher capital reserves than ordinary intermediaries. Another unique risk of financial conglomerates arises out of the possibility that a conglomerate's collective exposure to a certain risk—for example, a particular business or sector of the economy—may be greater than the exposure of each subsidiary firm; this would necessitate greater capital reserves at the consolidated level than at the entity level (see Jackson and Half, pp. 17–8.) A related concern is the "reputational" risk that an entity within a conglomerate structure faces when affiliates get into financial distress, a risk not borne by stand-alone intermediaries (see Jackson and Half 2002, p. 17). Finally, there is sometimes expressed a (frequently unsubstantiated) sense that financial conglomerates are more likely to exploit subsidiary firms than are the owners of independent entities and therefore require additional capital reserves; the idea is that by imposing capital requirements on conglomerates, regulators reduce the risk of such exploitation.[7]

While much could be said about the relative merits of these claims, these comments all appear with regularity in the literature about the regulation of financial conglomerates. A common implication of these arguments is that financial conglomerates that contain a collection of regulated intermediaries should maintain greater capital reserves than would be appropriate for a similar set of intermediaries operated as independent firms or for a financial conglomerate subject only to entity-level capital oversight.

Omission of Certain Diversification Effects in Entity-Level Regulation

Another advantage of consolidated capital regulation is that it takes into account diversification effects across the consolidated group. As explained in a recent article by Andrew Kuritzkes, Til Schuermann, and Scott Weiner (2003), the optimal capital required to support a group on a consolidated basis at a given level of insolvency risk may be at least 5% to 10% lower than the amount of capital required to support the group's constituent firms at the same level of insolvency risk. The reason for this difference is that entity-level capital requirements cannot reflect the value of offsetting risks in other constituent entities within the same corporate group. These intersectoral diversification benefits are in addition to the familiar benefits of portfolio diversification.[8] Capital requirements assessed at the level of the consolidated group thus offer a theoretically more complete measure of capital needs than do capital requirements imposed exclusively at the level of the regulated firm.

Misalignment with Internal Risk Management Procedures

A problem related to imposing capital requirements solely on regulated entities is that this traditional approach does not track the manner in which private enterprises themselves now engage in risk management and the allocation of economic capital.[9] Top management at the world's largest financial organizations is critically concerned with the overall risk profile of the group, not just the risk incurred within the group's constituent entities. Implicit in much of the discussion of consolidated supervision is the notion that, since capital requirements address many of the same risks that concern firm management, a similar consolidated approach should be taken to regulatory oversight, including capital regulation. Indeed, the impact of group-wide diversification effects on capital needs (described earlier) is simply one illustration of the types of insights regulatory officials might gain from emulating industry practices. For example, some of the unique risks of financial conglomerates mentioned earlier—among them, the aggregation of similar risks within different affiliates and the reputational costs of problems in one member of the group to affiliated firms—are also of concern to senior management and are already reflected in existing risk management techniques of private firms. (Other unique risks, such as concerns regarding the increased systemic risk of financial conglomerates, would not necessarily figure into management risk profiles, because the costs of systemic risks are borne by third parties.)

Conflicting Implications of the Justifications for Consolidated Capital Supervision

This quick review of the justifications for consolidated capital supervision suggests one of the reasons why there may be both consensus for imposing consolidated capital oversight and failure to reach easy agreement on how best to proceed. Experts may differ over the importance of the various justifications for consolidated capital oversight, but collectively the arguments in favor of extending capital oversight to financial conglomerates present a compelling case for some sort of consolidated capital supervision. But, if one ranks the four justifications outlined earlier on the basis of whether they suggest higher or lower capital requirements for consolidated firms, the result is instructive. The first two justifications—technical weaknesses in entity-level capital supervision and unique risks of financial conglomerates—both imply that capital standards for conglomerates should be higher than the sum of capital requirements set under entity-level capital oversight. The technical limitations of entity-level capital requirements imply that financial conglomerates can organize their activities in variety of ways that require lower levels of capitalization on a groupwide basis than consolidated capital regulation would permit. In addition, the unique risks supposedly associated with financial conglomerates suggest that the formulas used for devising capital requirements for conglomerates should be more demanding than those applicable to stand-alone regulated entities.

Diversification effects, on the other hand, point in the opposite direction. To the extent that financial conglomerates are less risky as a result of cross-sectoral diversification effects, the implication is that consolidated capital requirements for financial conglomerates should, on balance, be lower than those applicable to single-sector regulated entities or at least that the processes for determining the capital requirements for financial conglomerates should factor in these cross-sector diversification benefits. The implications of relying more heavily on private risk management technique are

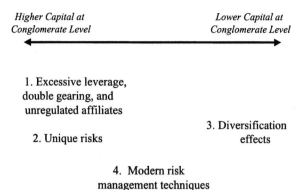

Higher Capital at
Conglomerate Level

Lower Capital at
Conglomerate Level

1. Excessive leverage,
double gearing, and
unregulated affiliates

2. Unique risks

3. Diversification
effects

4. Modern risk
management techniques

Figure 3.2. Justifications for Consolidated Capital Regulation.
Source: Author's compilation.

ambiguous, although most discussion of these management techniques seems
to assume that conglomeratewide risk management tends to reduce overall
risks and thereby reduces optimal levels for economic and regulatory capital.

In short, the justifications for imposing consolidated capital supervision
rest on conflicting assumptions regarding the effects of this reform (see
figure 3.2). Some of the justifications for consolidated capital supervision
imply that capital requirements for a consolidated entity should be higher
than the capital requirements of its constituent parts; other justifications
imply that consolidated capital requirements should be lower. As an a priori
matter, therefore, it is impossible to know whether a fully developed system
of consolidated capital supervision would tend to increase or decrease
overall capital requirements for particular institutions or the industry in
general. What is clear, a priori, is that a system of capital supervision designed to achieve all the potential benefits of consolidated oversight would
be extraordinarily complex (Cumming and Hirtle 2001). As it turns out, the
framers of the Basel II proposals were not nearly this ambitious.

HOW DOES BASEL II APPROACH THE PROBLEM OF
CONSOLIDATED CAPITAL SUPERVISION

Perhaps the most striking point about Basel II's approach to the problem of
consolidated capital supervision is the relatively modest scope of the proposal. As I explain in more detail shortly, if one lines up the concerns that
underlie the imposition of consolidated oversight of financial conglomerates
with the ambitions of the Basel II proposals, the modesty of the effort is clear.
The principal thrust of the proposal deals with the more technical problems
of excessive leverage, double gearing, and (less completely) unregulated
affiliates. The more subtle aspects of regulatory oversight of financial conglomerates are left unaddressed, though conceivably some of these might
be developed in the Accord's implementation of Pillar 2 standards for

supervisory oversight; this is where some of the additional supervisory techniques expounded in the Joint Forum's papers on conglomerate supervision might be implemented in the future.[10] Whether the modesty of the proposal's ambitions is a flaw or a strength is an important question, to which I will return at the close of this chapter.

But first let me briefly summarize Basel II proposal's key provisions.

Scope of Coverage

For purposes of consolidated capital supervision, the most important provision of the Basel II proposal is its scope of coverage. As illustrated in figure 3.3, reproduced from the April 2003 consultative document, the new

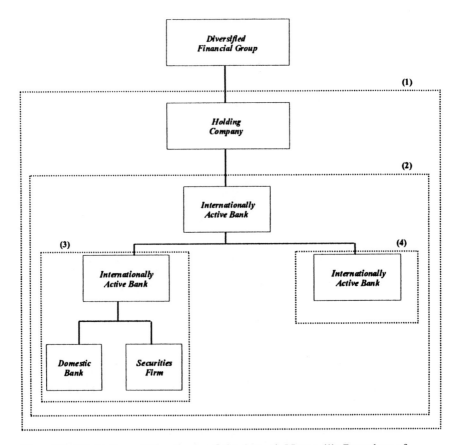

Figure 3.3. Illustration of New Scope of the Accord. Notes: (1): Boundary of predominant banking group. The Accord is to be applied at this level on a consolidated basis, i.e., up to the holding company level (paragraph 2). (2), (3), and (4): The Accord is also to be applied at lower levels to all internationally active banks on a consolidated basis. Source: BCBS (2003), p. 5 (available at http://www.bis.org/bcbs/cp3part1.pdf).

Accords are to apply at multiple levels of financial conglomerates that include internationally active banks. For purposes of complying with the new capital requirements, all internationally active banks will be required to take account of their downstream affiliates. In addition, any parent organization that controls an internationally active bank and that is "predominantly a banking group" must also comply with the Basel Accords. Thus, for the first time, the Basel Accords would be extended to the holding company structure.[11] The extension is, however, incomplete, since coverage would not reach financial groups that are not predominantly engaged in banking—that is, the consolidated capital rules do not extend to diversified financial groups.

This limitation of the scope of coverage presents an interesting design decision on the part of the framers of Basel II. On the one hand, to the extent one credits the concerns giving rise to consolidated oversight, the exception for diversified groups presents a substantial loophole. Diversified holding companies and unregulated affiliates that operate within such holding companies escape consolidated capital supervision. As a result, the problems of excessive leverage and unregulated affiliates persist in these organizational structures. On the other hand, the practical problems of applying regulatory capital standards to nonfinancial firms are great, and the ability of market mechanisms to provide adequate oversight is more plausible perhaps for fully diversified firms than for organizations that are predominantly engaged in banking. Still, the jurisdictional line here is potentially problematic, and anyone familiar with the difficulties that U.S. regulators have had in defining the business of banking over the past few decades cannot help but speculate that this jurisdictional boundary will be the focus of creative lawyering in the years ahead. In addition, it will be an area in which national authorities may have considerable latitude to articulate divergent interpretations.[12]

The Basel II treatment of insurance companies under its scope of coverage rules is also noteworthy. Insurance activities are not considered to be predominantly banking activities.[13] Thus, insurance companies—even ones with subsidiaries that constitute internationally active banks—would not be subject to the proposed Accord's consolidated capital provisions at the level of the parent insurance company; however, they would presumably be applied at the level of the internationally active bank subsidiaries. The decision to exclude parent insurance companies from the Accord's consolidated capital rules is understandable. Like diversified holding companies, insurance companies are not easily subject to the Basel II rules because the risks inherent in insurance underwriting are not fully addressed in the substantive requirements of the Basel Accords.[14] Moreover, the need to apply consolidated capital provisions to insurance companies as parents is less acute because these entities are subject to their own capital requirements, which reduce the likelihood of excessive leverage in such organizational structures. Allowing different capital standards to apply to insurance company parents does, however, allow eligible financial conglomerates to engage in a form of regulatory arbitrage. They can exploit differences between Basel II capital requirements applicable to downstream internationally active banks and insurance capital rules applicable to the parent insurance company by moving activities to the entity with the lowest capital requirements As I explain shortly, this form of regulatory arbitrage is also possible for financial conglomerates in which insurance companies are organized as subsidiaries of internationally active banks.

Three Rules of Consolidation: Full Consolidation, Deduction of Investments, and Risk Weighting of Investments

Another important feature of the Basel II proposals concerns the manner in which it imposes consolidated capital oversight. As it turns out, the proposals permit three different methods of consolidation—full consolidation, deduction of investments, and risk weighting of investments. Only the first of these methods—full consolidation—could in theory achieve the full range of benefits theoretically associated with consolidated capital supervision. However, a series of sensible and pragmatic considerations led the framers of Basel II to allow less stringent forms of consolidation in a variety of contexts.

In full consolidation, an entity's capital requirements are based on the fully consolidated financial statements of the entity and all of its downstream affiliates; investments in downstream entities and other intragroup transactions are eliminated, and then the substantive rules for capital requirements are applied to the balance sheet of the consolidated entity, including all the assets and liabilities of consolidated entities. The substantive capital rules are thus applied to the organization as if it were a fully integrated whole.

For the framers of Basel II, however, this ideal standard of full consolidation was not feasible in all contexts. The underlying Basel Accords themselves are designed principally for depository institutions and (as amended) can also be applied to securities firms, as they are in the European Union today. The Basel Accords are not, as noted, well suited to insurance companies or to certain other kinds of financial enterprises, much less to commercial firms. Accordingly, the Basel II proposal calls for full consolidation of only downstream banks, securities firms, and a limited number of financial affiliates other than insurance companies. Other downstream entities, most notably insurance companies, are dealt with under the deduction method whereby investments in these other entities are deducted from the parent organization's capital. Where local laws require (as, for example, in the United States under Gramm-Leach-Bliley), downstream securities affiliates and financial affiliates may also be dealt with in this manner.[15]

The proposal's approach to the issue of full consolidation reflects a pragmatic recognition that there exists today no comprehensive system of capital regulation. If, for example, insurance subsidiaries were consolidated with parent banks, the Basel II substantive rules would be ill equipped to generate appropriate capital reserves for risks peculiar to insurance companies. The deduction approach does, however, make insurance companies a bit of a stepchild to consolidated capital supervision, by permitting certain anomalies to persist. Most important, where there exist substantive differences in the capital requirements of unconsolidated affiliates and those of the Basel Accords (which govern consolidated affiliates), possibilities for capital arbitrage will arise.[16] For example, if loans made by insurance companies continue to have lower capital requirements than loans made by depository institutions, then conglomerates will have an incentive to move their lending activities to insurance affiliates, as noted in the previous section.[17] A regime of full consolidation of all affiliates would have reduced this incentive, but Basel II does not attempt this level of harmonization of capital standards.

A third approach to consolidation found within the Basel II framework is risk weighting of investments in certain subsidiaries. Under the risk-weighting approach, investments in downstream affiliates are treated like other assets under the Basel Accords; they are assigned a specific risk-weighting measure to be used to determine an entity's overall capital requirement. A risk-weighting approach is much more favorable to a regulated entity than the deduction approach, because the deduction approach essentially requires the investment to be 100% backed by regulatory capital of the regulated entity. With a risk weighting of 100%, a risk-weighted investment in a subsidiary typically would require only an 8% capital backing, and even a 150% risk weighting would require only 12% capital backing.

As explained later, the Basel II Accord permits risk weighting for certain investments in unregulated affiliates. It also, however, allows implementing countries to use risk weighting for certain insurance company subsidiaries. This authority appears to represent something of a political compromise based on the fact that, in some G-10 countries, investments by insurance companies in banks are subject to risk weighting. The framers of the Basel II Accords apparently concluded that competitive equality demands that banks in such jurisdictions also be permitted to use risk-weighted treatment for their investments in insurance companies. While one senses from the language describing this compromise that this authority was included with some reluctance, the result is that the Accord permits a degree of double gearing to persist at least for bank investments in insurance companies in jurisdictions that choose to take advantage of this exception.[18]

Basel II's three approaches to consolidation are summarized in figure 3.4. The purest form of consolidation—full consolidation—the Basel II proposals apply only to bank subsidiaries, as well as to securities and certain other financial subsidiaries in countries that (unlike the United States) do not have special rules that preclude consolidated capital treatment for these entities. Investments in insurance subsidiaries are generally subject to the deduction method but can be eligible for the more liberal risk-weighting approach in some circumstances.

Coverage of Unregulated Affiliates

The proposal's treatment of unregulated affiliates appears in several separate provisions and also encompasses a variety of alternative approaches. First, financial firms (other than banks, securities firms, and insurance companies)

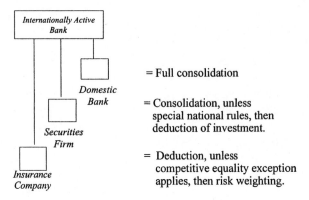

Figure 3.4. Alternative Approaches to Consolidation.
Source: Author's compilation.

that engage in "financial leasing, issuing credit cards, portfolio management, investment advisory, custodial and safekeeping services, and other similar activities that are ancillary to the business of banking" are generally required to be consolidated with parent banks, unless national rules require otherwise. Other affiliated entities are presumably treated as commercial enterprises. Where investments in commercial enterprises are material, these investments are deducted from the capital of parent banks; where nonmaterial, they are allowed the more lenient risk-weighted treatment, such as a 100% risk weighting under the standardized approach. Finally, for those unregulated affiliates that are held outside groups that predominantly engage in banking—that is, within diversified financial groups—the Basel II proposals do not apply.

This three-tiered approach to unregulated affiliates seems to leave considerable room for regulatory arbitrage. To the extent that the Basel II Accords present binding constraints, there will be strong incentives for conglomerates to move unregulated activities into commercial affiliates or diversified groups. One wonders how easy it will be for national authorities to determine how to categorize financial affiliates that engage in both listed and unlisted financial activities. Again, there will likely be considerable variation in the interpretation of these rules across national boundaries. Of course, for those who are skeptical as to the need for capital oversight of unrelated affiliates, the plasticity of Basel II may be a virtue. It does, however, further undermine the ability of the proposals to address the problem of unregulated affiliates.

Recognition of Diversification Effects at the Conglomerate Level

In light of the importance of diversification benefits in the theoretical case for consolidated capital supervision, it is perhaps surprising that the Basel II proposal's scope of coverage provisions do not expressly address this issue.

One has to dig into the substantive rules on credit risk, market risk, and operational risk in order to ascertain the extent to which diversification benefits at the conglomerate level will be recognized under the proposal. Although the proposal is not always clear on this issue, conglomerate diversification benefits will be allowed to only a very limited degree.

In the area of credit risk, for example, neither the standard approach nor the more complex internal models make allowances for additional diversification benefits that may occur at the conglomerate level. At root, the Accord's approach to credit risk is additive (Gordy 2002). So the credit risk portion of the capital requirement for a holding company with two banking subsidiaries will simply be the sum of the credit risk capital requirements of the subsidiary once intragroup transactions are eliminated.[19] To be sure, the credit requirements themselves are based on some assumed level of portfolio diversification. But this assumed level of diversification does not increase when the credit risk rules are applied at the holding company level; nor is there an explicit consideration of the intersector diversification benefits that may occur within a financial conglomerate.[20]

The market risk rules, in contrast, are designed in a manner that could theoretically recognize some of the benefits of additional portfolio diversification at the parent level. If, for example, a bank holding company had two bank subsidiaries with offsetting positions in certain kinds of securities transactions, the market risk rules applied on a consolidated basis might generate a lower capital requirement than the sum of the market risk capital requirement for the two bank subsidiaries. At least in the United States, bank holding companies are in fact permitted to recognize this intragroup diversification for purposes of the market risk rules. For purposes of calculating the market risk factor, the Federal Reserve Board allows trading activity to be measured on a consolidated basis.[21] As a result, the market risk measure for a bank holding company in the United States can be less than the sum of the market risk measures of downstream banks at which the actual trading activity is located.[22] Thus, market risk, in the United States, is not fully additive and recognizes some degree of conglomeratewide diversification benefits. The Basel II proposal does not address this aspect of the market risk calculations, and it is unclear whether other jurisdictions will follow U.S. practices in this area. The Federal Reserve Board's position is, however, likely to be influential, and, in any event, the Board's rules govern banking organizations subject to U.S. jurisdiction.

The only component of the Basel II proposals that recognizes expressly groupwide diversification benefits is the section that covers operational risk rules. In this area, at least with respect to the Advanced Measurement Approach (AMA), the framers of Basel II have recognized that risk correlations across the corporate group can be taken into account for purposes of determining operation risk capital requirements at the group level.[23] As result of this decision, the operational risk capital requirements for a consolidated group may be less than the sum of the operational risk requirements of the group's subsidiary banks.[24] So, at least in this area of

Basel II, conglomerate diversification benefits are recognized, albeit in an area that accounts for only a small fraction of total capital requirements under the Basel Accords.

Finally, the substantive Basel rules do not allow for the recognition of any diversification between or across the three building blocks of the capital requirements: credit risk, market risk, and operational risk. The three components are simply added together to determine an entity's or a group's total capital requirements.

In sum, although diversification benefits provide one of the theoretical justifications for imposing capital requirements on a consolidated basis, the Basel II proposals recognize those benefits only to a limited degree. While the operational risk rules and the market risk measure (if Federal Reserve Board policy is followed) do reflect some diversification benefits, the more important credit risk measures do not.

Other Technical Aspects of Implementation

Before presenting a tentative assessment of the Basel II proposals in this area, let me touch upon two other technical aspects of the proposal that raise interesting issues of implementation.

Regulated Entities with Surplus or Deficit Capital Positions

One conundrum for designers of consolidated capital rules is how to deal with subsidiaries that have either excess or inadequate capital. This is a particularly important problem for subsidiaries—such as insurance subsidiaries—that are generally subject to the deduction-of-investment method of consolidation. Consider, by way of illustration, a bank that has two $10 million investments in two different insurance affiliates—Insurance Co. A and Insurance Co. B (see figure 3.5). Under the Basel II proposal, investments in these subsidiaries

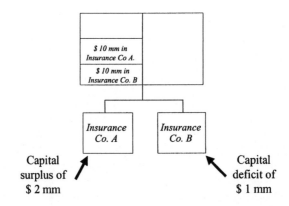

Figure 3.5. Bank with Over- and Undercapitalized Subsidiaries. Source: Author's compilation.

would be deducted from the parent organization's capital for purposes of determining compliance with the proposal's substantive rules. As ordinarily applied, these rules would call for two $10 million deductions from the parent bank's capital. However, suppose further that Insurance Co. A actually had $2 million more capital than required. Under Basel II, the deduction for investments in that insurance affiliate would generally be reduced by that $2 million surplus on the grounds that this surplus could be used to support other activities of the group. In other words, the excess capital at the insurance company level would be allowed to count towards the parent bank's capital.[25] Similarly, a $1 million deficit in Insurance Co. B's capital reserves, if not promptly corrected, would increase the amount of the deduction for the parent bank's investment in that firm on the theory that the parent bank might shortly have to cover the shortfall.

These accounting conventions have an internal logic and, in fact, comport with the manner in which subsidiary surpluses and deficits would be treated if the downstream affiliates were fully consolidated, but they raise an interesting question about the implementation of consolidated capital supervision. To what extent should surplus capital in one part of the organization be considered to be available to support activities in the consolidated group? In the late 1980s and early 1990s, this issue was a source of considerable controversy in the United States as regulatory officials sought with only limited success to force bank holding companies to infuse additional capital in to failing affiliates (see Jackson 1994). In the absence of clear regulatory authority to order such transfers, one might question whether it is appropriate for regulatory officials to rely on managerial cooperation to transfer capital reserves to failing affiliates in times of distress. On the other hand, if the Basel II rules failed to credit consolidated groups for surplus capital held in downstream affiliates, then financial conglomerates would have strong incentives to operate these affiliates with the minimum permissible capital.

Fractional Interests in Financial Affiliates

A final set of intriguing rules concerns the treatment of fractional interests in financial affiliates, as opposed to wholly owned subsidiaries. The proposal includes a separate set of rules for majority interests (such as the 60% investment in Subsidiary B in figure 3.6) and also substantial minority investments (such as the 30% investment in Subsidiary C in figure 3.6). For majority investments, the key interpretive issue is how to treat minority interests in affiliates when the parent bank owns only a majority interest. If the affiliates are fully consolidated, then the minority interests are treated as capital for purposes of the consolidated group. While the Basel II proposal permits such treatment, it also allows national authorities to exclude minority interests if these investments would not be readily available to the full group. It is not clear under which circumstances minority investments would be available to a consolidated group, but, at least in theory, the Basel II

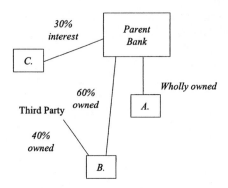

Figure 3.6. Fractional Interests.
Source: Author's compilation.

proposals seem to be imposing a standard similar to the one described earlier for surplus capital held in downstream insurance company affiliates. As the Basel II proposals penalize conglomerates for subsidiaries with capital deficits by requiring those deficits to be deducted from group capital, in a like manner a similar deduction is charged for minority interests in subsidiaries that would not be available to the consolidated group in times of crisis.[26]

In the case of significant minority interests in financial affiliates, the Basel II proposals permit two alternative approaches: such investments can be deducted under the deduction-of-investment method, or the subsidiaries can be consolidated on a pro rata basis. The latter option is available only if supervisory officials determine that the parent "is legally or de facto expected to support the entity on a proportionate basis only and other significant shareholders have the means and willingness to proportionately support it" (see BCBS 2003, at paragraph 9). Under both approaches, the goal seems to allow parent entities to maintain capital for only their proportionate interest in financial affiliates, provided there are not grounds to believe that the parent entity would be likely to support a greater share of the subsidiary's activities.[27]

The Basel II proposal's special rules for fractional interests highlight the conceptual difficulties for a regime of consolidated capital supervision when conglomerates hold less than controlling interests in affiliated organizations. Third-party investments in these affiliates are not fully available to the group while there remains the possibility that the parent organization will be called upon (or will have strong incentives) to support the affiliate in times of financial distress and that support may well go beyond the parent's pro rata share. Exactly how these competing concerns should be factored into consolidated capital rules presents difficult questions of regulatory design, a good portion of which the proposal has delegated to national authorities.

A PRELIMINARY ASSESSMENT OF THE BASEL II PROPOSALS

As suggested earlier, the ambitions of the Basel II proposal for consolidated capital supervision are quite modest. The proposals are concerned primarily with addressing the problem of excessive leverage and double gearing within groups that are predominantly engaged in banking (but not in diversified groups, which are exempt). The proposal is largely effective in these areas, although excessive leverage may still exist at the level of diversified groups that are not predominantly engaged in banking. In addition, the possibility of double gearing persists to the extent that countries permit investments in insurance subsidiaries to be accounted for under the relatively liberal risk-weighted approach. The proposal reaches, albeit in a somewhat less comprehensive way, the problem of unregulated affiliates. Internationally active banks and groups predominantly engaged in banking are subject to consolidated capital requirements for certain downstream financial affiliates. Consolidation, however, is required for only a limited range of financial affiliates and the exceptions for nonmaterial commercial affiliates and affiliates, within diversified groups may prove substantial.

The list of what the proposal does not attempt to do is much longer:

- The proposal does not eliminate the possibility of regulatory arbitrage between unconsolidated affiliates and parent banks; neither does it inhibit regulatory arbitrage between banks and subsidiaries that are consolidated under either the deduction or risk-weighting methods as long as those subsidiaries are subject to substantive capital requirements that differ from Basel II's substantive standards.
- The proposal makes almost no effort to adjust the capital requirements for financial conglomerates to their special characteristics: on the one hand, it does not increase the level of capital needed to offset the unique risks of financial conglomerates; on the other hand, it does not reduce in any substantial way the level of capital needed as a result of diversification effects, apart from the limited diversification effects for conglomerates recognized under the operational risk rules and market risk measures.
- More generally, the proposal does not incorporate any modern risk management techniques developed in the private sector, except those built into the VaR rules or the alternative credit models available to qualifying banks under other aspects of the proposal; even in these areas, the rules are implemented in a way that does not generally pick up diversification benefits at the conglomerate level.

Although the modesty of Basel II's aspirations is hardly inspiring, I wonder whether it is realistic to ask more of consolidated capital supervision. Many of the limitations of the Basel II proposal's approach to consolidated supervision are a direct result of limitations in the proposal's underlying substantive requirements. Consider, for example, the proposal's failure to address completely the problem of regulatory arbitrage. This shortcoming stems, principally, from the fact that the proposal exempts diversified financial groups from its coverage and also permits investments in insurance subsidiaries and sometimes securities firms to be consolidated under the deduction or risk-weighted methods. These limitations invite regulatory arbitrage by permitting financial conglomerates to move activities to affiliated entities with more liberal capital requirements. But the only way to forestall such regulatory arbitrage would be to impose a uniform set of capital requirements on all affiliates. The substantive rules of Basel II, however, do not provide such a comprehensive scheme of capital regulation, and as a result the framers of the Basel II Accord had little choice but to structure the system's coverage rules so as to allow some degree of regulatory arbitrage.

Another theoretical weakness of the Basel II approach is its failure to take account of diversification effects at the conglomerate level. While theoretical literature suggests that financial conglomerates enjoy some benefits from mingling banking, securities, and insurance activities, the Basel II rules of consolidation do not recognize these benefits. But the Basel II substantive rules were not written to address intersector diversification, and it is probably unreasonable to expect the drafters of Basel II to write in an entirely new set of rules to deal with an issue that arises only within financial conglomerates. The Basel II reforms are already plenty complex. Moreover, there is some rough justice in the fact that the Basel II proposal also omits some other factors that should in theory increase the capital requirements of financial conglomerates— for example, the unique risks of financial conglomerates that some analysts believe increase the likelihood of failures of regulated subsidiaries with this organizational form. So perhaps the two omissions balance out.

Yet another arguable shortcoming of the Basel II approach to consolidated capital regulation is its failure to provide any relief from capital regulation for regulated subsidiaries. If, after all, Basel II developed an effective system of consolidated capital supervision, capital regulation at the level of regulated subsidiaries would become redundant and could therefore be eliminated. Again, however, limitations in the underlying substantive rules of Basel II make such an adjustment inappropriate at this time. Consider the problem of a bank with both over- and undercapitalized regulated subsidiaries as illustrated in figure 3.5. If capital requirements were imposed only on a fully consolidated basis and not at the subsidiary level, one of the conglomerate's subsidiaries would be allowed to operate with less than adequate capital. Unless there were some obligation on the part of the parent organization to contribute capital to subsidiaries in times of distress—a source-of-strength requirement not written into the Basel II Accord—there would exist the possibility of insolvency on the part of the undercapitalized affiliate and potential risk to the financial system.[28] Because the Basel II substantive rules do not encompass a requirement of intragroup cross-guarantees, the Accord's coverage rules cannot be faulted for not relieving regulated subsidiaries of entity-level capital requirements.

Notwithstanding the foregoing limitations of Basel II—substantial though they are—I think there are plausible grounds for believing that the shortcomings of the Basel II proposals will ultimately do little harm. For one thing, if one looks around the world at the regulatory systems with the most experience dealing with financial conglomerates—in particular, those of the United States and the United Kingdom—consolidated capital rules are only a part of the supervisory process for conglomerates. Both the Financial Service Authority's "Qualitative Consolidated Supervision" program and the Federal Reserve Board's "Large Complex Banking Organizations" program require the monitoring and evaluation of internal risk management techniques of conglomerate managers. Such supervisory oversight may offer a more promising way to learn from the risk management techniques of private enterprise than would an effort to develop a more sophisticated system of consolidated capital supervision.[29] At a minimum, these supervisory techniques offer a check on the most obvious inadequacies of the Basel II consolidated capital rules. Moreover, even within the Basel II proposals, consolidated capital rules may not constitute the sole mechanism for policing financial conglomerates. Although not yet developed in this regard, the Pillar 2 (supervision) requirements could be fleshed out to require additional mechanisms for policing conglomerates and monitoring international risk management techniques. Indeed, much of the Joint Forum's work in this area addressed such supervisory standards, and this proposal could be grafted onto the new Basel Accords.

A further reason for equanimity with respect to the shortcomings of Basel II is the possibility that the rules may not constitute binding constraints for most firms. One of the most intriguing findings of recent studies on financial conglomerates is that current Basel requirements generally do not impose a binding constraint on major financial conglomerates. The actual capital that financial conglomerates now retain, tempered no doubt by market forces, is usually greater than the amount of capital required under Basel-based capital requirements. If true, this finding suggests that technical shortcomings of Basel II's consolidated capital rules may have little impact on the private behavior of most financial conglomerates for which the requirements are designed. Conceivably, only when capital levels of conglomerates fall beneath the requirements of internal models and market discipline—that is, in times of financial distress—will the new proposals have real bite. Thus, the costs (and benefits) of the new regime may be a good deal less significant than many commentators have assumed.

Acknowledgments Thanks to Cameron Half (HLS '02) and Jeffrey Robins (HLS '01), who provided valuable research assistance for my chapter.

Notes

1. See BCBS (1998). In the United States, bank holding companies have long been subject to consolidated capital requirements. In this regard, the U.S. capital

requirements have gone beyond the requirements of the original Basel Accords and anticipated the new proposals. See 12 C.F.R. § 225 App. A (2003).

2. A more complete discussion of the literature on this subject appears in Jackson and Half (2002). In this chapter, my goal is to identify the major themes underlying the case for consolidated capital supervision without delving into excessive detail.

3. To a degree, these problems could be addressed directly through the regulation of affiliated party transactions and restrictions on the withdrawal of capital, but it is possible that conglomerates are more likely to subvert these restrictions in times of financial distress than are independent financial institutions. The problem of excessive leverage is conceptually similar to some of the considerations discussed later in the section on unique risks of financial conglomerates.

4. As discussed later, there are two basic ways of implementing consolidated capital: full consolidation and deduction of investments. Either approach has the effect of eliminating any investment in covered subsidiaries from the calculation of the consolidated entity's capital, thereby solving the problem of double gearing. Under an entity-based system of capital regulation, the same result could be achieved by raising the risk weighting of investments in covered subsidiaries. With an 8% risk-weighted capital requirement, a 1250% risk weighting would be required to ensure that every dollar of investment in a covered subsidiary is backed by a dollar of capital at the parent level.

5. The decision of U.S. financial holding companies to locate over-the-counter derivatives activities in offshore affiliates is a familiar example of this phenomenon. Another form of regulatory arbitrage can occur if the capital requirements vary across different sectors of the financial services industry—for example, if the capital requirements for loans in insurance companies are different from those for loans in depository institutions. See chapter 2, "Capital Adequacy in Insurance and Reinsurance," by Scott Harrington, and chapter 1, "Capital Regulation for Position Risk in Banks, Securities Firms, and Insurance Companies," by Richard Herring and Til Schuermann. Such differences will encourage financial conglomerates to locate activities in the regulated entity with the lowest capital requirements.

Whether regulatory arbitrage of this sort presents a legitimate source of regulatory concern is a difficult question. On the one hand, it may seem inherently problematic for conglomerates to exploit differences in capacity requirements for the same activities in different units, and critics of regulatory arbitrage often seem to assume that private firms are exploiting supervisory errors in setting standards too low in some sectors. On the other hand, if the policy concerns are different in different contexts, then conceivably different capital requirements in different legal entities within the same conglomerate might be appropriate. If, for example, the social costs of failure for a depository institution were much higher than the costs of failure of other entities, such as insurance companies, then it might be appropriate to set capital standards lower for insurance companies than for depository institutions. Of course, were one to view the financial fate of affiliated entities as inexorably linked, then distinctions of this sort within similar financial groups could seems excessively legalistic.

6. The explanations given in the text are those commonly advanced for imposing consolidated capital rules. Implicit in these accounts is an often unstated premise that market mechanism do not provide an adequate independent restraint on inadequate capitalization at the holding company level. Zealous proponents of market discipline might well contest this premise.

7. See Jackson and Half 2002, p. 20. The empirical basis for claims of this sort are, in my view, weak (Jackson 1993, 1994).

8. The Kuritzkes-Schuermann-Weiner study suggests that the potential benefits of portfolio diversification are generally greater than the potential benefits of intersector diversification. It is, however, possible that financial conglomerates generally have more diversified portfolios than stand-alone entities, and thus some fraction of the potential benefits of portfolio diversification might properly be attributed to the conglomerate structure.

9. See illustrations of this approach to capital oversight in chapter 7, "The Use of Internal Models," by Michel Crouhy, Dan Galai, and Robert Mark. See also Kuritzkes, Schuermann, and Weiner 2003; Cummings and Hirtle 2001.

10. Together with the International Association of Insurance Supervisors and the International Organization of Securities Commissioners, the Basel Committee on Banking Supervision formed the Joint Forum on Financial Conglomerates, in 1996, to develop supervisory standards for financial conglomerates (see Jackson and Half, pp. 23, 30). Supervisory oversight of financial conglomerates was an important component of the Joint Forum's recommendations. (See Joint Forum on Financial Conglomerates 1999.)

11. Of course, some jurisdictions, most notably the United States, have long imposed capital requirements on many bank holding companies. See Jackson (1994, pp. 528–32).

12. Whether policymakers should be concerned about variation in national implementation of the Accords is a nice question. A chief justification for the original Basel Accords was to establish a level playing field among international banks. In the intervening years, commentators have recognized the difficulty of actually achieving uniformity. See Scott and Iwaraha (1994). In the current round of Basel proposals, international uniformity is less of a selling point, because the proposals themselves allow various approaches to credit risk and other issues. However, the ability of national regulators to implement identical provisions in substantially different ways does undermine, to some degree, one of the goals of harmonized capital standards.

13. Indeed, as explained later, insurance activities are not even considered to be financial for purposes of Basel II. See BCBS 2003, paragraph 5, n. 3.

14. See chapter 2, "Capital Adequacy in Insurance and Reinsurance," by Scott Harrington.

15. With the passage of the Gramm-Leach-Bliley Act, Congress determined that the capital rules applicable to U.S. bank holding companies would not extend to insurance companies and securities firms. See 12 U.S.C. § 1844(c)(3) 2003. The Basel II proposal's exception for local law grants U.S. regulators the discretion to treat securities firms under the deduction method, thereby avoiding direct application of Basel II's substantive rules to these firms.

16. As demonstrated in earlier papers of the Joint Forum, full consolidation and the deduction approach can reach the same results, but only if the requirements imposed on unconsolidated affiliates and consolidated affiliates are the same.

17. Conversely, if the downstream subsidiary's capital requirements were more stringent than the upstream parent's, the deduction approach could entail higher capital requirements than full consolidation.

18. An analogous sort of double gearing is also possible in jurisdictions that allow parent insurance companies to use the risk-weighted investment approach to investments in downstream banks.

19. The elimination of intragroup transaction does, of course, suggest that the actual credit risk capital requirement for the parent organization may be less than the sum of the credit risk capital requirements of its bank subsidiaries. This reduction does not, however, come from recognition of diversification benefits; it comes from the operation of the accounting rules of consolidation.

20. The absence of any recognition of intersectoral diversification in the credit risk models has been a source of criticism of Basel II from the financial services industry. See, for example, Letter from Jay S. Fishman, Chief Operating Officer, Financial and Risk, Citigroup, to William McDonough, Chairman, Basel Committee on Banking Supervision (May 31, 2001), available at www.bis.org/bcbs/ca/citigrou.pdf.

21. See 12 C.F.R. § 225 Appendix E n. 2 (2003). "Trading activity means the gross sum of trading assets and liabilities as reported in the bank holding company's most recent quarterly Y–9C Report."

22. When such a differential exists, a bank holding may have a capital requirement that is less than the sum of the capital requirements of its subsidiary banks, allowing it to maintain a greater degree of leverage.

23. See BCBS 2003: "Subject to the approval of its supervisor, a bank opting for partial use may determine which parts of its operations will use an AMA on the basis of business line, legal structure, geography, or other internally determined basis."

24. It is, apparently, still uncertain whether higher operational risk requirements will be imposed at the entity level when operational risk capital requirements are calculated for subsidiary banks. Although that result would occur if the operational risk rules were recalculated separately (and without regard to intragroup correlation of risks) for each subsidiary bank, it is possible that regulatory officials may permit conglomerates simply to allocate a portion of their operational risk capital requirements to all downstream subsidiaries, effectively granting subsidiary banks the diversification benefits of the group and making the operational risk capital requirements additive as well.

25. Application of this rule depends on national law, which would determine the extent to which such surpluses could be made available for other uses within the consolidated group.

26. Minority investments in other affiliates are subject to a different set of rules. In general, these investments are deducted by parent bank capital, but, if national laws permit, they may also be consolidated on a pro rata basis.

27. The proposal does not specifically address the treatment of insignificant investments in financial subsidiaries. The proposal does indicate that reciprocal cross-holdings of bank capital should be subjected to the deduction method. See BCBS 2003, note at paragraph 10. Otherwise, however, such investments might be eligible for the risk-weighted investment approach allowed for nonmaterial investments in commercial affiliates. Such treatment would allow for a certain degree of double gearing, but the amounts involved would presumably be relatively modest.

28. Particularly in countries such as the United States, where regulatory authority is divided across sectors of the financial services industry, it would be difficult to persuade national authorities (particularly banking regulators) that their regulated firms should be required to support failing affiliates in other sectors during times of financial distress.

29. Similarly, the European Union's new conglomerate directive relies to a significant degree on supervisory oversight of financial conglomerates. See Directive 2002/87/EC on the Supplementary Supervision of Credit Institutions, Insurance

Undertakings, and Investments Firms in A Financial Conglomerate (December 16, 2002), available at http://europa.eu.int/eur-lex/pri/en/oj/dat/2003/l_035/l_03520030211en00010027.pdf. See also Jan Meyers and David Ballegeer, What EU Rules Mean for Financial Conglomerates, *International Financial Law Review* (June 2003): 50.

References

Basel Committee on Banking Supervision (BCBS). 1988. International Convergence of Capital Measurement and Capital Standards. Basel Committee Publication No. 4. Available ta: www.bis.org/publ/bcbs04A.pdf.
―――. 2003b. Consultative Document: The New Basel Accord. Available at: www.bis.org/bcbs/cp3full.pdf.
Cumming, Christine M., and Beverly J. Hirtle. 2001. The Challenge of Risk Management in Diversified Financial Companies. *Federal Reserve Bank of New York Economic Policy Review* 7(1): 1–17. Available at: www.ny.frb.org/research/epr/01v07n1/0103cumm.pdf.
―――. 2002. Directive 2002/87/EC of the European Parliament and of the Council of 16 December 2002 on the Supplementary Supervision of Credit Institutions, Insurance Undertakings, and Investment Firms in a Financial Conglomerate and amending Council Directives 73/239/EEC, 79/267/EEC, 92/49/EEC, 92/96/EEC, 93/6/EEC and 93/22/EEC, and Directives 98/78/EC and 2000/12/EC of the European Parliament and of the Council.
Gordy, Michael B. 2002. A Risk-Factor Model Foundation for Ratings-Based Bank Capital Rules. Board of Governors of the Federal Reserve System FEDS Working Paper No. 2002-55. Available at: www.federalreserve.gov/pubs/feds/2002/200255/200255pap.pdf.
Herring, Richard J., and Anthony M. Santomero. 1990. The Corporate Structure of Financial Conglomerates. *Journal of Financial Services Research* 4: 471–497.
Jackson, Howell E. 1993. The Superior Performance of Savings and Loan Associations with Substantial Holding Companies. *Journal of Legal Studies* 22: 405–56.
―――. 1994. The Expanding Obligations of Financial Holding Companies. *Harvard Law Review* 107: 507–619.
Jackson, Howell E., and Cameron Half. 2002. Background Paper on Evolving Trends in the Supervision of Financial Conglomerates. Available at: www.law.harvard.edu/programs/pifs/pdfs/jackson_half.pdf.
Joint Forum on Financial Conglomerates. 1999. Supervision of Financial Conglomerates. Basel Committee Joint Publication No. 47. Available at: www.bis.org/publ/bcbs47.pdf.
Kuritzkes, Andrew P., Til Schuermann, and Scott M. Weiner. 2003. Risk Measurement, Risk Management, and Capital Adequacy in Financial Conglomerates. In *Brookings-Wharton Papers on Financial Services*, ed. Richard Herring and Robert E. Litan. Washington, D.C.: Brookings Institution Press.
Meyers, Jan, and David Ballegeer. 2003. What EU Rules Mean for Financial Conglomerates. *International Financial Law Review* 22 (6): 50–53.
Scott, Hal S., and Shinsaku Iwahara. 1994. In Search of a Level Playing Field: The Implementation of the Basel Accord in Japan and the United States. Washington, D.C.: Group of Thirty Occasional Paper No. 46.

4

Using a Mandatory Subordinated Debt Issuance Requirement to Set Regulatory Capital Requirements for Bank Credit Risks

PAUL KUPIEC

Important shortcomings limit the appeal of the direct use of bank internal models to set regulatory capital requirements for bank credit risks. Common approaches for calculating credit value for risk-based capital requirements produce biased estimates that do not control bank funding cost subsidies and the moral hazard externalities that mandate the need for bank capital regulation. If, alternatively, banks were required to issue subordinated debt that has both a minimum market value and maximum acceptable probability of default at issuance, banks would, thereby, be implicitly required to set their equity capital in a manner that limits both the probability of bank default and the expected loss on insured deposits. This mandatory subordinated debt issuance policy alone can control the externalities created by a government safety net without the need for a formal regulatory capital requirement for bank credit risk. It is demonstrated that the proposed subordinated debt requirement implicitly imposes a credit risk capital requirement that can be estimated using bank internal models. As such, the proposed subordinated debt policy can be viewed is an indirect way of imposing internal model based regulatory capital requirements for bank credit risks.

An important inference of the book is that market discipline should be elevated to the preferred method of setting bank capital. While noting the importance of market discipline, this chapter focuses on a mandatory subordinated debt requirement as being superior to reliance on bank internal models in determining the level of required risk capital to be held by banks. In addition, the chapter carries the strong suggestion that models would be more acceptable if bank subsidies, and the resulting moral hazard that accompanies them, were removed. A related point is that for insurance and securities firms, where subsidies are minimal, credit models would be more acceptable.

INTRODUCTION

This chapter explores the possibility of using a mandatory subordinated debt issuance policy *as a substitute* for an internal models approach for setting regulatory capital requirements for bank credit risks. Ostensibly, a system of regulatory capital requirements for credit risk that is based on bank internal model capital estimates would appear to solve the complex social welfare and moral hazard problems that arise in the context of bank capital regulation. In practice, the direct use of bank internal models for regulatory purposes has a number of important shortcomings that are not widely appreciated. As they are typically estimated, bank credit value-at-risk (credit VaR) capital estimates are biased measures of true buffer stock capital requirements.[1] Moreover, the accuracy of bank internal model estimates is difficult (if not impossible) to verify (Kupiec 1995), and capital requirements based on internal models do not remove the moral hazard incentives created by public depositor safety nets. As a consequence, banks that face internal models capital requirements for credit risk still face moral hazard incentives that distort their lending behavior.

Buffer stock capital requirements for credit risk can be accurately estimated using internal credit risk models by reformulating the credit VaR exposure measure and augmenting it with an estimate of the equilibrium interest payments required by bank debt holders (Kupiec 2002a). Unbiased internal model capital allocation procedures differ from those discussed in the credit VaR literature and in the Basel Committee on Banking Supervision (BCBS) consultative documents (1999) that survey bank practices. The importance of recognizing funding debt interest payment in buffer stock capital calculations provides the key for understanding how bank internal capital estimates are affected by the externalities that are created when banks benefit from underpriced safety net guarantees.

If depositor safety nets provide banks with funding cost subsidies, banks may use these subsidies to reduce their internal buffer stock capital allocations and still be able to satisfy a regulatory capital requirement based on an internal model. Because the magnitude of internal model capital "savings" engendered by a public guarantee is related to credit risk, these savings create distortions in a bank's optimal lending behavior. Kupiec (2002b) shows that even accurately constructed internal model capital estimates will not remove distortions in bank lending behavior induced by regulation.

While the direct use of bank internal models has significant shortcomings, the supposed benefits of an internal models approach can be realized under an alternative regulatory paradigm that uses a mandatory subordinated debt issuance requirement in place of a regulatory capital requirement. It is demonstrated that if a bank is required to fund its activities in part with a subordinated debt issue with specific characteristics, then it is possible to limit both the probability of bank default and the expected loss on insured deposits should the bank default. To accomplish this objective, the subordinated debt issue must have a minimum market value (for example, at least

2% of the bank's assets) and a maximum acceptable ex ante probability of default (for example, 20 basis points per year). This subdebt funding strategy largely removes any safety net funding cost subsidies that would otherwise be enjoyed by the bank.

The mandatory subordinated debt issuance requirement proposed herein indirectly imposes an equity capital requirement on the bank. The implicit equity capital requirement can be estimated using a modified credit VaR framework. While it is important that investors view bank subordinated debt issues as risky investments that are completely free from any government safety net guarantees, the subordinated debt regulation can be modified by increasing the magnitude of the minimum required subordinated debt issue if there is concern that subordinated debt holders benefit from "too big to fail" implicit guarantees.[2]

It has long been recognized that the junior standing of subordinated debt provides a capital cushion for the deposit insurer in bank liquidation. The 1988 Basel Capital Accord includes long-term subordinated debt in a bank's Tier 2 regulatory capital measure (up to a limit of 50% of a bank's Tier 1 capital), but neither the Accord nor U.S. banking regulations currently require that a bank issue subordinated debt.[3] Since a 1983 deposit insurance study by the Federal Deposit Insurance Corporation (FDIC 1983) recommended that banks be *required* to issue subordinated debt, a large literature has developed that investigates the potential use of bank subordinated debt as a supervisory tool.[4]

Those who advocate a mandatory subordinated debt issuance requirement argue that such a requirement has the potential to exert market discipline on banking operations. A staff study by the Federal Reserve Board (1999) reviews the mechanism through which this market discipline may promote bank safety and soundness. This mechanism includes (1) subordinated debt funding costs that increase as a bank increases the riskiness of its investments thereby reducing the gains that accrue to bank equity holders, (2) discipline exerted by bank counterparties who will monitor bank subordinated debt spreads and interpret them as a relative risk measure, and (3) regulatory discipline if specific supervisory actions are linked (formally or informally) to debt spreads or bank issuance irregularities.

The recommendations in this study differ from earlier subordinated debt proposals in that this proposal includes both minimum issuance requirements and a maximum allowable probability of default at issuance. The issuance requirements are used to indirectly set a bank's minimum regulatory equity capital requirement and are not a regulation that supplements a separate regulatory capital scheme. While it is possible that a mandatory subordinated debt policy may create additional restrictions on bank management behavior through increased market or supervisory discipline, this is *not* the primary operational function of subordinated debt in this proposal; mandatory subordinated debt issuance is recommended as a practical way to overcome the shortcomings associated with the direct use of bank internal models for setting regulatory capital requirements for credit risks.

THE APPEAL OF AN INTERNAL MODELS APPROACH FOR CAPITAL REGULATION

Regulatory capital requirements can be used to control the moral hazard risks that arise when banks benefit from mispriced safety net guarantees. Funding cost subsidies accrue to bank shareholders when bank deposits are covered by underpriced deposit insurance schemes or when bank funding costs are reduced by implicit "too big to fail" government guarantees. Other things equal, the magnitude of these subsidies is an increasing function of the risk of a bank's investment portfolio and the leverage gained from the guaranteed liabilities in a bank's capital structure.

Under the distortions created by safety net funding cost subsidies, banks may find it profitable to invest in risky negative net present value (NPV) investments that reduce social welfare. By controlling bank leverage, regulatory capital requirements can reduce funding cost subsidies, dull bank incentives to undertake high-risk investments, and thereby reduce the social welfare losses created when banks invest in negative NPV activities.

If a uniform regulatory capital requirement (a maximum leverage ratio) is set sufficiently high, it is possible to reduce the safety net-related benefits that create the moral hazard incentives that distort bank investment behavior. If banks bear costs when raising external capital and have monopolistic access to at least some forms of positive NPV lending activities, excessive regulatory capital requirements can, however, reduce social welfare by limiting banks' ability to profitably fund positive NPV investments.[5] Under a scheme of uniform regulatory capital requirements, a tradeoff arises between controlling moral hazard and limiting the social benefits associated with positive NPV lending activities.[6] The level of regulatory capital necessary to remove safety net subsidies and forestall moral hazard is positively related to the risk of a bank's investment opportunity set. As a consequence, a bank with overly risky investment possibilities (a potentially bad bank) requires higher regulatory capital requirements to control moral hazard than does a bank with a relatively safe set of investment options (a potentially good bank). To be effective, uniform regulatory capital requirements must be set high enough to control the behavior of bad banks, and yet this level of regulatory capital may limit the ability of good banks to make positive NPV loans.

By specifying bank-specific capital requirements that are linked to the risk of a bank's investment portfolio, risk-based capital requirements, in theory at least, can limit the social welfare loss that may be generated by capital regulation. Ideally, bank-specific capital requirements generated by a risk-based system should be large enough to remove moral hazard incentives generated by a bank's unique investment opportunity set without unnecessarily limiting its ability to fund its positive NPV loan investments.

Implementation of this regulatory ideal is problematic even if banking supervisors have complete discretion in setting individual bank regulatory capital requirements (and they typically don't). Kupiec and O'Brien (1998) show that supervisors need almost complete information about a bank's investment opportunity set if they are to attempt to set bank-specific capital requirements at a socially optimal level. One implication is that any practical scheme for setting risk-based capital requirements is likely to be socially suboptimal and that supervisors will always be selecting among competing second-best alternatives.

The 1988 Basel Accord established a uniform system for setting risk-based regulatory capital requirements for internationally active banks (BCBS 1988). The Accord's risk-insensitive regulatory capital scheme in time has given rise to moral hazard behavior that has come to be called "regulatory arbitrage." Banks originate high-quality loans to service customer relationships, securitize these loans to remove them from their balance sheets, retain the high-risk first-loss tranch of the securitization structures, and reduce their regulatory capital requirement in the process. Such behavior can be explained as a process whereby "good" banks with constrained regulatory capital free up additional funds to invest in additional positive NPV loans. Such behavior might also be exhibited by "bad" banks that are removing high-quality credits from their balance sheets in order to increase the risk of their portfolios and raise the capitalized value of their safety net-induced funding subsidies.

The New Basel Capital Accord (NBA), first made public by the BCBS in January 2001 (BCBS 2001), proposed significant revisions to the 1988 Accord's risk-weighted capital scheme. The newly proposed scheme specifies credit risk weights that are linked either to bank internal loan classification schemes, as in the internal rating-based (IRB) approaches, or to external credit ratings, as in the alternative standardized approaches. Both approaches set credit risk weights according to a credit's anticipated probability of default and are, at least in part, designed to mimic the techniques used internally by banks. In proposing the NBA, the BCBS's stated objective is to place "a greater emphasis on banks' own assessment of the risks to which they are exposed in the calculation of regulatory capital charges." (See BCBS 2001, paragraph 5.)

The regulatory capital schemes proposed in the NBA make capital requirements more sensitive to the credit risks in bank loan portfolios but do not allow the direct use of bank internal model estimates to set regulatory capital. In the standardized approaches, credit risk capital requirements are linked either to the external credit ratings of firms or to the credit rating of their sovereign. In the IRB approaches, credit risk weights are set according to a credit's anticipated probability of default. The regulatory capital approaches proposed in the NBA generate capital requirements that are much more sensitive to risks, but they only imperfectly account for portfolio effects and are calibrated without regard to the externalities generated by bank funding cost subsidies. Analysis in Kupiec (2001) shows that the proposed IRB approaches are not neutral with respect to bank risk-taking behavior, and they may create incentives for IRB banks to concentrate lending in the low-risk segment of the fixed-income market—a segment that has traditionally preferred bond issuance to bank finance.

The IRB regulatory capital proposals are envisioned by some as a partial step toward a regulatory structure in which banks are permitted to use their internal credit risk models for setting regulatory capital requirements for credit risk. In the early 1990s, banking interest groups convinced banking regulators to allow the use of bank internal-risk measurement models as a basis for setting market risk capital requirements (BCBS 1995); more recently, banking associations and risk management consultancies have argued that banks should be allowed to use their internal credit risk model estimates as a basis for setting credit-risk capital requirements. (See, inter alia, ISDA 2001; Institute of International Finance 2001; the Financial Services Roundtable 2001; KPMG 2001.) Those that advocate an internal models approach to regulation reason that the use of internal models will result in regulatory capital requirements that are more closely aligned with the so-called economic capital allocations set by bank managers for operational purposes and thereby lower regulatory compliance costs and create fewer distortions in credit and securities markets.

INTERNAL MODELS AND REGULATORY OBJECTIVES

An important issue that must be clarified before analyzing alternative approaches for setting regulatory capital is the objective function that underlies capital regulation. If the regulatory objective relates primarily to ensuring the safety of publicly guaranteed (implicitly or explicitly) bank deposits, then regulatory capital requirements may be aimed at limiting the probability that a bank's resources are insufficient to honor these claims without public (or perhaps a cooperative insurance scheme's) support.

Credit VaR buffer stock capital allocations ignore the losses that are generated when a bank defaults. They are not constructed to protect the value of depositor claims in bank default. Consequently, credit VaR buffer stock capital allocation techniques are inconsistent with typical depositor protection regulatory objectives or with supervisory mandates for least-cost resolution.[7]

If the regulator's objective is to protect the insured depositors *and* to limit the probability of bank insolvency to some de minimus level—as seems to be the case when regulators discuss the need to limit systemic risk—then capital models must focus on limiting the probability that a bank's resources are insufficient to honor all of its liabilities—including insured deposits, off-balance-sheet guarantees, derivatives, and subordinated debt. Standard credit VaR capital estimates are not designed to satisfy this multiple set of objectives.

In addition to issues related to regulators' primary objectives, there are extremely serious issues associated with the statistical validation of credit VaR model estimates. Kupiec (1995) discusses basic techniques that can be used for assessing the accuracy of risk measurement model estimates and analyzes the power of these statistical tests. These results and the results of subsequent analysis (Christofferson 1998) show that it is mathematically impossible to statistically validate the accuracy of a bank's internal risk management model with a high degree of confidence unless the monitoring sample size is exceptionally large. Because credit-VaR model estimates are typically based on horizons of one year, small sample sizes are unavoidable in model performance analysis.

Before formally analyzing the shortcomings of credit VaR capital allocations and considering modifications that may be necessary to satisfy regulatory goals, I introduce in the next section the formal framework that will be used in the analysis.

CREDIT RISK AND THE VALUE OF SAFETY NET GUARANTEES

Background

This section modifies the Merton (1977) framework to formally establish the value of an implicit or explicit safety net guarantee to bank shareholders under alternative approaches for setting regulatory capital requirements for bank credit risks. For modeling transparency, we assume the existence of a government agency that explicitly insures the value of banks' deposit liabilities. For simplicity, it is assumed that safety net guarantees are provided at a fixed ex ante rate normalized to 0, and so the safety net guarantee is costless to the bank.[8] While bank safety net funding cost benefits are modeled using a fixed-rate deposit insurance structure, similar issues arise when bank liabilities are only implicitly guaranteed under "too big" or "too important to fail" social arrangements. Following Merton (1977), the analysis does not consider information asymmetries that may arise in the context of the valuation of bank shares and assumes that the value of bank assets are transparent to equity market investors.

In order to analyze alternative internal model approaches for setting regulatory capital requirements for credit risk, it is necessary to consider the market value of stakeholder claims under an investment opportunity set that differs from the one considered in Merton (1977). While Merton (1977) implicitly restricted bank investment opportunity sets to traded equities, the analysis that follows restricts a bank's investment opportunity set to traded discount bonds with credit risk.

Asset Value Dynamics

Before considering specific expressions for the market values of stakeholder positions in these alternative settings, it is appropriate to consider the characteristics of the asset price dynamics that underlie all stakeholder valuations. In the Merton (1974, 1977) model, as in the Black and Scholes (1973) model that preceded it (henceforth, the structural model for credit risk is referenced as the Black-Scholes-Merton—BSM—model), a firm's underlying assets evolve in value, according to geometric Brownian motion:

$$dA = \mu A dt + \sigma A dz \tag{4.1}$$

where dz represents a standard Weiner process. If A_0 represents the initial value of the firm's assets, and A_T the value of the firm's assets at time T, Ito's lemma implies:

$$ln A_T - ln A_0 \sim \phi\left[\left(\mu - \frac{\sigma^2}{2}\right)T, \sigma\sqrt{T}\right] \tag{4.2}$$

where the functional notation $\phi[a, b]$ represents the normal density function with a first argument (the mean) of "a" and the second argument (the standard deviation) of "b." Equation (4.2) defines the physical probability distribution for the end-of-period value of the firm's assets:

$$\tilde{A}_T \sim A_0 e^{\left(\mu - \frac{\sigma^2}{2}\right)T + \sigma\sqrt{T}\tilde{\varepsilon}} \tag{4.3}$$

where $\tilde{z} \sim \phi[0,1]$ [OUP: please change $\tilde{\varepsilon}$ in equations 4.3 and 4.4 to $\tilde{z}$. I can't get into them.] and e represents the exponential function.

When the underlying assets or claims on these assets are traded, equilibrium absence of arbitrage conditions impose restrictions on the underlying asset's Brownian motion's drift term, $\mu = r_f + \lambda\sigma$, where λ is the market price of risk associated with the firm's assets and r_f represents the constant risk-free rate of interest. It will be useful subsequently to use this equilibrium relationship. Define $dA^\eta = (\mu - \lambda\sigma)A^\eta dt + A^\eta \sigma dz$. dA^η represents the "risk-neutralized" geometric Brownian motion process (the process after an equivalent martingale change of measure) that is used to value derivative claims. The probability distribution of the underlying end-of-period asset values after the equivalent martingale change of measure, $\tilde{A}_M^\eta$, is:

$$\tilde{A}_T^\eta \sim A_0 e^{\left(r_f - \frac{\sigma^2}{2}\right)T + \sigma\sqrt{T}\tilde{\varepsilon}} \tag{4.4}$$

Deposit Insurance Value

If the risk-free term structure is flat, and a firm issues only pure discount debt,[9] Black and Scholes (1973) and Merton (1974) demonstrated, among other things, that (1) the value of an uninsured firm's equity is equivalent to the value of a European (Black-Scholes) call option written on the firm's underlying assets; the call option has a maturity equal to the maturity of the firm's debt and a strike price equal to the par value of the firm's debt, and (2), the market value of the uninsured firm's debt issue is equal to the market value the issue would have if it were default-risk-free, less the market value of a Black-Scholes put option written on the value of the firm's assets; the put option has a maturity equal to the maturity of the debt issue and strike price equal to the par value of the discount debt.

If B_0 represents the discount bond's initial equilibrium market value and *Par* represents its promised payment at maturity date M, the BSM model requires:

$$B_0 = Par\, e^{-r_f M} - Put(A_0, Par, M, \sigma) \qquad (4.5)$$

where r_f represents the risk-free rate and $Put(A_0, Par, M, \sigma)$ represents the equilibrium value of a Black-Scholes put option on an asset with an initial value of A_0, a strike price of *Par*, a maturity of M, and an instantaneous return volatility of σ.

The default (put) option's value in expression (4.5) is a measure of the credit risk of the bond. The larger the bond's credit risk, the greater the discount in its market value relative to a default-riskless discount bond with identical par value and maturity.

Assume that the bank can issue discount debt claims that are insured by the government. If the bank's debt is insured, its initial equilibrium market value is $Par\, e^{-r_f M}$ because investors require only the risk-free rate of return on the debt issue. If the deposit insurer does not charge for insurance, the initial market value of the bank's equity is given by $Call(A_0, Par, M, \sigma) + Put(A_0, Par, M, \sigma)$, where $Call(A_0, Par, M, \sigma)$ represents the value of a Black-Scholes call option on an asset with an initial value of A_0, a strike price of *Par*, a maturity of M, and an instantaneous return volatility of σ.

The provision of costless deposit insurance provides the bank's shareholders with an interest subsidy on the bank's debt. This interest subsidy has an initial market value equal to $Put(A_0, Par, M, \sigma)$.[10] Absent any regulatory constraints or bank franchise value, it is well known that the bank shareholders maximize the ex ante value of their wealth by maximizing the present market value of the interest subsidy on their debt or, equivalently, by maximizing the value of $Put(A_0, Par, M, \sigma)$. By selecting the bank's investment assets and capital structure, the bank's shareholders maximize the value of their insurance guarantee by maximizing the credit risk of the insured debt claims issued by the bank.

The ex ante value of a deposit insurance guarantee was derived by Merton (1977) in the context of a bank that purchased assets that evolve in value according to geometric Brownian motion or equity-type investments. As a consequence, the Merton (1977) results do not characterize the deposit insurance value enjoyed by the shareholders of a bank that invests in fixed-income investments with credit risk where the payoffs in favorable return states are limited by the terms of its loan contracts. Using the intuition of the Merton results, the next section shows that one can then derive deposit insurance values that arise when banks invest in fixed-income assets with credit risk. In the absence of an insurance premium, the deposit insurance value is equal to the value of the implied default option on the bank's insured debt.

Insurance Value and Risky Discount Bond Investments

Assume that the bank can invest only in BSM risky discount bonds and that it funds these investments with equity and its own discount debt issue. Moreover, assume that the bank's investment opportunity set is restricted to discount bonds that are matched in maturity to the discount debt that the bank issues. The initial market value of the bank's bond investment is given by expression (4.5), but it is now necessary to distinguish between the par value of the bond that will be purchased and the par value of the bond issued to fund this investment. Let the purchased bond's initial market price be represented by:

$$B_0 = Par_P \, e^{-r_f M} - Put(A_0, Par_P, M, \sigma) \qquad (4.6)$$

where Par_P represents the par value of the purchased discount bond.

Define Par_F to be the par value of the discount bond that the bank issues to fund the bond purchase. In the absence of an insurance guarantee, if the maturity of the bank's funding debt matches the maturity of the firm's asset (both equal to M), then the end-of-period cash flows that accrue to the bank's debt holders are given by:

$$Min\left[Min(\tilde{A}_M, Par_P), Par_F\right] \qquad (4.7)$$

Because $\tilde{A}_M$ is the only source of uncertainty determining bank bond holder payoffs, the initial market value of the funding debt is given by discounting (at the risk-free rate) the expected value of (4.7) taken with respect to the equivalent martingale probability distribution of the end-of-period asset's value, $\tilde{A}_M^{\eta}$:[11]

$$E^{\eta}\left[Min\left[Min(\tilde{A}_M, Par_P), Par_F\right]\right]e^{-r_f M} \qquad (4.8)$$

where $E^{\eta}[\cdot]$ represents the expectations operator with respect to the probability density of $\tilde{A}_M^{\eta}$.

Applying the intuition of Merton (1977), if the bank's funding debt is costlessly guaranteed by the government, the value of the insurance guarantee that accrues to bank shareholders is given by:

$$Par_F \, e^{-r_f M} - E^{\eta}\left[Min\left[Min(\tilde{A}_M, Par_P), Par_F\right]\right]e^{-r_f M} \qquad (4.9)$$

Equation (4.9) represents the implicit value of the bank's default option on its own funding debt, which is equivalent to the interest subsidy it would receive if its funding debt were costlessly insured by the government.

CREDIT VAR AND BUFFER STOCK CAPITAL ALLOCATION

Unbiased Buffer Stock Capital Requirements

Recall that a buffer stock capital allocation is the equity portion of a funding mix that can be used to finance an asset or portfolio in a way that maximizes the use of debt finance subject to limiting the ex ante probability of default on the funding debt to some maximum acceptable rate.[12] Value-at-risk (VaR) techniques are commonly employed to estimate buffer stock capital allocations.

VaR is commonly defined to be the loss amount that could be exceeded by at most a maximum percentage of all potential future portfolio value realizations at the end of a given time horizon.[13] By this definition, VaR is determined by a specific lefthand critical value of a potential profit and loss distribution and by a right boundary against which the loss is measured. In the credit risk setting, the righthand boundary of the VaR measure is commonly set equal to the expected value of the portfolio's end-of-period value distribution. This VaR measure is said to estimate so-called unexpected credit loss.

When calculating credit VaR for buffer stock capital purposes, one must recall that the credit VaR horizon implicitly equals the maturity of the funding debt issue whose target insolvency rate is being set in the capital allocation exercise. It is only at maturity that the mark-to-market (MTM) value of the bank's liabilities can be ignored in a buffer stock capital calculation. Technical insolvency occurs when the market value of the bank's liabilities exceeds the market value of the bank's assets. When the VaR horizon is identical to the maturity of the bank's funding debt, the funding debt's market value in nondefault states is its par value.[14]

Consider the use of a 1%, one-year VaR measure—VaR(.01)—to determine the equity funding requirement under a buffer stock approach for capital. In buffer stock capital calculations, Kupiec (1999) demonstrates the importance of measuring VaR relative to the initial market value of the asset or portfolio that is being funded. If VaR is measured relative to the asset or portfolio's initial value, by definition, there is less than a 1% probability that the asset's value will ever post a loss that exceeds its 1% VaR risk exposure measure. While true as stated, this result is often misinterpreted as implying that, should a firm choose an amount of equity finance equal to its 1% VaR, there is less than a 1% chance that the firm will default on its debt.

Kupiec (2002a) discusses the bias implicit in the common VaR based measures of buffer stock capital requirements. Assume that a bank's equity financing share is set equal to a VaR(.01) measure (measured relative to initial portfolio value). Under this capital allocation, the amount of debt finance required to fund the bank's assets is $V_0 - VaR(.01)$. If the firm borrows $V_0 - VaR(.01)$ (and interest rates are positive), it must pay back more than $V_0 - VaR(.01)$ if it is to avoid default. While bank investment losses will exceed the bank's *initial* equity value with only 1% probability, this is not the event that determines whether or not the bank defaults, and the bank's actual default rate is greater than 1% under the VaR(.01) capital allocation rule. Kupiec (2002a) demonstrates that an unbiased buffer stock capital allocation rule is to set equity capital equal to 1% VaR (calculated from the portfolio's initial market value) plus the interest that accrues on the funding debt over the VaR horizon.

In contrast to the capital allocation procedures just described, typical discussions of credit risk capital allocation define VaR as the difference between the expected value of the end-of-period asset (portfolio) value distribution and the selected critical tail value associated with a target default rate. The difference between the mean end-of-period value and the portfolio's initial value substitutes for the interest payments that must be added to a properly constructed VaR measure. This increment, however, does not accurately estimate the equilibrium interest payments required by the funding debt holders, and so the VaR measure produces biased estimates of buffer stock capital requirements.

Calculating an Unbiased Buffer Stock Capital Estimate in the BSM Model

The credit VaR profit-and-loss distribution differs according to whether the funding horizon corresponds to the maturity of the credit-risky asset or to a shorter period of time. In this analysis, we consider the buffer stock capital allocation that is required in the absence of deposit insurance to limit the technical insolvency rate to α—the target default rate on the bank's funding debt. We consider the special case of capital allocation of a held-to-maturity (HTM) risky bond investment funded to maturity using a BSM risky discount bond.

At maturity, the payoff of the firm's purchased bond is given by $Min[Par_P, \tilde{A}_M]$. The credit VaR measure appropriate for credit risk capital allocation is given by:

$$VaR(\alpha) = B_0 - Min\left[Par_P, A_0 e^{\left[\mu - \frac{\sigma^2}{2}\right]M + \sigma\sqrt{M}\,\Phi^{-1}(\alpha)}\right] \qquad (4.10)$$

where B_0 is the initial market value of the purchased discount debt given by expression (4.6) and α is the target default rate on the funding debt. If α is sufficiently small (which is assumed), the expression $Min[Par_P, A_0 e^{[\mu - \sigma^2/2]M + \sigma\sqrt{M}\,\Phi^{-1}(\alpha)}]$ simplifies to $A_0 e^{[\mu - \sigma^2/2]M + \sigma\sqrt{M}\,\Phi^{-1}(\alpha)}$, and consequently, the expression for credit VaR in the HTM case is:

$$VaR(\alpha) = B_0 - A_0 e^{\left[\mu - \frac{\sigma^2}{2}\right]M + \sigma\sqrt{M}\,\Phi^{-1}(\alpha)} \qquad (4.11)$$

$B_0 - VaR(\alpha) = A_0 e^{[\mu - \sigma^2/2]M + \sigma\sqrt{M}\,\Phi^{-1}(\alpha)}$ determines the maximum par value of the funding debt that is consistent with the target default rate. The initial market value of this funding debt issue is given by:

$$E^\eta\left[Min\left[Min(\tilde{A}_M, Par_P), A_0 e^{\left[\mu - \frac{\sigma^2}{2}\right]M + \sigma\sqrt{M}\,\Phi^{-1}(\alpha)}\right]\right] e^{-r_f M} \qquad (4.12)$$

These relationships define the equilibrium required interest payment on the funding debt:

$$A_0 e^{\left[\mu - \frac{\sigma^2}{2}\right]M + \sigma\sqrt{M}\,\Phi^{-1}(\alpha)} - E^\eta\left[Min\left[Min(\tilde{A}_M, Par_P), A_0 e^{\left[\mu - \frac{\sigma^2}{2}\right]M + \sigma\sqrt{M}\,\Phi^{-1}(\alpha)}\right]\right] e^{-r_f M}$$

$$(4.13)$$

Expressions (4.11) and (4.13) imply that the initial equity allocation required to meet the target default rate α is given by:

$$B_0 - E^\eta \left[Min \left[Min(\tilde{A}_M, Par_P), A_0, e^{\left[\mu - \frac{\sigma^2}{2}\right]M + \sigma\sqrt{M}\Phi^{-1}(\alpha)} \right] \right] e^{-r_f M} \qquad (4.14)$$

SAFETY NET EXTERNALITIES AND INTERNAL MODELS CAPITAL ESTIMATES

A simple buffer stock capital allocation, even if it is completely accurate, does not remove the risk of default. If equity capital is set according to a buffer stock capital rule and the target solvency rate is positive, there is some chance the firm will default on its liabilities. If the firm happens to be a bank, the bank's resources in default may be insufficient to repay the bank depositors.

When safety nets are valuable to banks, investors view insured bank liabilities as if they are riskless (or at least less risky), and the initial market value of bank debt claims are increased relative to the value of identical claims issued by a noninsured entity. That is, for any given par value of a discount liability offered to investors by a bank, the initial market value of the discount issue will be greater if investors treat the claim as if it is insured. The reduction in interest expense engendered by the safety net guarantee allows bank shareholders to invest less equity (compared to a noninsured business) in order to establish a given target rate for insolvency. In other words, given two banks that are identical in all respects except that one is (costlessly) insured and the other is not, the insured bank's shareholder will be required to invest less in order to achieve a given insolvency rate.

Suppose that a regulatory authority mandates that an insured bank have sufficient capital so that, at the end of some specific horizon, the bank will remain technically solvent in at least $100*(1 - \alpha)\%$ of all outcomes. If the insured bank takes into account the safety net–related interest subsidy in its internal capital allocations, it can meet the regulatory mandated target solvency rate with less equity capital than would be required by an otherwise identical noninsured institution. The reduction in the buffer stock equity capital requirement is equal to the reduction in the interest cost on the bank's debt.

In the case of HTM buffer stock capital requirements for credit risk, Kupiec (2002b) shows that the interest subsidy on the bank's debt is given by:

$$A_0 e^{\left[\mu - \frac{\sigma^2}{2}\right]M + \sigma\sqrt{M}\Phi^{-1}(\alpha) - r_f M} - E^\eta \left[Min \left[Min(\tilde{A}_M, Par_P), A_0 e^{\left[\mu - \frac{\sigma^2}{2}\right]M + \sigma\sqrt{M}\Phi^{-1}(\alpha)} \right] \right] e^{-r_f M}$$

$$(4.15)$$

here M is the maturity of the fixed income asset, the funding debt, and the VaR horizon. The interest subsidy is identical to the deposit insurance guarantee value (expression (4.9)) evaluated at the par value of funding debt set by the regulatory determined minimum solvency rate, $Par_F = A_0 \, e^{[\mu-\sigma^2/2]M + \sigma\sqrt{M}\,\Phi^{-1}(\alpha)}$.

Expression (4.15) represents the deposit insurance values that a bank generates under internal model approaches for setting regulatory capital requirements for credit risk. The insurance subsidy is not uniform; its value can be altered by altering the risk characteristics of the equity or the discount bond in which the bank invests. Consequently, an internal models approach to setting regulatory capital may stimulate banks' demand for investments that offer attractive insurance subsidy benefits.

If equity markets are competitive and there are no asymmetric information costs associated with new equity issuance, existing bank shareholders will be able to capture the safety net subsidies associated with all new investments, and the existing shareholders will maximize their wealth by raising new equity capital and investing in all fair-valued investments that generate a positive safety net funding subsidy. If, however, there are costs associated with issuing new bank shares, existing bank shareholders will not capture the full value of the safety net funding subsidy and shareholders may not find it optimal to exploit all fair-valued investments with positive safety net subsidies. Instead, when raising outside bank equity capital is costly, the shareholder maximization problem must recognize the tradeoffs between the costs required to raise outside equity and the corresponding benefits that can be attained from exploiting available safety net guarantees. In the extreme case in which outside equity issuance costs are prohibitive, existing shareholders will allocate their equity capital across investments in order to maximize the value of the insurance subsidy per dollar of equity invested.

Consider the insurance value generated under an internal models approach to regulatory capital for credit risk when the maturity of the bank's bond asset is identical to the maturity of the insured bank liability and both asset and liability have a maturity of one year. In this HTM case, the value of the safety net subsidy generated under an internal models approach to credit risk capital—given by expression (4.15)—depends on specific characteristics of the purchased bond, including the bond's par value, the market value of the bond's supporting assets, including their return volatility, and the market price of risk.

The insurance value surface generated under a one-year, 1% internal models capital requirement for the one-year discount bonds is plotted in figure 4.1 under the assumption that the supporting assets have an initial market value of 100, the market price of risk is 10%, and the risk-free rate is 5%. In this example, credit risk is declining in the bond's par value and volatility, so the bonds in the northeast quadrant of the figure have the smallest credit risks. The peak of the insurance value surface corresponds to a set of discount bonds that have only modest credit risk because, under a 1% internal model capital constraint, these bonds allow the bank to use considerable funding leverage.

Figure 4.2 revisits the insurance value surface pictured in figure 4.1 and plots the surface when insurance value is measured in basis points per dollar

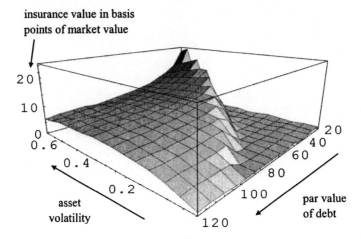

Figure 4.1. Insurance Value Under a HTM Internal Model Capital Requirement. Source: Author's calculation.

of required equity capital—the insurance value measure that is relevant for the shareholders of a capital constrained bank. The face of the cliff in figure 4.2 corresponds with the peak of the mountain ridge in figure 4.1. The high plateau at the top of the cliff corresponds with the bonds in figure 4.1 that populate the minimal credit risk "lowlands" in the northeast triangle-shaped region of figure 4.1. Under the 1% internal models capital requirement, the bonds in this region—bonds with minimal credit risk—can

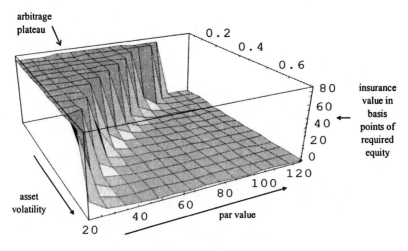

Figure 4.2. Insurance Value in Basis Points of Required Equity Capital. Source: Author's calculation.

be fully financed with insured deposits. Since bank shareholders make no investment but accrue fully the credit risk premium paid by these bonds (however small), the bonds on the plateau above the cliff face in figure 4.2 represent a pure arbitrage from the perspective of a bank's shareholders.

It is also possible to analyze the insurance values generated under an internal models buffer stock approach to regulatory capital for credit risk when banks may purchase longer term credits and fund them with shorter maturity liabilities. The insurance values and investment biases generated in such instances are qualitatively similar to those generated in figures 4.1 and 4.2 for the HTM internal models capital calculations. The interested reader is referred to Kupiec (2002b) for further details.

USING SUBORDINATED DEBT TO IMPLEMENT AN INTERNAL MODELS CAPITAL REGULATION

Requirements on Subordinated Debt

Many of the shortcomings inherent in the direct use of bank internal models for setting regulatory capital for credit risk can be mitigated if regulatory capital requirements are set indirectly through the use of a mandatory subordinated debt issuance requirement. If a bank is required to fund its credit risky assets with a minimum amount of subordinated debt that is free from safety net protections and this subordinated debt is required to have, at issuance, a maximum probability of default, then it is possible to both limit the probability of bank insolvency and control the expected losses on the bank's guaranteed liabilities should the bank default. Under this approach to setting regulatory capital, the bank can use its internal credit VaR models to estimate its equity capital and subordinated debt issuance requirements, and supervisors can use subordinated debt market values, agency ratings, and yield spreads as supplemental information when they attempt to verify the accuracy of bank internal models estimates.

Consider the following concrete example of this proposed approach. Assume that regulations require a bank to fund its assets, in part, with a subordinated debt issue that must, at issuance, have a market value that is at least 2% of the value of the bank's assets and may not have a probability of default that exceeds 20 basis points in its first year. The latter condition basically requires that the bank's subordinated debt be rated as investment grade when it is issued. For simplicity, the analysis focuses on a one-year regulatory horizon, and so the subordinated debt carries a maturity of one year and all bank internal models estimates are based on a one-year horizon. This subordinated debt issuance requirement implicitly determines a bank's regulatory capital requirement for shareholder's equity in a manner that includes both a buffer stock solvency constraint and a constraint that attenuates the safety net insurer's losses should a bank default.

Using Internal Models to Set Equity Capital Requirements under a Mandatory Subordinated Debt Issuance Requirement

A bank is technically insolvent when the market value of its existing assets are insufficient to discharge its liabilities when they mature. When the bank issues both insured deposits and subordinated debt, the maturity values of both claims must be taken into account when calculating internal model buffer stock capital allocations.

Recall that, when calculating the internal models buffer stock capital requirement in the simple case (single seniority class of debt), the critical value of the end-of-period probability distribution for the asset's value that is consistent with the target (maximum acceptable) insolvency rate determines the maximum par value of debt that can be issued by the bank. When the bank issues both insured deposits and subordinated debt, this critical asset value determines the total debt-related payments that can be promised by the bank if it is to remain within the required solvency rate margin.

Consider the case where the bank's credit has a maturity identical to that of the subordinated debt issue (one year). Let D represent the initial value of the guaranteed liabilities that the bank accepts (assumed to be discount instruments) and P_F represent the par value of the risky subordinated debt that is issued by the bank. The solvency rate restriction on the bank's subordinated debt issue requires:

$$P_F \leq Min\left[Par_P, A_0\, e^{\left[\mu - \frac{\sigma^2}{2}\right]M + \sigma\sqrt{M}\,\Phi^{-1}(\alpha)} \right] - De^{r_f} \qquad (4.16)$$

where the equality will hold when the bank faces incentives to maximize the use of leverage as will typically be the case if safety nets are valuable.[15]

Expression (4.16) shows that, given the risks in a bank's investment portfolio, the use of insured deposits restricts a bank's ability to issue subordinated debt. Similar to a buffer stock equity capital rule, expression (4.16) does not control the potential losses associated with a bank default, since the bank could set the par value of subordinated debt at a de minimus amount, say .01, issue subordinated debt, and satisfy the default rate condition. In this example, while subordinated debt holders would bear the first losses should the bank default, the depth of the losses they would absorb in default would be trivial, and default losses would be borne primarily by the bank deposit insurer. In this case, when the bank's assets fell in value to $A_0\, e^{[\mu - \sigma^2/2]M + \sigma\sqrt{M}\,\Phi^{-1}(\alpha)}$, the subordinated debt holders would become the bank's owners, but should the assets fall in value by just a penny more, the insured depositors would become the owners and would bear losses if a third-party insurer did not assume control, bear the losses, and pay the insured depositors their promised maturity payouts.

It is assumed that the payoff of all liabilities is required if a bank defaults on even its most junior debt obligation. If the subordinated debt tranche of the bank's capital structure is large enough to absorb bank credit risk losses, bank depositors may be paid in full in the event of default even in the absence of a safety net guarantee. More generally, the ex ante probability that the third-party deposit insurer will bear losses depends on both the ex ante probability of default on the bank's subordinated debt and the initial market value of the bank's subordinated debt issue. Given the probability of default on the subordinated issue, the larger its initial market value, the smaller is the probability that the deposit insurer will bear losses.

In the case of one-year subordinated debt, with $P_F < P_P$, the initial market value of the subordinated debt is given by:

$$E^n[Max[Min(\tilde{A}_1 - De^{r_f}, Par_F), 0]]e^{-r_f M} \qquad (4.17)$$

Assuming the leverage constraint on the bank's probability of insolvency is binding and expression (4.16) holds as an equality, expression (4.17) indicates that, in order for the bank to increase the market value of its subordinated debt issue, it must increase the par value of the issue *and* decrease the amount of insured deposits it accepts. Thus, an increase in the minimum required market value of the subordinated debt issue (holding constant its probability of default) forces subordinated holders to assume ownership (and bear losses) over a larger range of the bank's asset credit-loss distribution. This market value restriction controls the size of the wedge between the probability that the bank is insolvent and the probability that the deposit insurer bears losses. The larger the required market value of subordinated debt, the larger this wedge, and the smaller the probability that the deposit insurer bears losses.

When the regulatory capital requirement on the market value of the bank's subordinated debt is expressed as a minimum proportion, β, of the bank's asset value, the capital requirement can be formally written:

$$E^n[Max[Min(\tilde{A}_1 - De^{r_f}, Par_F), 0]]e^{-r_f M} \geq \beta A_0 \qquad (4.18)$$

It should be noted that the market value of the bank's subordinated debt and the value of the bank's assets (the book value at least) are observable quantities, and so verification issues are diminished over those that arise in the context of internal models capital regulation. While valuing bank loans may not be a trivial exercise without difficult complications, if banks are optimistic in their loan loss provisions and overstate loan values, they will be required to issue subordinated debt with greater market value.[16] The regulatory risks associated with overoptimistic bank loan valuations are in part attenuated by the requirement of a larger subordinated issue and thus a larger buffer for the deposit insurer.[17]

The bank sets its equity capital requirement by using its credit VaR models to estimate the critical value on its asset portfolio's future value distribution. In the case of the BSM discount bond examples used in this analysis, the critical value is given by $A_0 e^{[\mu - \sigma^2/2]M + \sigma\sqrt{M}\Phi^{-1}(\alpha)}$. Since it is in the bank shareholders' interest to maximize the use of guaranteed (interest subsidized) deposits, the bank will optimize its capital structure by choosing, simultaneously, the smallest value of P_F and the largest value of D that satisfy expressions (4.16) and (4.18). While the analysis has focused on the case in which the bank's investments and liabilities are maturity-matched, the extension to the MTM case, when the bank's investments have longer maturities than its liabilities, is straightforward and is omitted for the sake of brevity.

It should also be recognized that this analysis has assumed that subordinated debt investors price these liabilities as if they will bear full default losses without any benefit from the intervention of a safety net provider. If systemic risk concerns are sufficiently strong and safety nets are perceived to be sufficiently broad, subordinated debt investors may behave as if safety net benefits may, in some circumstances, be extended to subordinated debt holders.[18] In such a case, subordinated debt values are increased above their uninsured fair market values and their initial market value is no longer an accurate indicator of the degree of protection that subordinated debt will offer to the deposit insurer in the case of default. If this issue is important because of empirical evidence or historical precedent, the regulatory requirement for the minimum value of the subordinated debt issue can be increased to compensate for the safety net–engendered valuation bias in subordinated debt market value.

The probability associated with the critical value in the credit VaR calculation represents the probability of default on the most junior debt issue—in this case, the bank's subordinated debt. If, in addition to the quantitative requirement on the solvency rate on subordinated debt, a qualitative requirement were added that required the subordinated debt issue to be rated by an independent rating agency, the ratings would provide an indirect way (imperfect no doubt) to evaluate the probability of default on the subordinated debt issue that could supplement the direct examination verification procedures adopted by supervisors.

Example

Consider a specific example of the subordinated debt approach for implementing an internal models regulatory capital requirement for credit risk. Assume that regulations require that one-year subordinated debt be used to finance 2% of the value of the bank's assets and that the subordinated debt must have a probability of default that is less than 20 basis points. Assume that the bank's investment opportunity set includes only BSM risky discount bonds. For simplicity, assume that all these bonds have underlying assets with an initial market value of 100, a market price of risk of 5%, and par values of 108. Credit risk is varied in this example by varying the volatility of these bonds' supporting assets' values. The greater the volatility, the greater the credit risk of the BSM bond.

Table 4.1 reports on the efficacy of this capital regulation when banks are restricted to purchasing one-year BSM discount bonds. The first four rows of table 4.1 report on the market value and risk characteristics of the purchased bond. Rows 5–8 of the table report on various quantities that are

Table 4.1. Regulatory Capital Requirements for Maturity-Matched Debt

Asset volatility	0.05	0.10	0.15	0.20	0.25	0.30
Market value of purchased bond	99.06	97.18	95.21	93.22	91.22	89.23
Default option value of purchased bond	3.68	5.55	7.52	9.51	11.51	13.50
Market value discount for credit risk as a percentage of the risk-free value of par	3.58	5.41	7.32	9.26	11.20	13.14
Par value of funding subdebt	2.09	2.05	2.01	1.96	1.92	1.88
Market value of funding subdebt	1.98	1.94	1.90	1.86	1.82	1.78
Par value of insured deposits	89.07	73.04	62.79	53.81	45.97	41.14
Risk-free market value of insured deposits	84.72	73.04	62.79	53.81	45.97	39.14
Regulatory equity capital requirement	12.35	22.19	30.52	37.55	43.43	48.31
Regulatory equity capital requirement as percentage of market value of the asset	12.47	22.84	32.05	40.28	47.61	54.14
Market value of insured deposits without guarantee	84.72	73.04	62.79	53.80	45.96	39.13
Market value of safety net guarantee	0.00053	0.00199	0.00318	0.00392	0.00431	0.00454
Market value of safety net guarantee in basis points of asset market value	0.05	0.20	0.33	0.42	0.47	0.51

Note: Calculations are based on regulatory capital requirements for credit risk under a 2% minimum market value, 20 basis point maximum allowable default rate (over one-year) mandatory subordinated debt issuance requirement. The assumptions underlying the calculations are these: the initial value of the underlying assets = 100, the par value of the purchased bond = 108, bond maturity = one year, the risk-free rate = 5%, and the market price of risk = 5%.
Source: Author's calculations.

needed to calculate the bank's implied equity capital requirement. Rows 9–10 report the equity capital requirement in alternative basis, and the final three rows of the table report on the value of the safety net guarantee appropriated by bank shareholders.

The results reported in table 4.1 indicate that the proposed approach for setting regulatory capital requirements, even under the modest regulatory limits of the example, produces a risk-based regulatory capital requirement that (1) almost completely removes the safety net–funding cost subsidy, and (2) allows banks to generate very little variation in the funding cost subsidy by varying the credit risk of its assets. While the example does show that funding cost subsidies may rise slightly as asset credit risk is increased, the subsidy remains below one-half basis point of asset value in all cases considered, and these cases include alternatives with substantial credit risk. Not only are these subsidies small and likely to be insignificant compared to real-world uncertainties and transactions costs, but also they can be further decreased either by decreasing the regulatory minimum probability of default or by increasing the required share of subordinated debt funding.

CONCLUSIONS

Proposals that advocate the direct use of bank internal capital allocation models to set regulatory capital requirements ignore the importance of externalities generated by the safety net–funding cost subsidies. Unbiased buffer stock capital estimation requires the recognition of the interest costs on funding debt. When banks enjoy a funding cost subsidy because of implicit or explicit safety net guarantees on their liabilities, bank internal models will produce downward biased estimates of so-called economic capital requirements. Should bank internal models be used to set regulatory capital requirements, this bias ensures that bank shareholders earn safety net–engendered profits. Because the internal model capital bias is not uniform with respect to the risk profiles of alternative investments, an internal models approach for setting credit risk capital requirements will distort bank investment incentives.

It is possible to capture the intuitive promise of an internal models capital approach and mitigate many of the associated shortcomings by reformulating the way that capital regulation is implemented. If a bank is required to issue subordinated debt in addition to its senior insured liabilities, regulatory restrictions on the bank's subordinated debt issue can be used to replace internal models capital requirements. It is demonstrated that if a bank is required to fund its activities with a subordinated debt issue of a minimum market value with maximum acceptable ex ante probability of default, then it is possible to limit both the probability of bank default and the expected loss on insured deposits should the bank default and thereby largely remove any safety net–funding costs subsidies that would otherwise be enjoyed by a bank. This mandatory subordinated debt issuance requirement implicitly sets a bank's regulatory capital requirement. Bank safety net subsidies can be made arbitrarily small by altering the regulatory subordinated debt issuance requirements, and banks have only a limited ability to vary the subsidy by varying the risk characteristics of their investment portfolio.

Notes

1. Buffer stock capital is the amount of equity capital that is required to fund a portfolio of investments with the objective of maximizing the use of debt financing, subject to limiting the probability of default to a selected target level (for example, 1%).

2. Studies that include Avery, Belton, and Goldberg (1988), Gorton and Santomero (1990), Flannery and Sorescu (1996), and Sironi (2001) are consistent with the hypothesis that investors may sometimes behave as if bank subordinated debt issues benefit from safety net protections.

3. The capital regulation proposed in this study would not include subordinated debt in a bank's regulatory capital measure.

4. These studies include, inter alia, Benston et al. (1986), Horvitz (1983, 1986), Avery, Belton, and Goldberg (1988), Cooper and Fraser (1988), Wall (1989), Gorton and Santomero (1990), Osterberg and Thomson (1991), Evanoff (1993), Hassan, Karels, and Peterson (1994), Litan and Rauch (1998), Evanoff and Wall (2000), Calomiris (1997, 1999), Banker's Roundtable (1998), and the U.S. Shadow Financial Regulatory Committee (2000).

5. Gennotte and Pyle (1991), Rochet (1992), Chan, Greenbaum, and Thakor (1992), Craine (1995), and Kupiec and O'Brien (1998) consider models in which banks invest in positive NPV investments. The Kupiec and O'Brien (1998) analysis considers the most general set of bank investment opportunities and focuses on how the opportunity set affects the design of regulatory policy.

6. While all banks may share common investment opportunities (e.g., government bonds, market-traded bonds), if banks have monopoly access to some lending customers or markets (e.g., when a banking relationship is costly to establish but adds economic value), the risk-return characteristics of bank investment opportunity sets differ. These differences significantly complicate the design of socially optimal regulatory capital regulations.

7. The regulatory objective of least-cost resolution is the basis for prompt corrective action supervisory guidelines (12 U.S.C. §1831) and the guidelines that govern the U.S. FDIC's actions in insurance-related bank resolution activities (12 U.S.C. §1823c[4]).

8. As a point of comparison, it should be noted that the U.S. deposit insurance premium rate is currently 0 for well-capitalized banks.

9. Other assumptions include the absence of taxes and transaction costs, the possibility of short sales and continuous trading, and the assumptions that investors in asset markets act as perfect competitors and that the firm's assets evolve in value following geometric Brownian motion.

10. If the insurer were to charge an ex ante fee for insurance coverage, the market value of the insurance subsidy would be given by $Put(A_0, Par, M, \sigma)$ less the ex ante fee.

11. Alternatively, Geske (1977, 1979) provides a closed-form expression for the value of the compound option.

12. We make no claim that this objective function formally defines a firm's optimal capital structure—indeed, it almost certainly does not. It is, however, the objective function that is consistent with VaR-based capital allocation schemes and an approach commonly taken by banks, according to the BCBS's (1999) survey results.

13. This definition can be found, inter alia, in Duffie and Pan (1997), Hull and White (1998), Jorion (1995, 1997), and Marshall and Siegel (1997).

14. Prior to the maturity of the funding debt, in addition to valuing the bank's assets, the determination of technical insolvency requires an estimate of the market value of the funding liabilities.

15. When the bank invests in risky debt, it will be assumed that α is sufficiently small so that

$$Par_P > A_0\, e^{\left[\mu - \frac{\sigma^2}{2}\right]M + \sigma\sqrt{M}\,\Phi^{-1}(\alpha)}.$$

16. A full discussion of the specific operational and institutional details associated with implementation of the proposed approach, including its generalization to a

dynamic setting, is beyond the scope of this chapter. The difficulties associated with valuing bank assets and the differences between book and market valuations are discussed, for example, in Berger and Davies (1998) and in Berger, Davies, and Flannery (1998).

17. In this approach, loan-loss provisions should represent the difference between the book value of loans and an estimate of their fair market value. Loan-loss provisions that reduce the book value of loans reduce equity capital and are not a component of the regulatory capital measure proposed in this paper.

18. Historical data, for example, in Avery, Belton, and Goldberg (1988), Gorton and Santomero (1990), Flannery and Sorescu (1996), and Sironi (2001) are consistent with this behavior.

References

Avery, Robert B., Terrence M. Belton, and Michael A. Goldberg. 1988. Market Discipline in Regulating Bank Risk: New Evidence from Capital Markets. *Journal of Money, Credit, and Banking* 20 (4): 597–610.

Bankers Roundtable. 1998. *Market-Based Incentive Regulation and Supervision: A Paradigm for the Future*. Washington, D.C.: The Financial Services Roundtable (April).

Basel Committee on Banking Supervision (BCBS). 1988. International Convergence of Capital Measurement and Capital Standards. Basel Committee Publication No. 4. Available at: www.bis.org/bcbs/publ.htm#joint.

———. 1995. An Internal Model-Based Approach to Market Risk Capital Requirements. Basel Committee Publication No. 17. Available at: www.bis.org/bcbs/publ.htm#joint.

———. 1999. Credit Risk Modelling: Current Practices and Applications. Basel Committee Publication No. 49. Available at: www.bis.org/bcbs/publ.htm#joint.

———. 2001. The New Basel Capital Accord. Basel Committee Consultative Paper. Available at: www.bis.org/publ/bcbsca03.pdf.

Benston, George J., Robert A. Eisenbeis, Paul M. Horvitz, Edward J. Kane, and George G. Kaufman. 1986. *Perspectives on Safe and Sound Banking*. Cambridge, Mass.: MIT Press.

Berger, A., and S. Davies. 1998. The Information Content of Bank Examinations. *Journal of Financial Services Research* 14 (2): 117–44.

Berger, Allen N., Sally M. Davies, and Mark J. Flannery. 1998. Comparing Market and Supervisory Assessments of Bank Performance: Who Knows What When? Board of Governors of the Federal Reserve System FEDS Paper No. 1998-32. Available at: www.federalreserve.gov/pubs/feds/1998/199832/199832pap.pdf.

Black, Fischer, and Myron S. Scholes. 1973. The Pricing of Options and Corporate Liabilities. *Journal of Political Economy* 81 (3): 637–54.

Calomiris, Charles W. 1997. *The Postmodern Bank Safety Net: Lessons from Developed and Developing Economies*. Washington, D.C.: AEI Press.

———. 1999. Building an Incentive-Compatible Safety Net. *Journal of Banking and Finance* 23 (10): 1499–519.

Chan, Yuk-Shee, Stuart I. Greenbaum, and Anjan V. Thakor. 1992. Is Fairly Priced Deposit Insurance Possible? *Journal of Finance* 47 (1): 227–45.

Christoffersen, Peter F. 1998. Evaluating Interval Forecasts. *International Economic Review* 39: 841–62.

Cooper, S. Kerry, and Donald R. Fraser. 1988. The Rising Cost of Bank Failures: A Proposed Solution. *Journal of Retail Banking* (10): 5–12.

Craine, Roger. 1995. Fairly Priced Deposit Insurance and Bank Charter Policy. *Journal of Finance* 50 (5): 1735–47.

Duffie, Darrell, and Jun Pan, 1997. An Overview of Value at Risk. *Journal of Derivatives* 4 (3): 7–49.

Evanoff, Douglas D. 1993. Preferred Sources of Market Discipline. *Yale Journal on Regulation.* 10 (2): 347–67.

Evanoff, Douglas D., and Larry D. Wall. 2000. Subordinated Debt as Bank Capital: A Proposal for Regulatory Reform. *Federal Reserve Bank of Chicago Economic Perspectives* 24 (2): 40–53. Available at: www.chicagofed.org/publications/economicperspectives/2000/2qep3.pdf.

Federal Deposit Insurance Corporation (FDIC). 1983. Deposit Insurance in a Changing Environment: A Study of the Current System of Deposit Insurance Pursuant to Section 712 of the Garn-St. Germain Depository Institutions Act of 1982. A Report to Congress on Deposit Insurance (June). Washington, D.C.: The Federal Deposit Insurance Corporation.

Federal Reserve System Board of Governors. 1999. Using Subordinated Debt as an Instrument of Market Discipline. Board of Governors of the Federal Reserve System Staff Study 172. Available at: www.federalreserve.gov/pubs/staffstudies/1990-99/ss172.pdf.

Financial Services Roundtable. 2001. Re: The New Basel Accord: January 2001 Consultative Papers. Available at: www.fsround.org/PDFs/BaselcommentLetter .PDF.

Flannery, Mark J., and Sorin M. Sorescu. 1996. Evidence of Bank Market Discipline in Subordinated Debt Yields: 1983–91. *Journal of Finance* 51: 1347–77.

Gennotte, Gerard, and David Pyle. 1991. Capital Controls and Bank Risks. *Journal of Banking and Finance* 15 (4/5): 804–24.

Geske, Robert. 1977. The Valuation of Corporate Liabilities as Compound Options. *Journal of Financial and Quantitative Analysis* 12 (4): 541–52.

———. 1979. The Valuation of Compound Options. *Journal of Financial Economics* 7 (1): 63–81.

Gorton, Gary, and Anthony M. Santomero. 1990. Market Discipline and Bank Subordinated Debt. *Journal of Money, Credit and Banking* 22 (1): 119–28.

Hassan, M. Kabir, Gordon V. Karels, and Manfred O. Peterson. 1994. Deposit Insurance, Market Discipline, and Off-Balance-Sheet Banking Risk of Large U.S. Commercial Banks. *Journal of Banking and Finance* 18 (3): 575–93.

Horvitz, Paul M. 1983. Market Discipline Is Best Provided by Subordinated Creditors. *American Banker*, July 15.

———. 1986. Subordinated Debt Is Key to New Bank Capital Requirement. *American Banker*, December 31.

Hull, John C., and Alan D. White. 1998. Value at Risk When Daily Changes in Market Variables Are Not Normally Distributed. *Journal of Derivatives* 5 (3): 9–19.

Institute of International Finance (IIF). 2001. Report of the Working Group on Capital Adequacy. Washington, D.C.: Institute of International Finance.

International Swaps and Derivatives Association (ISDA). 2001. ISDA's Response to the Basel Committee on Banking Supervision's Consultation on the New Capital Accord. Available at: www.bis.org/bcbs/ca/isdaresp.pdf.

Jorion, Philippe. 1995. Risk^2: Measuring the Risk in Value-at-Risk. *Financial Analysts Journal* 52 (November): 47–56.

Jorion, Philippe. 1997. *Value at Risk: The New Benchmark for Managing Financial Risk*. New York: McGraw-Hill.

KPMG. 2001. The New Basel Accord: Response to Consultative Documents Dated January 2001. Available at: www.bis.org/bcbs/ca/kpmg.pdf.

Kupiec, Paul. 1995. Techniques for Verifying the Accuracy of Risk Measurement Models. *Journal of Derivatives* 3: 73–84.

———. 1999. Risk Capital and VaR. *Journal of Derivatives* 7 (2): 41–52.

———. 2001. Is the New Basel Accord Incentive Compatible? Available at: www.bis.org/bcbs/events/b2eakup.pdf.

———. 2002a. Calibrating Your Intuition: Capital Allocation for Market and Credit Risk. IMF Working Paper 02/99. Available at: www.imf.org/external/pubs/ft/wp/2002/wp0299.pdf.

———. 2002b. Internal Models-based Capital Regulation and Bank Risk-Taking Incentives. IMF Working Paper No. 02/125. Available at: www.imf.org/external/pubs/ft/wp/2002/wp02125.pdf.

Kupiec, Paul, and James M. O'Brien. 1998. Deposit Insurance, Bank Incentives, and the Design of Regulatory Policy. Board of Governors of the Federal Reserve System Finance and Economic Discussion Series Paper No. 1998-10. Available at: www.federalreserve.gov/pubs/feds/1998/index.html.

Litan, Robert E., and Jonathan Rauch. 1998. *American Finance for the 21st Century*. Washington, D.C.: Brookings Institution Press.

Marshall, Christopher, and Michael Siegel. 1997. Value-at-Risk: Implementing a Risk Measurement Standard. *Journal of Derivatives* 4 (3): 91–110.

Matten, Chris. 1997. *Managing Bank Capital: Capital Allocation and Performance Measurement*. Chichester: Wiley.

Merton, Robert C. 1974. On the Pricing of Corporate Debt: The Risk Structure of Interest Rates. *Journal of Finance* 29 (May): 449–70.

———. 1977. An Analytic Derivation of the Cost of Deposit Insurance and Loan Guarantees: An Application of Modern Option Pricing Theory. *Journal of Banking and Finance* 1 (1): 3–11.

Osterberg, William P., and James B. Thomson. 1991. The Effect of Subordinated Debt and Surety Bonds on the Cost of Capital for Banks and the Value of Federal Deposit Insurance. *Journal of Banking and Finance* 15 (4/5): 939–53.

Rochet, Jean-Charles. 1992. Capital Requirements and the Behavior of Commercial Banks. *European Economic Review* 36 (5): 1137–70.

Sironi, Andrea. 2001. An Analysis of European Banks' SND Issues and Its Implications for the Design of a Mandatory Subordinated Debt Policy. *Journal of Financial Services Research* 20 (2/3): 233–66.

U.S. Shadow Financial Regulatory Committee. 2000. *Reforming Bank Capital Regulation*. Washington, D.C.: American Enterprise Institute. Available at: www.aei.org/research/shadow/publications/pubID.16542,projectID.15/pub_detail.asp.

Wall, Larry D. 1989. A Plan for Reducing Future Deposit Insurance Losses: Puttable Subordinated Debt. *Federal Reserve Bank of Atlanta Economic Review* (July/August): 2–17.

5

No Pain, No Gain? Effecting Market Discipline via "Reverse Convertible Debentures"

MARK J. FLANNERY

The deadweight costs of financial distress limit many firms' incentive to include a lot of (tax-advantaged) debt in their capital structures. It is therefore puzzling that firms do not make advance arrangements to recapitalize themselves if large losses occur. Financial distress may be particularly important for large banking firms, which national supervisors are reluctant to let fail. The supervisors' inclination to support large financial firms when they become troubled mitigates the ex ante incentives of market investors to discipline these firms. This chapter proposes a new financial instrument that forestalls financial distress without distorting bank shareholders' risk-taking incentives. Reverse convertible debentures (RCD) would automatically convert to common equity if a bank's market capital ratio falls below some stated value. RCD provide a transparent mechanism for unlevering a firm if the need arises. Unlike conventional convertible bonds, RCD convert at the stock's *current* market price, which forces shareholders to bear the full cost of their risk-taking decisions. Surprisingly, RCD investors are exposed to very limited credit risk under plausible conditions.

This chapter assumes that market discipline is an important force in setting bank capital. To harness it for this purpose, the author proposes a new instrument, reverse convertible debentures. The chapter reflects a consistent theme of this book: the need for increased emphasis on market discipline rather than command and control rules.

The tradeoff theory of capital structure (leverage) posits that a firm balances the tax and agency benefits of debt against the costs of potential investment distortions and financial insolvency. Given the apparent tax benefits of debt, Almazan, Suarez, and Titman (2002) wonder why firms don't routinely operate with high leverage while routinely arranging *in advance* to recapitalize themselves if large losses occur. This chapter explores the potential for a new capital instrument: "reverse convertible debentures" (RCD) that can be converted into common stock if the issuing firm's capital ratio falls below some prespecified level.[1] RCD conversion would be triggered automatically; neither the issuer nor the investor would have an option regarding this conversion. Moreover, the debentures would convert at the *current* share price, rather than at some absolute price specified in the debenture agreement.[2]

Although any type of firm could incorporate RCD into its capital structure, I evaluate this instrument in the context of large banking firms, which pose difficult supervisory challenges. Many supervisors recognize that the condition of large international banks can no longer be evaluated in a timely manner using traditional supervisory techniques. The Basel Committee on Bank Supervision (BCBS) proposes three "pillars" of effective financial oversight of which the first two represent traditional supervisory tools: minimum capital requirements and regular review of a bank's risk management procedures. The third pillar is, however, qualitatively different: market discipline. The third pillar posits that uninsured counterparties— depositors, derivative traders, uninsured counterparties, and so forth—will evaluate a bank's default risk when deciding whether to deal with it. Greater perceived default risks will cause investors to demand higher rates on debt and/or more secure settlement arrangements for their trading relationships (BCBS 2000, 2001). These cost increases will also discourage bank shareholders from taking on risky investments that do not offer sufficiently high expected returns.

The fundamental flaw in this view of market discipline is that the issuing institution must fail in order to impose losses on uninsured claimants and to transfer ownership of the bank's assets to former debtholders. Yet most national supervisors are very reluctant to accept the market uncertainties associated with the failure of a "systemically important" financial firm. They contend that a large banking firm's failure could adversely affect the financial system and, through it, the real economy. Accordingly, rational conjectures about ex post support for large financial firms compromise the ex ante incentives of private investors to monitor and discipline these institutions.

Requiring each bank to maintain high levels of equity capitalization could substantially reduce the incidence of bank distress. However, bankers assert that binding capital requirements can make regulated firms uncompetitive because equity capital is more expensive than debt. In response to such pressures, supervisors have incorporated certain types of subordinated debentures (including trust-preferred stock) into regulatory capital. Although such debentures apparently protect the deposit insurance fund, they also expose the bank to more failure states because a smaller loss will render the bank insolvent. Moreover, the level of *equity* capital—not *regulatory* capital—determines whether bank shareholders can gain by increasing their portfolio risk. In short, including subordinated notes and debentures (SND) in regulatory capital increases the likelihood that supervisors will confront the systemic costs of a large financial firm's distress.[3]

Legal restrictions also limit the supervisors' ability to take prompt action when trouble first appears. Most banking laws specify a bank's condition in terms of its equity book value. Because book equity measures tend to lag behind market value measures when a bank first encounters distress, supervisors find it difficult to mandate new equity issues when a bank first encounters trouble. Supervisors have also overlooked low capital ratios, also known as "exercising forbearance." Pennacchi (1987) shows that permitting a bank to operate with low equity capital for extended periods of time substantially increases the value of safety net guarantees. For a sample of 23 large U.S. banks at the end of 1981, he estimates that the average actuarial value of deposit insurance was $0.47 per thousand dollars insured when the banks were *not* required to rectify capital shortages promptly. By contrast, if solvent banks had annually restored their capital to a fixed ratio, the mean insurance value would have dropped to $0.08 (Pennacchi 1987, table 3, p. 352). Clearly, supervisors' inability or unwillingness to force banks to recapitalize after losses substantially increases bank liability holders' expected default losses. (See also Duan and Yu 1999.)

The capital ratio that triggers RCD conversion should be measured using concurrent share prices to avoid the tendency of equity measures based on generally accepted accounting principles (GAAP) to delay supervisory actions. Issuing RCD as part of a bank's capital structure provides four benefits:

- It protects depositors and taxpayers via a transparent means of automatic recapitalization.
- It causes shareholders to internalize the costs of risk.
- It imposes no immediate tax penalty on bank shareholders.
- It reduces the incidence of costly failures.

Conversion of the RCD into equity shares would maintain a minimum equity ratio for the firm under a broad range of asset value declines. The issuing firms would therefore avoid distress in most circumstances, reducing the potential for their uninsured counterparties to "run" from the bank and make a bad situation worse.

This chapter is organized as follows. The first section ("Large Bank Failures") argues that rationally anticipated government interventions blunt private investors' incentives to monitor and influence large banking firms. The second section ("Reverse Convertible Debentures: Recapitalization Without Failure") then describes a new capital instrument—"reverse convertible debentures" (RCD)—that will convert into common stock when the firm's capital ratio falls. Because these RCDs convert at the current share price, shareholders internalize effectively all the costs associated with their risk taking. A short interval (e.g., one month) between capital ratio evaluation and conversion of RCD into stock could reduce bank failures by forcing banks to restore their capitalization promptly following large losses. At the same time, the banks could operate with less equity capital on the books because RCD provide an automatic means of replacing lost capital value. A key feature of RCD is the event(s) that trigger their conversion into common stock. Since triggers will be governed by all determinants of value, the third section ("Does Market Value Provide an Appropriate Trigger?")

argues that the trigger should be expressed in terms of equity's *market* value, not its book value. This section also discusses the importance of (potential) market pricing errors on the firm and provides some details concerning the computation of trigger ratios. The fourth section summarizes and points out the potential for applying RCD to nonfinancial firms.

LARGE BANK FAILURES

According to the textbook view of bankruptcy, a firm's failure is not a major event. Shareholders simply turn over the firm's assets to erstwhile bond-holders, who proceed to operate the firm in the most efficient manner available. In reality, however, the costs of distress and bankruptcy appear to be more substantial, particularly when a firm has multiple claimants, multiple classes of debt obligations, or assets that require specialized managerial expertise. Reorganization costs may be particularly important for large banking firms, because their credit worthiness plays a major role in some important types of business. A weak credit rating limits a bank's ability to trade foreign exchange or over-the-counter (OTC) derivatives or to extend credible lines of credit to borrowing customers. Although market participants have been working to substitute collateral and netting agreements for traditional payment conventions, a large international bank still cannot function without a solid credit rating.

A large banking firm's distress exposes many counterparties to great uncertainty. Large financial firms operate in many countries, under a variety of legal systems. Collateral, rights of offset, netting arrangements, and ring-fencing may each be treated differently in different jurisdictions. The pertinent case law is sketchy at best.[4] The importance of liquidity and credit-worthiness for interbank transactions makes such uncertainties particularly problematic. Once a bank's ability to perform has been questioned, many counterparties will seek alternate suppliers of financial services, and the bank's initial problem may compound rapidly.[5] If the bank were truly solvent, investors could stabilize the situation by adding new capital. However, the required due diligence for a complex international bank takes time. As long as the bank's survival remains in question, counterparties will depart from the institution. These losses diminish the firm's value to an acquirer, reducing the likelihood of successful recapitalization through traditional routes. Customer flight also forces the firm to unwind its security positions, perhaps at fire sale prices. Citing the situation of Long Term Capital Management in 1998, the Federal Reserve Board and other central banks fear that a troubled firm's market transactions may cause price movements that destabilize other large institutions.

Problem resolution in the banking sector is therefore caught between two forces. While supervisors would like to rely on market discipline to provide supplementary oversight, they find it extremely difficult to stand by when a large firm stumbles. The ex ante incentives of uninsured claimants to monitor and price risk may therefore be substantially compromised, rendering market discipline less effective for the world's most important financial firms. The situation could be salvaged if supervisors effectively disciplined large firms when their condition first began to deteriorate. Yet they are often prevented from interfering with a bank whose book capital exceeds statutory minima, even when the market (and hence the supervisors) clearly know that GAAP overvalues the firm's true equity.[6] A form of regulatory capital that permits supervisors to rely on market assessments of bank condition, while also forcing banks to maintain adequate levels of capital based on market valuations, could substantially improve supervisory oversight of large financial firms.

REVERSE CONVERTIBLE DEBENTURES: RECAPITALIZATION WITHOUT FAILURE

Reverse convertible debentures (RCD) can reduce failure probabilities and improve risk-taking incentives without imposing the immediate tax burden of equity capital.[7] RCD would have the following broad design features:

- They automatically convert into common equity if the issuer's capital ratio falls below a prespecified value.
- Unless converted into shares, RCD receive tax-deductible interest payments and are subordinated to all other debt obligations.
- The critical capital ratio is measured in terms of outstanding equity's *market* value. (See section 3.)
- The conversion price is the *current share price*. Unlike traditional convertible bonds, one dollar of debentures (in current market value) generally converts into one dollar's worth of common stock.
- RCD incorporate no options for either investors or shareholders; conversion occurs automatically when the trigger is tripped.
- When debentures convert, the firm must promptly sell new RCD to replace the converted ones.

RCD provide a "programmed unlevering" (Doherty and Harrington 1997, p. 28) when losses reduce a firm's capital ratio. The conversion of RCD short-circuits the usual tendency for bad events to feed upon themselves. If losses depress a firm's equity, counterparties know that RCD will automatically restore the firm's equity ratio if the decline continues.

A Simple Example

Table 5.1 illustrates the basic process of RCD conversion via bank balance sheets that apply to three points in time. The asset and liability quantities report *market* values, and I assume for the moment that share prices accurately reflect bank value.[8] Suppose adequate capital is set at 8% of assets and that regulatory capital includes only common stock. A new regulation requires that this banking firm maintain RCD liabilities equal to at least 5% of total assets.

Table 5.1. Mechanics of RCD Conversion

t = 0		t = ½		t = 1	
Assets	Liabilities	Assets	Liabilities	Assets	Liabilities
$100	$87 Deposits	$97	$87 Deposits	$97	$87 Deposits
	$5 RCD		$5 RCD		$2.24 RCD
	$8 Equity		$5 Equity		$7.76 Equity
$N = 10 \rightarrow P_S = \$0.80$		$P_S = \$0.50$		$N = 15.52 \rightarrow P_S = \$0.50$	

Source: Authors' calculation.

At $t = 0$ (date zero), the bank in table 5.1 starts out with a minimally acceptable 8% capital of $8.00, backed by RCD equal to an additional 5% of total assets. With ten shares ("N") outstanding, the initial share price ("P_S") is $0.80. By $t = ½$, the bank's asset value has fallen to $97, leaving equity at $5.00 and the share price at $0.50. The bank is now undercapitalized ($5/$97 = 5.15% < 8%). Required capital is $7.76 (= 8% of $97). The balance sheet for $t = 1$ shows that $2.76 of RCD converted into equity to restore capital to 8% of assets. Given that $P_S = \$0.50$ at $t = 1/2$, RCD investors receive 5.52 shares in return for their $2.76 of bond claims. These investors lose no principal value when their debentures convert; they can sell their converted shares at $0.50 each and use the proceeds to repurchase $2.76 worth of bonds. The initial shareholders lose the option to continue operating with low equity (Duan and Yu 1999) because they must share the firm's future cash flows with converted bondholders.

In this example, only a portion of the outstanding RCD convert. How would the converting debentures be selected? One possibility would be to select debentures at random or pro rata from each investor's holdings. However, it seems better to separate a bank's outstanding RCD into specific tranches that convert in a prespecified order (e.g., the longest-outstanding RCD convert first).[9] A subset of the outstanding RCD would bear most of the conversion uncertainty, and investors who are strongly averse to receiving equity might sell their RCD as the probability of conversion increases. Conversely, it might be easier to sell new RCD if they were less likely to be converted in the near future.

The bank at $t = 1$ is again adequately capitalized, but it has only $2.24 of remaining RCD. Restoring the firm's available RCD to 5% of total assets therefore requires that some deposits be replaced with new RCD. At what rate can new debentures be sold? Since the bank has 8% equity capital in place, the new debentures are just as safe as their predecessors were.[10] The promised return on these bonds need not include a large default risk premium.

Generalizing the Example: Continuous Asset Returns

When asset returns follow a continuous distribution, RCD have positive effects on bank investment incentives and failure rates.[11] Moreover, frequent

Hunt Library
Carnegie Mellon University

02/02/09
12:35 pm

Item:Deposit insurance around the world :
issues of design and implementation
Due Date: 5/3/2009,23:59

Item:Capital adequacy beyond Basel :
banking, securities, and insurance
Due Date: 5/3/2009,23:59

Email Renewals: library-renew@cmu.edu

Items subject to recall after 7 days

Have a great day!

trigger evaluations tend to make the credit risk of newly issued RCD quite low.

Consider a stylized bank with the initial ($t = 0$) balance sheet presented in table 5.1. Recall that the indicated assets and liabilities are presented at their market (not book) values. The minimum required capital ratio is 8% of assets, and the firm starts out with just that ratio.[12] For simplicity, assume that the only change over time is the asset portfolio's market value; no new assets or liabilities are added to the firm, nor do the initial securities mature or change their market value. Realized asset values follow a known, continuous (e.g., normal) distribution. If the bank's market equity ratio is below 8% when the trigger is evaluated, just enough RCD are converted to restore the bank to the 8% required minimum ratio.

The equity trigger is examined at some time $t > 0$. If the asset value ($\tilde{A}_t$) exceeds its initial level ($100), equity value exceeds $8 and the bank remains sufficiently capitalized. The bank could then pay dividends or repurchase shares if it wished to reduce its capital ratio to 8%. However, if the asset value ($\tilde{A}_t$) has fallen, the bank's capital ratio becomes inadequate. RCD convert until the capital ratio is restored to 8%, or until all the initial RCD have converted (whichever comes first). Figure 5.1 illustrates the bank's time t capital ratio as a function of the asset portfolio's value. With conventional bonds outstanding, the firm's capital ratio falls with asset value. When $\tilde{A}_t$ < $92 the firm fails, and its fixed-income claimants are left to absorb the costs of reorganization. The narrow line in figure 5.1 shows the bank's capital ratio with subordinated note and debenture (SND) obligations. By contrast, the thicker line traces the bank's capital ratio when it has issued RCD. For relatively small losses, the converting RCD maintain the bank's capital ratio at 8%. Capital becomes "inadequate" only if $\tilde{A}_t$ falls below $94.56, where the $2.56 of remaining initial equity plus the $5 of converted RCD become insufficient to maintain an 8% capital ratio.

If $\tilde{A}_t$ falls to $92, the initial equity holders are wiped out, but the RCD conversion leaves the bank's capital ratio at $\left(\frac{\$5}{\$92}\right) = 5.43\%$. The firm fails

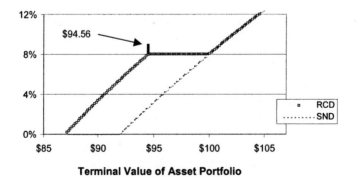

Figure 5.1. Capital Ratio. Source: Author's calculation.

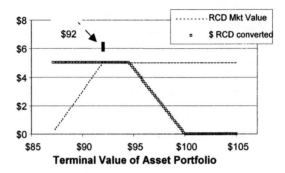

Figure 5.2. RCD Conversion and Value. Source:
Author's calculation.

only if $\tilde{A}_t$ < \$87 when both the initial capital and the RCD are exhausted.[13]
Ex ante, the expected deadweight costs associated with bankruptcy are
lower with RCD than with conventional SND, provided that RCD do not
induce shareholders to take on additional risk. I argue later that RCD do
not encourage risk taking if the equity trigger is appropriately designed.

Figure 5.2 illustrates how RCD conversion provides this additional equity protection. The thin line in figure 5.2 traces the value of outstanding
RCD at time t, as a function of the realized asset value. RCD receive the
standard type of risk bond payoff. At high asset values ($\tilde{A}_t \geq$ \$100), bonds
are fully repaid in cash. For \$92, < $\tilde{A}_t$ < \$100 the bonds are fully repaid
with a combination of cash and shares.[14] These shares are sold to converting
bondholders at a price that reflects the realized value of bank assets, and
hence the RCD investors receive the full amount of their promised repayment over this range of asset values. When $\tilde{A}_t$ < \$92, all RCDs convert, but
the resulting equity claims are worth less than the bonds' promised repayment. That is, the bondholders suffer default losses. However, the firm's
ownership is passed from shareholders to bondholders *without* an event of
default or the costs associated with default.

To summarize, the innovative contribution of RCD to firm capitalization
takes two forms. First, bankruptcy is avoided for asset realizations in the
range [\$87, \$92]. RCD therefore provide the risk absorption of equity
without the ex ante tax burden. Second, limited conversions maintain the
bank's equity capital ratio in the wake of small losses. If the initial equity
holders are not wiped out, RCD investors are fully repaid, although the
form of that repayment (cash versus shares) is uncertain. Because the absolute conversion price is not specified ex ante, shareholders do not know
what proportion of the firm's shares will be transferred to RCD investors
upon conversion. The shareholders' uncertainty permits RCD claimants to
be free of credit risk over a wide range of asset values.

Surprisingly, figure 5.3 indicates that the payoff to the bank's initial equity
holders takes the same (familiar) form for *either* RCD or conventional SND.

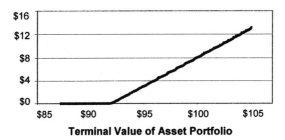

Figure 5.3. Equity Value (SND or RCD).
Source: Author's calculation.

Does this imply that RCD and SND have similar effects on shareholders' risk-bearing incentives?[15] The answer depends on the probability that the loss on initial assets exceeds the value of initial equity. Moral hazard occurs when shareholders do not bear the full downside of their investment decisions. The key to undistorted investment incentives is therefore to make the initial level of equity capital large, compared to the relevant asset volatility. A market-based conversion trigger can be evaluated very frequently—that is, we can make the time interval "*t*" quite short—which limits the range of likely asset values at the time conversion can next occur.[16]

This turns out to be a very important design advantage of the proposed RCD. Since the asset value's volatility rises with the square root of the time between evaluations, a shorter interval between evaluations makes large asset declines quite unlikely. For example, consider an annual bank asset volatility (σ_A) of 5.72%, which is the median of large U.S. bank holding companies' asset volatilities in 1998–2000 as computed by Flannery and Rangan (2003). With annual examinations and normally distributed asset values, the probability of an 8% decline in asset value (enough to wipe out initial equity) is about 8.1%. Now suppose that RCD might be converted at the end of every month, based on month-end share prices. The asset return's one-month value has a standard deviation of 1.65% $\left(= \left(\frac{5.72\%}{\sqrt{12}}\right)\right)$, and the probability that asset value falls enough to wipe out the firm's initial 8% equity is effectively zero (6.34E−07). By shortening the interval between possible RCD conversions, we make the shareholders' payoff in figure 5.3 linear over (effectively) the entire range of possible asset values. The beginning-of-month shareholders fully bear any decline in asset values, just as they accrue all of the asset appreciation. In other words, shareholders confront undistorted risk-bearing incentives.

Figure 5.3 shows that RCD investors in a bank with 8% initial capital and monthly trigger evaluations bear effectively no risk of loss. If the bank starts out at its minimum capital level, there is a high probability (something less than 50%) that at least some RCD will convert into common shares, but those investors are still very likely to be paid the full value of their debentures.

Further Design Issues

Effect on Bank Share Prices

Replacing traditional fixed claims with RCD will lower the call option component of bank equity value. RCD could still increase share values if they permit banks to operate with lower equity ratios. Suppose again that the typical annual asset volatility is 5.72%. Initial equity capital of 8% implies an 8.1% probability of a credit loss for RCD with annual trigger dates. By reviewing the triggers monthly instead of annually, the RCD have the same default probability (8.1%) with only 2.3% initial capital. Setting initial capitalization to 5% (for example) gives the RCDs triggered each month a default probability of 12 basis points (0.12%). Bankers could therefore reduce their equity capital from (say) 8% to 5%, add another 5% of relatively safe and short-term RCDs, and substantially lower their default probability. The tax treatment of RCD "capital" and a reduction in expected default costs would tend to raise equity value, offsetting at least some of the lost option value.

Equity Market Imperfections

Share prices can fluctuate for reasons other than changes in the firm's underlying asset value. It is therefore comforting to know that the RCDs' low default risk does not require that shares be valued in a perfect market. As the probability of RCD conversion increases, share prices will change to reflect the net effect of additional shares on each outstanding share's value. One might anticipate that the firm's shares would fall in value in several cases:

- Because of a downward sloping demand schedule for the bank's equity.
- Because each share's voting right becomes less valuable when there are more shares outstanding.
- Because the firm will become less levered.

Suppose the net effect is negative. The market price per share in table 5.1 would then be less than $0.50 and RCD investors would get more than 5.52 shares for their $2.76 of converting RCD. The initial shareholders would be left with a smaller proportion of the firm. Market imperfections therefore affect only the initial shareholders, who thereby bear the full effect of poor investment outcomes.

Maturity of the RCD

Conventional subordinated debentures protect senior (deposit) claimants only if they are not redeemed before bankruptcy occurs. Accordingly, SND must have long maturities in order to count as regulatory capital.[17] The situation is very different for RCD, which protect senior bank claimants by adding equity following small losses. RCD serve this function so long as they cannot mature before the next possible conversion date—say, the end of each month. Casual reflection suggests that the costs of maintaining a portfolio of RCD would be lower if the debentures' maturity substantially exceeded the conversion interval. (A longer maturity would probably make it easier to replace converted RCD with new ones.) However, the important point is that an initial maturity of one to two years seems sufficient if trigger evaluations occur monthly. Since high-quality bonds with relatively short maturities have a liquid market, banks could continue borrowing in their traditional maturity habitat. Their issues of RCD would thus benefit from marketing scale economies, and selling new RCD to replace the converted ones should be relatively easy.

Monitoring with Debenture Spreads

If the proposed RCD are generally quite safe, one might wonder whether their interest rates could be used to monitor bank condition or to constrain supervisory discretion. To some extent, the answer is straightforward: if trigger intervals are short and initial equity levels are high, banks are very safe, and a low spread on RCD should be the norm. If RCD investors perceive an increase in asset volatility that raises default risk, bond values will fall. The observed yield premia will continue to provide information about the market's view of a bank's capital sufficiency. Consequently, supervisors can continue to infer information from RCD investors, even if that information simply attests to the low probability of a bank's default.

Jumps in Asset Returns

The discussion in this section has assumed a continuous distribution of asset values. Clearly, a jump component to asset returns makes capital problems more likely and thus increases the probability that RCD investors will suffer default losses. However, RCD still prevent failure more effectively than conventional SND. In figure 5.1, $\tilde{A}_t < \$92$ forces bankruptcy if the firm has issued SND, while RCD would keep the firm solvent (though perhaps undercapitalized) for asset value realizations down to $87. In addition, RCD continue to maintain bank capitalization better than SND for relatively small losses. Although jumps in asset returns make it more difficult to maintain bank solvency, RCD retain substantial advantages over current arrangements.

A Means of Issuing Equity

A low equity ratio can occur because losses depress equity value (a bad thing for the firm) or because asset growth is rapid (probably a good thing). In the absence of RCD, a regulated firm's growth is constrained by its retained earnings plus new securities issued. Large, intermittent equity issuance involves a well-known lemons problem in which firms issue equity when insiders believe the shares are overvalued in the market (Myers and Majluf 1984). RCD might permit managers to finance growth with equity without

controlling when that equity is issued. As suggested by Hillion and Vermaelen (2001), therefore, issuing equity through RCDs may improve the
price at which new equity is sold.

Summary

RCD triggered by a low market capital ratio will maintain the issuing firm's
equity ratio over a wide range of asset value losses. Consequently, uninsured
counterparties need not run as a bank's equity falls, and losses at a large
financial firm need not generate the type of downward spiral that presently
elicits supervisory intervention. Frequent trigger evaluations eliminate moral
hazard incentives and expose the RCD to surprisingly low default risk. This
added protection imposes no immediate tax burden on shareholders, because unconverted debentures are paid tax deductible interest. With sufficiently high (conservative) trigger points, RCD are very safe, and new ones
can readily be issued to replace converted debentures. Although RCD will
deprive financial firms' shareholders of some option value, the firms will
benefit from lower expected bankruptcy costs and from their ability to
maintain a given solvency standard with less equity capital on the books.

DOES MARKET VALUE PROVIDE AN APPROPRIATE TRIGGER?

Supervisory personnel have historically formed their own assessments of
bank condition, frequently via on-site visits. These assessments influenced
capital adequacy judgments. However, supervisors have been increasingly
willing to utilize market information in assessing regulated financial firms.
The models-based approach to assessing credit risk exposures in Basel II
substantially delegates capital adequacy judgments to the regulated firms
themselves. Even the standardized approach anticipated for smaller banks
defines required capital in terms of the borrowers' (privately produced) credit
ratings. Still, many supervisors feel that market prices are not always accurate. Market prices can reflect only information that is available to investors,
and even then the prices are correct only *on average*. We must therefore
consider the implications of security pricing errors. This section considers
whether market prices or book valuations are more accurate and whether
pricing errors would imply large costs for the RCD conversion scheme.

Market versus GAAP Measures of Bank Capitalization

The issuers' equity ratio seems to be a reasonable trigger for a convertible
security designed to maintain adequate capitalization. A bank's equity can
be valued according to GAAP or at current market prices, and these two
estimates can diverge substantially. Both valuations probably include errors.
However, an efficient market's bank stock valuation errors should have zero
mean and no serial correlation. By contrast, GAAP provides managers with
options to inflate their firm's value, and supervisory restrictions on book
equity ratios sometimes provide strong incentives to do this.[18] Relying on

GAAP capital ratios to trigger RCD conversion seems problematic if book equity value is biased upward when the firm is closest to distress. This appears to be the case.[19]

The data in table 5.2 suggest that book equity ratios are overstated for the most highly levered U.S. bank holding companies (BHC). These data describe the 100 largest U.S. large bank holding companies with traded common equity over the period 1986–2000 (Flannery and Rangan 2003). The reported book equity ratio is the book value of common stock divided by the book value of total (on-book) assets. The market value equity ratio is the market value of common stock divided by the sum of (the book value of total liabilities plus the market value of common stock). The dataset includes 151 BHC with at least one year's data. An individual BHC could appear up to 15 times among the dataset's 1,288 observations. Across the entire sample, 17% of BHC-years report a book equity ratio above the corresponding market ratio, but this is much more likely to occur for BHC with low capital.

Table 5.2 compares book and market-valued equity ratios for the 100 largest U.S. bank holding companies (BHC) over the period 1986–2000.[20] Clearly, book equity ratios are most likely to be overstated for the weakest BHCs. The first row of panel A identifies 84 (out of 1,288) BHC-years with book capital less than 5% of assets. Of those 84 BHC-years, more than 63% had a book equity exceeding the corresponding market valuation of equity. By contrast, only 13.79% of the BHC-years with book capital above 5% showed higher book than market equity values. This result is consistent with the hypothesis that regulatory pressure leads banks to use accounting options more aggressively to show higher book capital. Qualitatively similar patterns occur when the sample is divided at higher capital ratios. BHC-years with book equity below 8% are seven times as likely to have relatively low market valuations as those with book ratios that exceed 8%. When the sample is divided at a book ratio of 10%, the low-capital banks are more than three times as likely to have book equity value exceed market. Panel B of table 5.2 divides the sample's 1,288 BHC-years on the basis of their *market* equity ratios. Now the results are even more dramatic: banks with low market capitalization are more than 10 times as likely to report book equity ratios that exceed the market's assessment.

The biases in book equity valuations will lead supervisors to close banks too late or too infrequently. With book valuations most likely to be overstated for the firms attracting supervisory attention, a bank's true (market-based) asset value can easily be lower than liabilities' value, while book value remains positive. Such firms have strong incentives to gamble for resurrection. The same bias makes the book equity ratio a poor trigger for RCD conversions, unless the required capital ratio is set very high.

Must Share Prices Be Perfectly Accurate?

In an efficient market, current asset prices are the best indicators of future values. Because market valuations incorporate informed expectations about

Table 5.2. Relation Between Book and Market Capitalization for 100 Largest U.S. Bank Holding Companies, 1986–2000

Panel A: 1,288 BHC-Years Divided According to Book Equity Ratio[a]

Critical Capital Ratio	BHC-Years Below Critical Ratio		BHC-Years Above Critical Ratio	
	Total Number	Proportion with Book Ratio Above Market Ratio (%)	Total Number	Proportion with Book Ratio Above Market Ratio (%)
< 5%	84	63.10	1204	13.79
< 8%	888	23.20	400	3.25
< 10%	1225	17.63	63	4.76

Panel A: 1,288 BHC-Years Divided According to Market Equity Ratio[b]

Critical Capital Ratio	BHC-Years below Critical Ratio		BHC-Years above critical ratio	
	Total Number	Proportion with Book Ratio Above Market Ratio (%)	Total Number	Proportion with Book Ratio Above Market Ratio (%)
< 5%	142	92.96	1146	7.59
< 8%	375	57.07	913	0.55
< 10%	576	37.85	712	0.14

[a] Book Equity Ratio = the book value of common stock divided by the book value of total (on-book) assets.
[b] Market Equity Ratio = the market value of common stock divided by the sum of (the book value of total liabilities plus the market value of common stock).
Note: Annual data describe BHC capital ratios during 1986–2000 (1,288 BHC-year observations).
Source: Author's compilation.

a firm's future cash flows, they seem well suited to the role of RCD trigger proposed here. However, security markets are probably not "strong form" efficient (Fama 1970). Market investors may lack important information or may misinterpret the publicly available data.[21] Nor do efficient prices imply perfect accuracy at all times. Bank regulators often feel that on-site supervisory inspections generate important information that is not available to the public or that investors do not act rationally when a bank is in financial distress. Given the possibility that market share prices contain valuation errors, few supervisors are prepared to rely on market valuations for important decisions. This view may be quite appropriate for some purposes, but pricing errors have a relatively benign effect on RCD.

Pricing errors can be evaluated in the context of a forecasting problem. Supervisors seek to identify banks that need to be closed or forced to recapitalize. Investors seek to identify banks whose current share prices do not reflect their true prospects. Supervisors and investors both wish to estimate a banking firm's true (but unobservable) condition, and such estimates generally include forecast errors. Both supervisors and investors must recognize the presence of these errors when deciding how to respond to new information. In some cases, the potential for valuation errors makes it optimal to act slowly. Consider the case of a bank closure. Banks are appropriately closed when their liabilities exceed the value of assets in place plus future growth options. Supervisors perceive (probably quite appropriately) that closing a bank is socially costly, even with a safety net. By contrast, the cost of permitting an insolvent bank to continue operating for a while seems less onerous. A supervisor should therefore consider the incidence *and cost* of Type I and Type II classification errors when making a closure decision. With asymmetric costs of misclassification and symmetrical pricing errors, the optimal closure decision will occur not when the estimated bank value is zero but rather when it is negative.[22]

While mistakenly closing a bank entails deadweight costs, an RCD conversion caused by a share pricing error only redistributes value between shareholders and RCD investors, and the associated risk should be diversifiable. A small share pricing error generates (or avoids) only a small RCD conversion. As asset prices fluctuate or the bank's assets grow, conversions may happen fairly often. With unbiased share prices, bank shareholders expect to sell their shares at a "fair" average price. The cumulative value of these redistributions should be close to zero and the associated deadweight costs correspondingly small. Contrast this with the present-day situation, where supervisors tolerate capital insufficiency for a while, then pressure the bank to make a large securities issuance. (The large fixed costs of security underwriting also tend to make seasoned equity offerings relatively large.) With infrequent, large security issues, pricing errors affect a bank's expected welfare more than if the bank converted small amounts of RCDs at many points in time. Potential share pricing errors are much less important if RCD are converted gradually on the basis of a market equity ratio, when the firm is not in financial distress.

A second type of valuation error also affects the number of shares con-veyed to converting bondholders: the RCD's market value.[23] If a bank's RCDs trade in an active market, those prices provide the obvious estimate of bond value for conversion purposes. However, bonds can also be valued via the type of matrix pricing used to compute a bond mutual fund's daily net asset value. Errors in either share prices or estimated RCD values will affect the number of shares per dollar of converted RCD. Yet, the potential for bond misvaluation adds little to the preceding discussion, which has already treated uncertainty about the exchange ratio when shares may be mispriced. Furthermore, the stock and bond pricing errors are likely to be positively correlated, with (imperfectly) offsetting effects on the number of shares per converted bond.

Trigger Design

Several main elements of RCD design depend on how the trigger ratio is computed and how often it is evaluated. Without this information, one cannot compute a required minimum equity capital, a minimum RCD ratio, or the required speed of replacing converted RCD. The discussion to this point has assumed a "relevant" market equity ratio, and the mechanism for computing this ratio warrants further consideration.

First, how should this ratio be computed? Initially, one might think to use the last trading day's closing price for the issuer's equity. However, noisy market prices may imply that share prices should be averaged over some interval. Likewise, the potential for price manipulation by an interested party seems to support the use of an average. (Recall how option cash values were initially based on closing prices, but that this practice was subsequently changed to use instead an average over some time period.) On the other hand, averaging share prices over too long an interval diminishes the speed with which a firm can be recapitalized. Because the intended RCD issuers are large, important financial firms, their share prices seem difficult to ma-nipulate for very long.

Second, how often should the market equity ratio be evaluated for large banks? A market equity ratio trigger could be evaluated weekly; equity prices are available daily, and many large banks already report their total liabilities on a weekly basis. For example, in the United States, all banks with more than $17 billion in total assets are asked to complete the Weekly Report of Assets and Liabilities for Large Banks (form FR 2416). Although participation in this survey is voluntary and the individual banks' data are at present confidential, it seems reasonable to require a weekly statement of total liabilities from large holding companies so that their market equity ratios can be computed. Although I have not analyzed this issue in detail, further discussion may be aided by a specific suggestion. Therefore, I pro-pose that the closing market value of equity be averaged over the last five business days of each month.[24] Issuing BHC would report their closing liability balances over the same five days, and the trigger ratio would be the simple ratio of average equity value to (average liabilities plus average equity value). If the trigger were tripped, shares would convert on the first trading day of the (immediately ensuing) month.[25] Supervisors could require that converted RCDs be replaced within a week.

In an efficient stock market, it is quite possible that a bank's market value would rise again shortly after some RCDs were converted, making its capital more than adequate at the subsequent trigger evaluation. The bank could choose to hold this equity as a cushion, or (if the price reversal were large) it could pay out some excess equity via dividends or share repurchases, subject to the minimum permissible level of equity's market capitalization.

Could This Process Lead to Costly Strategic Behaviors?

The process of converting some debt to equity when the borrowing firm becomes poorly capitalized provides several benefits to firm claimants. It also raises some corporate control issues. Such conversions would expose both shareholders and RCD investors to new types of expropriation.

Encouraging Short Sellers

Hillion and Vermaelen (2001) studied a set of 487 "death spiral convertibles" issued in the United States before August 1998. These bonds or preferred stock could be converted to equity at the investor's option, generally at a conversion price below the shares' market value on the conversion date. Many issues also included a look-back option in the form of a conversion price based on a trailing average market value. Hillion and Vermaelen give the example of a gold mining company that issued convertible preferred stock in 1997. The preferred shares were convertible (at their face value) into common shares. The conversion price was between 8.5% and 39% of the common shares' recent average (past 15–60 days) market value. They find that 85% of the firms that issued such convertible bonds had negative abnormal returns in the subsequent year, and a great many failed. They conclude that this poor ex post performance was largely due to contract design flaws that encouraged short-selling by the convertible investors. Since the investor could obtain shares through conversion, she could increase her expected returns by selling short the underlying common (Hillion and Vermaelen 2001, p. 3). The selling pressure might drive down share prices. Anticipating such a decline, professional short sellers sought out companies with convertible bonds or preferred shares.

The RCD proposed here differ from Hillion and Vermaelen's death spiral convertibles in several important ways. First, RCD investors have no riskless arbitrage opportunity because they have no option to convert, or even to time a conversion mandated by a low capital ratio. Second, conversion occurs at the current market price, not at a discount. Short sellers cannot lock in a riskless profit based on their option to convert at a discount to market value (Shleifer and Vishny 1997). Third, many of Hillion and Vermaelen's sample securities were converted at their par value. My proposed RCD convert at their (actual or estimated) market value, which eliminates the loss to existing shareholders when conversion occurs. Unlike the death spiral convertibles, RCD conversion causes no systematic transfer from shareholders to bond investors. Despite the fact that RCD appear less likely to encourage shorting the issuer's equity, it is worth evaluating the impact of RCD issuance on stock price dynamics, particularly as the firm's assets fall in value.

Aiding Corporate Raiders

Could RCD become a vehicle for gaining control of a firm cheaply? Perhaps a corporate raider could accumulate a firm's outstanding RCDs, then short-sell the stock to force conversion at an artificially low price. One obvious response to the fear of market manipulation is to make the trigger apply to an average share price, as opposed to any one day's price. Another response is to observe that RCD are designed for large, systemically important financial firms, whose shares trade in broad and deep markets.

Entrenching Management

Management is often replaced when a firm fails or is taken over. By avoiding financial distress, RCD would also circumvent this mechanism for replacing weak management. This constitutes a deadweight cost of RCDs, which is more important in industries whose managerial talent more strongly affects firm value. If RCDs increased managerial entrenchment, it would constitute a deadweight cost of including them in a firm's capital structure. Still, shareholders (including the newly converted ones) could vote management out.

Timing the Conversion of Shares

It is often alleged that managers offer new shares to the market when they feel their shares are overvalued (Myers and Majluf 1984; Ritter 1991). If management felt its shares were overvalued when the firm was close to its equity ratio trigger, it could pay a large dividend or repurchase shares in order to drive the ratio below the trigger. The value of such behavior is limited, however, by the fact that new shares are issued to RCD investors only in proportion to the equity shortfall. It seems that large share issues through this channel are unlikely at any one trigger date.

On the other side, managers might take extraordinary (and costly) steps to *avoid* triggering conversion if they wished to protect their current shareholders from the attendant dilution. Impending conversion might cause managers to continue paying normal dividends despite falling sales, to underreport expected future loan losses, and so forth. Although these possibilities deserve serious consideration, the fact that falling a little below the trigger level causes only a little conversion (and hence a little dilution) seems likely to limit the deadweight costs that shareholders would bear in order to avoid conversion.[26] Both of these possible share manipulation strategies deserve further consideration.z

Unresolved Issues

I have not fully analyzed all of the important features of a capital policy based on RCD. Omitted issues include the following:

- *Mandated ratios.* What level of equity capital should be required, and how would it be determined? How should the volume of outstanding RCD affect the required amount of equity?
- *Replenishment.* How quickly should a bank be required to replace converted RCD?
- *Maturity.* Should supervisors care about the maturity of RCD?
- *Pricing errors.* For what set of large financial firms might actual pricing errors (for the shares or for the RCDs) cause serious problems?
- *Tax treatment.* I have assumed that RCD interest will be tax deductible and that conversion is not a taxable event. Is this correct?
- *Market.* Is there likely to be a deep market for RCD?
- *Scope.* How large a banking firm should be required to maintain outstanding RCD? Is it possible to implement an RCD scheme for a bank without traded equity? With only thinly traded equity?
- *Ownership restrictions.* At least in the United States, supervisors must approve the identity of anyone who controls a banking firm. Similarly, a controlling firm becomes subject to regulation as a BHC or financial services company (FSC). Finally, the SEC requires investors to report when they control 5% of a traded firm's shares. Would such ownership restrictions limit the market for RCD? Is there a sufficient grace period within which an RCD owner can dispose of his shares in order to avoid such regulations?

If reverse convertible debentures become a serious candidate for regulatory capital, these questions will need more extensive consideration.

SUMMARY AND CONCLUSIONS

Bankruptcy costs tend to discourage many firms from operating with high leverage. This must reflect some deadweight cost of raising new equity in the wake of substantial losses. A security that reduces the deadweight costs of financial distress could therefore permit firms to operate with more debt and hence (perhaps) a lower cost of capital. Reverse convertible debentures (RCD) expand shareholders' financing opportunities by automatically reducing leverage when it becomes too high. RCD provide a transparent and time-consistent means of programmed unlevering that requires that no new securities be sold to the public when a firm has been suffering losses. Many types of firms might be able to use RCD in place of conventional debt to increase their financial leverage quite substantially.

RCD could have special benefits for the financial supervisors who might like to rely on market discipline but prefer to avoid significant financial failure. The BCBS intention to make market discipline an important component of supervisory oversight is commendable (BCBS 2000, 2001). However, relying on market discipline for systemically important institutions is probably not a time-consistent policy, given supervisors' and central bankers' concerns about the social costs of a large financial firm's failure. Exhortations from academics and others to "let the market work" in these situations are doomed to fail, because the people in charge believe that the market works poorly when a large firm becomes distressed. If large bank failures are believed to be socially costly, ex post incentives to bail out the creditors of a large bank will interfere with market incentives to monitor and discipline such firms. Yet these are precisely the firms for which market disciplinary forces have the greatest value, because traditional supervisory practices are least efficacious.

A security that keeps banking firms adequately capitalized in most situations could be preferable to traditional practice. A firm whose outstanding debt includes reverse convertible debentures (RCD) would have established a transparent means by which relatively large capital losses could be absorbed without involving depositors, counterparties, or taxpayers. RCD circumvent the human or legalistic tendencies to forbear when a firm experiences minor difficulties; they automatically make the decision to increase the firm's equity capital whenever it becomes inadequate. Triggered by a frequently evaluated ratio of the equity's market value to assets, RCD could be nearly riskless to the initial investors, while transmitting the full effect of poor investment outcomes to the shareholders who control the firm. In short, some features of RCD appear to be extremely attractive to issuing banks, market investors, and supervisors.

APPENDIX: SOME PRECEDENTS FOR REVERSE CONVERTIBLE DEBENTURES

The RCD instrument proposed here reflects earlier proposals regarding SNDs and closure rules.

Horvitz (1983) observed that deposit insurance would be unnecessary if banks could be closed as soon as their asset values fell below their promised liability payments. This argument is correct provided that asset values follow a continuous statistical process (no jumps), that deadweight closure costs are zero, that supervisors can observe bank asset values continuously, and that supervisors can close insolvent firms promptly even if they have positive book value. Horvitz's intuition clearly indicates that efficient bank closures should involve frequent inspections and rapid supervisory action.

Wall (1989) proposed that banks issue subordinate debentures with an embedded put option; investors could demand repayment (at par) at any time for any reason. The put option would substitute for traditional restrictive covenants and hence avoid the need to specify untoward events ex ante. Puttable debt also would addresses some of the problems of book value supervisory intervention. A solvent bank should be able to replace the redeemed debentures. If a bank could not do so promptly, it would have to close. This feature would give market investors a lot of power over whether and when to terminate a distressed banking firm. Some would count the resulting constraints on supervisors' options as a benefit. It may also have discouraged official support for the idea.

Bankruptcy studies note that distressed firms have three avenues for improving their situation. First, they can go through statutory bankruptcy (or the financial firm equivalent), which entails substantial deadweight costs that seem to be particularly large for banking firms (James 1991). Second, they can try to unlever the firm by exchanging debt for shares. This is a relatively low-cost transaction, but it is difficult to implement with many atomistic bondholders. Finally, the firm can negotiate a prepackaged bankruptcy restructuring and then use the bankruptcy law's cram-down feature to impose the deal on minority shareholders (Betker 1997; McConnell and Servaes 1991; Tashjian, Lease, and McConnell 1996). RCD resemble a state-dependent prepackaged bankruptcy: if equity falls, some bonds will be converted to shares to unlever the firm. Programmed unlevering not only reduces expected bankruptcy costs but also changes the incentive structure for new project selection by reducing debt overhang. Importantly, the firm needs to raise no new money at a time when managers frequently believe that their securities are undervalued.

Almazan, Suarez, and Titman (2002) try to explain why firms do not counteract the potential distress costs of high leverage by committing to sell new equity if leverage gets too high. Their model includes a negative expected effect on firm value when information is revealed through the due diligence process. (These costs reflect an assumed asymmetry in workers' wage demands to the information revealed.) Early in their paper (fn. 2), Almazan, Suarez, and Titman acknowledge that some forms of convertible debt may circumvent these negative information effects while reducing the uncertainties associated with the bankruptcy process.

Doherty and Harrington (1997) propose a reverse convertible debenture that is the most direct antecedent of the security I propose here. Starting from a risk management perspective, the authors define an RCD as subordinated debt that can be repaid with either cash or common shares at a *prespecified price* at the *option of the issuing firm*. They derive the impact of such a debt instrument on risk-taking incentives and conclude that these securities can be valuable for any sort of firm. (See also Doherty 2000a, chapter 13.) The RCD I analyze here differs from the Doherty-Harrington security in two important features. First, my RCDs convert at current market prices, rather than at a predetermined price. Second, the Doherty-Harrington security provides shareholders with an option to repay debenture holders with shares only at maturity, while my RCDs convert automatically whenever the trigger is tripped. These two features make my RCDs relatively safe and provide shareholders with extremely good incentives for making new investments. A few capital market instruments already exist to recapitalize firms following specified events. Some insurance companies have issued "catastrophe bonds" that are canceled following a large loss (Doherty 2000a, pp. 609–13). "Contingent capital" contracts give an insured firm the right to sell equity instruments (usually preferred stock) to an insurance company under prespecified conditions (Shimpi 2001, chapter 9; Culp 2002, chapter 21). The investment trade press describes a limited number of bonds that can be repaid with either cash or shares, at the issuer's option. These bonds generally offer maturities of one to three years, are sold to retail investors, and offer a high coupon rate to compensate for the embedded put. Doherty (2000b) points out that these instruments serve a risk-management function: when the firm's share price is depressed, part of the outstanding debt is (effectively) forgiven.

A similar-looking, but puzzling, instrument provides the issuer with an option to repay principal with *another* company's stock. For example, ABN-Amro has outstanding a number of reverse exchangeable securities: medium-term notes repayable either in cash or in a fixed number of shares of another company's stock, at the option of ABN-Amro. Outstanding reverse exchangeable securities permit payment with the stock of Walt Disney Co., Citigroup, General Electric, and Home Depot, among others. Perhaps these securities constitute a means of selling underpriced put options to retail investors.

Acknowledgments I would like to thank the project participants (particularly Paul Kupiec) who have provided many helpful comments and suggestions. Norah Barger, George Benston, Rob Bliss, John Connelly, Diana Hancock, George Kaufman, and Prakash Shimpi have also offered valuable comments and suggestions, as have seminar participants at Case Western Reserve University and the Federal Reserve Board.

Notes

1. Paul Kupiec initially suggested this security to me in the context of the U.S. housing government-sponsored enterprises (GSEs). As noted in the appendix, others have previously written about similar instruments, although the conversion features proposed here appear to be novel.

2. The section on "Generalizing the Example" demonstrates that this feature has the surprising effect of making RCD very low-risk securities.

3. The Shadow Regulatory Committee (2000) would permit banks to operate with any desired combination of equity and debenture "capital" because equity and debentures are both subordinate to depositors and the deposit insurance fund. However, equity capital prevents insolvency, while debenture "capital" does not. The two are equivalent only if insolvency is costless.

4. In discussing the mechanisms available to resolve "large complex banking organizations," Bliss (2003, p. 18) states: "This patchwork of laws governing termination and netting of derivatives contracts provides some protections but remains the source of legal uncertainty."

5. This possibility is often discussed in terms of a "depositor run," but the process is not confined to depositors. In fact, depositor preference laws provide quite a senior claim to even the uninsured depositors of a large financial institution. Merton (1990) differentiates between a firm's customers and its creditors. When a customer must also be a creditor (e.g., in an unsecured derivatives transaction), the firm's condition affects the demand for its services.

6. The case of Manufacturers Hanover (MH) in 1990 illustrates the problem. The bank had issued $85 million in "mandatory preferred stock," which was scheduled to convert to common shares in 1993. An earlier conversion would be triggered if MH's share price closed below $16 for 12 out of 15 consecutive trading days (Hilder 1990). Such forced conversion appeared possible in December 1990. In a letter to the Federal Reserve Bank of New York concerning the bank's capital situation, MH's CFO, Peter J. Tobin, expresses the bank's extreme reluctance to permit conversion or to issue new equity at current prices. At yearend 1990, MH's book ratio of equity capital to total (on-book) assets was 5.57%, while its market equity ratio was 2.53%. The bank was also adamant in announcing that it would *not* omit its quarterly dividend. Despite the low market capital ratio, the New York Fed appeared unable to force MH to issue new equity. Chemical Bank acquired Manufacturers Hanover at the end of 1991.

7. The appendix describes some antecedents of this idea.

8. Equity market "imperfections" are discussed in the second section under "Further Design Issues."

9. Even with multiple tranches, the marginal tranche will not generally be converted in its entirety, although a covenant could require this.

10. This statement makes several key assumptions about the potential extent of asset value losses and the timeliness of RCD conversion, discussed later. I return to the question of RCD credit quality in the section "Further Design Issues."

11. A jump component to asset returns complicates the ensuing analysis but does not affect most of the RCD features derived here. See the section "Further Design Issues."

12. Presumably, banks would aim for some cushion above this minimum required equity level.

13. This statement assumes that RCD convert even if the initial equity has been fully depleted.

14. Bond investors with no expertise in evaluating bank equities may choose to sell their shares immediately upon conversion, or the RCD most likely to convert might be sold to specialists.

15. Green (1984) shows that standard convertible bonds eliminate the incentives of equity to undertake excessive risk, under at least some theoretical conditions. Positive outcomes are shared with convertible bondholders, while the expected value of negative outcomes are paid by shareholders in the form of a higher coupon rate (or lower conversion price). However, convertible bonds share the costly feature of regular debentures that the issuer must fail in order for debenture losses to be imposed. These costs can be avoided with RCD.

16. Pyle (1986) makes this point: that riskier assets could or should be accompanied by a shorter interval between examinations.

17. Under current U.S. capital regulations, the proportion of a debenture that counts for regulatory capital declines linearly in the last five years of its scheduled life.

18. For example, many BHCs sold their headquarters buildings in the 1980s, booked a capital gain, and then leased it back from the purchaser. A bank can also

"cherry-pick" its securities portfolio to enhance its book equity, realizing the gains on appreciated securities while postponing the sale of assets with unrealized losses. Finally, loan provisioning offers a notorious means of inflating equity value for troubled banking firms, because managers have substantial latitude about how much inside information to reflect in their reported loan loss allowance. Note that each of these transactions raises the present value of taxes paid, which lowers equity market value (*ceteris paribus*) even while it boosts book value.

19. Peek and Rosengren (1996, p. 57) contend, "Reported capital ratios are lagging indicators of bank health, in part because some banks have not fully reflected likely future losses in their loan loss reserve." See also Jones and King (1995).

20. The dataset, taken from Flannery and Rangan 2002, describes the 100 largest BHC each year with traded equity. A total of 151 BHC are represented in the dataset, with each individual BHC appearing between 1 and 15 times among the dataset's 1,288 bank-year observations.

21. Some banking writers contend that banks are unusually difficult for outsiders to value. Flannery, Kwan, and Nimalendran (2004) provide some evidence that contradicts the hypothesis for "normal" times, although the question remains whether bank valuation errors become unusually large when the bank is in distress.

22. Acharya and Dreyfus (1989) derive an optimal closure rule with "early" closure—the bank is closed while asset value still exceeds liabilities.

23. Recall that table 5.1 presents the *market* values of bank assets and liabilities. An RCD conversion based on book debenture values could generate large value redistributions, which would affect investors' ex ante behaviors.

24. This average should probably be weighted by shares traded to help alleviate the potential for low-volume price manipulations.

25. Inserting a few days between the trigger evaluation and the conversion date—as suggested in the introduction—would permit bond investors to sell their bonds to traders with lower costs of liquidating the converted shares.

26. When Manufacturers Hanover confronted a possible conversion of preferred stock in late 1990 (see note 6), it considered redeeming the issue using cash on hand. Such a "plan" works only if a supervisor will accept it. Under a market value trigger, such redemption would have to be financed by issuing equity; otherwise, the redemption would further lower the capital ratio. Another important feature of the MH convertible preferred issue was that the *entire issue* converted if common share prices were even $0.01 too low over the specified time interval.

References

Acharya, Sankarshan, and Jean-Francois Dreyfus. 1989. Optimal Bank Reorganization Policies and the Pricing of Federal Deposit Insurance. *Journal of Finance* 44 (5): 1313–33.

Almazan, Andres, Javier Suarez, and Sheridan Titman. 2002. Capital Structure and Transparency. University of Texas Working Paper (September). Available at: http://papers.ssrn.com/sol3/papers.cfm?abstract_id = 331860.

Basel Committee on Banking Supervision (BCBS). 2000. A New Capital Adequacy Framework: Pillar 3 Market Discipline. Consultative Paper. Available at: www.bis.org/publ/bcbs65.pdf.

———. 2001. Pillar 3—Market Discipline. Basel Committee Working Paper No. 7. Available at: www.bis.org/publ/bcbs_wp7.pdf.

Betker, Brian L. 1997. The Administrative Costs of Debt Restructurings: Some Recent Evidence. *Financial Management* 26 (Winter): 56–68.

Bliss, Robert R. 2003. Bankruptcy Law and Large Complex Financial Organizations: A Primer. *Federal Reserve Bank of Chicago Economic Perspectives* 1Q: 48–58. Available at: www.chicagofed.org/publications/economicperspectives/2003/1qeppart4.pdf.

Culp, Christopher L. 2002. *The Art of Risk Management*. New York: Wiley.

Doherty, Neil A. 2000a. *Integrated Risk Management: Techniques and Strategies for Managing Corporate Risk*. New York: McGraw-Hill.

———. 2000b. Insurance and Finance: New Vehicles for Driving Value. *Financial Times*, May 16, 4.

Doherty, Neil A., and Scott E. Harrington. 1997. Managing Corporate Risk with Reverse Convertible Debt. Wharton School Working Paper.

Duan, Jin-Chuan, and Min-Teh Yu. 1999. Capital Standard Forbearance and Deposit Insurance Pricing Under GARCH. *Journal of Banking and Finance* 23 (11): 1691–1706.

Fama, E. F. 1970. Efficient Capital Markets—Review of Theory And Empirical Work. *Journal of Finance* 25 (2): 383–417.

Flannery, Mark J., and Kasturi Rangan. 2003. What Caused the Bank Capital Buildup of the 1990s? University of Florida Working Paper. Available at: http://www3.unicatt.it/unicattolica/dipartimenti/segesta/allegati/Bank_Capital.pdf.

Flannery, Mark J., Simon H. Kwan, and M. Nimalendren. 2004. Market Evidence on the Opaqueness of Banking Firms Assets. *Journal of Financial Economics* 71 (3): 419–60.

Green, Richard C. 1984. Investment Incentives, Debt, and Warrants. *Journal of Financial Economics* 13 (1): 115–36.

Hilder, David B. 1990. Hanover Bank's Managers to Urge Usual Dividend. *The Wall Street Journal*, November 2, A2.

Hillion, Pierre, and Theo Vermaelen. 2004. Death Spiral Convertibles. *Journal of Financial Economics* 71(2): 381–415.

Horvitz, Paul M. 1983. Market Discipline Is Best Provided by Subordinated Creditors. *American Banker*, July 15, 4.

James, Christopher. 1991. The Losses Realized in Bank Failures. *Journal of Finance* 46 (4): 1223–42.

Jones, David S., and Kathleen Kuester King. 1995. The Implementation of Prompt Corrective Action: An Assessment. *Journal of Banking and Finance* 19 (3/4): 491–510.

McConnell, John J., and Henri Servaes. 1991. The Economics of Prepackaged Bankruptcy. *Journal of Applied Corporate Finance* 4 (2): 93–97.

Merton, Robert C. 1990. *Continuous-Time Finance*. Cambridge: Basil Blackwell.

Myers, Stewart C., and Nicholas S. Majluf. 1984. Corporate Financing and Investment Decisions When Firms Have Information That Investors Do Not Have. *Journal of Financial Economics* 13 (2): 187–221.

Peek, Joe, and Eric S. Rosengren. 1996. The Use of Capital Ratios to Trigger Intervention in Problem Banks: Too Little, Too Late. *Federal Reserve Bank of Boston New England Economic Review* (September/October): 49–58.

Pennacchi, George G. 1987. A Reexamination of the Over- (or Under-) Pricing of Deposit Insurance. *Journal of Money, Credit and Banking* 19 (3): 340–60.

Pyle, David H. 1986. Capital Regulation and Deposit Insurance. *Journal of Banking and Finance* 10 (2): 189–201.

Ritter, Jay R. 1991. The Long-Run Performance of Initial Public Offerings. *Journal of Finance* 46 (1): 3–27.

U.S. Shadow Financial Regulatory Committee. 2000. *Reforming Bank Capital Regulation.* Washington, D.C.: American Enterprise Institute. Available at: www .aei.org/research/shadow/publications/pubID.16542,projectID.15/pub_detail.asp.

Shimpi, Prakash A. 2001. *Integrating Corporate Risk Management.* New York: Texere.

Shleifer, Andrei, and Robert W. Vishny. 1997. The Limits of Arbitrage. *Journal of Finance* 52 (1): 35–55.

Tashjian, Elizabeth, Ronald C. Lease, and John J. McConnell. 1996. An Empirical Analysis of Prepackaged Bankruptcies. *Journal of Financial Economics* 40 (1): 135–62.

Wall, Larry D. 1989. A Plan for Reducing Future Deposit Insurance Losses: Puttable Subordinated Debt. *Federal Reserve Bank of Atlanta Economic Review* 74 (4): 2–17.

6

The Use of Internal Models: Comparison of the New Basel Credit Proposals with Available Internal Models for Credit Risk

MICHEL CROUHY, DAN GALAI, AND ROBERT MARK

This chapter presents the New Capital Adequacy Accord proposed by the Basel Committee on Banking Supervision (Basel II) to replace the current 1988 Capital Accord (Basel I) by a more risk-sensitive framework for the measurement of credit risk. Basel II offers a menu of approaches: the "standardized" approach and the "internal ratings based" (IRB) approach with two variants: the "foundation" and the "advanced" approaches. These approaches are reviewed and their shortcomings are discussed. The standardized approach presents similar flaws to Basel I. The regulatory capital attribution according to the IRB approach is compared with the economic capital allocation from the industry-sponsored credit portfolio models, including CreditMetrics, KMV, and CreditRisk+. This comparison shows that the capital attribution for investment grade facilities from the IRB approach, although much lower than for the standardized approach, is still too high compared with the allocation from internal models. For subinvestment grade portfolios, the opposite is true where the IRB approach allocates more capital than the standardized approach, but still much less than the internal models. We also note that when the various credit portfolio models are calibrated with consistent parameters they produce capital attributions that are relatively close to one another. It is clear from these conclusions that regulatory arbitrage will prevail as banks will be incentivized, as under Basel I, to shed away their high-quality assets through loan sales and securitization, and keep on their balance sheet the more risky loans for which regulatory capital underestimates the actual economic risk.

This chapter shows why the Basel II command and control approach to regulatory capital for credit risk, based on a "Basel model," may be inferior to the use of models actually used by banks to determine economic capital. It thus underscores an important conclusion of this book: bank credit models (which take into account correlation of risk) may be superior to the Basel approach.

INTRODUCTION

Global competition is now affecting banks everywhere, both in developed and in emerging market countries. Regulators need to make sure that the regulatory framework does not inadvertently drive a competitive wedge between G-10 and non-G-10 competing banks. Over the past 10 years, the risk profile of banks has changed dramatically, and the methodologies used to describe risks now make strong supervision and enhanced market discipline important complements to capital regulation (McDonough 1998).

Banks' regulators also recognize that the biggest risk facing commercial banks is the oldest risk of all, that is, credit risk, rather than the risk of rogue traders losing fortunes in the capital markets. Recent high-profile trading losses, even including the significant losses of Allied Irish Bank or Barings bank at the hands of Nick Leeson, amount to a few billion dollars. The damage caused by reckless lending at Credit Lyonnais in the 1980s amounted to more than $20 billion. The credit losses incurred by banks in Japan and East Asia reach hundreds of billions of dollars.

In June 1999, the Basel Committee on Banking Supervision (Basel Committee or BCBS) released a proposal to replace the 1988 Accord, also referred to as Basel I, with a more risk-sensitive framework for the measurement of credit risk. In addition, the new framework proposes for the first time a measure of operational risk, while the market risk measure for traded securities remains unchanged. However, the measurement of market risk in the banking book for regulatory capital purpose has been postponed. This chapter focuses on the credit risk measurement methods and on the attribution of capital (Pillar 1).[1]

The new Accord (Basel 2001a), also referred to as Basel II, offers a menu of approaches to measure credit risk: the standardized approach, which is an improved version of the current 1988 Accord, and the internal ratings–based (IRB) approach, which has two variants: the foundation and the advanced approaches, the latter applying to the most sophisticated banks. The description and critique of the standardized and internal ratings–based approaches is given later in this chapter in the sections headed "The Standardized Approach" and "The New Internal Ratings–Based Approach," respectively.

The rules of the 1988 Accord (Basel I) are generally acknowledged to be flawed.[2] First, the Accord does not address complex issues such as portfolio effects, even though credit risk in any large portfolio is bound to be partially offset by diversification across issuers, industries, and geographical locations. For example, a bank is required to set aside the same amount of regulatory capital for a single $100 million corporate loan as for a portfolio of 100 different and unrelated $1 million corporate loans.

Second, the current rules assume that a loan to a corporate counterparty generates five times the amount of risk as does a loan to an OECD bank, regardless of their respective credit worthiness. For example, a loan to General Electric Corporation, an AAA-rated entity, has to be supported by five times as much regulatory capital as a similar loan to a Mexican (BB) or Turkish bank (B). General Electric is also considered to be infinitely more risky than the sovereign debt of Turkey or Mexico. Clearly, this is the opposite of what one might think appropriate.

Third, regulatory rules assume that all corporate borrowers pose an equal credit risk. For example, a loan to an AA-rated corporation requires the same amount of capital as a loan to a B-rated credit. This is also clearly inappropriate.

Fourth, revolving credit agreements with a term of less than one year do not require any regulatory capital,[3] while a short-term facility with 366 days to maturity bears the same capital charge as any long-term facility. The bank is clearly at risk from offering short-term facilities, yet so long as the term is less than one year no regulatory capital is required. This has led to the creation of the 364-day facility, in which banks commit to lend for 364 days only, but the loan is then continuously rolled over. Such a facility attracts no capital, even if the terms of the facility are such that if the commitment is canceled, the obligor then has the right to payback the drawn amount over a number of years.

Finally, the Accord does not allow for netting and does not provide any incentive for credit risk mitigation techniques such as the use of credit derivatives.

These shortcomings have produced a distorted assessment of actual risks and have led to a misallocation of capital. In some instances, they have even led financial institutions to take too much risk. The problem is that as the definition of regulatory capital drifts further away from the bank's understanding of the economic capital needed to support a position, the bank faces a strong incentive to play the game of "regulatory arbitrage." Banks are tempted to incur lower capital charges while still incurring the same amount of risk by using financial engineering constructs such as, for example, securitization through various types of collateralized debt obligations (CDOs) and the use of credit derivatives. In the process, banks transfer high-grade exposures from their banking book to their trading book, or outside the banking system, and the quality of the assets remaining in the books deteriorates, putting into question the purpose of the Accord. The elimination of the kind of regulatory arbitrage we just mentioned can be achieved only by a better alignment of regulatory and economic capital.

These problems have led the banking industry to suggest that banks should be allowed to develop their own internal credit portfolio models to determine value at risk (VaR) for credit in lieu of the standards set by Basel I. Credit VaR models would be approved by regulators and used by the industry to calculate the minimum required regulatory credit risk capital to be associated with the traditional loan products in the banking book.

Over the past few years, a series of industry-sponsored credit VaR methodologies have been devised, including CreditMetrics, developed by the investment bank J.P. Morgan, now JPMorganChase, and CreditRisk+, developed by Credit Suisse Financial Products (CSFP), now Credit Suisse First Boston (CSFB). Credit VaR models have also been developed by various software and consultancy firms: the KMV approach is now in use at many U.S. financial institutions.[4] These models are reviewed in some details in the appendix. Here, it is worth noting that a major challenge facing every model developer is to ensure that proprietary credit VaR formulas are comprehensible and practical enough to be accepted by the regulatory community. It is also essential to ensure that enough reliable data are available to both calibrate and backtest the credit portfolio models.

With the advent of products such as credit derivatives, the financial community is moving toward valuing loans and loan-type products on a mark-to-market/mark-to-model basis. Moreover, in measuring the credit risk of products whose value is driven mostly by changes in credit quality, we see an increasing trend toward applying quantification techniques similar to those used to measure market risk.

A related but separate challenge is to develop an integrated approach to calculating market VaR and credit VaR, taking into account correlations between market and credit factors such as credit migration and default events, as well as spread risk. Typically, most financial institutions still use one set of rules to value trading products and another set of rules to value loan products. The integration of market risk and credit risk is at the leading edge of a new wave of risk management. The sections that follow assess the new Basel proposals for standardized and IRB approaches. They are discussed in the context of the banks' own suggestions for the use of internal models and the Basel Committee's Quantitative Impact Studies, QIS2 and QIS3. QIS2 was initiated in April 2001, and its results were released on November 5 of the same year. That study assesses the impact of the new proposals for capital adequacy requirements of the second consultative paper (CP2), released in January 2001, and involves banks across the G-10 and beyond. Based on the results of QIS2 that clearly show that there was no incentive for banks to adopt the more risk-sensitive IRB approaches, the Basel Committee proposed a new calibration of the IRB formula in November 2001. This calibration remains the same for large corporate and mid-market (SME)[5] loans in the third consultative paper (CP3), which was released in April 2003, together with the results of QIS3. QIS3 was a full-scale impact study, much more detailed and comprehensive than QIS2, undertaken by a total of 188 banks in the 13 G-10 countries and an additional 177 banks from 30 other countries, during the period October–December 2002. QIS3 is based on new standards and calibrations set out in the Quantitative Impact Study technical guidance note issued by the Basel Committee in October 2002. We conclude by assessing the likely effectiveness of the banks' own proposals for meeting the new requirements.

THE NEW BASEL ACCORD—DEFINITION OF CAPITAL

The new framework maintains both the current definition of capital and the minimum capital requirement of 8% of the risk-weighted assets:

$$\frac{Total\ Capital}{Credit\ Risk + Market\ Risk + Operational\ Risk} = Capital\ Ratio\ (minimum\ 8\%)$$

$$(6.1)$$

where risk weighted assets are the sum of the assets subject to market, credit, and operational risk.

The new Basel Accord incorporates both expected and unexpected losses into the calculation of capital requirements, in contrast to the BIS 98, which is concerned only with unexpected loss for market risk in the trading book.[6] The justification for including expected losses in the capital requirement is that loan loss reserves are already counted as Tier 2 capital and are constituted to protect the bank against credit losses.[7]

However, in the current regulatory framework, loan loss reserves are eligible for Tier 2 capital only up to a maximum of 1.25% of risk weighted assets, and Tier 2 capital cannot exceed more than 50% of total regulatory capital, which is the sum of Tier 1 and Tier 2 capital. Banks, through their professional advocacy groups, are asking for the removal of these constraints in the final version of the new Basel Accord.

In order to compare the economic capital attribution produced by internal models and regulatory capital from the new Basel Accord's various approaches, one needs to gross up economic capital by the expected loss.

THE STANDARDIZED APPROACH

The standardized approach is conceptually the same as the present Accord (Basel I), but is more risk-sensitive. The bank allocates a risk weight to each of its assets and off-balance-sheet positions and produces a sum of risk-weighted asset values. For example, a risk weight of 50% means that an exposure is included in the calculation of risk-weighted assets at 50% of its full value, which then translates into a capital charge equal to 8% of that value, or, equivalently, to 4% of the exposure.

Individual risk weights depend both on the broad category of borrower, that is, whether it is a sovereign, a bank, or a corporate, and on the rating provided by an external rating agency (table 6.1). For banks' exposures to sovereigns, the Basel Committee proposes the use of published credit scores of export credit agencies, which are considered more accurate than the creditworthiness assessments produced by the rating agencies.

For claims on corporations, the new Accord proposes to retain a risk weight of 100% except for highly rated companies, that is, those rated AAA to A- and noninvestment grade borrowers rated below BB-. Highly rated companies would benefit from a lower risk weight of 20%–50%. Non-

Table 6.1. Standardized Approach—New Risk Weights, January 2001 (percentage)

Claim	Assessment					
	AAA to AA−	A+ to A−	BBB+ to BBB−	BB+ to BB− (B−)[a]	Below BB− (B−)[a]	Unrated
Sovereigns	0	20	50	100	150	100
Banks						
Option 1[b]	20	50	100	100	150	100
Option 2[c]	20	50[d]	50[c]	100[c]	150	50[c]
Corporates	20	50	100	100	150	100
Securitization tranches	20	50	100	150	Deduction from capital	Deduction from capital

[a]B− is the cutoff rating for sovereigns and banks. It is BB− for corporates and securitization tranches.

[b]Risk weighting based on risk weighting of sovereign in which the bank is incorporated. Banks incorporated in a given country will be assigned a risk weight one category less favorable than that assigned to claims on the sovereign with a cap of 100% for claims to banks in sovereigns rated BB+ to BB−.

[c]Risk weighting based on the assessment of the individual bank.

[d]Claims on banks of a short original maturity, for example, less than three months, would receive a weighting that is one category more favorable than the usual risk weight on the bank's claims, subject to a floor of 20%.

Source: Basel Committee on Banking Supervision 2001a.

investment-grade companies rated below BB− are attributed a risk weight of 150%. Short-term revolvers, with a term less than a year, would be subject to a capital charge of 20%, instead of zero under the current 1988 Accord. The new proposal would put highly rated corporate claims on the same footing as the obligations of bank and government sponsored enterprises.

Our view is that the proposed standardized approach presents flaws similar to those of the 1988 Accord. Banks will have the same incentive as before to play the regulatory arbitrage game for the following reasons:

- There is not enough differentiation among credit categories: six credit categories (including unrated) are not sufficient; for example, the same risk weight (100%) is attributed to a corporate investment grade facility rated BBB and a noninvestment grade facility rated BB−.
- The unrated category receives a risk weight of 100%, which is less than that attributed to noninvestment grade facilities rated below BB−. This does not make much sense. There will be no incentive for high-risk institutions to be rated since, by remaining unrated, they will benefit from the same treatment they would receive if they were investment grade. Clearly, the highest risk weight should apply to any firms that elect to remain unrated.
- The standardized approach attributes too much capital—more than they need for security—to investment-grade facilities (e.g., 1.6% for AA facilities) and not enough to noninvestment-grade debt (e.g.,

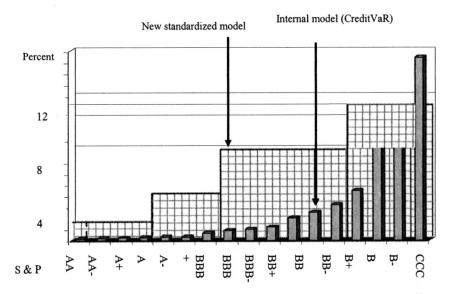

Figure 6.1. Capital Weights According to the New Standardized Approach versus a Typical Internal Credit VaR Model. Source: Author.

12% to B facilities). Figure 6.1 compares capital weights according to the new proposal to those generated by a typical internal credit value-at-risk model for a well-diversified portfolio of corporate loans; there is a huge discrepancy between the two.

In their empirical study, which covers the period 1981–1999, Altman, Bharath, and Saunders (2002) reach conclusions similar to our own. Their analysis, matched against the standardized approach, shows that the capital requirements of the latter are far too high for investment-grade obligors and about right for the noninvestment-grade bucket below BB. Their calculations are based on a Monte Carlo simulation with the loss data coming from Professor Altman's database on bond losses and recoveries. The Monte Carlo methodology involves creating a large number of random portfolios drawn from the actual universe of all bond issues across the period 1981–1999. Simulated losses are calculated at the 99.5% confidence level, that is, the capital target chosen by the Basel Committee:

- First, in the period 1981–1999 there has not been one single default, within one year, on bonds rated AAA to AA, corresponding to the first bucket of the standardized approach, yet the standardized approach attributes 1.6% of capital.[8]
- Second, in the A bucket, the 99.5% loss rate is only 0.35%, versus 4% under the standardized approach.
- Third, in the BBB–BB bucket, the 99.5% loss rate is 1.7%, versus 8% under the standardized approach.

- Fourth, in the below BB bucket the 99.5% loss rate is 11%, versus 12% under the standardized approach.

During the recession period 1989–1991, the actual 99.5% loss rates were 0% for the AAA–AA bucket, 0.99% for the A bucket, 2.3% for the BBB–BB bucket, and 13.1% for the below-BB bucket. The corresponding capital charges in the standardized approach are as noted earlier.

Another important flaw in the standardized approach is the degree to which capital ratios may be affected by the excessive procyclicality of capital that can result from the inherently lagging nature of agency ratings. A good example is the downgrading by the rating agencies of Enron to junk status less than one month before the company filed for Chapter 11 bankruptcy protection, in December 2001. This procyclicality could cause capital ratios to move too slowly during a recessionary period and to reach their maximum after the peak of the recession, when loan defaults are already on the decline.

THE NEW INTERNAL RATINGS–BASED APPROACH

Under the internal ratings–based (IRB) approach to assessing risk capital requirements proposed by Basel, banks will have to categorize banking-book exposures into at least six broad classes of assets with different underlying credit risk characteristics; the classes include corporates, banks, sovereigns, retail, project finance, and equity.[9] Today, there is clarity on the approach, but not necessarily on the calibration of the proposed credit model, only for the first four asset classes. Distinct analytical frameworks are provided for different types of loan exposures, for example, corporate and retail lending, whose loss characteristics are different. The focus of this chapter is on corporate debt, since internal models, so far, apply essentially to corporate loans and bonds.

Banks that adopt the IRB approach will be allowed to use their own internal ratings methodology to assess credit risk, subject to the approval by the regulator of the bank's internal rating system and the validation of key risk parameters such as the probability of default (PD) for each rating category, the loss given default (LGD), and exposure at default (EAD) for loan commitments. Under the IRB, the calculation of the potential future loss amount, which forms the basis of the minimum capital requirement, encompasses both expected and unexpected losses. It is derived from a formula whose key inputs are the PD, LGD, EAD, and maturity, M, of the facility. In the foundation approach, banks estimate the PD associated with each borrower, and the supervisors supply the other inputs, as follows:

- $LGD = 50\%$ for senior unsecured facilities and 75% for subordinated claims; reduced by the existence of collateral
- $EAD = 75\%$ for irrevocable undrawn commitments[10]
- $M = 3$ years

In the IRB advanced approach, banks that meet more rigorous capital standards, that is, those that have a sufficiently developed internal ratings system and a robust capital allocation process, will be permitted to set the values of all the necessary inputs. They will not be restricted to *PD* but can include *LGD*, *EAD*, and *M*. Still, the Committee is stopping short of permitting banks to calculate their capital requirements on the basis of their own credit risk portfolio models.

Under both the foundation and the advanced IRB approaches, however, the range of risk weights is far more diverse than that in the standardized approach, resulting in greater risk sensitivity. The IRB approach allocates capital facility by facility and does not allow explicitly the capture of portfolio effects.[11]

Credit Model for Corporate Exposures—The January 2001 Proposal

Risk weights for each facility in CP2 are derived from formula (6.2); it uses the input parameters mentioned earlier, that is, the probability of default (*PD*) of the obligor, the exposure at default (*EAD*), loss given default (*LGD*) and maturity (*M*) of the facility:[12]

$$RW_C = EAD*(LGD/50)*BRW_C(PD)*[1+b(PD)*(M-3)] \qquad (6.2)$$

or $12.5 * EAD * LGD$, whichever is smaller. In expression (6.2), RW_C denotes the corporate risk weight attributed to a facility, which translates into a capital charge, CC_C, of:

$$CC_C = 8\%*RW_C \text{ that is capped at the maximum loss, that is, } EAD*LGD$$
$$(6.3)$$

BRW_C denotes the corporate benchmark risk weight associated with a given *PD*, which is calibrated for an *LGD* of 50%, so that a three-year loan with a PD equal to 70 basis points (bp) has a BRW_C of 100% and a capital requirement of 8%. Capital requirements are calibrated to a loss coverage target of 99.5% and an average asset return correlation of 20%.

The expression in brackets represents the maturity adjustment that applies for the advanced approach; for the foundation approach *M* is set arbitrarily to three years. The maturity adjustment is a multiplicative scaling factor, linear in *M*, where the adjustment factor $b(PD)$ is a function of *PD*:

$$b(PD) = \frac{0.0235*(1-PD)}{PD^{0.44}+0.0470*(1-PD)} \qquad (6.4)$$

According to CP2, the risk weight for a three-year benchmark loan to a borrower having a probability of default, *PD*, and a 50% *LGD* is:

$$BRW_C(PD) = 976.5*N(1.118*G(PD)+1.288)*(1+0.0470*(1-PD)/PD^{0.44}) \qquad (6.5)$$

where

- $N(x)$ denotes the cumulative distribution function for a standard normal random variable, that is, the probability that a normal

random variable with mean zero and variance of one is less than or equal to x
- $G(z)$ denotes the inverse cumulative distribution function for a standard normal random variable, that is, the value x such that $N(x) = z$

Expression (6.5) is the product of three terms:

- $N(1.118*G(PD) + 1.288)$, which represents the sum of expected and unexpected losses associated with a hypothetical, infinitely granular portfolio of one-year loans having an LGD of 100%, using a so-called Merton credit model in which there is a single systematic risk factor and the values of the borrower's assets are assumed lognormally distributed. The coefficients in this expression are calibrated to a loss coverage target of 99.5% and an average asset return correlation of 20%.
- $(1 + 0.0470*(1 - PD)/PD^{0.44})$ is an adjustment to reflect that the maturity of the benchmark security is 3 years.
- The scaling factor 976.5 is calibrated so that the benchmark risk weight is exactly 100% for a PD of 0.7% and an LGD of 50%.

Numerical applications of the risk weight formula (6.2) and the comparison of the capital charges according to the various approaches are given later in sections headed "Comparison of the Standardized and the Foundation IRB Approaches" and "Comparison of the Internal Models Approach and the IRB Approach."

Results of the Second Quantitative Impact Study (QIS2)

As noted earlier, in April 2001, the Basel Committee initiated a Quantitative Impact Study (QIS2) in order to assess the impact of the new proposals for capital adequacy requirements. For the group of institutions representative of diversified, internationally active banks, the application of the standardized approach would generate a 6% increase in the capital requirement for credit risk only, relative to the current Accord. Apparently, the reduction in capital requirements for investment grade exposures relative to the 1988 Accord is outweighed by the higher risk weight of 150% for facilities rated below BB–, as well as the increased capital charge on short-term commitments.

The impact of the IRB foundation approach on regulatory capital for credit risk would be an increase of 14%. The IRB advanced approach, on the contrary, would lead to a reduction in regulatory capital attributed to credit risk of 5%.

Comparison of the Standardized and the Foundation
IRB Approaches

By applying formula (6.3) to loans issued by obligors of different credit standing and comparing the capital charge derived from the standardized

Table 6.2. Capital Charges According to the Standardized and Foundation IRB Approaches

		Standardized		Foundation	
S&P Rating	1-Year Historical Default Probability %	Risk Weight %	Capital Charge per $100 of Asset Value	Corporate BRW[a] Risk Weight %	IRB Capital Charge per $100 of Asset Value (LGD = 50%)	Foundation Capital Charge Divided by Standardized Capital Charge (Ratio)
AAA	0.01	20	1.6	7	0.56	0.35
AA	0.03	20	1.6	14	1.12	0.70
A	0.04	50	4.0	17	1.34	0.34
BBB	0.22	100	8.0	48	3.83	0.48
Benchmark	0.70	100	8.0	100	8.00	1.00
BB	0.98	100	8.0	123	9.87	1.23
B	5.30	150	12.0	342	27.40	2.28
CCC	21.94	150	12.0	694	(55.52)50[b]	4.17

[a]BRW = Benchmark Risk Weight
[b]The capital charge is capped to the maximum loss of 50
Note: Capital Charge for Standard and Poor's Rating Categories.
Source: Author.

approach (table 6.2), we find that for noninvestment-grade facilities, the foundation IRB approach charges more capital than the standardized approach; the reverse is true for investment-grade facilities. For example, a B-rated facility is charged 27.4% according to the foundation IRB approach, while it is charged only 12% under the standardized approach. For an A-rated loan, the capital charges are 1.34% and 4%, respectively. Both examples assume an *LGD* of 50%.

Table 6.2 shows a detailed comparison of the standardized and foundation IRB approaches. Figure 6.2 is the graphical representation of the results exhibited in table 6.2.

COMPARISON OF THE INTERNAL MODELS (IIF/ISDA) APPROACH AND THE IRB APPROACH

In 2000, the International Institute of Finance (IIF) and the International Swap and Derivatives Association (ISDA) conducted an experiment with six participating banks: Barclays, Chase, CSFB, CIBC, Dresdner, and J.P. Morgan. The purpose was to compare the economic capital charges according to the internal models used by the participating banks. All the currently available methodologies noted earlier—CreditMetrics and other proprietary models based on the credit migration framework, KMV, and CreditRisk+—were used among the different banks. To make the comparison meaningful,

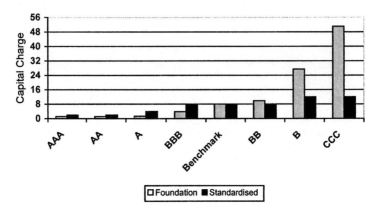

Figure 6.2. Capital Charges According to the Standardized and Foundation IRB Approaches. Source: Author.

the banks agreed on a benchmark portfolio of corporate bonds and loans, well diversified across industrial sectors, with obligors well distributed across the rating spectrum, and maturities from 6 months to 10 years. Input parameters were harmonized to make them consistent across models as much as possible.

The models were run at the 99.5% confidence level. The average results are summarized in table 6.3 for an *LGD* of 100%. The numbers in this grid are the relative capital weights for each facility by default probability bucket and maturity, relative to a benchmark security that is a **BBB** loan, whose default probability falls in the range 16.5–25.5 bp, with a three-year maturity. The average economic capital charge for this benchmark loan was 3.45%.

From this table it is easy to determine the capital charge for a loan of a given maturity and default probability. It is the product of the relative capital weight given in table 6.3, times 3.45%, times the *LGD*.[13] For example, the capital charge according to this grid for a 5-year loan in the benchmark portfolio with an *LGD* of 40%, issued by an obligor whose *PD* is 30 bp, is $CC = 1.68*3.45\%*0.40 = 2.32\%$. Applying formula (6.3), we can compare the capital charges according to the foundation IRB approach and the internal model (IIF/ISDA) approach shown in table 6.4. The capital charge corresponding to the current calibration of the foundation IRB approach is more than twice the average capital charge produced by internal models. The primary driver for this difference is the 1.5 multiplier embedded in formula (6.5).

Table 6.3. IIF/ISDA Relative Capital Weights at the 99.5% Confidence Level and 100% LGD

Prob.	Def.%	0.5 yr.	0.5–1 yr.	1–2 yr.	2–3 yr.	3–4 yr.	4–5 yr.	5–6 yr.	6–7 yr.	7–8 yr.	8–9 yr.	> 9 yr.
0.00	0.025	6	8	12	17	21	25	28	32	36	40	43
0.025	0.035	9	12	17	23	29	35	40	46	51	56	60
0.035	0.045	13	17	24	31	38	46	52	58	66	73	80
0.045	0.055	16	20	28	36	44	52	59	65	74	81	89
0.055	0.065	18	24	32	41	49	58	65	73	81	89	98
0.065	0.085	22	29	38	47	56	65	73	81	91	100	109
0.085	0.115	27	34	45	56	66	76	85	94	104	114	123
0.115	0.165	36	46	59	72	86	97	108	119	130	140	151
0.165	0.255	48	60	80	100	118	134	149	164	178	191	203
0.255	0.405	72	86	108	130	150	168	186	202	216	230	241
0.405	0.635	100	119	145	172	195	216	236	254	269	283	294
0.635	0.915	140	163	190	215	238	257	275	292	305	317	327
0.915	1.335	181	207	231	253	273	290	307	321	331	342	351
1.335	1.945	240	271	293	312	330	345	359	371	379	388	395
1.945	3.875	370	409	420	430	440	450	457	463	466	473	476
3.875	7.705	662	716	719	721	724	726	727	727	727	727	727
7.705	14.995	1083	1163	1164	1166	1166	1166	1166	1166	1166	1166	1166
14.995	20.000	1619	1718	1718	1718	1718	1718	1718	1718	1718	1718	1718

Note: 100 is set for a **BBB**-rated bond with a three-year duration, for which the capital charge is 3.45%. Weights are average values derived by 6 international banks (Barclays, Chase, CSFB, CIBC, Dresdner, and J. P. Morgan).

Source: Author's compilation based on data from IIF/ISDA (2000).

Table 6.4. Capital Charges at 99.5% Confidence Level:Foundation IRB and Internal Model (IIF/ISDA) Approaches Compared

S&P rating	1-Year Historical Default Probability %	*Foundation IRB* Corporate BRW Risk Weight[a] %	IRB Capital Charge per $100 of Asset Value (LGD = 50%)	*IIF/ISDA* Capital Charge[b] (LGD = 50%)	Foundation IRB Capital Charge divided by IIF/ISDA Capital Charge (Ratio)
AAA	0.01	7	0.56	0.22	2.5
AA	0.03	14	1.12	0.43	2.7
A	0.04	17	1.34	0.57	2.4
BBB	0.22	48	3.83	1.95	2.0
Benchmark	0.70	100	8.00	4.41	1.8
BB	0.98	123	9.87	5.34	1.8
B	5.30	342	27.40	17.74	1.5
CCC[c]	21.94	694	50.00	50.00	1.0

[a]BRW = Benchmark Risk Weight

[b]Capital charge for the internal models approach based on IIF/ISDA's Table 5.1—illustration for the case $PD = 0.7$:

Unexpected loss (UL) = LGD × (entry in table 5.1/100) × 3.45% × EAD = 50% × 2.15 × 3.45% = 3.71% × EAD

Expected loss (EL) = PD × EAD = 0.7% × EAD

Capital charge $(CC) = UL + EL = (3.71\% + 0.7\%)$ × EAD = 4.41% × EAD

[c]For the CCC facilities, the maximum charge is capped at the LGD for both the internal models and the IRB approaches.

Source: Author.

REVISED FOUNDATION IRB APPROACH—NOVEMBER 2001 PROPOSED MODIFICATIONS

During the consultative period that followed the release of CP2, the major international banks, through their advocacy groups, voiced their concern about the huge gap between the internal models and the IRB foundation approaches. The quantitative study (QIS2), published in November 2001, only corroborated the results illustrated in table 6.4.

The response of the Basel Committee was published in November 2001 in the form of potential modifications to the risk weight curve (BRW). It also differentiates $LGDs$ for various types of collateral and security (BCBS 2001b). The response reflects some of the industry feedbacks and additional research by the Committee's working group.

The new Benchmark Risk Weight (BRW) curve differs from the formula proposed in CP2 (see formulas 6.1 to 6.4) in several ways. First, it no longer contains the 1.5 scaling factor that was embedded in the original formula, but the loss coverage target has now been increased from the 99.5 to a 99.9% confidence level. Second, the new formula tries to accommodate both large corporations and middle-market firms or SMEs by making asset return correlations a function of *PD*. The new formula assumes that asset correlation declines with *PD*. It is the highest (20%) for the lowest *PD* values, assumed to characterize the largest obligors, and it is the lowest (10%) for the highest *PD* values, assumed to be more representative of commercial borrowers.[14] Third, there is a greater recognition of physical collateral and receivables.

The proposed calibration in CP3 is the same as in the revised November 2001 formula for large corporates (see later discussion). SMEs in CP3 benefit from a size adjustment that can lead to a reduction in capital of up to 20% compared to that for a similar large corporate exposure with the same *PD*.

Revised Calibration of the IRB Approach

The modified Benchmark Risk Weight function, *BRW*, is:[15]

$$BRW_C = 12.5*LGD*M*N\left[(1-R)^{-0.5}*G(PD)+\left(\frac{R}{1-R}\right)^{0.5}*G(0.999)\right]$$
(6.6)

where the maturity adjustment factor, M, is the same as in the January 2001 proposal and reflects that the maturity of the benchmark security is three years:

$$M = 1 + 0.047\left(\frac{1-PD}{PD^{0.44}}\right)$$
(6.7)

and the correlation function, R, ranging from 0.20 for the lowest PD value to 0.10 for the highest *PD* value, is:

$$R = 0.10\left(\frac{1-e^{-50PD}}{1-e^{-50}}\right)+0.20\left(1-\frac{1-e^{-50PD}}{1-e^{-50}}\right)$$
(6.8)

The risk-weighted assets, RW, is:

$$RW = \frac{LGD}{50}*BRW$$
(6.9)

where $LGD = 75\%$ for a subordinated loan; $LGD = 50\%$ for an unsecured loan; $LGD = 45\%$ for a loan fully secured by physical, non-real-estate collateral; and $LGD = 40\%$ for a loan fully secured by receivables.

Table 6.5 illustrates the capital requirements that would apply for a senior unsecured loan ($LGD = 50\%$), using both the CP2 formula (6.1 to 6.4) and the November 2001 modified risk formula (6.6 to 6.7). Table 6.5 also shows the capital attribution from internal models according to the IIF/ISDA table produced for a confidence level of 99.9%.[16]

From table 6.5 it appears that the capital charge for investment grade facilities is higher under the modified November proposal. But the ratio of the capital charges from the modified IRB approach and the internal models approach, as proposed by IIF/ISDA, remains approximately the same.

Table 6.5. Capital Charges at 99.9% Confidence Level:Foundation IRB (Modified November 2001) and Internal Model (IIF/ISDA) Approaches Compared

		Foundation IRB		IIF/ISDA	
S&P rating	1-Year Historical Default Probability %	Corporate BRW Risk Weight[a] %	IRB capital Charge per $100 of Asset Value (LGD = 50%)	Capital Charge[b] (LGD = 50%)	Foundation IRB Capital charge divided by IIF/ISDA Capital Charge (Ratio)
AAA	0.01	10 (7)	0.83	0.33	2.5
AA	0.03	18 (14)	1.45	0.57	2.5
A	0.04	21 (17)	1.68	0.74	2.3
BBB	0.22	50 (48)	4.00	2.49	1.6
Benchmark	0.70	86 (100)	6.88	5.40	1.3
BB	0.98	99 (123)	7.90	6.46	1.2
B	5.30	190 (342)	15.20	21.75	0.7
CCC[3]	21.94	392 (694)	31.30	50.00	0.6

[a]In parentheses are the BRWs from the initial foundation IRB proposed in January 2001 (see table 6.4)
[b]The IIF/ISDA table derived at the 99.9% confidence level is not shown here.
Source: Author.

Indeed, the increase in capital in the modified IRB proposal is compensated for by approximately the same proportional increase in capital under the internal models approach as the confidence level increases from 99.5 to 99.9%.

There is a substantial decrease in capital for subinvestment grade facilities under the modified IRB proposal. In addition, the ratio of the capital charges from the IRB and the internal models approaches is dramatically reduced. For facilities rated BB– and below, this ratio becomes less than one, that is, the capital charge from the modified IRB approach is less than the capital attribution from the internal models approach.

Results of the Third Quantitative Impact Study (QIS3)

The new calibration proposed by the Basel Committee in November 2001 and published in April 2003 creates a greater incentive to follow it with the following average percentage changes in capital requirements from Basel I:

Standardized approach: 0% (+11% overall, with operational risk),
IRB foundation approach: −7% (+3% overall, with operational risk), and
IRB advanced approach: −13% (−2% overall, with operational risk)

For banks that adopt the advanced IRB approach, there should be on average a slight reduction in total capital, including the new capital charge for operational risk, compared with the current situation.

THE INTERNAL MODELS FOR CREDIT RISK—OVERVIEW
AND MODELS COMPARISON

Over the past few years, a number of new approaches to credit portfolio modeling have been made public. Among others, we discuss here the ones used in the IIF/ISDA study. CreditMetrics from J.P. Morgan, first published in 1997, is based on the analysis of credit migration, that is, the probability of moving from one credit quality to another, including default, within a given time horizon (often arbitrarily taken to be one year). CreditMetrics models the full forward distribution of the values of any bond or loan portfolio, say one year forward, where the changes in values are related to credit migration only; interest rates are assumed to evolve in a deterministic fashion.

The credit VaR of a portfolio is then derived in a similar fashion as for market risk. It is the value on the cumulative distribution of the future value of the portfolio such that the probability of being below it is set in advance, for example, 1%. The required capital is the distance from the mean of the forward distribution to the VaR at the desired confidence level. (This definition applies to all credit risk models and is independent of the underlying theoretical framework.)

Tom Wilson (1997a, 1997b) proposes an improvement to the credit migration approach by allowing default probabilities to vary with the credit cycle. In this approach, default probabilities are a function of macrovariables such as unemployment, the level of interest rates, the growth rate in the economy, government expenses, and foreign exchange rates. These macrovariables are the factors that, to a large extent, drive credit cycles.

Over the past few years, KMV Corporation, a firm that specializes in credit risk analysis, has developed a credit risk methodology and an extensive database to assess default probabilities and the loss distribution related to both default and migration risks. KMV's methodology differs from CreditMetrics in that it relies upon the expected default frequency, or *EDF*, for each issuer, rather than upon the average historical transition frequencies produced by the rating agencies for each credit class. The KMV approach is based on the contingent claim approach for the valuation of corporate debt, originally proposed by Merton (1974); the main difference is the simplifying assumptions required to facilitate the model's implementation. It remains to be seen whether these compromises prevent the model from capturing the real complexity of credit (Vasicek 1997).

At the end of 1997, Credit Suisse Financial Products (CSFP) released an approach, CreditRisk+, that is based on actuarial science and that focuses on default alone rather than on credit migration. CreditRisk+ assumes that the dynamics of default for individual bonds or loans follows a Poisson process.

Finally, the "reduced form" approach, currently the foundation of credit derivatives pricing models, is not reviewed in this chapter, since we are not aware of any existing commercial application based on this framework that is actively used by financial institutions. These models allow one to derive the term structure of default probabilities from credit spreads, while assuming an exogenous and somewhat arbitrary recovery rate.[17]

Table 6.6 summarizes the key features of all the models mentioned here. The key input parameters common to all are credit exposures, recovery rates (or, equivalently, the "loss given default"), and default correlations. Default correlations are listed in the row entitled "Correlation of credit events." They are captured in a variety of ways. KMV derives default correlations from asset returns correlations; CreditMetrics relies on a similar model but employs equity returns correlations as a proxy for asset returns, which are not directly observable. In the other models, the default probabilities are conditional on common systemic or macro factors. Any change in these factors affects all the probabilities of default, but to a different degree, depending on the sensitivity of each obligor to each risk factor.[18]

The current state of the art does not allow for the full integration of market and credit risk. Market risk models disregard credit risk, and credit risk models assume that credit exposures are determined exogenously. The next generation of credit models should remedy this.

In the appendix we review the framework, the strengths, and the limitations of the three most common credit portfolio models used by banks to measure and manage their credit risk exposure: CreditMetrics, KMV, and CreditRisk+. In this section, we compare CreditMetrics, KMV, and Credit Risk+ by applying them to the same benchmark bond/loan portfolio diversified across all rating categories; the assumptions for each application have been kept consistent as much as possible. The results show that the models produce similar estimates of value-at-risk.

Portfolio Specifications and Input Parameters

In order to facilitate the comparison of the results across models, and between the different models and the standardized and IRB approaches, we have kept the benchmark portfolio small. We created a hypothetical portfolio composed of 22 bonds, or loans, diversified across all rating categories.[19] There are two facilities for each of the 11 rating categories. All facilities are zero-coupon bonds with:

- A notional value of $1m
- A stochastic *LGD* with a mean of 50% and a standard deviation of 25%
- A maturity of one year and three years depending on the simulations

Obligors are real names diversified across various industry sectors. In order to match parameters as closely as possible between CreditMetrics and KMV, we used the same correlation matrix for both models.[20]

Default Probabilities and Current EDFs for KMV

Table 6.7 gives the default probabilities for each rating grade. Investment-grade obligors are rated 1 to 5, and ratings 7 to 11 are attributed to sub-investment-grade borrowers. The column "standard deviation" shows the

Table 6.6. Key Features of Credit Risk Models

Characteristic	Credit migration approach		Contingent claim approach	Actuarial approach	Reduced-form approach
	CreditMetrics	*CreditPortfolio View*	*KMV*	*CreditRisk+*	*Kamakura*
Software					
Definition of risk	Δ Market value	Δ Market Value	Δ Market value	Default losses	Default losses
Credit events	Downgrade/default	Downgrade/default	Δ Continuous default probabilities (EDFs)	Δ Actuarial default rate	Δ Default intensity
Risk drivers	Asset values	Macrofactors	Asset values	Expected default rates	Hazard rate
Transition probabilities	Constant	Driven by macro factors	Driven by: • Individual term structure of EDF • Asset value process	N/A	N/A
Correlation of credit events	Standard multivariate normal distribution (equity-factor model)	Conditional default probabilities function of macrofactors	Standard multivariate normal asset returns (asset factor model)	Conditional default probabilities function of common risk factors	Conditional default probabilities function of macrofactors
Recovery rates	Random (beta distribution)	Random (empirical distribution)	Random (beta distribution)	Loss given default deterministic	Loss given default deterministic
Interest rates	Constant[a]	Constant	Constant	Constant	Stochastic
Numerical approach	Simulation/analytic Econometric	Simulation Econometric	Analytic/simulation Econometric	Analytic	Tree-based/simulation Econometric

[a]See Vasicek (1997).
Note: Delta = change in.
Source: Author.

Table 6.7. Credit Ratings and Default Rates

	Credit Rating	S&P Equivalent	Default Rate Mean (%)	Default Rate Standard Deviation (%)
Investment grade	1	AAA	0.01	0.00
	2	AA	0.02	0.01
	3	A	0.08	0.04
	4	BBB	0.24	0.12
	5	BBB−	0.54	0.27
	6	BB	1.14	0.57
Subinvestment grade	7	BB−	2.07	1.03
	8	B	3.92	1.96
	9	B−	7.00	3.50
	10	CCC	13.70	6.85
	11	CCC−	29.40	14.68
		Default	100	N/A

Source: Author.

volatility of the default probabilities: for example, 50% of the mean default probability, when CreditRisk+ is run with stochastic default rates. Default rates are assumed to be stochastic only in CreditRisk+. These default probabilities are common to all three models.

Transition Matrix

Table 6.8 shows the transition matrix used in CreditMetrics to determine rating changes. There is migration risk only when models are run with facilities with more than one-year maturity. When the facilities have a one-year term, their terminal value at the one-year horizon is either the nominal value (i.e., $1 million) or LGD * Nominal value (i.e., $0.5 million) if the obligor defaults. (See appendix for a description of credit migration as used by CreditMetrics.)

Valuation Methodologies

The valuation of facilities in CreditMetrics is based on yield curves, using zero-coupon spot curves at current time and forward zero-coupon curves at the credit horizon, say one year. Table 6.9 shows the spot zero-coupon curves used in CreditMetrics for each rating category.

KMV uses a different valuation technique, called "risk comparable valuation," or RCV, which is based on the risk-neutral valuation framework. The term "structure of risk-neutral EDFs" is derived from the current EDF and the term structure of credit spreads at the credit horizon.

CreditRisk+ is a pure actuarial model with no endogenous valuation. The value of the facility at the credit horizon is an input to the model. It is

Table 6.8. Transition Matrix—One-Year Horizon

Initial
Rating Rating at Year End (%)

	1	2	3	4	5	>6	7	8	9	10	11	D
1	87.70	12.06	0.24	0	0	0	0	0	0	0	0	0.01
2	0.50	89.57	9.71	0.14	0.07	0	0	0	0	0	0	0.02
3	0.04	1.89	92.30	3.38	1.69	0.39	0.19	0.03	0.01	0	0	0.08
4	0.02	0.20	5.32	86.00	3.20	2.99	1.49	0.32	0.16	0.07	0	0.24
5	0.11	0.25	3.84	4.18	82.47	3.01	1.50	2.14	1.07	0.80	0.08	0.54
6	0.29	0.34	0.87	1.52	3.05	76.33	5.25	5.79	2.89	2.27	0.25	1.14
7	0.32	0.40	0.87	1.26	2.51	6.96	70.14	7.48	3.74	3.88	3.70	2.07
8	0.38	0.52	0.87	0.72	1.44	5.44	10.87	59.37	8.75	7.11	0.61	3.92
9	0.35	0.48	0.71	0.60	1.19	4.35	8.69	10.70	54.43	10.02	1.48	7.00
10	0.28	0.39	0.39	0.35	0.71	2.15	4.29	5.26	10.52	58.75	3.22	13.69
11	0.35	0.17	0.52	0.23	0.46	1.15	2.30	2.53	5.07	9.84	48.02	29.36
D	0	0	0	0	0	0	0	0	0	0	0	100.00

Source: Author.

either *EAD*, if there is no default, or *EAD* * *LGD* if the obligor defaults. The *EAD* for each facility in all three models is set to the mark-to-market value at the credit horizon.

Credit Horizon

The credit horizon is assumed to be one year in all cases.

Capital Attributions Under the Standardized and IRB Approaches

The capital attributions to the reference portfolio under the standardized approach and the IRB approaches—the January 2001 (IRB-Jan) proposal

Table 6.9. Zero-Coupon Credit Curves

Term   Credit Rating

	1	2	3	4	5	6	7	8	9	10	11
1	6.8	6.8	7.0	7.3	7.5	8.0	8.8	9.5	11.8	13.2	19.7
2	6.8	6.8	7.1	7.3	7.5	8.2	9.2	9.7	12.0	13.4	20.0
3	6.8	6.9	7.1	7.4	7.6	8.4	9.4	9.9	12.2	13.6	20.4
5	6.9	7.0	7.3	7.6	7.8	8.5	9.5	10.3	12.6	14.0	21.2
7	6.9	7.1	7.4	7.7	8.0	9.0	9.7	10.5	12.8	14.2	21.5
10	7.0	7.3	7.9	8.1	8.4	9.5	11.2	12.1	14.4	15.8	24.6
15	7.0	7.3	7.8	8.1	8.4	9.8	11.6	12.5	14.8	16.2	25.4
20	7.0	7.3	7.9	8.2	8.5	10.1	12.3	13.4	15.7	17.1	27.1
30	7.1	7.4	7.9	8.4	8.8	11.6	16.6	20.3	22.6	24.0	40.9

Source: Author.

and the revised November 2001 (IRB-Nov) formula—are presented in table 6.10.

Comments similar to our observations when analyzing the results of tables 6.4 and 6.5 apply here. First, the capital charge for investment-grade facilities is much higher under the standardized approach (4.6%) than under the IRB approaches, which come to 2.8% for IRB-Jan and 2.9% for IRB-Nov. On average, the standardized approach is 60% more onerous than the IRB approaches. When comparing the capital attribution of IRB-Jan and IRB-Nov, we observe that under IRB-Nov, the higher capital charge to the obligors with the highest credit quality is compensated for by the lower capital charge to obligors rated BBB–. If we eliminate the exposures rated BBB–, then the capital charges become 3.8% under the standardized approach and 1.3% and 2.1% under the IRB-Jan and IRB-Nov, respectively.

Second, for subinvestment-grade facilities and contrary to investment-grade facilities, the standardized approach appears much less onerous (9.7%) than the IRB approaches, which are 29.5% for the IRB-Jan and 18.3% for the IRB-Nov. The IRB-Nov formula produces, on average, capital attributions 40% lower than the original IRB-Jan.

Capital Attributions Under the Internal Models

CreditMetrics, KMV, and CreditRisk+ were applied using the assumption that all facilities had the same maturity of either one year or three years. The simulation with one-year facilities was designed to assess the impact on capital allocations of structural differences in the modeling of credit risk across models. To conduct a fair comparison of internal models with the regulatory approaches, we also ran the credit models with three-year facilities, three years being the average maturity assumed in the IRB foundation approach.

To be consistent with the definition of capital in the new Basel Accord, the capital charge (CC) to any facility and at the portfolio level is the sum of the expected loss (EL) and unexpected loss (UL):

$$CC = EL + UL \tag{6.10}$$

In our implementation of CreditMetrics and KMV, we applied the same methodology for capital attribution at the facility level. The EL is calculated as:

$$EL = E(V_H/ND) - E(V_H) \tag{6.11}$$

where:

- V_H denotes the value of the portfolio, or any facility, at the credit horizon, H, say one year in our numerical applications
- $E(V_H/ND)$ is the expected value of the portfolio, or facility, at the credit horizon, conditional on no default
- $E(V_H)$ is the unconditional value of the portfolio, or facility, at the credit horizon

Table 6.10. Capital Attributions Under the Standardized and the IRB Approaches

S&P Equivalent	Internal Rating	Default Probability (%)	Exposure ($)	Standardized Approach (%)	($)	IRB-Jan (%)	($)	IRB-Nov (%)	($)
AAA	1	0.01	2 MM	1.6	32,000	0.4	8,000	0.6	12,000
AA	2	0.02	2 MM	1.6	32,000	0.9	18,000	1.2	23,600
A	3	0.08	2 MM	4.0	80,000	2.0	40,000	2.4	48,000
BBB	4	0.24	2 MM	8.0	160,000	4.0	80,000	4.2	84,000
BBB–	5	0.54	2 MM	8.0	160,000	6.8	136,000	6.2	123,000
Investment-Grade Portfolio				4.6	464,000	2.8	282,000	2.9	290,600
BB	6	1.14	2 MM	8.0	160,000	10.9	213,000	8.4	167,400
BB–	7	2.07	2 MM	8.0	160,000	15.8	316,000	10.4	208,000
B	8	3.92	2 MM	12.0	240,000	23.0	460,000	13.3	265,200
B–	9	7.00	2 MM	12.0	240,000	32.0	640,000	17.4	347,600
CCC	10	13.70	2 MM	12.0	240,000	45.1	902,000	24.8	495,200
CCC–	11	29.40	2 MM	12.0	240,000	50.0	1,000,000	35.8	715,400
Subinvestment-Grade Portfolio				9.7	1,160,000	29.5	3,536,000	18.3	2,198,800
Total Portfolio				7.4	1,624,000	17.3	3,818,000	11.3	2,489,400

Source: Author.

For a portfolio of securities, UL is defined as the distance to the unconditional mean—$E(V_H)$—from the percentile of the distribution of the portfolio values at the credit horizon, derived at the specified confidence level.[21] For each facility, UL is defined as the risk contribution of the facility to the overall risk of the portfolio, taking into account the default correlation structure. The risk contribution, UL_i, of a facility, i, is defined as:[22]

$$UL_i = \frac{UL_P}{\sigma_P}\frac{\partial \sigma_P}{\partial w_i} = \frac{UL_P}{\sigma_P}\frac{\text{cov}(V_{i,H},P_H)}{\sigma_P} \qquad (6.12)$$

where:

- UL_P denotes the unexpected loss for the portfolio
- σ_P is the standard deviation of the distribution of the portfolio values at the credit horizon
- w_i is the weight of facility i in portfolio P
- $\frac{\partial \sigma_P}{\partial w_i}$ is the delta standard deviation of facility i and is measured as the effect of adding a small amount of facility i on the standard deviation σ_P of the portfolio. It satisfies the property:

$$\sum_i \frac{\partial \sigma_P}{\partial w_i} = \sigma_P \qquad (6.13)$$

- $\text{cov}(V_{i,H},P_H)$ denotes the covariance of the value of the facility i, $V_{i,H}$, with the value P_H of the portfolio at the credit horizon, H. It follows from expressions (6.12) and (6.13) that the sum of the risk contributions of all the facilities is equal to the unexpected loss for the portfolio.[23]

In CreditRisk+, expected loss, EL, is simply defined as the product of the default probability, PD, and the exposure at risk, $EAD * LGD$. The risk contribution for each facility is defined in a similar fashion as described earlier, although it already contains the expected loss component and, therefore, does not need to be adjusted to derive the capital charge. (See Credit Suisse 1997, p. 53.)

Parameters are most closely matched with the one-year credit horizon when all facilities have a one-year maturity. For this case, we also assume that all obligors are uncorrelated, there is no uncertainty on LGDs (standard deviation is set to zero), and default probabilities are constant in Credit Risk+. This is equivalent to running CreditMetrics and KMV in a pure default mode, with no migration risk, so that they can best be compared with CreditRisk+, which is a pure default model. The simulation results are shown in table 6.11.

The models were run at the 99%, 99.5%, and 99.9% confidence levels. For investment-grade facilities, the results are quite similar across models. For subinvestment-grade facilities, results are quite close for both CreditMetrics and KMV but differ substantially for Credit Risk+. CreditRisk+ attributes more capital than the other models to subinvestment-grade facilities at the 99.5% and the 99.9% confidence level. The difference between

Table 6.11. Capital Attributions Under the Internal Models (1-year facilities)

	CreditMetrics			KMV			CreditRisk+		
Confidence Level	99.00	99.50	99.90	99.00	99.50	99.90	99.00	99.50	99.90
Portfolio	9.10	9.20	11.40	8.60	8.70	10.80	9.10	11.40	13.60
Facility Rating									
1	0.02	0.02	0.02	0.01	0.01	0.02	0.02	0.02	0.03
2	0.04	0.04	0.05	0.04	0.04	0.05	0.03	0.04	0.05
3	0.16	0.16	0.20	0.15	0.15	0.19	0.14	0.17	0.21
4	0.48	0.49	0.61	0.46	0.46	0.58	0.41	0.52	0.62
5	1.09	1.12	1.37	1.02	1.04	1.29	0.93	1.16	1.40
6	2.30	2.40	2.90	2.20	2.20	2.70	2.00	2.50	3.00
7	4.10	4.30	5.20	3.90	3.90	4.90	3.60	4.50	5.30
8	7.70	7.90	9.70	7.20	7.40	9.10	6.80	8.40	10.10
9	13.40	13.90	16.80	12.60	12.80	15.90	12.10	15.00	18.10
10	24.70	25.20	31.00	23.40	23.80	29.40	23.60	29.40	35.30
11	46.10	46.90	57.20	43.70	44.30	54.10	50.60	63.10	75.80

Source: Author.

Credit Risk+ and the other models tends to increase with the default probability (DP). The reason for this discrepency is technical and relates to the simplification made in CreditRisk+ where $\log(1 + DP)$ is approximated by DP. This approximation is legitimate only for investment-grade facilities characterized by low default probabilities. But, for high default probabilities, the model overestimates risk.[24]

Table 6.12 shows the results when all the facilities have three-year maturities. For these simulations we assume stochastic LGDs, stochastic default probabilities in CreditRisk+, and correlated asset returns, that is, correlated default events.

Results for CreditMetrics and KMV are relatively close, except for very-high-default-probability facilities (rated 10 and 11), for which CreditMetrics allocates more capital than KMV. The difference between CreditMetrics and KMV for facilities rated 10 and 11 comes from the following technical feature in KMV: KMV caps the unexpected loss to $LGD*EAD$ at 50% of the mark-to-market value. When the unconstrained capital allocation is greater than 50%, then the truncated amount is allocated back to the rest of the facilities.

Capital charges are higher for three-year facilities (table 6.12) than for one-year facilities (table 6.11). This is due to credit migration risk that is captured by both models, which produces an additional capital charge to the one relative to pure default risk.[25]

CreditRisk+ produces results for three-year facilities that are similar to those produced in table 6.11 with one-year facilities. The capital charges are slightly higher in table 6.12 as we assume stochastic default probabilities, except for low-rated facilities (ratings 9, 10, and 11). As a consequence,

Table 6.12. Capital Attributions Under the Internal Models (3-year facilities)

	CreditMetrics			KMV			CreditRisk+		
Confidence Level	99.00	99.50	99.90	99.00	99.50	99.90	99.00	99.50	99.90
Portfolio	12.00	13.80	17.70	10.60	12.20	15.30	8.30	9.90	11.90
Facility Rating									
1	0.13	0.15	0.19	0.31	0.37	0.49	0.02	0.02	0.03
2	0.28	0.33	0.43	0.44	0.54	0.72	0.04	0.05	0.06
3	0.61	0.71	0.93	0.94	1.13	1.51	0.16	0.19	0.23
4	1.55	1.81	2.36	1.76	2.11	2.81	0.48	0.57	0.69
5	3.34	3.88	5.08	3.71	4.45	5.91	1.08	1.29	1.55
6	5.80	6.70	8.70	6.20	7.40	9.80	2.30	2.70	3.20
7	9.10	10.60	13.70	10.30	12.30	16.30	3.90	4.70	5.60
8	12.90	14.80	19.10	12.90	15.30	20.00	7.20	8.60	10.40
9	21.00	24.10	31.10	21.40	25.30	33.20	12.30	14.60	17.60
10	30.50	35.00	44.60	27.40	32.20	34.70	23.00	27.30	32.80
11	47.30	53.90	68.20	31.20	33.30	43.20	41.30	49.00	58.50

Source: Author.

except for junk loans (rating 11), the capital charges under CreditRisk + are much lower than those produced under CreditMetrics and KMV. This is a result of the fact that CreditRisk+ is a pure default model that does not capture migration risk.

Table 6.13 gives a high-level summary of the differences between the capital attributions under the standardized approach, the revised IRB approach, and the three internal models. In the following discussion, we eliminate CreditRisk+ from the comparison since its results are dramatically different from those for the other two models. In order to match assumptions as closely as possible between the regulatory approaches and the internal models, CreditMetrics and KMV are run at the 99.9% confidence level, which corresponds to the confidence level in the revised IRB formula; the maturity of all facilities is three years. As a general conclusion, the capital attribution of the regulatory approaches for investment-grade facilities is too high compared with the internal models, especially for the standardized approach.

The opposite is true for subinvestment-grade facilities, where the internal models are more onerous than the regulatory models. In particular, the standardized approach attributes a far-too-low capital charge compared with both the revised IRB approach and the internal models. The capital charges from all the various approaches are relatively close only for BB–rated facilities.

It is clear from these conclusions that regulatory arbitrage prevails as long as banks have incentives, as under the current 1988 Accord, to shed their high-quality assets through loan sales and securitization and to keep on their balance sheet the more risky loans for which regulatory capital underestimates the actual economic risk.

Table 6.13. Summary Comparison of Capital Attributions Under the New Basel Accord and the Internal Models

			Standardized Approach (%)	IRB Nov (%)	CreditMetrics 99.9 (%)	KMV 99.9 (%)	CreditRisk+ 99.9%
	Portfolio		7.4	11.3	17.7	15.3	11.9
Facility Rating							
S&P Equivalent	*Internal Rating*	*Default Probability*					
AAA	1	0.01	1.6	0.6	0.2	0.5	0.03
AA	2	0.02	1.6	1.2	0.4	0.7	0.06
A	3	0.08	4.0	2.4	0.9	1.5	0.2
BBB	4	0.24	8.0	4.2	2.4	2.8	0.7
BBB–	5	0.54	8.0	6.2	5.1	5.9	1.6
Investment-Grade Portfolio			4.6	2.9	1.8	2.3	0.5
BB	6	1.14	8.0	8.4	8.7	9.8	3.2
BB–	7	2.07	8.0	10.4	13.7	16.3	5.6
B	8	3.92	12.0	13.3	19.1	20.0	10.4
B–	9	7.00	12.0	17.4	31.1	33.2	17.6
CCC	10	13.70	12.0	24.8	44.6	34.7	32.8
CCC–	11	29.40	12.0	35.8	68.2	43.2	58.5
Subinvestment-Grade Portfolio			9.7	18.3	30.9	26.2	21.4

Source: Author.

IMPLEMENTATION OF INTERNAL MODELS AND VALIDATION ISSUES

Some practitioners are concerned about applying credit risk models to nontraded loans because of the scarcity of data on their default frequencies and recovery rates (and the lack of good spread data). (Such data already exist for corporate bonds and loans, at least for the United States and Canada.) The major international banks are currently making real efforts to collect data, and, at an industry level, projects are under way to pool data regarding default, losses, and recovery rates by asset classes.

For their middle-market portfolios, banks should rely on their internal rating system rather than external ratings, since it is hard to compare small nonpublic firms with large public firms. Middle-market loan portfolios are specific to each bank, and banks often have better information on their borrowers than do the rating agencies.

The use of credit models for allocating bank economic capital should be the first step in improving capital allocation for credit risk. Banks have to convince the regulators that they trust their models enough to use them to manage their loan portfolios before there is a real chance their internal models will be approved for regulatory capital calculations for the banking book.

Credit models are hard to validate because default is a rare event. The direct testing of any credit risk methodology imposes an impossible demand on the available data.[26] This does not mean, however, that models cannot be tested at all.

First, models can be tested against cumulative credit profit and losses (P&L). This requires banks to record P&L separately for market and credit risks, which is a daunting task. A more realistic alternative is to use the "static P&L" methodology to disentangle the portion of the P&L that is related to market and credit risk. To this end, at the end of the previous day we can determine the "theoretical" market risk P&L that applies to the end-of-previous-day portfolio on the basis of observed changes in market factors. Assuming that the position remains constant over the next day, we can determine the change in the value of the position from the change in the value of the market risk factors. This gives a proxy for the P&L that is related strictly to market risk. Taking the difference between the observed P&L and the theoretical P&L related to market risk produces a proxy for the credit risk–related P&L. This proxy is good only when the portfolio remains stable from one day to the next.[27]

Second, if direct testing is impossible, it is worth exploring indirect testing. That is, the model input, as opposed to the output, can be validated. For instance, the accuracy of the default rates fed into the model can be tested. Default prediction models have been around for at least 30 years. These models incorporate accounting and market data in order to predict default events.

Internal credit rating methodologies developed for the middle market can be tested in the same way as default prediction models. A similar comment applies to credit card portfolios. It should also be noted that repeated sampling using replacement methodologies can help overcome the problem of insufficient data. Lopez and Saidenberg (1999) propose a backtesting methodology based on cross-sectional simulation. Specifically, models are evaluated not only for their forecasts over time but also in terms of their forecasts at a given point in time for simulated portfolios. The problem with this approach is that the statistical test used to assess the quality of the expected loss forecasts is not powerful (Crnkovic and Drachman 1996). Finally, it might be argued that a more appropriate test of a credit risk model is a stress test, or sensitivity analysis, that identifies those areas where the model may be more likely to generate inappropriate results.

APPENDIX: INTERNAL MODELS FOR CREDIT RISK: FRAMEWORK, STRENGTHS, AND LIMITATIONS

THE CREDIT MIGRATION APPROACH TO MEASURING CREDIT RISK—CREDITMETRICS

CreditMetrics is a methodology that is based on the estimation of the forward distribution of changes in the value of a portfolio of loan- and bond-type products at a given time horizon, usually one year.[28] The changes in value are related to the migration, upward and downward, of the credit quality of the obligor, as well as to default.

In comparison to market VaR, credit VaR poses three challenges. First, the portfolio distribution is far from being a normal distribution. Second, measuring the portfolio effect due to diversification is much more complex than for market risk. Third, the information on loans is not as complete as it is for traded instruments such as bonds.

While it may be reasonable to assume that changes in portfolio values are normally distributed when due to market risk, credit returns are by their nature highly skewed and fat-tailed (figure 6.3). An improvement in credit quality brings limited "upside" to an investor, while downgrades or defaults bring with them substantial "downsides." Unlike market VaR, the percentile levels of the distribution cannot be estimated from the mean and variance only. The calculation of VaR for credit risk thus demands a simulation of the full distribution of the changes in the value of the portfolio.

To measure the effect of portfolio diversification, we need to estimate the correlations in credit quality changes for all pairs of obligors. However, these correlations are not directly observable. CreditMetrics bases its evaluation on the joint probability of equity returns. This entails making some strong simplifying assumptions about the capital structure of the obligor and about the process that is generating equity returns. We elaborate on this key feature of the model later on.

Finally, CreditMetrics, like KMV and CreditRisk+, makes no provision for market risk; forward values and exposures are derived from deterministic

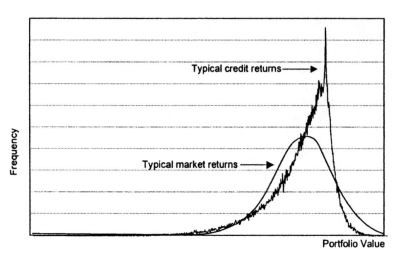

Figure 6.3. Comparison of the Probability Distributions of Credit Returns and Market Returns. Source: Author.

forward curves. The only uncertainty in CreditMetrics relates to credit migration, that is, the process of moving up or down the credit spectrum.

Credit VaR for a Bond

The first step is to specify a rating system, with rating categories, together with the probabilities of migrating from one credit quality to another over the credit risk horizon.

This transition matrix is the key component of the credit VaR model proposed by J.P. Morgan. The matrix may take the form of the rating system of Moody's or Standard & Poor's, or it might be based on the proprietary rating system internal to the bank. A strong assumption made by Credit-Metrics is that all issuers within the same rating class are homogeneous credit risks. They have the same transition probabilities and the same default probability. (KMV departs from CreditMetrics in the sense that in KMV's framework each issuer is specific and is characterized by its own asset returns distribution, its own capital structure, and its own default probability.)

Second, the risk horizon should be specified. This is usually taken to be one year. When one is concerned about the risk profile over a longer period of time, as for long-dated illiquid instruments, multiple horizons can be chosen, such as 1 to 10 years.

The third step consists of specifying the forward discount curve at the risk horizon(s) for each credit category. In the case of default, the value of the instrument should be estimated in terms of the "recovery rate," which is given as a percentage of face value, or "par." In the final step, this information is translated into the forward distribution of the changes in the portfolio value consecutive to credit migration.

Step 1: Specify the Transition Matrix

The rating categories, as well as the transition matrix, are chosen from an external or internal rating system (table 6.14).

In the case of Standard & Poor's, there are seven rating categories. The highest credit is AAA, the lowest, CCC. Default is defined as a situation in which the obligor cannot make a payment related to a bond or a loan obligation, whether the payment is a coupon payment or the redemption of the principal. "Pari passu" clauses are such that when an obligor defaults on one payment related to a bond or a loan, the obligor is technically declared in default on all debt obligations.

The bond issuer in our example currently has a BBB rating. Table 6.14 shows the probability, as estimated by Standard & Poor's, that this BBB issuer will migrate over a period of one year to any one of the eight possible states, including default. Obviously, the most probable situation is that the obligor will remain in the same rating category, that is, BBB; this has a probability of 86.93%. The probability of the issuer's defaulting within one year is only 0.18%, while the probability of its being upgraded to AAA is also very small, 0.02%. Such a transition matrix is produced by the rating agencies for all initial ratings and is based on the history of credit events that have occurred to the firms rated by those agencies. (Default is taken to be an "absorbing state;" that is when an issuer is in default, it stays in default.)

Moody's publishes similar information. The probabilities published by the agencies are based on more than 20 years of data across all industries. Obviously, these data should be interpreted with care, since they represent average statistics across a heterogeneous sample of firms and over several business cycles. For this reason, many banks prefer to rely on their own statistics, which relate more closely to the composition of their loan and bond portfolios.

Table 6.14. Transition Matrix: Probabilities of Credit Rating Migrating from One Rating Quality to Another Within One Year

Initial Rating	Rating at year-end (%)							
	AAA	AA	A	BBB	BB	B	CCC	Default
AAA	90.81	8.33	0.68	0.06	0.12	0	0	0
AA	0.70	90.65	7.79	0.64	0.06	0.14	0.02	0
A	0.09	2.27	91.05	5.52	0.74	0.26	0.01	0.06
BBB	0.02	0.33	5.95	86.93	5.30	1.17	1.12	0.18
BB	0.03	0.14	0.67	7.73	80.53	8.84	1.00	1.06
B	0	0.11	0.24	0.43	6.48	83.46	4.07	5.20
CCC	0.22	0	0.22	1.30	2.38	11.24	64.86	19.79

Source: Standard & Poor's (1996).

Table 6.15. One-Year Forward Zero-Curves for Each Credit Rating (%)

Category	Year 1	Year 2	Year 3	Year 4
AAA	3.60	4.17	4.73	5.12
AA	3.65	4.22	4.78	5.17
A	3.72	4.32	4.93	5.32
BBB	4.10	4.67	5.25	5.63
BB	5.55	6.02	6.78	7.27
B	6.05	7.02	8.03	8.52
CCC	15.05	15.02	14.03	13.52

Source: CreditMetrics (1997).

Step 2: Specify the Credit Risk Horizon

The risk horizon is usually set at one year and is consistent with the transition matrix shown in table 6.14. But this horizon is arbitrary and is dictated mostly by the availability of the accounting data and the financial reports processed by the rating agencies. In KMV's framework, which relies on market data, as well as on accounting data, any horizon can be chosen, from a few days to several years. Indeed, market data can be updated daily; it is assumed that the other characteristics of the borrowers remain constant (until new information for these, too, becomes available).

Step 3: Specify the Forward Pricing Model

The valuation of a bond is derived from the zero-curve that corresponds to the rating of the issuer. Since there are seven possible credit qualities, seven "spread" curves are required to price the bond in all possible states. All obligors within the same rating class are then marked-to-market with the same curve. The spot zero-curve is used to determine the current spot value of the bond. The forward price of the bond one year from the present is derived from the forward zero-curve, one year ahead, which is then applied to the residual cash flows from year one to the maturity of the bond. Table 6.15 gives the one-year forward zero-curves for each credit rating.

The one-year forward price, V_{BBB}, of the five-year, 6% coupon bond, if the obligor stays BBB, is then:

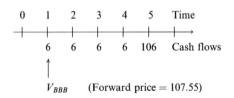

Table 6.16. One-Year Forward Values for a BBB Bond

Year-End Rating	Value ($)
AAA	109.37
AA	109.19
A	108.66
BBB	107.55
BB	102.02
B	98.10
CCC	83.64
Default	51.13

Source: CreditMetrics (1997).

$$V_{BBB} = 6 + \frac{6}{1.041} + \frac{6}{(1.0467)^2} + \frac{6}{(1.0525)^3} + \frac{106}{(1.0563)^4} = 107.55$$

where the discount rates are taken from table 6.15. If we replicate the same calculations for each rating category, we obtain the values shown in table 6.16.[29]

We do not assume that everything is lost if the issuer defaults at the end of the year. Depending on the seniority of the instrument, a recovery rate of par value is recuperated by the investor. These recovery rates are estimated from historical data by the rating agencies. Table 6.17 shows the expected recovery rates for bonds by different seniority classes as estimated by Moody's (Carty and Lieberman 1996). In our example, the recovery rate for senior unsecured debt is estimated to be 51.13%, although the estimation error is quite large and the actual value lies in a fairly large confidence interval.

When the loss distribution is derived from a Monte Carlo simulation, it is generally assumed that the recovery rates are distributed according to a beta distribution with the same mean and standard deviation as shown in table 6.19.

Table 6.17. Recovery Rates by Seniority Class *(% of face value, i.e., "par")*

Seniority Class	Mean (%)	Standard Deviation (%)
Senior secured	53.80	26.86
Senior unsecured	51.13	25.45
Senior subordinated	38.52	23.81
Subordinated	32.74	20.18
Junior subordinated	17.09	10.90

Source: Carty and Lieberman (1996).

3

Capital Adequacy Beyond Basel

Step 4: Derive the Forward Distribution of the Changes in Portfolio Value

The distribution of the changes in the bond value, at the one-year horizon, as a result of an eventual change in credit quality is shown table 6.18 and figure 6.4. This distribution exhibits a long "downside tail." The first percentile of the distribution of ΔV, which corresponds to credit VaR at the 99% confidence level, is -23.91. It is a much lower value than if we computed the first percentile assuming a normal distribution for ΔV. In that case, credit VaR at the 99% confidence level would be only -7.43.[30]

Credit-VaR for a Loan or Bond Portfolio

First, consider a portfolio composed of two bonds with an initial rating of BB and A, respectively. Given the transition matrix shown in table 6.14, and assuming no correlation between changes in credit quality, we can then derive easily the joint migration probabilities shown in table 6.19. Each entry is simply the product of the transition probabilities for each obligor. For example, the joint probability that obligor #1 and obligor #2 will stay in the same rating class is the product of the probability that bond A will remain at its current rating at the end of the year, 91.05%, and the probability that bond BB will remain as BB, or 80.53%: 73.32% = 80.53% × 91.05%. Unfortunately, when we need to assess the diversification effect on a large loan or bond portfolio, this table is not very useful in practice. In reality, the correlations between the changes in credit quality are not zero. And it is shown in a later section that the overall credit VaR is quite sensitive to these correlations. Their accurate estimation is therefore one of the key determinants of portfolio optimization.

Default correlations might be expected to be higher for firms within the same industry or in the same region than for firms in unrelated sectors. In addition, correlations vary with the relative state of the economy in the

Table 6.18. Distribution of the Bond Values and Changes in Value of a BBB Bond in One Year

Year-end Rating	Probability of State: p(%)	Forward Price: V($)	Change in Value: $\Delta V(\$)$
AAA	0.02	109.37	1.82
AA	0.33	109.19	1.64
A	5.95	108.66	1.11
BBB	86.93	107.55	0.00
BB	5.30	102.02	−5.53
B	1.17	98.10	−9.45
CCC	0.12	83.64	−23.91
Default	0.18	51.13	−56.42

Source: CreditMetrics (1997).

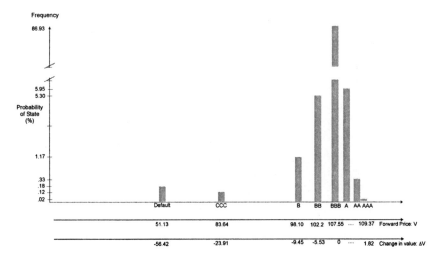

Figure 6.4. Histogram of the One-Year Forward Prices and Changes in Value of a BBB Bond. Source: Author.

business cycle. If there is an economic slowdown in the economy, or a recession, most of the assets of the obligors will decline in value and quality, and the likelihood of multiple defaults will increase substantially. The opposite happens when the economy is performing well: default correlations go down. Thus, we cannot expect default and migration probabilities to stay stationary over time. There is clearly a need for a structural model that relates changes in default probabilities to fundamental variables.

For the sake of simplicity, CreditMetrics makes use of the stock price of a firm as a proxy for its asset value as the true asset value is not directly

Table 6.19. Joint Migration Probabilities with Zero Correlation for Two Issuers Rated BB and A *(percentage)*

Obligor #1 (BB)		*Obligor #2 (single-A)*							
		AAA	AA	A	BBB	BB	B	CCC	Default
		0.09	2.27	91.05	5.52	0.74	0.26	0.01	0.06
AAA	0.03	0.00	0.00	0.03	0.00	0.00	0.00	0.00	0.00
AA	0.14	0.00	0.00	0.13	0.01	0.00	0.00	0.00	0.00
A	0.67	0.00	0.02	0.61	0.40	0.00	0.00	0.00	0.00
BBB	7.73	0.01	0.18	7.04	0.43	0.06	0.02	0.00	0.00
BB	80.53	0.07	1.83	73.32	4.45	0.60	0.20	0.01	0.05
B	8.84	0.01	0.20	8.05	0.49	0.07	0.02	0.00	0.00
CCC	1.00	0.00	0.02	0.91	0.06	0.01	0.00	0.00	0.00
Default	1.06	0.00	0.02	0.97	0.06	0.01	0.00	0.00	0.00

Source: Author.

Table 6.20. Balance Sheet of Merton's Firm

	Assets	*Liabilities/Equity*
	Risky assets: V_t	Debt: $B_t(F)$
		Equity: S_t
Total:	V_t	V_t

Source: Author.

observable. (This is another simplifying assumption in CreditMetrics that may affect the accuracy of the approach.) CreditMetrics estimates the correlations between the equity returns of various obligors, then infers the correlations between changes in credit quality directly from the joint distribution of these equity returns.

The theoretical framework underlying all this is the option pricing approach to the valuation of corporate securities first developed by Merton (1974). The basic model is presented in a later section of this appendix, and it is described in more detail in the section that follows, since it forms the basis for the KMV approach. In Merton's model, the firm is assumed to have a very simple capital structure; it is financed by equity, S_t, and by a single zero-coupon debt instrument maturing at time T, with face value F and current market value B_t. The firm's balance sheet is represented in table 6.20, where V_t is the value of all the assets and $V_t = B_t(F) + S_t$. In this framework, default occurs at the maturity of the debt obligation only when the value of assets is less than the promised payment, F, to the bondholders. Figure 6.5 shows the distribution of the assets' value at time T, the maturity of the zero-coupon debt, and the probability of default (i.e., the shaded area on the left side of the default point, F).

Merton's model is extended by CreditMetrics to include changes in credit quality, as illustrated in figure 6.6. This generalization consists of slicing the

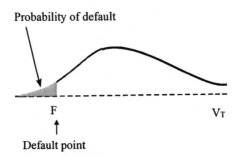

Figure 6.5. Distribution of the Firm's Assets Value at Maturity of the Debt Obligation. Source: Author.

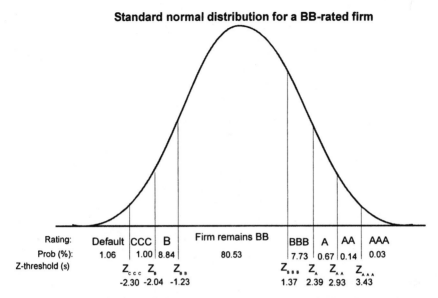

Figure 6.6. Generalization of the Merton Model to Include Rating Changes.
Source: Author.

distribution of asset returns into bands in such a way that, if we draw randomly from this distribution, we reproduce exactly the migration frequencies as shown in the transition matrices that we discussed earlier. Figure 6.6 shows the distribution of the normalized assets' rates of return one year ahead. The distribution is normal, with mean zero and unit variance. The credit rating "thresholds" correspond to the transition probabilities in table 6.14 for a BB–rated obligor. The right tail of the distribution, down to Z_{AAA}, corresponds to the probability that the obligor will be upgraded from BB to AAA, that is, 0.03%. Then, the area between Z_{AA} and Z_{AAA} corresponds to the probability of being upgraded from BB to AA, and so on. The left tail of the distribution, on the left side of Z_{CCC}, corresponds to the probability of default, that is, 1.06%. Table 6.21 shows the transition probabilities for two obligors rated BB and A respectively, and the corresponding credit quality thresholds. The thresholds are given in terms of normalized standard deviations. For example, for a BB–rated obligor, the default threshold is -2.30 standard deviations from the mean rate of return.

This generalization of Merton's model is quite easy to implement. It assumes that the normalized log-returns over any period of time are normally distributed, with a mean of 0 and a variance of 1, and that the distribution is the same for all obligors within the same rating category. If p_{Def} denotes the probability that the BB–rated obligor will default, then the critical asset value V_{Def} is such that $p_{Def} = \Pr[V_t \leq V_{Def}]$, which can be translated into a normalized threshold Z_{CCC}, such that the area in the left tail below Z_{CCC} is p_{Def}. Z_{CCC} is simply the threshold point in the standard

Table 6.21. Transition Probabilities and Credit Quality Thresholds for Rated BB and A Obligors

	Rated-A Obligor		Rated-BB Obligor	
Rating in One Year	Probabilities (%)	Thresholds: $Z(\sigma)$	Probabilities (%)	Thresholds: $Z(\sigma)$
AAA	0.09	3.12	0.03	3.43
AA	2.27	1.98	0.14	2.93
A	91.05	−1.51	0.67	2.39
BBB	5.52	−2.30	7.73	1.37
BB	0.74	−2.72	80.53	−1.23
B	0.26	−3.19	8.84	−2.04
CCC	0.01	−3.24	1.00	−2.30
Default	0.06		1.06	

Source: Author.

normal distribution, $N(0,1)$, corresponding to a cumulative probability of p_{Def}. Then, on the basis of the option pricing model, the critical asset value V_{Def} that triggers default is such that $Z_{CCC} = -d_2$. This critical asset value is also called the "default point."[31]

Note that only the threshold levels are necessary to derive the joint migration probabilities, and one can calculate these without having to observe the asset value and to estimate its mean and variance. To derive the critical asset value V_{Def} we only need estimate the expected asset return, μ, and the asset volatility, σ. Accordingly, Z_B is the threshold point corresponding to a cumulative probability of being either in default or in rating CCC, that is, $p_{Def} + p_{ccc}$, and so on.

We mentioned that, because asset returns are not directly observable, CreditMetrics makes use of equity returns as their proxy. Yet, using equity returns in this way is equivalent to assuming that all the firm's activities are financed by means of equity. This is a major drawback of the approach, especially when it is being applied to highly leveraged companies. For those companies, equity returns are substantially more volatile, and possibly less stationary, than the volatility of the firm's assets. Now, assume that the correlation between the assets' rates of return is known and is denoted by ρ, which is assumed to be equal to 0.20 in our example. The normalized log-returns on both assets is assumed to follow a joint normal distribution. We can then compute the probability that both obligors will be in any particular combination of ratings. For example, we can compute the probability that they will remain in the same rating classes, that is, BB and A, respectively: $\Pr(-1.23 < r_{BB} < 1.37, -1.51 < r_A < 1.98) = 0.7365$, where r_{BB} and r_A are the instantaneous rates of return on the assets of obligors BB and A, respectively. If we implement the same procedure for the other 63 combinations, we obtain table 6.22. We can now compare table 6.22 and table 6.19, which

Table 6.22. Joint Rating Probabilities (%) for BB- and A-Rated Obligors when Correlation Between Asset Returns Is 20%

Rating of First Company (BB)	Rating of Second Company (A)								
	AAA	*AA*	*A*	*BBB*	*BB*	*B*	*CCC*	*Def*	*Total*
AAA	0.00	0.00	0.03	0.00	0.00	0.00	0.00	0.00	0.03
AA	0.00	0.01	0.13	0.00	0.00	0.00	0.00	0.00	0.14
A	0.00	0.04	0.61	0.01	0.00	0.00	0.00	0.00	0.67
BBB	0.02	0.35	7.10	0.20	0.02	0.01	0.00	0.00	7.69
BB	0.07	1.79	73.65	4.24	0.56	0.18	0.01	0.04	80.53
B	0.00	0.08	7.80	0.79	0.13	0.05	0.00	0.01	8.87
CCC	0.00	0.01	0.85	0.11	0.02	0.01	0.00	0.00	1.00
Def	0.00	0.01	0.90	0.13	0.02	0.01	0.00	0.00	1.07
Total	0.09	2.29	91.06	5.48	0.75	0.26	0.01	0.06	100

Source: CreditMetrics (1997).

was derived under the assumption that there was zero correlation between the companies. Notice that the joint probabilities are different.

Figure 6.7 illustrates the effect of asset return correlation on the joint default probability for the rated BB and A obligors. If the probabilities of default for obligors rated A and BB are $P_{def}(A) = 0.06\%$ and $P_{def}(BB) = 1.06\%$, respectively, and the correlation coefficient between the rates of return on the two assets is $\rho = 20\%$, it can be shown that the probability of default is $P(def1, def2) = 0.0054\%$. The correlation coefficient between the two default events is corr$(def1, def2) = 19\%$. Asset returns correlations are

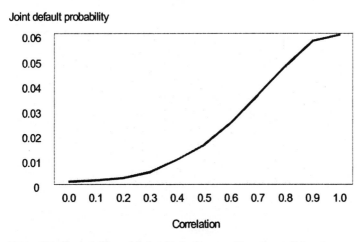

Figure 6.7. Probability of Joint Defaults as a Function of Asset Return Correlation. Source: CreditMetrics (1997).

approximately 10 times larger than default correlations for asset correlations in the range of 20% to 60%. This shows that the joint probability of default is in fact quite sensitive to pair-wise asset return correlations, and it illustrates how important it is to estimate these data correctly if one is to assess the diversification effect within a portfolio. The impact of correlations on credit VaR is quite large. It is larger for portfolios with relatively low-grade credit quality than it is for high-grade portfolios. Indeed, as the credit quality of the portfolio deteriorates and the expected number of defaults increases, this number is magnified by an increase in default correlations.

APPENDIX 2: THE CONTINGENT CLAIM OR STRUCTURAL APPROACH TO MEASURING CREDIT RISK—KMV

What we will call the "structural" approach offers an alternative to the credit migration approach. Here, the economic value of default is presented as a put option on the value of the firm's assets. The merit of this approach is that each case can be analyzed individually on the basis of its unique features. But this is also the principal drawback, since the information required for such an analysis is rarely available to the bank or the investor.

Various ways to implement the structural approach have been proposed in the literature, all of which are consistent with arbitrage-free pricing methodologies. The option-pricing model approach, introduced by Merton (1974) in a seminal paper, builds on the limited-liability rule that allows shareholders to default on their obligations while they surrender the firm's assets to the various stakeholders, according to prespecified priority rules. The firm's liabilities are thus viewed as contingent claims issued against the firm's assets, with the payoffs to the various debt holders completely specified by seniority and safety covenants. Default occurs at debt maturity whenever the firm's asset value falls short of debt value at that time. In this model, the loss rate is endogenously determined and depends on the firm's asset value, the volatility of the assets, and the default-free interest rate for the debt maturity.[32]

The model presented in this section assumes a simple capital structure with one type of (zero-coupon) debt. It can, however, be easily extended to the case where the firm has issued senior and junior debts. In this case, the loss rates for each type of debt are endogenously derived, together with the default probability.[33]

MERTON'S MODEL (1974)

Consider the simple case of a firm with risky assets V, which is financed by equity, S, and by one debt obligation, maturing at time T with face value (including accrued interest) of F and market value B. The loan to the firm is subject to credit risk, namely the risk that at time T the value of the firm's assets, V_T, will be below the obligation to the debt holders, F. Credit risk exists as long as the probability of default, Prob $(V_T < F)$, is greater than zero. This implies that at time 0, $B_0 < Fe^{-rT}$, or equivalently that the yield to maturity on the debt, y_T, is higher than the risk-free rate, r, where $\pi_T = y_T - r$ denotes the default spread that compensates the bond holders for the default risk that they bear. If we assume that markets are frictionless, with no taxes, and there is no bankruptcy cost, then the value of the firm's assets is simply the sum of the firm's equity and debt:

$$V_0 = S_0 + B_0 \qquad (6.14)$$

From the viewpoint of a bank that makes a loan to the firm, this gives rise to a series of questions. Can the bank eliminate/reduce credit risk, and at what price? What is the economic cost of reducing credit risk? And, what are the factors affecting this cost?

In this simple framework, credit risk is a function of the financial structure of the firm, that is, its leverage ratio $LR \equiv Fe^{-rT}/V_0$ (where V_0 is the present value of the firm's assets and Fe^{-rT} is the present value of the debt obligation at maturity), the volatility of the firm's assets, σ, and the time to maturity of the debt, T.

To determine the value of the credit risk arising from this bank loan, we first make two assumptions: that the loan is the only debt instrument of the firm and that the only other source of financing is equity. In this case, the credit value is equal to the value of a put option on the value of assets of the firm, V, at a strike price of F, maturing at time T. If the bank purchased such a put option, P, it would completely eliminate the credit risk associated with the loan (see table 6.23).

To put this another way, by purchasing the put on V for the term of the debt, with a strike price equal to the face value of the loan, the bank can completely eliminate all the credit risk and convert the risky corporate loan into a riskless loan with a face value of F. If the riskless interest rate is r, then in equilibrium, it should be that $B_o + P = Fe^{-rT}$, where P is a put option maturing at time T and with exercise price F.

Thus, the value of the put option is the cost of eliminating the credit risk associated with providing a loan to the firm. If we make the assumptions

Table 6.23. Bank's Payoff Matrix at Times 0 and T for Making a Loan and Buying a Put Option

Time	0	T	
Value of Assets	V_0	$V_T \leq F$	$V_T > F$
Bank's position:			
(a) make a loan	$-B_0$	V_T	F
(b) buy a put	$-P_0$	$F - V_T$	0
Total	$-B_0 - P_0$	F	F

Source: Author.

that are needed to apply the Black and Scholes (1973) model to equity and debt instruments, we can write the value of the put as:

$$P_0 = -N(-d_1)V_0 + Fe^{-rt}N(-d_2) \qquad (6.15)$$

where P_0 is the current value of the put, $N(.)$ is the cumulative standard normal distribution, and

$$d_1 = \frac{\ln(V_o/F) + (r + \frac{1}{2}\sigma^2)T}{\sigma\sqrt{T}} = \frac{\ln(V_o/Fe^{-rT}) + \frac{1}{2}\sigma^2 T}{\sigma\sqrt{T}}$$

$d_2 = d_1 - \sigma\sqrt{T}$ and σ is the standard deviation of the rate of return of the firm's assets.

The model illustrates that the credit risk, and its costs, is a function of the riskiness of the assets of the firm σ, and that this risk is also a function of the time interval until debt is paid back, T. The cost is also affected by the risk-free interest rate r; the higher r is, the less costly it is to reduce credit risk. The cost is a homogeneous function of the leverage ratio, $LR = Fe^{-rT}/V_0$, which means that it stays constant for a scale expansion of Fe^{-rT}/V_0.

We can now derive the yield to maturity for the corporate discount debt, y_T, as follows:

$$y_T = -\frac{\ln\frac{B_0}{F}}{T} = -\frac{\ln\frac{Fe^{-rT} - P_0}{F}}{T}$$

so that the default spread, π_T, defined as $\pi_T = y_T - r$, can be derived from equation (6.15) as follows:

$$\pi_T = y_T - r = -\frac{1}{T}\ln\left(N(d_2) + \frac{V_0}{Fe^{-rT}}N(-d_1)\right) \qquad (6.16)$$

The default spread can be computed exactly as a function of the leverage ratio, $LR \equiv Fe^{-rT}/V_0$, the volatility of the underlying assets, σ, and the debt maturity, T. The numerical examples in table 6.25 show the default spread for various levels of volatility and different leverage ratios.

Note that when the risk-free rate, r, increases, the credit spread, π_T, declines, that is, $\frac{\partial \pi_T}{\partial r} < 0$. Indeed, the higher is r, the less risky is the bond and the lower is the value of the put protection. Therefore, the lower is the risk premium, π_T.

In table 6.24, by using the Black-Scholes model when $V_0 = 100$, $T = 1$, $r = 10\%$ and also $\sigma = 40\%$ with the leverage ratio $LR = 70\%$,[34] we obtain for the value of equity $S_0 = 33.37$ and for the value of the corporate risky debt $B_0 = 66.63$. The yield on the loan is equal to $77/66.63 - 1 = 0.156$ that is, there is a 5.6% risk premium on the loan to reflect the credit risk.

The model also shows that the put value is $P_0 = 3.37$. Hence, the cost of eliminating the credit risk is $3.37 for $100 worth of the firm's assets, where the face value (i.e., the principal amount plus the promised interest rate) of the one-year debt is 77. This cost drops to 25 cents when volatility decreases

Table 6.24. **Default Spread for Corporate Debt** *(for $V_0 = 100$, $T = 1$, and $r = 10\%$)*[a]

Leverage Ration: LR	Volatility of Underlying Asset: σ			
	0.05	0.10	0.20	0.40
0.5	0	0	0	1.0%
0.6	0	0	0.1%	2.5%
0.7	0	0	0.4%	5.6%
0.8	0	0.1%	1.5%	8.4%
0.9	0.1%	0.8%	4.1%	12.5%
1.0	2.1%	3.1%	8.3%	17.3%

[a]10% is the annualized interest rate discretly compounded, which is equivalent to 9.5% continuously compounded.

Source: Author.

to 20%, and to 0 for 10% volatility. The riskiness of the assets as measured by the volatility, σ, is a critical factor in determining credit risk.

To demonstrate that the bank eliminates all its credit risk by buying the put, we can compute the yield on the bank's position as $F/(B_0 + P) = 77/(66.63 + 3.37) = 1.10$, which translates to a riskless yield of 10% per annum.

PROBABILITY OF DEFAULT, CONDITIONAL EXPECTED RECOVERY VALUE, AND DEFAULT SPREAD

From equation (6.15) one can extract the probability of default for the loan. In a risk-neutral world, $N(d_2)$ is the probability that the firm's value at time T will be higher than F, and $1 - N(d_2) = N(-d_2)$ is the probability of default.

By purchasing the put, P_0, the bank buys an insurance policy whose premium is the discounted expected value of the expected shortfall in the event of default. Indeed, equation (6.15) can be rewritten as:

$$P_0 = \left[-\frac{N(-d_1)}{N(-d_2)} V_0 + Fe^{-rT} \right] N(-d_2) \qquad (6.17)$$

Equation (6.17) decomposes the premium on the put into three factors. The absolute value of the first term inside the bracket is the expected discounted recovery value of the loan, conditional on $V_T \leq F$. It represents the risk-neutral expected payment to the bank in the case where the firm is unable to pay the full obligation F at time T. The second term in the bracket is the current value of a riskless bond promising a payment of F at time T. Hence, the sum of the two terms inside the brackets yields the expected shortfall in present value terms, conditional on the firm's being bankrupt at time T. The final factor that determines P_0 is the probability of default, $N(-d_2)$. By multiplying the probability of default by the current value of the expected shortfall, we derive the premium for insurance against default.

Using the same numerical example as in the previous subsection (i.e., $V_0 = 100$, $T = 1$, $r = 10$ percent, $\sigma = 40$ percent, $F = 77$, and $LR = 0.7$), we obtain:

Discounted expected recovery value $= \dfrac{0.137}{0.244} \times 100 = 56.1$

Value of riskless bond $\qquad\qquad = 77 \times e^{-0.0953} = 70$

Expected shortfall $\qquad\qquad\qquad = 70 - 56.1 = 13.9$

Probability of default $\qquad\qquad\quad = 24.4\%$

Cost of default[35] $\qquad\qquad\qquad = 0.244 \times 13.9 = 3.39$

These results are based on an assumption of risk neutrality. For the general case, when the assumption of a risk-neutral world is removed, the probability of default is given by $N(-d_2^1)$, where $d_2^1 = [\ln(V_0/F)+(\mu - 1/2\sigma^2)T]/(\sigma\sqrt{T})$ and where μ is the expected rate of return on asset V and V is assumed to be log-normally distributed. Referring to our numerical example, the risk-neutral probability of default is 24.4%. If we assume that the discrete time μ is 16%, the probability of default is 20.5%. The expected recovery value is now: $N(-d_1^1)/[N(-d_2^1)]V_0 = \frac{0.110}{0.205} \cdot 100 = 53.7$.

From (6.17) we can compute the expected loss, EL_T, in the event of default, at maturity date T:

$$EL_T = \text{probability of default} \times \text{loss in case of default}$$
$$= N(-d_2)F - N(-d_1)V_0 e^{rT} = F - N(d_2)F - N(-d_1)V_0 e^{rT}$$
$$= F\left(1 - N(d_2) - N(-d_1)\frac{1}{LR}\right) \qquad\qquad (6.18)$$

Again, using our previous numerical example we obtain $EL_T = 0.244 \times 77 - 0.137 \times 100 e^{0.0953} = 3.718$

This result is consistent with the definition of the default spread and its derivation in (6.16). Indeed, from (6.18), the expected payoff from the corporate debt at maturity is:

$$F - EL_T = F\left(N(d_2) + N(-d_1)\frac{1}{LR}\right)$$

so the expected cost of default, expressed in yield, is:

$$-\frac{1}{T}\ln\left(\frac{F}{F - EL_T}\right) = -\frac{1}{T}\ln\left(\frac{F\left(N(d_2) + N(-d_1)\frac{V_0}{Fe^{-rT}}\right)}{F}\right) = \pi_T$$

which is identical to (6.16).

The result in equation (6.18) is similar to the conclusion in Jarrow and Turnbull's (1995) model, which is used to price credit derivatives, that the credit spread is the product of the probability of default and the loss in the event of default. However, in their model they assume that the term structure of credit spread is known and can be derived from market data. The forward spread can then be easily derived. By assuming that the recovery factor is given and exogenous to the model, they can imply the forward probability of default.

In the contingent claim model, we reach the same conclusion, but both the probability of default and the recovery rate are simultaneously derived from equilibrium conditions. From equation (6.16) and (6.17), it is clear that the recovery rate cannot be assumed to be constant: it varies as a function of time to maturity, and according to the value of the firm's assets.

ESTIMATING CREDIT RISK AS A FUNCTION OF EQUITY VALUE

We have shown that the cost of eliminating credit risk can be derived from the value of the firm's assets. A practical problem arises over how easy it is to observe V. In some cases, if both equity and debt are traded, V can be reconstructed by adding the market values of both equity and debt. However, corporate loans are not often traded, and so, to all intents and purposes, we can observe only equity. The question, then, is whether the risk of default can be hedged by trading shares and derivatives on the firm's stock.

In our simple framework, equity itself is a contingent claim on the firm's assets. Its value can be expressed as:

$$S = VN(d_1) - Fe^{-rT}N(d_2) \tag{6.19}$$

Equity value is a function of the same parameters as the put calculated in equation (6.15).

A put can be created synthetically by selling short $N(-d_1)$ units of the firm's assets and buying $FN(-d_2)$ units of government bonds maturing at T, with face value of F. If one sells short $N(-d_1)/N(d_1)$ units of the stock, S, one effectively creates a short position in the firm's assets of $N(-d_1)$ units, since:

$$\frac{-N(-d_1)}{N(d_1)} S = -VN(-d_1) + Fe^{-rT}N(d_2)\frac{N(-d_1)}{N(d_1)}.$$

Therefore, if V is not directly traded or observed, one can create a put option dynamically by selling short the appropriate number of shares. The equivalence between the put and the synthetic put is valid over short time intervals and must be readjusted frequently with changes in S and in time left to debt maturity.

Using the data from the previous numerical example

$$\frac{-N(-d_1)}{N(d_1)} = \frac{-0.137}{0.863} = -0.159.$$

This means that in order to ensure against the default of a one-year loan with a maturity value of 77, for a firm with a current market value of assets of 100, the bank should sell short 0.159 of the outstanding equity. (Note that the outstanding equity is equivalent to a short-term holding of $N(d_1) = 0.863$ of the firm's assets. Shorting 0.159 of equity is equivalent to shorting 0.863 of the firm's assets.)

The question now is whether we can use a put option on equity in order to hedge the default risk. It should be remembered that equity itself reflects the default risk, and as a contingent claim its instantaneous volatility, σ_S, can be expressed as:

$$\sigma_S = \eta_{S,V}\sigma \qquad (6.20)$$

where $\eta_{S,V} = N(d_1)\frac{V}{S}$ is the instantaneous elasticity of equity with respect to the firm's value and $\eta_{S,V} \geq 1$.

Since σ_S is stochastic, changing with V, the conventional Black-Scholes model cannot be applied to the valuation of puts and calls on S. The Black-Scholes model requires σ to be constant or to follow a deterministic path over the life of the option. However, it was shown by Bensoussan, Crouhy, and Galai (1994, 1995) that a good approximation can be achieved by employing equation (6.20) in the Black-Scholes model.

In practice, for long-term options, the estimated σ_S from (6.20) is not expected to change widely from day to day. Therefore, equation (6.20) can be used in the context of Black-Scholes estimation of long-term options, even when the underlying instrument does not follow a stationary lognormal distribution.

KMV APPROACH

KMV derives the estimated default frequency or default probability, the EDF, for each obligor from the Merton (1974) type of model. The probability of default is thus a function of the firm's capital structure, the volatility of the asset returns, and the current asset value (Vasicek 1997; Kealhofer 1995, 1998). The EDF is firm-specific and can be mapped onto any rating system to derive the equivalent rating of the obligor. EDFs can be viewed as a "cardinal ranking" of obligors relative to default risk, instead of the more conventional "ordinal ranking" proposed by rating agencies (which relies on letters such as AAA, AA, and so on).

Unlike CreditMetrics, KMV's model does not make any explicit reference to the transition probabilities, which, in KMV's methodology, are already embedded in the EDFs. Indeed, each value of the *EDF* is associated with a spread curve and an implied credit rating.

Credit risk in the KMV approach is essentially driven by the dynamics of the asset value of the issuer. Given the capital structure of the firm,[36] and once the stochastic process for the asset value has been specified, then *the actual probability of default* for any time horizon, one year, two years, and so forth, can be derived. Figure 6.8 schematizes how the probability of default relates to the distribution of asset returns and the capital structure of the firm.

We assume that the firm has a very simple capital structure. It is financed by means of equity, S_t, and a single zero-coupon debt instrument maturing at time T, with face value F and current market value B_t. The firm's balance sheet can be represented as follows: $V_t = B_t(F) + S_t$ where V_t is the value of all the

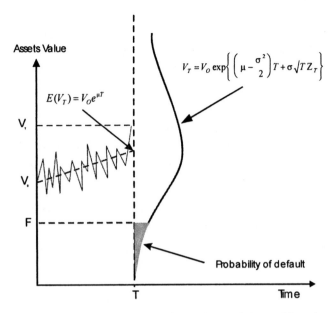

Figure 6.8. Distribution of the Firm's Assets Value at Maturity of the Debt Obligation. Source: Author.

assets. The firm's assets value, V_t, is assumed to follow a standard geometric Brownian motion (see earlier discussion of Merton's model). In this framework, default occurs only at maturity of the debt obligation, when the value of assets is less than the promised payment, F, to the bondholders. Figure 6.8 shows the distribution of the assets' value at time T, the maturity of the zero-coupon debt, and the probability of default (i.e., the shaded area below F).

The KMV approach is best applied to publicly traded companies, where the value of the equity is determined by the stock market. The information contained in the firm's stock price and balance sheet can then be translated into an implied risk of default, as shown in the next section. The derivation of the actual probabilities of default proceeds in three stages:

- Estimation of the market value and volatility of the firm's assets
- Calculation of the distance to default, which is an index measure of default risk
- Scaling of the distance to default to actual probabilities of default using a default database

Using a sample of several hundred companies, KMV observed that firms default when the asset value reaches a level that is somewhere between the value of total liabilities and the value of short-term debt. Therefore, the tail of the distribution of asset values below total debt value may not be an accurate measure of the actual probability of default. Loss of accuracy may also result from factors such as the nonnormality of the asset return distribution and the

simplifying assumptions about the capital structure of the firm. This may be
further aggravated if a company is able to draw on (otherwise unobservable)
lines of credit. If the company is in distress, using these lines may (unexpectedly) increase its liabilities while providing the necessary cash to honor
promised payments.

For all these reasons, KMV implements an intermediate phase before
computing the probabilities of default. As shown in figure 6.9, which is
similar to figure 6.8, KMV computes an index called "distance to default"
(DD). DD is the number of standard deviations between the mean of the
distribution of the asset value and a critical threshold, the "default point,"
set at the par value of current liabilities, including short-term debt to be
serviced over the time horizon, plus half the long-term debt.

Given the lognormality assumption of asset values, the distance to default
is expressed in unit of asset return standard deviation at time horizon T:

$$DD = \frac{\ln \frac{V_0}{DPT_T} + (\mu - 1/2\sigma^2)T}{\sigma\sqrt{T}} \qquad (6.21)$$

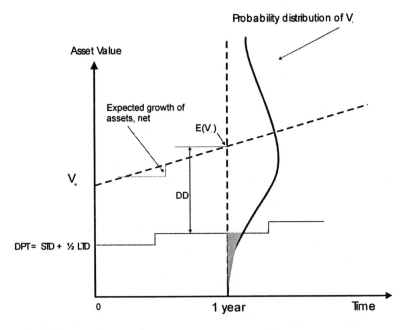

Figure 6.9. Distance to Default (DD). Source: Author. Note: STD = short-
term debt; LTD = long-term debt; DPT = default point = $STD + 1/2\ LTD$;
DD = distance-to-default, which is the distance between the expected
asset value in one year, $E(V_1)$, and the default point, DPT, expressed in
standard deviation of future asset returns: $DD = \frac{E(V_1) - DPT}{\sigma_\sigma}$.

where

V_0	= current market value of assets
DPT_T	= default point at time horizon T
μ	= expected return on assets, net of cash outflows
σ	= annualized asset volatility

It follows that the shaded area below the default point is equal to $N(\text{-}DD)$.

This last phase consists of mapping the "distance-to-default" (DD) to the actual probabilities of default, for a given time horizon (see figure 6.10). KMV calls these probabilities "expected default frequencies," or EDFs.

Using historical information about a large sample of firms, including firms that have defaulted, one can estimate, for each time horizon, the proportion of firms of a given ranking, say $DD = 4$, that actually defaulted after one year. This proportion, say 40bp, or 0.4 percent, is the EDF, as shown in figure 6.10. Then, $DD = \frac{1,200 - 800}{100} = 4$. Assume that among the population of all the firms with a DD of 4 at one point in time, for example, 5,000 firms, 20 defaulted one year later. Then, $EDF_{1year} = \frac{20}{5,000} = 0.004 = 0.4\%$ or 40 bp. The implied rating for this probability of default is BB^+. The next example is provided by KMV and relates to Federal Express on two different dates: November 1997 and February 1998.

This last example illustrates the main causes of changes for an EDF, which are variations in stock price, debt level (leverage ratio), and asset volatility (i.e., the perceived degree of uncertainty concerning the value of the business).

THE ACTUARIAL APPROACH TO MEASURING CREDIT RISK—CREDITRISK+

In the structural models of default that we discussed earlier, default time is jointly determined by the stochastic process of the firm's assets and its

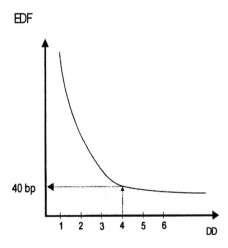

Figure 6.10. Mapping of the Distance to Default into the EDFs, for a Given Time Horizon. Source: Author.

Table 6.25. Example 1

Current market value of assets	$V_0 = 1,000$
Net expected growth of assets per annum	20%
Expected asset value in one year	$V_0 (1.20) = 1,200$
Annualized asset volatility, σ	100
Default point	800

Source: Author.

capital structure. Default occurs when the asset value falls below a certain boundary, such as a promised payment, as in, for example, the Merton (1974) framework.

By contrast, CreditRisk+ and the "reduced form" models that are analyzed in this chapter treat the firm's bankruptcy process, including recovery, as exogenous. CreditRisk+, released in late 1997 by the investment bank Credit Suisse Financial Products (CSFP), is a purely actuarial model. This means that the probabilities of default that the model employs are based on historical statistics on default experience by credit class. CreditRisk+ assumes that the probability distribution for the number of defaults over any period of time follows a Poisson distribution. Under this assumption, CreditRisk+ produces a loss distribution of a bond or loan portfolio based on the individual default characteristics of each security and their pair-wise default correlations. The reduced form approaches also use a Poisson-like process to describe default.

The Probability of Default

CreditRisk+ applies an actuarial science framework to the derivation of the loss distribution of a bond/loan portfolio.[37] Only default risk is modeled; downgrade risk is ignored. Unlike the KMV approach to modeling default,

Table 6.26. Example 2: Federal Express (billions of US$)

	November 1997	*February 1998*
Market capitalization (price shares outstanding)	$7.7	$7.3
Book liabilities	$4.7	$4.9
Market value of assets	$12.6	$12.2
Asset volatility	15%	17%
Default point	$3.4	$3.5
Distance to default (*DD*)	$\dfrac{12.6 - 3.4}{0.15 \cdot 12.6} = 4.9$	$\dfrac{12.2 - 3.5}{0.17 \cdot 12.2} = 4.2$
EDF	0.06% (6bp) $\equiv$ AA$^-$	0.11%(11bp) $\equiv$ A$^-$

Source: Author.

CreditRisk+ makes no attempt to relate default risk to the capital structure of the firm. Also, it makes no assumptions about the causes of default; an obligor A is either in default with probability P_A or is not in default with probability $1-P_A$. It does make these assumptions:

- For a loan, the probability of default in a given period, say one month, is the same as in any other month.
- For a large number of obligors, the probability of default by any particular obligor is small, and the number of defaults that occur in any given period is independent of the number of defaults that occur in any other period.

Under these assumptions, the probability distribution for the number of defaults during a given period of time (say, one year) is represented well by a Poisson distribution:[38]

$$P(n \text{ defaults}) = \frac{\mu^n e^{-\mu}}{n!} \quad \text{for } n = 0,1,2,\ldots \tag{6.22}$$

where $\mu =$ average number of defaults per year ($\mu = \sum_A P_A$). The annual number of defaults, n, is a stochastic variable with mean μ and standard deviation $\sqrt{\mu}$. The Poisson distribution has a useful property: it can be fully specified by means of a single parameter, μ.[39] For example, if we assume $\mu = 3$, then the probability of "no default" in the next year is $P(0 \text{ default}) = \frac{3^0 e^{-3}}{0!} = 0.05 = 5\%$, while the probability of exactly three defaults is $P(3 \text{ defaults}) = \frac{3^3 e^{-3}}{3!} = 0.224 = 22.4\%$. The distribution of default losses for a portfolio is derived in two stages.

Frequency of Default Events

So far, we have assumed that a standard Poisson distribution approximates the distribution of the number of default events. If this were the case, we should expect the standard deviation of the default rate to be approximately equal to the square root of the mean, $\sqrt{\mu}$, where μ is the average default rate. However, the actual standard deviation for all ratings is higher than the square root of the average default rate. In these circumstances, the Poisson distribution underestimates the probability of default. This is not surprising if we observe the variability of default rates over time. (Intuitively, we expect the mean default rate to change over time depending on the business cycle.)

This suggests that the Poisson distribution can be used to represent the default process only if, as CreditRisk+ suggests, we make the additional assumption that the mean default rate is itself stochastic, with mean μ and standard deviation σ_μ.[40] Figure 6.11 shows what happens when we incorporate this assumption. The distribution of defaults becomes more skewed and exhibits a "fat tail" on the right side of the figure.

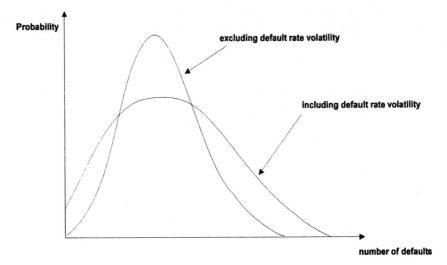

Figure 6.11. Distribution of Default Events. Source: Author.

Severity of the Losses

In the event of default by an obligor, the counterparty incurs a loss that is equal to the amount owned by the obligor (his exposure is the marked-to-market value, if positive, otherwise zero (if negative, at the time of default) less a recovery amount.

In CreditRisk+, the exposure for each obligor is adjusted by the anticipated recovery rate in order to calculate the "loss given default." These adjusted exposures are exogenous to the model and are independent of market risk and downgrade risk.

Distribution of Default Losses for a Portfolio

In order to derive the loss distribution for a well-diversified portfolio, the losses (exposures, net of the recovery adjustments) are divided into bands. The level of exposure in each band is approximated by means of a single number.

As an example, suppose the bank holds a portfolio of loans and bonds from 500 different obligors, with exposures of between \$50,000 and \$1 million. In table 6.27, we show the exposures for the first six obligors. The unit of exposure is assumed to be $L = \$100,000$. Each band $j, j = 1, \ldots, m$, with $m = 10$, has an average common exposure: $v_j = \$100,000 \times j$. In CreditRisk+, each band is viewed as an independent portfolio of loans/bonds, for which we introduce the following notation:

Obligor	A
Exposure	L_A

Table 6.27. Exposure per Obligor

Obligor A	Exposure ($) (Loss Given Default) L_A	Exposure (in $100,000) V_j	Round-Off Exposure (in $100,000) v_j	Band j
1	150,000	1.5	2	2
2	460,000	4.6	5	5
3	435,000	4.35	5	5
4	370,000	3.7	4	4
5	190,000	1.9	2	2
6	480,000	4.8	5	5

Source: Author.

Probability of default $\qquad\qquad P_A$

Expected loss $\qquad\qquad \lambda_A = L_A \times P_A$

Then, by definition we have $\varepsilon_j = v_j \times \mu_j$. Hence:

$$\mu_j = \frac{\varepsilon_j}{v_j} \tag{6.23}$$

Denote by ε_A the expected loss for obligor A in units of L, that is, $\varepsilon_A = \lambda_A / L$. Then, the expected loss over a one-year period in band j, ε_j, expressed in units of L, is simply the sum of the expected losses ε_A of all the obligors that belong to band j, that is, $\varepsilon_j = \sum_{A:v_A = v_j} \varepsilon_A$.

From (6.23) it follows that the expected number of defaults per annum in band j is:

$$\mu_j = \frac{\varepsilon_j}{v_j} = \sum_{A:v_A = v_j} \frac{\varepsilon_A}{v_j} = \sum_{A:v_A = v_j} \frac{\varepsilon_A}{v_A}$$

Table 6.28 provides an illustration of the results of these calculations. To derive the distribution of losses for the entire portfolio, we need to fulfill the following three steps.

Step 1: Probability-Generating Function for Each Band

Each band is viewed as a separate portfolio of exposures. The probability generating function for any band, say band j, is by definition: $G_j(z) = \sum_{n=0}^{\infty} P(loss = nL)z^n = \sum_{n=0}^{\infty} P(n \ defaults)z^{nv_j}$ where the losses are expressed in the unit L of exposure.

To derive the distribution of losses for the entire portfolio, we proceed as follows. Since we have assumed that the number of defaults follows a Poisson distribution, then:

Table 6.28. Expected Number of Defaults per Annum in Each Band

Band: j	Number of Obligors	ε_j	μ_j
1	30	1.5	1.5
2	40	8.0	4.0
3	50	6.0	2.0
4	70	25.2	6.3
5	100	35.0	7.0
6	60	14.4	2.4
7	50	38.5	5.5
8	40	19.2	2.4
9	40	25.2	2.8
10	20	4.0	0.4

Source: Author.

$$G_j(z) = \sum_{n=0}^{\infty} \frac{e^{-\mu_j}\mu_j^n}{n!} z^{n v_j} = e^{-\mu_j + \mu_j z^{v_j}} \qquad (6.24)$$

Step 2: Probability-Generating Function for the Entire Portfolio

Since we have assumed that each band is a portfolio of exposures, independent of the other bands, the probability-generating function for the entire portfolio is simply the product of the probability-generating function for each band:

$$G(z) = \prod_{j=1}^{m} e^{-\mu_j + \mu_j z^{v^j}} = e^{-\sum_{j=1}^{m}\mu_j + \sum_{j=1}^{m}\mu_j z^{v_j}} \qquad (6.25)$$

where $\mu = \sum_{j=1}^{m} \mu_j$ denotes the expected number of defaults for the entire portfolio.

Step 3: Loss Distribution for the Entire Portfolio

Given the probability-generating function (6.25), it is straightforward to derive the loss distribution, since

$$P(loss\ of\ nL) = \frac{1}{n!}\frac{d^n G(z)}{dz^n}\Big|_{z=0}\ for\ n = 1, 2, \ldots$$

These probabilities can be expressed in closed form and depend on only two sets of parameters: μ_j and η_j.(See Credit Suisse 1997, p. 26.)

Extensions of the Basic Model

CreditRisk+ proposes several extensions of the basic one-period, one-factor model. First, the model can be easily extended to a multiperiod framework;

second, the variability of default rates can be assumed to result from a number of "background" factors, each representing a sector of activity. Each factor, k, is represented by a random variable, X_k, which is the number of defaults in sector k and which is assumed to be gamma distributed. The mean default rate for each obligor is then supposed to be a linear function of the background factors, X_k. These factors are further assumed to be independent.

In all cases, CreditRisk+ derives a closed-form solution for the loss distribution of a bond/loan portfolio.

Advantages and Limitations of CreditRisk+

CreditRisk+ has the advantage that it is relatively easy to implement. First, as we mentioned above, closed-form expressions can be derived for the probability of portfolio bond/loan losses, and this makes CreditRisk+ very attractive from a computational point of view. In addition, marginal risk contributions by the obligor can be easily computed. Second, CreditRisk+ focuses on default, and therefore it requires relatively few estimates and "inputs." For each instrument, only the probability of default and the exposure are required.

Its principal limitation is the same as for the CreditMetrics and KMV approaches: the methodology assumes that credit risk has no relationship to the level of market risk. In addition, CreditRisk+ ignores what might be called "migration risk"; the exposure for each obligor is fixed and is not sensitive to possible future changes in the credit quality of the issuer or to the variability of future interest rates. Even in its most general form, where the probability of default depends upon several stochastic background factors, the credit exposures are taken to be constant and are not related to changes in these factors.

Finally, like the CreditMetrics and KMV approaches, CreditRisk+ is not able to cope satisfactorily with nonlinear products such as options and foreign currency swaps.

ELEMENTS OF MERTON'S MODEL

The firm's assets value, V_t, is assumed to follow a standard geometric Brownian motion, that is:

$$V_t = V_0 \exp\left\{(\mu - \frac{\sigma^2}{2})t + \sigma\sqrt{t}Z_t\right\} \tag{6.26}$$

with $Z_t \sim N(0,1)$, μ and σ^2 being respectively the mean and variance of the instantaneous rate of return on the assets of the firm, $\frac{dV_t}{V_t}$. V_t is lognormally distributed, with expected value at time t of, $\overline{V_t} = E(V_t) = V_o \exp\{\mu t\}$. The dynamics of $V(t)$ is described by $\frac{dV_t}{V_t} = \mu dt + \sigma dW_t$ where W_t is a standard Brownian motion, and $\sqrt{t}Z_t \equiv W_t - W_0$ is normally distributed with a zero mean and a variance equal to t.[41] It is assumed that the firm has a very simple capital structure, as it is financed only by equity, S_t, and by a single zero-coupon debt instrument maturing at time T, with face value F and current market value B_t. (table A4.1). The value of the assets of the firm is denoted by V_t: $V_t = S_t + B_t$.

Denote by p_{Def} the probability of default, that is, $p_{Def} = \Pr[V_t \leq V_{Def}]$ where V_{Def} is the critical asset value below which default occurs. According to (6.26), default occurs when Z_t satisfies:

$$p_{Def} = \Pr\left[\frac{\ln\left(\frac{V_{Def}}{V_0}\right) - \left(\mu - \frac{\sigma^2}{2}\right)t}{\sigma\sqrt{t}} \geq Z_t\right]$$

$$= \Pr\left[Z_t \leq -\frac{\ln\left[\frac{V_0}{V_{Def}}\right] + \left[\mu - \frac{\sigma^2}{2}\right]t}{\sigma\sqrt{t}}\right] = N(-d_2) \qquad (6.27)$$

where the normalized return:

$$r = \frac{\ln\left(\frac{V_t}{V_0}\right) - \left(\mu - \frac{\sigma^2}{2}\right)t}{\sigma\sqrt{t}} \qquad (6.28)$$

is $N[0,1]$. Z_{CCC} is simply the threshold point in the standard normal distribution, $N(0,1)$, corresponding to a cumulative probability of p_{Def}. Then, the critical asset value V_{Def} which triggers default is such that $Z_{CCC} = -d_2$ where:

$$d_2 \equiv \frac{\ln\left(\frac{V_0}{V_{Def}}\right) + \left(\mu - \frac{\sigma^2}{2}\right)t}{\sigma\sqrt{t}} \qquad (6.29)$$

and is also called "distance to default."[42]

If we denote by r_{BB} and r_A the instantaneous rates of return on the assets of obligors that are rated BB and A, respectively, and by ρ the instantaneous correlation coefficient between r_A and r_{BB}, then the normalized log-returns on both assets follow a joint normal distribution:

$$f(r_{BB}, r_A; \rho) = \frac{1}{2\pi\sqrt{1-\rho^2}}\exp\left\{\frac{-1}{2(1-\rho^2)}\left[r_{BB}^2 - 2\rho r_{BB} r_A + r_A^2\right]\right\}$$

This joint normal distribution is useful in calculating the joint-migration matrix for the two obligors initially rated A and BB. Consider two obligors whose probabilities of default are P_{def1} and P_{def2}, respectively. Their asset return correlation is ρ. The events of default for obligors 1 and 2 are denoted $def1$ and $def2$, respectively, and $P(def1, def2)$ is the joint probability of default. Then, it can be shown (Lucas 1995) that the default correlation is:

$$corr(def1, def2) = \frac{P_{1,2} - P_1 P_2}{\sqrt{P_1(1-P_1)P_2(1-P_2)}} \qquad (6.30)$$

The joint probability of both obligors defaulting is, according to Merton's model:

$$P(def1, def2) = \Pr\left[V_1 \le V_{def1}, V_2 \le V_{def2}\right] \qquad (6.31)$$

V_1 and V_2 denote the asset values for both obligors at time t, and V_{def1} and V_{def2} are the corresponding critical values that trigger default. Expression (6.31) is equivalent to:

$$P(def1, def2) = \Pr\left[r_1 \le d_2^1, r_2 \le d_2^2\right] = N_2\left(-d_2^1, -d_2^2, \rho\right) \qquad (6.32)$$

where r_1 and r_2 denote the normalized asset returns for obligors 1 and 2, respectively, and d_2^1 and d_2^2 are the corresponding distance to default as in (A4.4). $N_2(x, y, \rho)$ denotes the cumulative standard bivariate normal distribution where ρ is the correlation coefficient between x and y.

Notes

1. The new proposal refers to three pillars of risk supervision and control: Pillar 1 focuses on minimal capital requirements, Pillar 2 addresses the issue of risk control and risk management, and Pillar 3 focuses on disclosure.

2. See Crouhy, Galai, and Mark (2001), chapter 2, for a detailed presentation of the 1988 Accord.

3. A revolver is a facility that allows one to borrow and repay the loan at will within a certain period of time.

4. KMV is a trademark of KMV Corporation. The initials KMV stand for the first letter of the last names of Stephen Kealhofer, John McQuown, and Oldrich Vasicek, who are the founders of KMV Corporation.

5. SME stands for small and medium-size entities, which, according to Basel II, are firms with sales for the consolidated group of less than 50 million Euros.

6. In April 1995, the Basel Committee issued a consultative proposal to amend the 1988 Accord, which became known as BIS 98 after it was implemented in January 1998. BIS 98 requires financial institutions with significant trading activities to measure and hold capital to cover their exposure to the market risk associated with debt and equity positions in their trading books, and foreign exchange and commodity positions in both the trading and banking books (see BCBS 1996).

7. Regulatory capital is broader than equity capital. It has three components: Tier 1, or core capital, which includes commonstockholders' equity, noncumulative perpetual preferred stock, and minority equity interests in consolidated subsidiaries, less goodwill and other deductions; Tier 2, or supplementary capital, which includes hybrid capital instruments such as cumulative perpetual preferred shares; and Tier 3, or subsupplementary capital, which consists of short-term subordinated debt with an original maturity of at least two years.

8. The only exceptions occurred just after the close of the study, in the first quarter of 2001, when Southern California Edison and Pacific Gas & Electric defaulted on their bonds, which were rated AA- as of December 31, 2000.

9. Others may be included, such as credit cards, residential mortgages, and commercial mortgages.

10. The credit conversion factor is 0% only for unconditionally and immediately cancellable commitments.

11. Portfolio effects are indirectly captured in the proposed formula through the average asset correlation embedded in the calculation of the risk weights.

12. A 1% *PD* in these formula should be input as 0.01.

13. The actual relationship between economic capital and *LGD* is not exactly linear and varies across models. However, the linearity assumption is a good approximation.

14. Note that there is still discussion in the industry about whether this assumption is legitimate. Some banks propose instead to make the correlation an increasing function of size. But the size of a typical commercial borrower in North America, in Europe, or in Asia is quite different, so that it seems difficult to propose a unique calibration for all countries.

15. The notation for *N(x)* and *G(z)* have already been defined in (6.5). A 1% *PD* in these formulas should be input as 0.01.

16. This IIF/ISDA table is similar to the one shown in table 6.3 but is generated at the higher confidence level of 99.9% instead of 99.5%. We don't show it here.

17. Kamakura, a consulting firm with Professor Robert Jarrow as a principal of the company, is currently working on a commercial model based on this framework. Professor Jarrow is one of the pioneers of the reduced form approach.

18. Note that, conditional on the current realized value of the common risk factors, default events are independent across obligors. This greatly facilitates the derivation of the loss distribution.

19. We have eliminated the exposure to rating 0 (government securities), whose default probability is zero.

20. KMV calculates asset returns correlations that are derived from a proprietary multifactor model, while CreditMetrics calculates equity returns correlation (see appendix).

21. Note that, in KMV's jargon, *UL* denotes the standard deviation of the distribution of the portfolio values (σ_P).

22. An alternative, and more intuitive, measure of the risk contribution for each facility is $\frac{\partial UL_P}{\partial w_i}$. It also satisfies the property that the sum of the risk contributions is equal to the unexpected loss for the portfolio. However, there is no analytical derivation of this quantity, and numerical calculations based on Monte Carlo simulations prove to be very unstable and inaccurate.

23. The risk contributions as defined by (6.8) are calculated analytically.

24. See formula (33) p. 40 in Credit Suisse (1997).

25. There is an anomaly in the results for KMV as the capital attribution for risk rating 11 is lower for the three-year than for the one-year facilities. Note that in table 6.5 default correlations are assumed to be zero.

26. Validation of portfolio loss probabilities over a one-year horizon at the 99% confidence level implies 100 years of data. This is clearly not feasible.

27. This is the backtesting methodology that we use at CIBC for the implementation of CIBC's value-at-risk model in the trading book.

28. CreditMetrics' approach applies primarily to bonds and loans, which are both treated in the same manner. It can be easily extended to any type of financial claims such as receivables and financial letters of credit, for which we can derive easily the forward value at the risk horizon for all credit ratings. For derivatives such as swaps or forwards, the model needs to be somewhat adjusted or "twisted," since

there is no satisfactory way to derive the exposure, and the loss distribution, within the proposed framework (since it assumes deterministic interest rates).

29. CreditMetrics calculates the forward value of the bonds, or loans, cum compounded coupons paid out during the year.

30. The mean, m, and the variance, σ^2, of the distribution for ΔV can be calculated from the data in Table 6.19 as follows:

$$m = mean(\Delta V) = \sum_i p_i \Delta V_i$$

$$= 0.02\% \times 1.82 + 0.33\% \times 1.64 + \ldots + 0.18\% \times (-56.42)$$

$$= -0.46$$

$$\sigma^2 = variance(\Delta V) = \sum_i p_i(\Delta V_i - m)^2$$

$$= 0.02\%(1.82 - 0.46)^2 + 0.33\%(1.64 - 0.46)^2 + \ldots + 0.18\%(-56.42 - 0.46)^2 = 8.95$$

and

$$\sigma = 2.99$$

The first percentile of a normal distribution N (m, σ^2) is $(m - 2.33 \sigma)$, or -7.43.

31. Note that d_2 is different from its equivalent in the Black-Scholes formula, since, here, we work with the "actual" instead of the "risk-neutral" return distributions, so that the drift term in d_2 is the expected return on the firm's assets, instead of the risk-free interest rate, as in Black-Scholes.

32. In what follows, "exogenous" refers to the assumptions specified outside the model and that constitute a given in the model derivation, while "endogenous" characterizes results derived from the model.

33. The model builds on Black and Cox's extension (1976) of Merton's model (1974).

34. A leverage factor equal to 0.7 can be presented by a face value $F = 77$.

35. The computed cost of default is slightly different from the put value due to rounding errors.

36. The composition of its liabilities: equity, short-term and long-term debt, convertible bonds, and so on.

37. CreditRisk+ is a trademark of Credit Suisse Financial Products (CSFP), now reorganized into CSFB. CreditRisk+ is described in a CSFP publication; see Credit Suisse (1997).

38. In any portfolio, there is, naturally, a finite number of obligors, say n; therefore, the Poisson distribution, which specifies the probability of n defaults, for $n = 1, \ldots, \infty$ is only an approximation. However, if the number of obligors, n, is large enough, then the sum of the probabilities of $n + 1, n + 2, \ldots$ defaults becomes negligible.

39. Expression (6.1) can be derived from the probability-generating function for a portfolio of independent obligors (see Credit Suisse 1997, pp. 34–35).

40. CreditRisk+ assumes that the mean default rate is gamma distributed. Mean default rate volatility may also reflect the influence of default correlation and background factors, such as a change in the rate of growth in the economy, which may in turn affect the correlation of default events.

41. In fact, the process for the market value of the firm should be written as $dV_t = (\mu V_t - C)dt + \sigma V_t dW_t$ where C denotes the net dollar payout by the firm to shareholders and bondholders. Here, we assume that no dividend and no coupon are paid out; debt is in the form of a zero coupon.

42. Note that d_2 is different from its equivalent in the Black-Scholes formula, since, here, we work with the "actual" instead of the "risk-neutral" return distributions, so that the drift term in d_2 is the expected return on the firm's assets, instead of the risk-free interest rate as in Black-Scholes.

References

Altman, Edward I., Sreedhar T. Bharath, and Anthony Saunders. 2002. Credit Ratings and the BIS Capital Adequacy Reform Agenda. *Journal of Banking and Finance* 26 (5): 909–21.

Basel Committee on Banking Supervision (BCBS). 1996. Amendment to the Capital Accord to Incorporate Market Risks. Basel Committee Publication No. 24. Available at: www.bis.org/publ/bcbs24.pdf.

———. 2001a. The New Basel Capital Accord. Basel Committee Consultative Paper. Available at: www.bis.org/publ/bcbsca03.pdf.

———. 2001b. Potential Modifications to the Committee's Proposal. The New Basel Capital Accord Quantitative Impact Study 2. Available at: www.bis.org/bcbs/capotenmodif.pdf.

Bensoussan, Alain, Michel Crouhy, and Dan Galai. 1994. Stochastic Equity Volatility Related to the Leverage Effect I: Equity Volatility Behavior. *Applied Mathematical Finance* 1: 63–85.

———. 1995. Stochastic Equity Volatility Related to the Leverage Effect II: Valuation of European Equity Options and Warrants. *Applied Mathematical Finance* 2: 43–60.

Black, Fischer, and John C. Cox. 1976. Valuing Corporate Securities: Some Effects of Bond Indenture Provisions. *Journal of Finance* 31 (2): 351–67.

Black, Fischer, and Myron S. Scholes. 1973. The Pricing of Options and Corporate Liabilities. *Journal of Political Economy* 81 (3): 637–54.

Carty, Lea V., and Dana Lieberman. 1996. Defaulted Bank Loan Recoveries. Moody's Investors Service Global Credit Research Special Report. Available at: http://riskcalc.moodysrms.com/us/research/lied/20641.pdf.

CreditMetrics. 1997. Technical Document: The Benchmark for Understanding Credit Risk. J.P. Morgan.

Credit Suisse. 1997. CreditRisk+: A Credit Risk Management Framework. Available at: www.csfb.com/institutional/research/assets/creditrisk.pdf.

Crnkovic, Cedomir, and Jordan Drachman. 1996. Quality Control. *Risk* 9 (9): 138–43.

Crouhy, Michel, Dan Galai, and Robert Mark. 2001. *Risk Management*. New York: McGraw-Hill.

Institute of International Finance, Inc. and International Swaps and Derivatives Association (IIF/ISDA). 2000. Modeling Credit Risk: Joint IIF/ISDA Testing Program (February).

Jarrow, Robert A., and Stuart M. Turnbull. 1995. Pricing Derivatives on Financial Securities Subject to Credit Risk. *Journal of Finance* 50 (1): 53–85.

Kealhofer, Steven. 1995. Managing Default Risk in Portfolios of Derivatives. In *Derivative Credit Risk: Further Advances in Measurement and Management*, ed. David Lando, 49–66. London: Risk Books.

———. 1998. Portfolio Management of Default Risk. *Net Exposure* 1 (2).

Lopez, Jose A., and Marc R. Saidenberg. 1999. Evaluating Credit Risk Models. Federal Reserve Banks of San Francisco Working Paper No. 99-06. Available at: www.frbsf.org/econrsrch/workingp/wp99-06.pdf.

Lucas, Douglas J. 1995. Default Correlation and Credit Analysis. *Journal of Fixed Income* (March): 76–87.

McDonough, William J. 1998. Issues for the Basel Accord. Speech delivered before the Conference on Credit Risk Modeling and Regulatory Implications, London (September). Reproduced in the 1998 Annual Report of the Federal Reserve Bank of New York.

Merton, Robert C. 1974. On the Pricing of Corporate Debt: The Risk Structure of Interest Rates. *Journal of Finance* 29: 449–70.

Standard & Poors. 1996. *Credit Week* (April 15).

Vasicek, Oldrich A. 1997. Credit Valuation. *Net Exposure* 1 (1).

Wilson, Thomas C. 1997a. Portfolio Credit Risk I. *Risk* 10 (9): 111–17.

———. 1997b. Portfolio Credit Risk II. *Risk* 10 (10): 56–61.

7

Sizing Operational Risk and the Effect of Insurance: Implications for the Basel II Capital Accord

ANDREW P. KURITZKES AND HAL S. SCOTT

This chapter addresses the issue of whether and to what extent banks should be required by regulation to hold capital against operational risks. It argues that the types of operational risk for which Basel II requires capital, internal or external event risks, are and should be dealt with by other means—better controls, loss provisions, or insurance. Basel's definition of "operational risk" excludes the major category of nonfinancial risk for which banks do hold capital—namely, business risk. According to the chapter's estimates, business risk accounts for slightly more than half of a bank's total nonfinancial risk, which, in turn, averages about 25 to 30% of economic capital. Analyzing legal risk, as a type of operational risk, the chapter shows the difficulties in defining or predicting such risk, and that the amount of such risk will vary depending on the legal jurisdictions to which a bank is subject. It also argues that the Basel II limit of 20% on capital mitigation achievable through insurance is arbitrary and creates a perverse incentive for banks to be underinsured. It generally concludes that banks should not be required by regulation to hold capital for operational risks; the issue would be better dealt with through supervision and market discipline.

This chapter shows the difficulty of regulating bank capital for operational risk. Basel excludes business risk from the definition of operational risk even though business risk is the primary operational risk for which banks actually hold capital. Basel has acknowledged the difficulties in its approach by giving more latitude to the use of bank models for operational risk under the advanced management approach (AMA) than for credit risk under the IRB approach; this is despite there being as yet no tested models for operational risk. The fact that banks routinely hold more capital than Basel requires can be explained by the demands of the market that banks have adequate capital to deal with business risk. The case for regulatory capital is undermined if the market generally demands more capital than does regulation.

This chapter addresses the issue of regulatory capital for operational risk, focusing on the Bank for International Settlements (BIS) proposals for banking organizations—the New Basel Capital Accord, or Basel II. The chapter is organized into four parts. The first part defines "operational risk" and examines how a financial firm should determine how much operational risk capital to hold.[1] The second part looks at legal risk as a microcosmic example of operational risk. The third part examines how the presence of insurance should affect this issue. The fourth part summarizes key conclusions and draws policy implications from the analysis.

CAPITAL FOR OPERATIONAL RISK

The General Problem

Basel II calls for the introduction of bank regulatory capital requirements for operational risk. The operational risk proposals are among the most significant provisions of Basel II, since they would extend bank regulatory capital to nonfinancial risks for the first time. These proposals have significantly changed over time.

The Earlier Proposals

When the second consultative package of the Basel Accord was released in January 2001 (CP2), it incorporated a capital charge for operational risk that would amount, on an industrywide basis, to 20% of the total regulatory capital (BCBS 2001a). The level of required capital was criticized on a number of grounds, one of which was that it did not take into account the fact that banks held insurance policies for many of the risks that were included in the new capital charge. Under the revised proposal of September 2001, the total charge was lowered to an average 12% of current regulatory capital, partly in response to the existing insurance coverage (BCBS 2001b, p. 1). CP2 proposed three approaches to operational risk, depending on the sophistication of the bank. Under the basic indicator approach, banks were required to hold capital for operational risks equal to a fixed percentage of gross income. Under the more sophisticated standardized approach, they were to hold capital based on their gross income for eight different business lines. Under the advanced management approach (AMA), banks could use their own models to determine necessary capital, subject to holding capital equal to at least 75% of what would be required under the standardized approach. This meant that the maximum reduction in capital from the level required under the standardized approach, as a result of the use of models *and* insurance, was 25%. It also meant that banks that used the basic indicator or standardized approach could achieve no reduction in capital through the use of insurance. The 75% floor of the AMA approach was subsequently dropped in 2002 after much criticism from both academics and industry (BIS 2002).

Changes in the Current Proposal

The latest proposal, of April 2003, makes three important changes. First, it gives banks that use the AMA approach more flexibility in the use of models; second, it puts a limit of 20% on the amount of capital reduction that banks that use the AMA approach can obtain through the use of insurance (BCBS 2003a). In addition, the committee will allow supervisors to permit banks to use an alternative standardized approach (ASA) "to the extent supervisors are satisfied that it provides an improved basis by, for example, avoiding double counting of risks" (BCBS 2003a, paragraph 94).[2] The ASA is the same as the standardized approach except for two business lines, retail and commercial banking. For these lines, total loans and advances (an asset rather than an income measure) are multiplied by a fixed factor to determine the capital charge. (BCBS 2003b, paragraph 122).

Banks that use the standardized or AMA approaches must qualify by meeting certain requirements: (1) the bank's board of directors and senior management, as appropriate, must be actively involved in the oversight of the operational risk management framework; (2) the bank must have a risk management system that is conceptually sound and implemented with integrity; and (3) the bank must have sufficient resources in the use of the approach in major business lines as well as in control and audit areas. Supervisors can require an initial monitoring period before the standardized approach can be used, but, apparently, before AMA can be used, initial monitoring is obligatory (BCBS 2003b, paragraphs 620–22).

For a given bank, the capital charges for operational risk will be incremental to existing requirements for credit and market risk—the two sources of bank risk that are already subject to minimum capital rules. The overall calibration for credit and market risk, however, has been adjusted to keep the total amount of regulatory capital in the banking system unchanged. It is expected that the operational risk capital charge will be 12% of current minimum regulatory capital. To accommodate BCBS's objective of not increasing overall capital requirements, the new capital requirement for operational risk has led to a corresponding reduction in capital for credit risk. According to the most recent quantitative impact exercise, known as QIS 3, it is expected that banks that use the AMA approach would have a 14% decline in the capital requirement for credit risk, offset by the 12% increase for operational risk, for a net decline of 2% (BCBS 2003c, p. 26).

Basel II would become effective in January 2007.

U.S. Implementation

On February 27, 2003, the Federal Reserve Board announced how it would implement Basel II operational risk requirements at the end of 2006.[3] At that time, the United States would mandate the 10 largest internationally active U.S. banks to use the advanced internal ratings approach (A-IRB) for credit risk and the AMA for operational risk. The Fed is developing criteria to identify these banks on the basis of asset size and foreign activities. Other banks could continue to use the current Basel rules, which include no charge for operational risk, or they could seek supervisory approval to use A-IRB and AMA. The Fed has stated that it expects an additional 10 banks to do so.[4] The Fed has also stated that it expects the cushion built into the current Basel rules for credit risk to be adequate to cover operational risks for those banks that do not use the new Basel rules where a separate operational risk charge is assessed. It is expected that the 20 banks that use Basel II will account for approximately two-thirds of all U.S. banking assets. In addition, those U.S. banks are expected to account for about 99% of all foreign assets held by the top 50 domestic U.S. banking organizations, with the 10 mandatory banks themselves accounting for about 95% (Ferguson 2003).

This section now turns to a series of questions that are raised by the Basel II proposals:

- *Definition*: What risks are captured within the Basel II definition of operational risk? While the term "operational risk" is commonly used to refer to all nonfinancial risks, the Basel II definition applies to only a subset of nonfinancial risks—those resulting from the failure of "internal processes, people, or systems" or from external events (BCBS 2001b, p. 1). The starting point for evaluating the Basel II proposals is to place the definition of operational risk in the context of a broader taxonomy of bank risks.

- *Bottom-up measurement*: How can operational risks be measured in terms of intrinsic—or economic—capital requirements? Are there unique challenges in trying to quantify operational risk? The ability to allocate capital to operational risk will ultimately hinge on the ability to measure it. If the purpose of risk-based capital allocation is to reflect differences across banks in business mix and risk profile, then operational risk measurement will need to be supported bottom-up within individual institutions.

- *Relative magnitude*: Given available top-down estimates, how big a problem is operational risk relative to other sources of bank risk? Is operational risk, as defined by Basel II (see figure 7.1), the main driver of nonfinancial earnings volatility? A preliminary sizing of operational risk helps address whether the problem is worth the regulatory candle: in effect, is this where regulators (and banks) should be spending resources on risk and capital measurement?

- *Effectiveness*: On the basis of the evidence, is capital the appropriate regulatory mechanism for protecting banks against operational risk? Unlike most financial risks, operational risk can be mitigated through improved "processes, people, and systems" and/or transferred to third parties through insurance. To the extent that operational risks are difficult to quantify and can be controlled ex ante, alternative approaches to capital regulation may be more effective at protecting banks against operational losses.

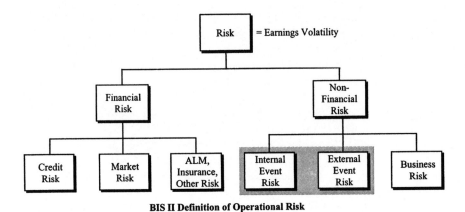

BIS II Definition of Operational Risk

Figure 7.1. Taxonomy of Bank Risk. Source: Authors' compilation.

Definition of Operational Risk

The first step in analyzing the new capital requirements is to fit operational risks within a broader bank risk and capital framework.

"Risk" for a bank is defined in terms of earnings volatility. Earnings volatility creates the potential for loss. Losses, in turn, need to be funded, and it is the potential for loss that imposes a need for banks to hold capital. Capital provides a balance sheet cushion to absorb losses, without which a bank subjected to large (negative) earnings swings could become insolvent.

Risk can be divided into two main sources of earnings volatility: financial risk and nonfinancial risk. Financial risks are risks that a bank assumes directly in its role as a financial principal or intermediary. They can be classified into the familiar categories of credit and market risk, as well as asset/liability mismatch risk, liquidity risk, and, potentially, insurance underwriting risk. The assumption of financial risk is one of the defining characteristics of a financial institution—and the dominant reason why banks hold capital.

Unlike financial risk, nonfinancial risk is not a distinctive feature of financial institutions but is common to all firms. Nonfinancial risk arises because a firm may incur an operating loss due to nonfinancial causes—in other words, for reasons other than unexpectedly large credit losses, market trading losses, asset liability mismatch losses, or insurance underwriting losses. The cause of a nonfinancial operating loss could be a drop in revenues, a surge in costs, an internal operating failure, or an uncontrollable external event. Whatever the cause, a firm needs to hold sufficient capital to fund the loss. The need for capital is analogous to the role of equity in a nonfinancial company—and explains why commercial firms cannot operate with infinite leverage.

Nonfinancial risk can be subdivided into categories on the basis of risk factors or causes of loss. Three main categories include the following:

- *Internal event risk.* These risks refer to losses from internal failures, such as fraud, operating errors, systems failures, and legal liability and compliance costs. A recent example of an internal event risk is the $700 million loss suffered by Allied Irish in February 2002 as a result of unauthorized trading at its Allfirst subsidiary.
- *External event risk.* These risks refer to losses from uncontrollable external events such as earthquakes or other natural catastrophes, terrorism, war, and acts of God. A stark example of an external event risk is the $85 million loss reported by the Bank of New York—a major securities processing bank headquartered in lower Manhattan—as a result of the terrorist strike on September 11.
- *Business risk.* This category refers to residual nonfinancial earnings volatility not attributable to internal or external events. Business risk is a catchall that covers losses from such factors as a drop in volumes, a shift in demand, a price squeeze, a cost surge, regulatory changes, or technological obsolescence. A recent example of business risk is the $1 billion loss reported by Credit Suisse First Boston (CSFB) in the fourth quarter of 2001, because of the collapse in investment banking activity in that period.[5]

Significantly, the Basel II definition of operational risk does not refer to all sources of nonfinancial risk but defines operational risk as "the risk of loss resulting from inadequate or failed internal processes, people, and systems, or from external events" (BCBS 2001b, p. 2). This definition is underinclusive in two key respects: First, it ignores business risk—the catchall category of risk that results when a firm runs a loss for ordinary economic reasons. CSFB's $1 billion loss, like that of other Wall Street firms in the fourth quarter of 2001, would be excluded from the Basel II definition.

Second, as clarified in the most recent BIS working paper on operational risk, only the direct losses associated with internal and external events are captured within the scope of the Basel II definition. Specifically excluded are strategic and reputation risks, as well as any opportunity costs associated with operational failures. Thus, in terms of the three categories of nonfinancial risk, the BIS definition can be reduced to direct losses associated with internal or external events.

While the Basel II definition may be a practical attempt to put a boundary around the scope of nonfinancial risk, a key problem in restricting the definition is that the categories of nonfinancial risks are inherently overlapping. Internal and external events can quickly bleed into business risk; in fact, the knock-on effects can often be greater than the initial loss. The events of September 11 provide an obvious example. Under the Basel II definition, operational risk would capture the direct losses to a bank from the terrorist attacks, including loss of life, injury to workers, damage to property, and other direct costs (e.g., systems failures). But the definition would exclude the costs of business disruption that affected banks around the world (the U.S. stock markets were closed for four days), let alone any broader economic impact triggered by the event. To see this point, one has only to compare the $85 million direct loss for September 11 reported by the Bank of New York with the $1 billion business loss reported by CSFB the following quarter.[6] The case is equally true with internal event risks: the real threat to Arthur Andersen from the shredding of Enron documents was not the financial penalty at stake in the government's criminal prosecution but the implosion of the firm's business caused by massive client attrition.

As these examples illustrate, the direct losses of internal and external events may not be the most significant source of nonfinancial risk. The Basel II focus on internal and external events may have more to do with the ease with which they can be classified for purposes of monitoring and reporting losses than with their actual contribution to earnings volatility.

Bottom-Up Measurement

Ultimately, the question of how much capital should be allocated to operational risk is a problem of measurement. Within banking, economic capital has become the accepted standard for measuring the intrinsic capital needed to support risk taking. Indeed, the Basel II proposals specifically adopt economic capital as the relevant metric for calculating operational risk "bottom-up" under the advanced measurement approach.

The theory of economic capital is easy to state. As shown in figure 7.2, economic capital defines risk at a common point—or confidence interval—in

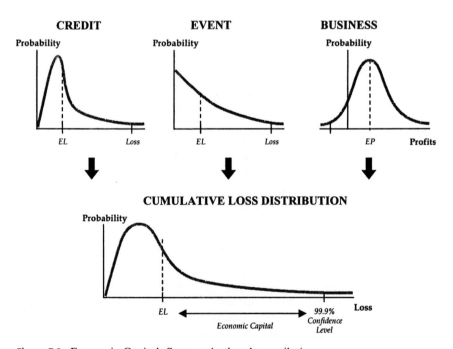

Figure 7.2. Economic Capital. Source: Authors' compilation.

a loss (or value) distribution. Typically, the confidence interval is tied to the bank's solvency standard; for example, a bank that holds sufficient capital to protect against losses at the 99.9% level has a .10% risk of default—about the same solvency standard (or default risk) as an A-rated bond. By defining risk in probabilistic terms, economic capital establishes a common currency for risk that allows exposures to be directly compared across different risk classes, such as credit risk, event risk, and business risk. It also allows risk to be aggregated across different risk classes (on the basis of underlying correlations) to create a cumulative loss distribution for the institution as a whole. These relationships are shown in figure 7.3.

It is important to note that, because capital is needed only to absorb unexpected swings in earnings, economic capital is attributed to the difference between the mean of the loss distribution (EL) and the designated confidence interval. Mean, or expected, losses are already reflected in expected earnings. They are not considered risk per se but rather a cost of the business. Expected losses are either accounted for through reserves, as in the case of credit provisions, or budgeted into the expense base, as in the case of routine operational errors. It is only variations in expected loss that create earnings volatility—in particular, the larger than expected losses that are responsible for downside volatility.

The division of the loss distribution into "expected loss" (covered by reserves or expected expenses) and "unexpected loss" (covered by capital) has significant implications for operational risk. As shown in figure 7.3, internal and external events can be characterized in a two-by-two matrix according to (1) whether they are high or low frequency events, and (2)

	Low severity	High severity
High frequency	Expected loss e.g., routine processing errors	N/A
Low frequency	Expected loss e.g., branch robbery	Capital (self-insure) or insurance, e.g., 9/11

Figure 7.3. Measuring Operational Risk. Source: Authors.

whether the impact of the event is high or low in terms of loss severity. Capital for operational risk is not required for high-frequency, low-severity events, such as routine processing errors in a high-volume business, since these will be budgeted for in the expense base and reflected in expected earnings. Capital, however, is necessary to backstop against low-frequency, high-severity events—the rare events that threaten the solvency of the institution and contribute to the "tail" of the bank's loss distribution. (Low-frequency, low-severity events are, by definition, immaterial. High-frequency, high-severity events are assumed to be a null category, since repeated high losses would put a bank out of business.)

In practice, economic capital for operational risk is very difficult to estimate internally.[7] There are a number of reasons for this:

- *Paucity of data.* The first—and most fundamental—reason is that data for operational losses are limited. By nature, low-frequency, high-severity losses seldom occur within any one bank. While there are well-known examples of extreme operational losses, such as the unauthorized trading losses that led to the collapse of Barings in 1995, most banks lack data on exactly the type of loss events that are most relevant for estimating economic capital. For this reason, the Basel II proposals require that banks that use the advanced measurement approach supplement internal data sources with external data on extreme events.

- *Endogeneity.* External data, however, may often not be strictly comparable to a bank's own loss potential because operational losses are, to a significant degree, endogenous. Management can take steps to prevent or mitigate operational losses, through improved business processes, audit, and controls. The problem with applying external data is in judging how relevant another bank's extreme loss is to a bank's own internal operations. From the perspective of a well-run institution, is a bank that incurred a large operational loss unlucky or just poorly managed? The question of comparability becomes even more acute the longer the time series used to estimate event losses, because industry practices—for example, segregation of front- and back-office activities in trading rooms, systems backup and contingency planning—evolve in response to previous events.

- *Insurance.* To the extent that operational losses cannot be mitigated by internal processes and controls, they often can be insured by third parties. This is particularly true of external event risks. As discussed in the next section, any measurement framework for operational losses must take into account the effects of insurance—both on historical experience (e.g., how did insurance affect realized losses reported in internal or external data?) and on prospective exposure.

- *Definitional problems.* As noted, operational losses do not fit neatly into a single category. Not only can internal and external event risks bleed into business risk, but operational risks can also overlap with credit and market risk. For example, a documentation error that leads to a lower recovery on a defaulted loan is, in principle, part credit risk, part operational risk. But segregating the causes is likely to prove difficult from a measurement perspective, especially when working with historical data.

- *Correlations.* To the degree that internal and external risk events can be discretely estimated, a further problem lies in aggregating individual events into a cumulative loss distribution. Portfolio theory is clear that unless perfectly correlated, the whole will be less than the sum of the parts. Since many operational risks reflect random occurrences, cross-event correlations are likely to be low. This suggests that aggregate capital should be significantly less than that implied for individual events on a stand-alone basis. A bottom-up economic capital model for operational risks needs to have an explicit method for taking correlations into account.

Reflecting these challenges, operational risk measurement is at a much more primitive stage of evolution than credit or market risk measurement. Banks are only now beginning to collect data systematically, both internally and externally, and to experiment with techniques for modeling operational risks. Ironically, these modeling techniques appear to be at a much earlier stage of development—and are likely to be more unstable—than the credit portfolio models considered and rejected by the Basel Committee for use in setting credit risk capital requirements (BCBS 1999). It is an open question whether the models will be sufficiently robust to support meaningful internal capital allocation for operational risk by the 2006 implementation deadline.

Top-Down Estimates of Nonfinancial Risk

Given the difficulty of estimating low-frequency, high-severity events for individual banks, an alternative approach is to develop top-down estimates for a group of banks that use market data. This admittedly "back of the envelope" approach can be applied to answer some basic questions about the magnitude of nonfinancial risk:

- How large is nonfinancial risk as a proportion of banks' total earnings volatility?
- What is the size of the internal and external event risks ("operational risk" as defined by BIS) relative to business risk?
- How do top-down market estimates of nonfinancial risk compare to the internal economic capital calculations used by large banks?

Top-Down Estimate of Total Nonfinancial Risk

By definition, total nonfinancial risk (inclusive of event and business risk) is measured by residual earnings volatility once financial risks have been stripped out. Nonfinancial risk can therefore be estimated by deviations in a return measure, such as return on risk-weighted assets (RORWA), provided returns are neutralized for the impact of financial volatility. As a proxy, this can be done by adding back credit provisions and subtracting trading gains/(losses) from RORWA to yield an adjusted measure, RORWA*:

RORWA* = RORWA + credit provisions $-/+$ trading gains (losses)

Figure 7.4 shows an analysis of deviation in RORWA* for a sample of 45 of the 50 largest U.S. banks for an eight-year period, from 1994 through 2001.[8] On the basis of the distribution (360 data points), the standard deviation of RORWA* is calculated to be 50 bp of assets. Given the skewness in the distribution, the 99.9% confidence interval is roughly five times the standard deviation, or 2.5% of assets.

This result—2.5% of risk-weighted assets (RWA)—can be directly compared to existing regulatory capital requirements, since BIS capital requirements are defined as 8% of RWA. It suggests that at the 99.9% level—the same solvency standard set for operational risk under the advanced measurement approach—economic capital for total nonfinancial risk is roughly 31% of the BIS' total capital requirement (2.5% divided by 8.0%).

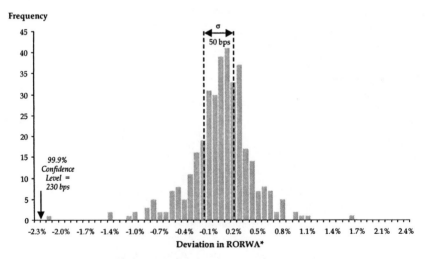

- Top 50 US banks
- 8 years (1994–2001), 360 observations
- RORWA*= RORWA – Credit Provisions – Trading Gains
- σ = 50 bps x 5⇒ Economic Capital≈ 2.5% of Assets

Figure 7.4. Top-Down Estimate: Nonfinancial Risk. Source: Bank Regulatory Reporting OWC Analysis.

Top-Down Estimates of Event Risk

Unlike nonfinancial earnings volatility, economic capital for internal and external event risk is difficult to estimate by conventional distribution analysis because event risks are highly skewed, with a large number of high-frequency, low-severity events and a small but appreciable number of low-frequency, high-severity events. Data drawn from the mode of the distribution are not very useful for characterizing the behavior of the tail in the region relevant for economic capital.

An alternative approach is to focus directly on the tail of the distribution by applying extreme value theory to large, reported event losses. While only limited information is publicly disclosed about operational losses, extreme losses, such as rogue trading scandals or major compliance failures, are reported in the press and included as extraordinary items in financial statements. A recent study by de Fontnouvelle, DeJesus-Rueff, Jordan, and Rosengren at the Federal Reserve Bank of Boston (de Fontnouvelle et al. 2003) uses two external databases of large, publicly reported event losses to quantify operational risk. While the de Fontnouvelle study attempts to model the full operational loss distribution through a random truncation model, a simpler, "back of the envelope" approach can be used to calculate the frequency of large event losses from a known sample of reporting banks.

Figure 7.5 shows a distribution of large reported losses from one of the two external databases, OpRisk Analytics, for a consistent sample of the global top 100 banks over a 10-year period, from 1992 to 2001.[9] This sample yields 1,000 loss years of observation. The losses are scaled as a percentage of RWA, the same scalar used in the nonfinancial earnings volatility analysis of RORWA*.[10] Applying a (simplified) version of extreme value theory, the losses in the distribution can be ordered from the right, or most extreme, observation—Standard Chartered's Indian fraud in 1993, which cost the bank 1.44% of RWA—to the left. The 99.9% loss event in the distribution is 1.05% of RWA, which is roughly equivalent to the second most extreme observation, the Daiwa trading loss in 1995.

The 1.05% estimate of event risk is 13% of the BIS total bank capital requirement of 8% of RWA, in line with the proposed 12% calibration for operational risk under Basel II. But recall from the RORWA* analysis that the total estimate of nonfinancial earnings volatility is 2.5% of RWA. This implies that internal and external event risks account for only 42% of total nonfinancial risk. The residual—or business risk—is worth the other 58% and is actually the bigger driver of nonfinancial risk.

Internal Economic Capital Benchmarks

The top-down estimates of total nonfinancial, event, and business risk can be compared to bottom-up calculations of internal economic capital requirements for a sample of large banks. Figure 7.6 shows the results of a benchmarking study conducted by Oliver, Wyman & Company in 2001 of the internal economic capital attributions of 10 large, internationally active

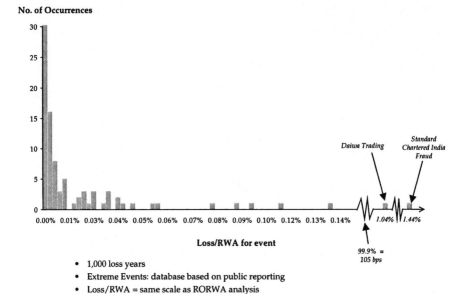

No. of Occurrences

Loss/RWA for event

- 1,000 loss years
- Extreme Events: database based on public reporting
- Loss/RWA = same scale as RORWA analysis
- 99.9% = 105 bps

Figure 7.5. OpRisk Analytics: Publicly Reported Losses, Top 100 Banks, 1992–2001. Source: OpRisk Analytics, OWC Analysis.

INSTITUTION	CREDIT	MARKET/ ALM	NON FINANCIAL
Bank A	47	27	27
Bank B	61	24	16
Bank C	43	25	32
Bank D	37	27	36
Bank E	63	8	29
Bank F	58	16	26
Bank G	46	28	26
Bank H	55	24	21
Bank I	45	24	31
Bank J	71	7	22
Average	53	21	26

Figure 7.6. Oliver, Wyman & Company Benchmarks Percentage of Total Risk Capital. Source: OWC database. (N.B.: The sources for OWC Analytics and OWC databases cannot be accessed by readers.)

U.S. and European banks. On average, the economic capital attributed by these banks to nonfinancial risk was 26%, which is very close to the 31% estimate of nonfinancial risk implied by the top-down RORWA analysis. Not surprisingly, the range in internal nonfinancial risk capital across the banks is fairly wide, from 16% to 36% of total economic capital. More significant, however, 9 of the 10 banks in the sample allocated economic capital for both business and event risks. This suggests that banks that use internal economic capital models recognize the importance of business risk as a driver of nonfinancial risk. Finally, of those banks in the sample that reported the breakout between the two risks, the split between event and business risk was 44% versus 56%—again, very close to the results of the top-down analysis (42% versus 58%).

These results support the following tentative conclusions:

- Nonfinancial risk is a significant source of bank risk, accounting for roughly 25–30% of economic capital.
- However, Basel II operational risk accounts for less than half of the nonfinancial risk total. The bigger driver of nonfinancial risk is business risk.
- Accepting the narrow definition of operational risk, the Basel II calibration of 12% of total economic capital appears to be confirmed by the top-down analysis.
- The range in nonfinancial capital allocation across banks suggests that, even if right on average, the calibration for operational risk could be wrong in practice unless supported by effective, bottom-up allocation.

LEGAL RISK AS A MICROCOSM OF OPERATIONAL RISK

It may be useful to look at a particular type of operational risk to get a better idea of the difficulties of devising a capital framework for operational risk. Legal risk is not a separate category of operational risk under the Basel approach. It cuts across the various Basel categories of inadequate or failed internal processes, people and systems, and external events. It is thus unclear where it actually fits in the Basel analysis.

Defining and Predicting Legal Risk

Like operational risk generally, legal risk is difficult to define. Losses from legal risk depend on how the law (including the law of contract) allocates risk between banks and other transactors and on the extent to which banks actually have to bear losses not allocated to other transactors. Obviously, not all losses depend on how the law allocates risk. For example, it is not a legal risk as to whether an institution bears the risk of having its employees embezzle funds (assuming there is no contract requiring third-party insurers to bear that risk). It is a legal risk that an insurance contract that does cover such risk could be interpreted, contrary to the intention of the bank, not to cover the embezzlement.

Loss allocation can be of two types. Primarily it is between financial institutions and other private contractors. But the government can also play a role by assuming losses, as is the case with terrorism reinsurance, or by imposing losses on banks, as occurs when it fines banks for regulatory violations. Particular legal risks are often exceedingly difficult to predict. Their incidence depends not only on whether the event giving rise to the risk will occur, for example, the breach of the contract but also on who will bear the loss of the event if it occurs.

As with other types of operational risk, some risks are high frequency and low impact; most credit card fraud falls into that category. Others are low frequency and low impact and are by definition unimportant, as when an employee is entitled to severance pay after a court determines that her firing was unjustified. The most important events are low frequency, high impact occurrences, such as 9/11, where there is an insurance dispute, or the Orange County claims against derivative dealers.

One can get a sense of the range of risks by looking at a sample of decided cases in federal district courts from October 2000 through October 2001 in table 7.1. This is not a representative sample because it includes only litigated cases that were not settled and only deals with a short period of time. Nonetheless, it shows the variety of cases in federal court.

Notice that the cases cover a wide range of issues, from antitrust violations to consumer protection, to the Holocaust, to conflicts over patents and trademarks. How would one predict the likelihood of low-frequency, high-severity events like the Holocaust? Surely it would not be on the basis of gross income, as under the prescribed Basel methodologies. And it is also far from clear how a bank's internal model could predict exposure to such claims.

We have also collected a sample of state appellate court cases in California, New York, and Texas over the same period of time. The data are given in table 7.2.

The interesting feature of this table is that the incidence of litigation can depend on the state in which a bank is located. This is also obviously the case for countries, as well. It is probably true that U.S. banks are more likely to be exposed to legal risk than foreign banks because of the litigious nature of the United States, the availability of class actions, and the significant statutory impediments to disclaiming risk. U.S. banks are probably much more exposed, as well, to costly regulatory sanctions. This raises the question of how to apply any standardized operational risk methodology across countries. Even apart from legal risk, one can well imagine that other types of operational risk, such as computer failure or employee theft, might well have different incidences in different jurisdictions.

One way of getting an insight into the incidence of high-impact legal risk is to look at what disclosures banks make about material litigation. Table 7.3 shows the disclosures of the top 100 banking companies in 2000.

Banks tend to disclose when an event can have an impact on 5%–10% of earnings. Such disclosures were made by 21% of banks in 2000. This is surprisingly a high number, but even this level of exposure significantly

Table 7.1. Federal District Court Cases Against Banks, 2000–2001

Type of Case		Number
Banks as trustee		4
Antitrust		2
Checks		9
Consumer protection		54
Truth in lending	21	
Fair debt collection	9	
Other	24	
Contracts		31
Discrimination		24
Customer	6	
Employees	18	
Fraud		15
Holocaust compensation		1
Indian land claims		2
Mortgage or foreclosure dispute		8
Patent infringement		2
RICO		10
Securities fraud		17
Fraud	8	
Disclosure	9	
Third party		32
Deposit holder or trustee	18	
Finance provider or debt holder	4	
Mortgage or lien holder	10	
Torts		4
Trademark		2
Other		7
TOTAL		224

Source: Authors' compilation.

understates the level of major risk litigation, since, if banks had already set aside reserves to cover cases with probable losses, there would be no material impact on earnings when the cases were actually brought. Table 7.3 does reflect, however, the kinds of cases that were difficult enough to predict so that reserves were not set aside in advance.

INSURANCE AGAINST OPERATIONAL RISK

This section of the chapter addresses the question of insurance coverage for operational risk and how the availability of such coverage should affect capital requirements (Bunge 2002). We begin by discussing the problem of insurance coverage.

Table 7.2. **State Appellate Court Cases Against Banks, 2000–2001**

Type of Case	California	New York	Texas
Banks as trustee	3	0	4
Checks	1	4	7
Consumer protection	1	0	5
Contracts	1	9	13
Conversion	0	1	4
Employment discrimination	2	3	0
Fraud	0	4	5
Mortgage/foreclosure	1	1	2
Personal injury	0	10	1
Securities	0	0	2
Third party	2	9	8
Other	1	1	4
TOTAL	13	41	55

Source: Authors' compilation.

Coverage

Let us focus again on figure 7.3. Generally, banks insure against low-frequency, high-intensity events. Expected losses of low severity, such as routine processing errors, are planned for in the budget process and are expensed as they occur. Low-frequency, low-severity events are dealt with through contingencies. Not only are these events not insured against, but, as

Table 7.3. **Material Litigation Disclosures by 100 Top Bank Holding Companies, 2000**

Type of Case	Number
Breach of fiduciary duty	3
Consumer protection	6
Conversion and fraud	2
Derivative suit	2
Employment	1
Environmental	2
Lender Liability	1
Merger related suits	2
Patent infringement	1
Securities violation	3
Unspecified	1
TOTAL	24

Source: Authors' compilation.

we argued earlier, they should not be subject to mandatory capital requirements. As before, we also assume that high-frequency, high-severity events are a null set. Thus, the decision to insure externally applies to low-frequency, high-severity events like 9/11, and, in principle, insurance is a direct substitute for capital. Institutions would compare insurance costs against the cost of capital. The cost of capital is influenced significantly by regulation if regulation requires that one hold more capital than one would otherwise do (Insurance Working Group 2001). Banks might not be willing or able to purchase insurance for all low-frequency, high-severity events. Policies may be too expensive. It appears that rogue trader insurance has not become popular because banks believe the policies are too expensive and would rather rely on internal controls (*Insurance Journal* 2002). Due to information asymmetries, it may be difficult and costly for an insurance company to differentiate between risky and safe banks. To mitigate the effect of moral hazard, a deductible may be included in the insurance policy. The effect of such deductible is set out in figure 7.7.

This deductible effectively means that part of the risk is uninsured. Also, insurance policies may have a cap on liability. Such caps, like deductibles, may give banks incentives to manage risk, but they also mean that such risks are uninsured. In addition, many insurance policies exclude certain events, such as risk from war or nuclear attacks, from coverage. This creates further gaps in coverage. Insurance policies are often written in extremely technical and complicated language, and it may be difficult in advance to specify which risks are covered and which are excluded. This problem is further intensified by the number of different policies that may cover different types of risks, each with its own set of deductibles, caps, and exclusions. For example, there are the following kinds of policies: Bankers' Blanket Bond or Financial Institutions Bond, Computer Crime, Unauthorized Trading, Property Insurance, Bankers' Professional Indemnity, Commercial General Liability, Employment Practice Liability, Director's and Officer's Liability, Electronic Insurance, and Environmental Protection.

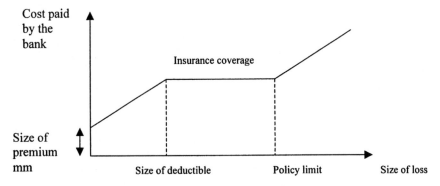

Figure 7.7. Effect of Deductible. Source: Marshall (2001), p. 436.

These complications may also result in disputes about whether policies actually do cover particular loss events. A notable recent example is the litigation over the extent of insurance coverage for the destruction of the World Trade Center.[11]

There have been some important developments in reducing such complications by the introduction of a broader and more complete "blanket" policy. For example, Swiss Re has introduced a policy for Financial Institutions Operational Risk Insurance (FIORI) that covers liability, fidelity and unauthorized activities, technology risks, asset protection, and external fraud. However, there is a $100 million deductible for every loss and a requirement that the insured bank have at least a $20 billion balance sheet and be listed on an exchange.

It is widely acknowledged that there is an indirect benefit of insurance coverage. The presence of insurance causes the insurer, in cooperation with the insured, to monitor and try to reduce risk. This protects the insurer against moral hazard and generally reduces its exposure. From a capital point of view, this might be thought to be irrelevant, since, if the risk is covered, it will be borne by the insurer. Monitoring may reduce the insurer's exposure, but lack of monitoring does not increase the insured's exposure. This may not be true if there are deductibles and caps. Insurance company monitoring may reduce the insured's exposure for the uninsured portion of the risk. Basel has suggested no way in which the quality of insurance company monitoring would affect capital for partially insured risk.

Insurance Payoffs

Even if a bank is insured, it may not be able to collect on its insurance. This may result from a default of the insurance company, although one would assume that the probability of default of a highly rated insurance company on a given policy is quite small. A more difficult issue is posed by the fact that the insurance company might not promptly pay its claims. This could be the result of conscious stalling, but the reputational consequences of nontimely bill paying can be severe. However, there may be legitimate issues about the extent of coverage that delay prompt payments. One might think that this would be of special concern to banks that may need to draw on the funds immediately. However, third parties or the insurance company itself should be willing to finance delayed but clearly expected payments. Under the FIORI policy, Swiss Re agrees to solve the liquidity problem by buying treasury shares from the bank once a claim for loss is made. This provides Swiss Re with security against the return by the bank of any insurance payments that are ultimately decided not to be due.

The Basel Committee has attempted to collect some data on insurance coverage through the Quantitative Impact Study (BCBS 2002), but its data are generally unsatisfactory because they were collected from only 30 banks from 11 countries over three years. The committee had a limited ability to capture tail events represented by low-frequency, high-severity events, which are those that should be insured. Thus, when it found that only 2.4% of loss events (out of a total of 7,463) had an insurance payoff, this indicates not that insurance is not important but, rather, that only a small portion of operational risk is insured. Most loss events, as we have discussed, are expensed and pose no threat to capital. The study also reports that the average recovery rate for insured losses was only 80% of loss amounts. This does not necessarily mean that payoffs are unreliable but may rather reflect deductibles and caps.

If Basel insists on factoring in the willingness of insurance companies to pay into the amount of capital reduction achievable through insurance, it might permit banks to rely on willingness to pay ratings, such as the Financial Enhancement Ratings, issued by Standard & Poor's since 2000.

Insurance for Legal Risk

As previously discussed, there is a range of different policies that cover operational risk. Not all such policies cover legal risk. For example, the Bankers' Blanket Bond covers losses through acts of dishonest employees, which is not a legal risk. It is also unclear to what extent any of the policies that might cover legal risks of some kind, for example, Bankers' Professional Indemnity or Commercial General Liability, would cover some of the major legal risks (e.g., the Holocaust or Indian land claims). This might be because such claims were specifically excluded or exceeded caps. Often, however, it occurs because no one anticipated the claims involved and therefore no one sought to insure against them. This could be remedied by blanket policies, but, again, cost would be a major consideration. The unpredictability of events that might give rise to legal risk is of an order of magnitude of uncertainty that is beyond the unpredictability of known risks such as, for example, rogue trading. Indeed, such unpredictability of the types of events calls into question the whole operational risk exercise.

As with other risks, there is also the question of the dependability of insurance payoffs for legal risk. But there is the additional issue of legal risk about the payoffs themselves. This is the issue in the World Trade Center litigation. The destruction of the WTC was a nonlegal operational risk, but legal risk affects the validity and the extent of insurance.

The Basel Committee Approach

Neither the basic indicator approach, under which banks are required to hold capital for operational risk equal to a fixed percentage of gross income, nor the standardized approach, under which they are required to hold capital in an amount based on their gross income for eight different business lines, allows any reduction in required capital for the amount of insurance. Only the AMA permits insurance to reduce required capital, and then only to the extent of 20%. The committee originally envisioned developing parameters that would affect the actual extent that insurance could reduce capital, such as criteria relating to timeliness of payment, certainty of coverage, length of contract, credit rating of the insurer, and use of reinsurance, but it abandoned this in favor of an absolute limitation of 20%. It also refused to take insurance into account at all under the basic indicator and standardized approaches. This will be irrelevant to U.S. banks to which these two approaches will not apply.

We see no economic justification for the 20% limit on insurance under AMA. Given that regulators are letting banks use models to determine capital risk for operational risks generally, they should also have permitted them to do so with respect to insurance mitigation.[12] Indeed, this limit may have the perverse effect of reducing the incentives of banks to obtain insurance and thus increase banking losses. It may create further disincentives for those U.S. banks that have substantial operational risks but that are not in the core 10 mandated to adopt A-IRB and AMA. This would be particularly true for banks like State Street that focus on processing and have virtually no consumer or commercial loans. The negative prospect of a 12% operational capital charge combined with limits on insurance mitigation could more than outweigh the nonexistent savings of reductions in capital for credit risk. Indeed, such banks might well decide not to adopt Basel II even with full mitigation from insurance.

The insurance industry has suggested using a premium or limits approach (Insurance Companies 2001). Under the premiums approach, the sum of insurance policy premiums is used as a single indicator proxy for measuring capital relief. The total amount of premiums is multiplied by a prescribed fixed percentage and a ratio to reduce the expected loss portion of the risk transferred. The foundation for the use of premiums is that insurance premiums are directly correlated with the amount of risk transferred; the higher the premiums, the higher the level of risk transfer. The key is the fixed percentage adjustment. It is unclear whether and to what extent such a fixed percentage could be determined with any reasonable reliability. The ratio adjustment would adjust the level of premiums for the limits of coverage and the credit rating of the insurer; the latter appears more feasible than the former.

The second method proposed by the industry is the limits approach. Under this approach, the insurance premiums paid are assumed to represent the portion of the risk applicable to the expected loss. Thus, the policy limit less the insurance premium should be the amount of the policy limit related to unexpected loss that is actually insured against. This amount would be discounted by a coverage breadth factor. To the extent that coverage breadth was coextensive with the operational risks identified by the Basel Committee, this factor would be close to 1.0; to the extent it was much less, the factor would approach 0. This determination would be aided by a mapping exercise in which the Basel-identified risks would be mapped to particular insurance policies and empirical data. As the industry points out, there are aggregate and specific loss limits in policies, an aggregate overall limit and a limit on specific risks. It is unclear how these different limits are taken into account. Further, the mapping process seems difficult, given the problems in generally defining operational risk, as well as in defining the specific components.

CONCLUSION: IS CAPITAL A CURE-ALL FOR RISK?

Given the modest impact of Basel II operational risk on bank earnings volatility, the question becomes whether capital is the appropriate regulatory mechanism for protecting banks against internal and external events. Unlike financial risks, which a bank consciously assumes in the expectation of financial return, operational risks are an unwanted by-product of the business. At the same time, banks can take significant steps to mitigate exposure to operation risks ex ante, rather than relying on capital to absorb losses ex post. The tradeoff a bank faces in managing operational risks is not risk versus return but risk versus the costs of avoidance.

The approach to avoiding operational risks differs for internal and external event risks. Internal event risks, by their nature, are endogenous; they result from the failure of internal processes, people, or systems. The first line of defense against internal event risks should be management controls. The history of quality control in industrial manufacturing demonstrates that there are effective measures banks can take to reduce operational losses. The key determinant of how safe a bank is against operational failures is not the level of capital it holds but how well managed the bank is in the first instance. In fact, in a few spectacular cases of operational failures, incremental capital would have made no difference to the firm's survivability. If Barings had held more capital, arguably all that would have happened is that trading losses would have continued to mount until the firm ran out of capital.

External event risks, by contrast, are caused by exogenous incidents outside the control of the firm. Because of this, external events have little moral hazard and tend to be uncorrelated, which makes them good candidates for insurance. For most firms, insurance is the first line of defense against external event risks. And, while insurance transfers exposure to a third party, banks can also take steps internally to mitigate the consequences of external events. As an example, at a recent Oliver, Wyman & Company-Wharton Risk Roundtable on operational risk, several participants discussed how their firms managed through the events of September 11. It became clear that the financial heroes of September 11 were firms, such as Morgan Stanley and Depository Trust & Clearing Corporation (DTCC), that had invested heavily in safety measures, contingency planning, and back-up systems and that were prepared to cope with a catastrophic event whose nature was entirely unpredictable ex ante. No amount of capital would have made a difference to the ability of these firms to withstand the business disruption and uncertainty surrounding September 11.

The one category of nonfinancial risk that cannot be effectively mitigated by management controls or insured against is classic business risk. This is the reason that firms like CSFB need to hold capital to absorb the potential for loss from a business downturn—similar to the need for equity in nonfinancial companies. It is ironic that the source of nonfinancial risk that is best protected by capital is ignored by Basel II.

It is clear that insurance is a substitute for capital. It is thus highly unclear why insurance should not be taken into account in setting capital requirements under the basic indicator and standardized approaches of Basel II. Also, a 20% limit on capital reduction achievable under AMA may give many banks a perverse incentive to underinsure. There is no established formula or methodology for determining the degree of substitution. This counsels against Basel II's establishing any arbitrary limit. Financial institutions should be free to adopt their own substitution approach, subject to regulators's review of the thoughtfulness of the process that led to the substitution approach. There is no reason to give banks this freedom for operational risk in general and then to limit it with respect to insurance substitution.

The U.S. implementation of Basel II is troubling. In the first place, it creates significant competitive problems in the United States among large banks with significant operational risk that Basel I sought to diminish.[13] For example, banks with low credit risk and high operational risk (as defined by Basel) that are required to adopt Basel II will be at a disadvantage compared to banks that are not required to adopt Basel II, since, for the former group of banks, overall capital will increase. This competitive problem also has an international dimension. The E.U. Capital Adequacy Directive (CAD), based on Basel I, applies to all E.U. banks. If the European Union applies its revised CAD, based on Basel II, to all E.U. banks, the low-credit-risk and high-operational-risk U.S. banks not subject to Basel II will have a potential competitive advantage over European banks. This could lead the disadvantaged Basel II banks to change their business mix or to sell off their operations to advantaged banks.

For these reasons, we believe that operational risk should be dealt with under Pillar 2 and not Pillar 1. This view has been strengthened by the consequences of the U.S. approach to the implementation of Basel II under which some but not all banks with major operational risks will be subject to operational risk charges.

As a second-best solution, we recommend that the European Union follow the U.S. lead by eliminating operational risk charges for most banks. In addition, we think that a better method should be devised to determine the core U.S. banks that will have mandatory operational risk charges or that the adoption of AMA should be entirely voluntary, as Basel II envisions. By making Basel II mandatory for certain banks, the United States is going farther than Basel II requires. Given our fundamental disagreement with the approach of Basel II to operational risk, we see no reason to compel banks to use it. While it is true that banks can use their own models in AMA, the limit on insurance mitigation significantly limits this freedom. At the least, the arbitrary 20% ceiling should be removed.

We note with interest that a bipartisan group of U.S. representatives has sponsored a bill that would require reports to Congress concerning the Basel

II process and that would permit the U.S. Treasury, rather than the Fed, to control U.S. policy on Basel capital requirements.[14] Whether or not this bill passes, its mere filing and the hearings that preceded it indicate that this entire process will become more political in the future. This is perhaps an inevitable result of the adoption of highly contestable policies with significant competitive implications.

Acknowledgments We would like to acknowledge Scott Weiner and Sugata Ray for their research assistance on the empirical analysis (although we accept personal responsibility for any errors or omissions).

Notes

1. The first part of the chapter is a revised version of an earlier article, Kuritzkes (2002).

2. Also, banks that qualify for AMA may use either the basic indicator approach or the standardized approach for some parts of their operations and an AMA approach for others (BCBS 2003a, paragraph 91).

3. The Federal Reserve Board issued an advance notice of formal rule making to implement its earlier statements on July 3, 2003. No formal rule-making proposal has yet been advanced. (See Ferguson 2003.)

4. It is unclear how one can mandate the use of AMA for certain banks without the banks themselves qualifying for AMA, a basic requirement of Basel II. Perhaps the Fed envisions requiring these banks to develop systems that do qualify for AMA.

5. Of CSFB's Q4 2001 loss, $850 million was related to an extraordinary charge taken to cover the cost of severance packages and business disinvestment attributable to the business slowdown.

6. A significant portion of the capital markets slowdown in Q4 2001 resulted from the knock-on effects of September 11. Commentary on CSFB blames September 11 for much of the loss in corporate finance and equities revenues.

7. This point is also made in a recent Federal Reserve Bank of Boston study by de Fontnouvelle, DeJesus-Rueff, Jordan, and Rosengren (2003). The authors rely on external databases of publicly reported operational risk events to quantify operational risk. Although de Fontnouvelle et al. conclude that "using external data is a feasible solution for understanding the distribution of ... large [operational] losses," their estimates still result in a wide range of outcomes. In their model, the key variable for estimating a bank's operational risk capital requirement is the annual number of internal losses that exceed $1 million. The bank's loss distribution is then assumed to follow the same (Pareto) form as that for the external data. The authors report that "a typical large internationally active bank experiences an average of 50 to 80 losses above $1 million per year." However, depending on the exponential parameter assumed in their model, the 50 to 80 losses translate into an operational risk capital requirement at the 99.9% confidence interval of between $500 million and $4.9 billion—or a difference of 10 to 1. For a bank with 60 reported losses, the range is only slightly smaller—between $600 million and $4 billion.

8. Five banks were dropped from the analysis because of incomplete data.

9. The OpRisk Analytics database is considered to be comprehensive for large publicly reported losses (>$10 million) going back at least 10 years.

10. The OpRisk Analytics database reports losses as a percentage of assets, not risk-weighted assets. However, for comparability with the RORWA* analysis, assets were converted to risk-weighted assets. For the sample of 45 banks used in the RORWA* analysis, risk-weighted assets were 78% of total assets. This conversion factor was applied to the OpRisk Analytics results.

11. See, for example, World Trade Center Properties LLC et al. v. Travelers Indemnity Company, 01 Civ.12738 (June 3, 2002).

12. The argument against the 20% cap applies even though many banks with economic capital models have yet to integrate insurance into their models. There are two reasons that existing economic capital models fail to take account of insurance. First, "bottom-up" models for operational risk are still at an early stage of development, for the reasons stated in the section on bottom-up measurement. The current focus of modeling efforts is on the underlying operational risk exposure rather than on risk mitigation through insurance, in the same way that credit exposure measurement for derivatives focused first on *gross* exposure, and then on *net* exposure with individual counterparties. Given the Basel II mandate, however, banks are accelerating development of bottom-up models under the AMA, and they will inevitably seek to integrate the effects of insurance once the underlying exposure is measured. Second, existing economic capital approaches to operational risk are often calibrated using external benchmarks of capital levels for nonfinancial company analogs. The external benchmarks reflect the prevailing level of insurance cover among the analog companies. As banks move from an external benchmark approach to calibration to an internal modeling approach consistent with the AMA, they will need to factor insurance into their internal capital calculations or risk potentially overstating capital.

13. In our view, however, the ability of the Accord to reduce competitive inequality is quite limited (Scott and Iwahara 1994).

14. H.R. 2043, 108th Cong. 1st Sess. (2003).

References

Bank for International Settlements (BIS). 2002. *Basel Committee Reaches Accord on New Capital Accord Issues.* Press Release (July 10). Available at: http://www.bis.org/press/p020710.htm#pgtop.

Basel Committee on Banking Supervision (BCBS). 1999. Credit Risk Modelling: Current Practices and Applications. Basel Committee Publication No. 49. Available at: www.bis.org/bcbs/publ.htm#joint.

———. 2001a. Consultative Document: Operational Risk, Supporting Document to the New Basel Capital Accord. Available at: http://www.bis.org/publ/bcbsca07.pdf.

———. 2001b. Regulatory Treatment of Operational Risk. BIS Working Paper No. 8. Available at: www.bis.org/publ/bcbs_wp8.pdf.

———. 2002. The Quantitative Impact Study for Operational Risk: Overview of Individual Loss Data and Lessons Learned. Available at: http://www.bis.org/bcbs/qis/qisopriskresponse.pdf.

———. 2003a. Consultative Document: Overview of the New Basel Capital Accord. Available at: www.bis.org/bcbs/cp3ov.pdf.

———. 2003b. Consultative Document: The New Basel Accord. Available at: www.bis.org/bcbs/cp3full.pdf.

————. 2003c. Quantitative Impact Study 3—Overview of Global Results. Available at: www.bis.org/bcbs/qis/qis3results.pdf.

Bunge, Aino. 2002. Operational Risk Insurance—Treatment Under the New Basel Accord. Paper written for Seminar on International Finance, Harvard Law School. Available at: www.law.harvard.edu/programs/pifs/pdfs/aino_bunge.pdf.

de Fontnouvelle, Patrick, Virginia DeJesus-Rueff, John Jordan, and Eric Rosengren. 2003. Using Loss Data to Quantify Operational Risk. Federal Reserve Bank of Boston Working Paper (April). Available at: www.bos.frb.org/bankinfo/oprisk/articles.htm.

Ferguson, Roger W., Jr. 2003. Statement Before the Subcommittee on Domestic and International Monetary Policy, Trade, and Technology. Committee on Financial Services, United States House of Representatives (February 27). Available at: http://financialservices.house.gov/media/pdf/022703rf.pdf.

Insurance Journal. 2002. Most Banks Don't Have Rogue Trader Insurance. February 11. Online. Available at: www.insurancejrnl.com/html/ijweb/breakingnews/international/in0202/in0211022.htm.

Insurance Working Group of the Operational Risk Research Forum. 2001. Insurance as a Mitigant for Operational Risk: A Report Submitted to the Basel Committee on Banking Supervision (May 31). Available at: www.bis.org/bcbs/ca/oprirefo.pdf.

Insurance Companies. 2001. Insurance of Operational Risk Under the New Basel Accord. Working Paper submitted to the Basel Committee (November). Available at: www.bos.frb.org/bankinfo/conevent/oprisk/basel.pdf.

Kuritzkes, Andrew. 2002. Operational Risk Capital: A Problem of Definition. *Journal of Risk Finance* 4 (1): 47–56.

Marshall, Christopher L. 2001. *Measuring and Managing Operational Risks in Financial Institutions: Tools, Techniques, and Other Resources.* Chichester: Wiley.

Scott, Hal S., and Shinsaku Iwahara. 1994. In Search of a Level Playing Field: The Implementation of the Basel Accord in Japan and the United States. Washington, D.C.: Group of Thirty Occasional Paper No. 46.

8

Enforcement of Risk-Based
Capital Rules

PHILIP A. WELLONS

This chapter examines the role of enforcement for capital adequacy regulation in U.S. banking and securities markets. Very little is known about how enforcement works: What broken rules are being enforced? By whom? How serious are the violations? How effective is enforcement, which presumably should discourage others from breaking important capital rules? The data are from enforcement actions over the last 6 to 10 years by U.S. regulators, who are unique in publishing them. Even though the capital adequacy rules differ for banks and securities firms, the approaches to enforcing them overlap enough to allow rough comparison.

This chapter finds a very low number of formal enforcement actions. Most target the small firms or individuals, not the big firms. Formal actions are particularly rare against the largest banks and securities firms, those that pose the greatest threat to the financial system. All but one of the capital adequacy violations resulted from fraud, theft, or other forms of operational risk. Only one resulted from credit risk. The chapter examines possible explanations of the findings, such as the relatively strong economy during much of the period and the possibility that very effective supervision catches almost all firms before their capital falls too low. Evidence from case studies of failed banks suggests that supervisors need to do a better job relating a bank's apparently adequate capital to its risk exposure and to force banks to implement proposals regulators make to remedy deficiencies. Perhaps the very limited enforcement against large firms reflects a regulatory bias in their favor rather than their underlying strength and adequate capital.

As the chapter effectively argues, any regulation must be enforced to be effective. This chapter shows very low levels of enforcement of capital requirements for securities firms and banks in the United States between 1993 and 2001, particularly for larger firms. Of course, this may result from the fact that such firms are adequately capitalized. The low level of enforcement of capital requirements for securities firms may be explained by the relatively low level of concern with their failure. The chapter points out the lack of available data on enforcement of capital requirements abroad. This situation needs to be improved.

INTRODUCTION

This chapter examines the role of enforcement of capital adequacy regulation. Enforcement is what the regulator does when someone breaks the rules; the regulator penalizes financial institutions that do not comply. Enforcement or its threat is essential to regulation. If the rules are not enforced, people do not obey them.

The chapter maps the topography of enforcement of capital adequacy rules in U.S. banking and securities markets. Very little is known about how enforcement works. What broken rules are being enforced? By whom? How serious are the violations? How effective is enforcement, which presumably should discourage others from breaking important capital rules? Since little or no scholarly work exists on this topic, much of this chapter is exploratory. It gives the lay of the land.

The data are from official reports of enforcement actions on the U.S. capital adequacy rules for banks and securities companies. U.S. regulators publish data that show the type and number of enforcement actions and allow some comparison, even if it is sometimes uneven. The United States is unique among developed financial markets in the extent to which it publishes this information. Countries in Europe, Germany for example, do not do so. In these two sectors, the United States offers a rich vein of data to be mined. It may be useful for other countries that do not.

Even though the capital adequacy rules differ for banks and for securities firms, the approaches to enforcing them overlap, also allowing rough comparison. The goals of the rules do differ by type of financial institution, however (GAO 1998). For commercial banks, the conventional regulatory goal is to ensure the "continued operation of the banking system," preserving the payments system and the lending function, according to a 1998 study by the U.S. General Accounting Office (GAO 1998). For securities companies, the goal is to guarantee sufficient liquidation value to meet claims of customers and others in the market.[1] Rules that govern the two types of firms differ in their approach to risk. For U.S. banks, risk-based capital regulation has increasingly focused on discrete risks, such as credit risk, market or position risk, foreign exchange risk, operational risk, and many others. But for broker-dealers, the U.S. capital rules are comprehensive, and include credit risk, market risk, and operational risk, among others, in one measure.

The methodology is straightforward. Actions by regulators enforcing capital adequacy rules that govern banks and securities firms were identified, and time series were developed. Information about the actions was gathered to identify the type, nature of the rule violation, penalty, and amounts involved. The results appear in tables and as case studies throughout the chapter. The raw data for this primary research are formal actions within the administrative agency or self-governing body or before the courts; examples of formal actions are cease-and-desist orders, termination of insurance, and removal of officers or directors.[2] The sources of these enforcement actions are the regulatory agencies themselves, which report formal actions on their own web sites.

Each major bank regulator has an engine on its web site that allows the reader to search formal enforcement actions using key words such as "prompt corrective action" (PCA). The Office of the Comptroller of the Currency (OCC), for example, has the enforcement actions search.[3] Federal Deposit Insurance Corporation (FDIC) gives the full text of enforcement decisions and orders against financial institutions it regulates or their affiliates.[4] The Federal Reserve Board has its list of enforcement actions.[5] Major secondary sources about bank regulators are case studies, done by the Office of the Inspector General in the FDIC, of prompt corrective action that preceded bank failures that require substantial payouts of deposit insurance and a historic analysis of the actions toward troubled banks by the FDIC. (See FDIC 1996, p. 473–74.)

For securities firms, the primary sources for data are enforcement or disciplinary actions that involve violation of the net capital rules, found through searches of the web sites of the Securities Exchange Commission (SEC), the New York Stock Exchange (NYSE), and the National Association of Securities Dealers (NASD). The major secondary source is a study by the General Accounting Office of prompt corrective action (GAO 2001). Despite the differences among regulators, this study found that enforcement of capital rules for the two types of firms is similar in the relative number of formal actions, the size of the firms involved, and the type of violations that are sanctioned. It differs in the kind of enforcement tools used.

Enforcement of capital adequacy rules is often part of a larger enforcement action. For example, a person who commits fraud or theft may leave his firm with capital below the regulatory minimum. Regulators attack the fraud or theft as their primary target and often add a count for violating capital adequacy standards almost as an afterthought. Obviously, any behavior that diminishes capital below the legal floor is reprehensible. But the solutions to it are found in criminal law for fraud and theft and are not likely to apply to deficient capital due to misjudgments of creditworthiness or the risk of adverse market movements. As a practical matter, researchers can find it hard to segregate enforcement of capital adequacy rules from other rules against fraud or theft.

The research for this chapter revealed that there have been very few formal actions to enforce capital adequacy rules that govern banks and securities firms. Indeed, at least among banks, the need for enforcement is low because most banks are reported to be well capitalized. Most formal enforcement targets the small players, not the big ones. Formal actions are particularly rare against the largest banks and securities firms, those that pose the greatest threat to the financial system. The net effect, therefore, is to place responsibility for enforcing the capital rules with the regulators who supervise the smaller financial firms.

The chapter first gives the relevant capital adequacy standards and the institutions that enforce them. It explains the enforcement triggers for banks and securities companies, as well as the techniques and tools that regulators use to intervene. It then presents the low numbers of formal enforcement actions and explores reasons for them. Are informal enforcement processes a substitute? Apparently not. What is the role of the economic cycle? It certainly helps explain the low enforcement. Is strong supervision a substitute for enforcement? Despite the low aggregate numbers, case studies highlight situations in which supervisors do not fully implement existing rules. They raise the possibility that the low number of formal enforcements is not a result of impeccable supervision. The chapter finds that enforcement actions target usually small firms and rarely large ones. The events that lead to enforcement actions usually involve fraud or theft and, secondarily, simple misreporting. Among all enforcement actions, only one took place because markets reduced capital below the base levels; that is, operational risk rather than market risk generated the actions.

The chapter concludes with observations about the findings, supervisory discretion, the limited role of enforcement for regulatory capital, and puzzles that emerge.

ENFORCEMENT: RULES, INSTITUTIONS, PROCESS

The Capital Adequacy Standards

U.S. banks are subject to the risk-weighted capital adequacy rules of Basel 1, well known and much debated, while securities firms must comply with liquid capital rules imposed by the SEC. These are less broadly known and therefore are summarized here.

U.S. broker-dealers must calculate their minimum capital against two different measures, meeting the higher in each case (GAO 1998). The first measure is an absolute minimum level of capital set in dollars, the amount rising as the broker-dealer handles the money or securities of others. The minimum is $5,000 for broker-dealers that do not receive or hold the funds or securities of customers or others. Many small brokers are in this category. Capital serves as a cushion against their very limited liabilities. The brokers do not incur market risk, so they do not need capital to protect against it. At the next stage, the minimum is $25,000 for broker-dealers in registered shares of mutual funds who only take orders by wire or phone. A $100,000 minimum capital exists for broker-dealers that carry customer accounts but do not hold customer funds or securities or that trade only for their own account. Finally, the minimum is $250,000 for broker-dealers that do hold customer accounts or funds for other brokers or dealers. This protects customers and other broker-dealers who are players in the securities markets. If they were to incur losses when a broker-dealer fails, the market would not function smoothly. The New York Stock Exchange (NYSE) and the National Association of Securities Dealers (NASD) use the SEC capital standard as their base rule but set higher standards as early-warning markers. For example, NASD rules make any firms with net capital below 150% of the SEC's minimum net capital subject to corrective action for members that experience financial or operational difficulties.[6] The National Securities Clearing Corporation (NSCC) rules for its members' capital apply to the clearing brokers and to those correspondents whose business is a significant portion of clearing broker's capital. The NSCC's capital rules are also based on the SEC's rules but are more stringent.[7]

The second measure of capital is a ratio that takes two forms, permitting the broker-dealer to relate capital either to its liabilities or its assets. The basic method requires that a broker-dealer's adjusted net capital never be less than 6.67% of its adjusted liabilities. Net capital is a modified form of net worth, namely liquid assets less most liabilities. Net capital is reduced by haircuts that vary roughly according to the volatility of the different types of securities the broker-dealer holds. Haircuts are also said to adjust for other risks, such as liquidity and operational risk, although the allowances made for these risks are not identified or quantified separately (GAO 1998). Any amount above the required net capital is called excess capital. The alternative method allows broker-dealers to hold, instead, minimum capital equal to 2% of adjusted amounts due from customers, which are assets. This makes the alternative method more akin to the Basel rules for banks, which also relate capital to assets. Smaller firms tend to use the basic method and larger ones the alternative method.

The capital adequacy rule for securities firms uses three major elements to determine the level of capital: the extent of financial obligations to customers and other broker-dealers, the size of liabilities, and the degree of market risk. The rule also brings in other less salient factors, such as charges when the selling broker cannot deliver on time because its customer failed to deliver.

The two measures for minimum capital mesh. The absolute capital rules set minimum capital levels that increase as the broker-dealer takes on financial obligations to market players. The ratio replaces the absolute rule as liabilities increase.

Small broker-dealers find the absolute level of capital higher than the ratio, while large broker-dealers must meet the ratio rather than the absolute minimum. This distinction turns out to be important for much of the SEC's enforcement, as discussed later. The larger firms can also choose the alternative method of computing net capital against liabilities. To use it, they must meet the $250,000 absolute minimum.

A simple example is a very small broker that does not take positions or receive or hold funds or securities of customers or others. Assume the broker has liquid assets of $50,000 and adjusted liabilities of $40,000. Its net worth is $10,000. This is well above the $5,000 required by the absolute test and the $2,668 (6.7% of $40,000) required by the ratio. As the broker's liabilities grow, the ratio approaches the $5,000 absolute capital requirement and equals it when liabilities are $75,000, since 6.7% of $75,000 is $5,000. Above that, the ratio sets the minimum regulatory capital.

When the broker-dealer takes positions in securities, the rule varies the amount of capital required, according to some idea of the risk of those securities.

The goal of this capital rule is to allow the regulator to close insolvent broker-dealers quickly and cleanly because net capital will be sufficient to absorb the amount by which the likely liabilities of the firm exceed its assets. This permits the players to avoid the delays and pitfalls of formal bankruptcy. The rule is designed to let the fast-moving securities market continue to operate without pause for failed brokers. It is administered and enforced to achieve this goal.

These are minimum capital levels. The SEC wants to know before a broker-dealer hits these minimums, so it has an early-warning system, described later.

Who Enforces: Most Net Capital Enforcement Actions Are by NASD

The distribution of enforcement actions among the supervisors reflects their responsibility in the regulatory system. Those responsible for the small and medium-size firms do more, and the securities regulators enforce more actions than the bank regulators.

In the securities markets, the SEC leaves most net capital enforcement to others. The SEC chooses to carry out fewer exams, in more depth and on its own initiative or as an appeal from a self-regulatory organization (SRO), as was the case in many of its 44 capital enforcement actions. The SEC selects matters that have broad policy implications, in order to make a point about, for example, compliance. Supplementing the SROs are market players that help enforce the capital rules. Clearing brokers are an example; they clear and settle trades for brokers that are not members of an exchange. In this capacity, they make sure the nonclearing brokers maintain adequate capital.

NASD disciplines the many small players in the securities markets. Perhaps two-thirds of NASD's members are firms of five or fewer people (the smallest broker-dealer needs minimum capital of only $5,000). NASD also regulates Nasdaq and the OTC market. It is NASD's job to police them, and it sees itself as the "cop on the beat." As a result, most net capital actions are carried out by NASD, which accounts for 122, or almost 60%, of the 209 actions involving banks (27) or brokers (182) identified here. However, even 20 a year during 1996 through 2001 is not huge, given the small size of most firms, the easy entry, and the number (about 5,500) of broker/dealers.

NYSE, which regulates the high end of the market, accounted for only 16 actions. Its member firms are much bigger than most firms in NASD, and they have more capital than many NASD members. NYSE sets a higher capital standard, so its members are better capitalized. Under these circumstances, it is not surprising that NYSE plays a minor role.

On the banking side, the regulators are also responsible for supervising different types of banks—national, state Federal Reserve member, state nonmember—but these types do not correlate with firm size as reliably as do securities firms. As the supervisor for most of the biggest U.S. banks, the OCC might be analogous to the NYSE as up-market regulator.[8] Because big banks were not subject to prompt corrective action (PCA), one might expect the OCC to have a very small share of these enforcement actions. But the OCC reported 44% of the PCAs between 1993 and 2001, 12 of the 27, and more than either the Fed or FDIC. The national banks it supervises also include many small and medium-size ones.

The FDIC appears to be more analogous to NASD. It supervises small banks, those state banks that are not members of the Federal Reserve System. These account for 17% of all bank assets, 23% of deposits, and 26% of offices. But they only account for a minuscule 1.4% of the assets of the top 25 banks, 2.4% of deposits, and 3.7% of offices (Greenspan 1999). The FDIC enforced 37% of the PCAs, 10 of 27. It was not the dominant bank enforcer, but it played an important role.

The Federal Reserve supervises state-chartered member banks, which held only 24% of all bank assets but included almost all the rest of the biggest U.S. banks: 37% of assets, 17% of domestic deposits, and 7% of U.S. offices. The Fed's small 19% share of all PCAs is consistent with its role as a regulator of big banks.

Venue: Where the Enforcement Takes Place

A part of the enforcement tool kit is the forum, the place where the action takes place. Here the options are the supervisory agency itself, a higher forum (e.g., the SEC on appeal from NASD), or a court. Almost all capital adequacy enforcement is done through the internal administration of the regulator; all PCA by bank regulators is internal to the regulator. Among the supervisors of securities firms, the SROs act through their own internal institutions only on their own initiative; a few of their decisions are appealed to the SEC. The SEC, in addition to its internal enforcement, litigates in federal district courts and reviews actions on appeal from the SROs. So all NASD and NYSE actions enforcing capital adequacy rules were internal; while most SEC actions were also internal, almost one-quarter took place in federal courts.

Intervention Triggers for Enforcement

In order not to be caught flat-footed when a financial firm violates the capital adequacy rules, both bank and securities firm regulators use early-warning triggers. As a firm moves toward clear and serious noncompliance, milestones alert the supervisors, who are expected to act. These enforcement triggers vary mainly according to whether the firm is a bank or securities firm but also among regulators. The triggers for bank supervisors are more finely graded than those for the regulators of securities firms.

Triggers for Bank Supervisors

Regulators classify banks according to standard criteria, then use the tools already described to make those banks that have weak classifications improve. U.S. bank regulators apply a uniform system to rate banks (Board of

Governors of the Federal Reserve System 2002, p. 7). Their criteria are six tests known collectively as CAMELS: capital, assets, management, earnings, liquidity, and sensitivity to changes in market conditions. For each measure, banks are classified along a sliding scale from strong to weak.

Capital is the first element of the CAMELS test and classifies banks' capital in relation to the risk profile of the bank. U.S. regulators use measures of capital based on the Basel risk-based capital rules for Tier 1 and Tier 2. Classifications that are below adequate levels prompt the regulator to require increasingly drastic action. The regulator's power to impose these actions grows as the bank's capital worsens. The following paragraphs set out the rules in more detail because they serve as triggers for enforcement.

The ratings of capital adequacy are as follows:[9]

- A #1 rating indicates that the bank is well capitalized, that capital is strong relative to the risk: for Tier 1, capital exceeds 6%, the total risk-based ratio exceeds 10%, and the leverage ratio exceeds 5%.[10]
- A #2 rating indicated that the bank is adequately capitalized, so capital is "satisfactory" relative to risk. This rating requires the ratio to exceed 4% for Tier 1, 8% for Tiers 1 and 2, and 4% as the leverage ratio (3% if the CAMELS rating is the highest).
- A #3 rating means that the bank is undercapitalized, which means that capital is less than satisfactory relative to the bank's risk and needs to improve: for Tier 1, is below 4%, the total risk-based ratio is below 8%, or the leverage ratio is below 4% or 3%.
- A #4 rating means that the bank is significantly undercapitalized. Capital is so low that the deficiency may threaten the firm's viability. More capital may be needed from shareholders or others outside the firm. For Tier 1, capital is below 3%, the total risk-based ratio is below 8%, and the leverage ratio is below 3%.
- A #5 rating means that the bank is critically undercapitalized. Capital is so deficient that it does threaten the firm's viability. Outside capital support is needed immediately. The leverage ratio is below 2%.

If the supervisor finds that the bank is engaged in unsafe or unsound practices measured against standards set in Section 39 of the FDIC Improvement Act (FDICIA 1991), then it must lower the capital adequacy rating at least one step. The supervisor also may require other actions on the part of the bank and may even close the bank.

The FDICIA required specific zones for determining the cost of deposit insurance and need for prompt corrective action. At each stage of capitalization, as violations progress from minor to life threatening, PCA requires regulators to enforce certain action by the bank and gives them the discretion to make the bank take more drastic action, as described by the U.S. General Accounting Office (GAO 2001):

> If a bank is undercapitalized, three actions are mandatory. The bank must submit an acceptable plan to restore capital (CRP) and the regulator must

monitor closely the bank's condition and compliance with the plan. The bank must limit its asset growth. Any new acquisition, branch, or business line must be approved by the regulator. In addition, the regulator may do anything it could do with a significantly undercapitalized bank on a showing that the action is necessary.

If a bank is significantly undercapitalized, or is undercapitalized but fails to submit or materially implement a plan, the regulator has broader powers. It must require the bank to raise equity or debt capital; merge with or be acquired by another insured depository institution if grounds exist to appoint a conservator or receiver; restrict affiliate transactions; or restrict interest on deposits. Only if the acts would not promote the goals of prompt corrective action can the regulator not carry them out. In that case, it may restrict growth of assets, restrict activities that are too risky, require better management, which may include removing senior managers, stop the bank from accepting deposits from its correspondents, require regulator approval for the holding company to distribute capital, force the bank to divest assets in certain cases, or require any other action that would achieve the prompt corrective action goals, including those for critically undercapitalized firms.

If a bank is critically undercapitalized, the regulator must ensure that the bank complies with FDIC rules that limit "material transactions outside the normal course of business," lending for "highly leveraged transactions," "amending the charter or by-laws," "material change in accounting methods," "covered transactions with affiliates," excessive pay, and above-market interest rates on liabilities.[11] The regulator must also require the bank to stop servicing subordinated debt or even accept the regulator's appointment of a receiver if it would help achieve PCA goals or the institution is critically undercapitalized 270 or more days (unless the regulators certify they do not expect the institution to fail).

If a bank is unsafe or unsound, the regulator may appoint a conservator or receiver, or close the bank.

These requirements also give rough standards against which to judge supervisors' efforts to implement the capital adequacy rules and to prompt corrective action.[12]

Triggers for Supervisors of Securities Companies

Compared to bank supervisors, SEC regulators have simpler triggers and more discretion. The early-warning system alerts regulators in the SEC and the self-regulating organization to which the broker-dealer belongs that the broker's capital is near the legal minimum. The system simply requires the broker-dealer to inform the SEC and its SRO when its net capital falls below 125% of the required net capital if the basic method is used or 120% if the absolute dollar method is used (see table 8.1). If the broker-dealer uses the alternate method, relying on customer receivables, it must give notice when the actual net capital falls below 250% of required net capital, which is calculated with a different base, customer receivables, and is not included in the table.

The SEC and the SRO, in addition, review periodic reports by the broker-dealer that include its capital condition. SROs must notify the SEC when

Table 8.1. Early-Warning System as Broker-Dealer Net Capital Declines: Using the Basic Method to Calculate Net Capital

	Actual Net Capital as % of:		
Method	Required Net Capital	Aggregate Debt	Required Action
Basic	< 125	< 8.33	Notify SEC and SRO in 24 hours
Dollar	< 120	< 8.00	Notify SEC and SRO in 24 hours, no capital withdrawals by shareholders
All	= 100	= 6.67	(Minimum permissible net capital)
All	< 100	< 6.67	Notify SEC and SRO and stop operations immediately

Source: GAO (1998), p. 136, Exchange Act Rule 17a-11(c). Notice is telegraphic or by facsimile. Rule 17a-11(g).

they discover that a broker-dealer's net capital is at or below the early warning point.[13]

The regulators may act when they learn that net capital is close to or below the warning point. They have mandatory and discretionary powers. At the early warning point, 125% or 120% above the minimum net capital, the regulators instruct the broker-dealer to take steps to reverse the trend. Regulators watch the broker-dealer more closely than before. The SRO may restrict operations even more than the SEC. "For example, the New York Stock Exchange's rule 326 restricts the business activities of member broker-dealers that are approaching financial or operational difficulties" (GAO 1998, p. 136).

If the broker-dealer's capital is below the minimum net capital, the SEC requires the broker dealer to stop operating immediately. The SEC may either allow the broker-dealer to raise capital or require it to liquidate (GAO 1998, p. 136).

Techniques of Intervention

Regulators enforce the rules with various tools. After briefly distinguishing formal actions from informal ones, and supervision from enforcement, this section presents the range of tools available to regulators. These vary depending on whether the regulator is part of the executive branch of government or a self-regulation organization.

Formal versus Informal Actions

Supervisors take formal action to discipline financial firms when important violations have taken place. One securities regulator interviewed could not imagine an informal action for a major or material deficiency. Bank regulators apply formal enforcement actions mainly to banks with composite CAMELS ratings of 4 (serious weaknesses that could impair the bank's viability) or 5 (likely to fail soon). The tools of formal action are presented later.

Informal actions, including cease-and-desist orders, termination of insurance, and removal of officers or directors, address less serious problems. Informal actions leave open the possibility that the regulator will abuse—or be perceived to abuse—its discretion. To deal with this, regulators have rules for the use of informal actions. Despite this concern, one regulator—NASD—wants to increase the share of informal actions, allowing violations of minor rules to be resolved informally. Net capital rules would probably not, however, be treated as minor.

Another form of informality may correct potential capital problems of some banks with strong ratios but higher-than-normal risk. For example, when a bank needs regulatory approval for some desired action, the supervisor might require the bank to strengthen capital as a condition for granting approval. In such a case, formal or even informal action might be unwarranted because nominally the bank's capital is sound.[14] This informality is not caught in the data analyzed by this chapter. However, later cases presented in the chapter give examples in which supervisors failed to identify the higher risk. It is not possible to know whether the catches exceed the misses.

When banks fail, the FDIC generally forces mergers or arranges for other banks to assume the assets and deposits. Much more rarely, it closes the bank and acts as conservator or arranges for a bridge bank. At this point, the time for prompt corrective action has passed.

Frequent and Full Reports and Examinations

Supervision methods are not the subject of this chapter, so it is enough to note that supervision consists of on-site examinations and off-site analysis and reviews based on electronic reports from the firms. The mixes vary by regulator and according to whether the entity is a bank or securities firm. Since annual field exams are costly, supervisors do not visit every institution every year, but they see the importance of these examinations. Frequent electronic filing helps give regulators an early warning.

The informal actions described earlier for both banks and securities companies are a tool more of supervision than of enforcement, if such a distinction is useful. They are the regulators' signal to firms that can still turn around their performance that they must comply. When they are not sufficient, there are triggers for enforcement. Supervisors apply these triggers.

Enforcement Tools Allow Supervisors to Fine-Tune

The regulators' enforcement tools expanded from the mid-1960s to the late 1980s. Regulators now have the ability to tailor directives to individual financial institutions. Securities regulators do so; the bank regulators, however, have a standardized approach to PCA directives that they modify a bit for each bank.

The most important tools for capital adequacy enforcement are fines, censure, and suspension for securities firms and directives for how to increase capital for banks. The range of available tools is much broader than what is actually used.

Available Tools Vary Among Regulators

Enforcement tools are distributed unequally among the supervisors. Government regulators have a very broad range of tools to enforce capital adequacy rules. As table 8.2 shows, the SROs, which do most of the work, are quite limited in what they can do to discipline their members. Bank regulators and the SEC, as government agencies, differ little in their enforcement tools. Both may use the mildest form of action, a formal agreement with the firm that it will mend its ways, or they may tighten the screws; issuing cease-and-desist orders to firms and affiliated parties that force them to end unsafe or unsound practices or behavior that violates laws, rules, or written conditions of any regulatory action (e.g., a license granted to a bank). Cease-and-desist orders may include an order to correct conditions, rather than simply a demand that a bank stop activity that breaks the capital rules. For example, the FDIC can direct a bank to increase its capital by a set time without even holding a hearing.[15] Government regulators can also issue injunctions, levy civil penalties, order funds returned to affected parties, limit licenses or revoke charters, remove officers or directors, close firms, seek more stringent civil penalties through courts, and pursue criminal actions.

Among the enforcement actions examined here, all 16 of those by the NYSE were internal, as were all 122 of the NASD's actions. The SEC, in contrast, brought 9 actions through the courts, 4 of which were criminal. The SEC turned to the courts to decide cases involving fraud, theft, and market manipulation. Of the 31 actions in this category (see table 8.5), 8 were brought by the SEC to federal courts. This means, however, that the SEC dealt with most—21—internally. Another 12 SEC cases dealt with bad management. Of these, only 1 was before the court. The majority—7—were before the SEC on appeal from the SROs. The SEC emerges as a versatile supervisor that can and does use its tools selectively.

Constraints on government regulators' use of these tools do not seem to hinder regulators' ability to enforce the rules. The existence of ceilings on fines does not significantly restrict the regulators in cases involving small and medium-size firms that are the main targets, but they do serve as constraints in cases involving the largest firms. However, although a penalty of even $1 million a day may not deter leading securities firms, a penalty of 1% of assets would surely attract the attention of the biggest banks.

Some of the tools are specific to the sector. Denial of insurance, even temporarily, could have disastrous consequences for a bank, whose depositors will flee, but such a penalty would have a smaller impact on a broker's customers. On the other hand, temporary or permanent loss of membership in an exchange could be devastating for brokers.

Table 8.2. Range of Enforcement Tools for Bank and Securities Regulators

Enforcement Tool	Bank Regulators	SEC	SROs
Subpoena	Yes	Yes	
Access to records	Yes	Yes	
Re-educate			Yes. Compliance committee, re-educate, relicense
Censure		Yes	Yes
Remove membership privileges temporarily		Yes	Yes. Suspend, bar temporarily from access to members (can reapply), limit broker activities
Formal agreement between regulator, firm	Yes. Enforceable as cease-and-desist order	Yes	Yes
Cease-and-desist order (permanent or temporary, including removal of officers or directors)	Yes, to insured + affiliates for unsafe/unsound acts or violating any rule. Includes order to correct conditions	Yes, if violating rules, may order to correct conditions, temporary restraining orders (with court review), mandamus, injunction, and order to comply or make member comply	
Civil penalties without court	Yes. Three tiers: 1. to $5K/day if violate rule 2. to $25K/day for patterns of misconduct	Same 3 tiers as with court (below) if willful violation or fraud, or if fail to supervise	Fine (to any amount: NYSE)

Account, pay to affected people	3. to $1m/day or 1% of assets if knowing violation + harm, even recklessness	Yes	Yes
Litigate independently	Yes	Yes	No
End insurance (even temporarily)	Yes. For unsafe, unsound practice by firm, directors, accountants	Not relevant	Not relevant
Close firm	Appoint conservator or receiver for critically undercapitalized, with PCA	Appoint a conservator through a court	
Removal and prohibition	Yes, for bank affiliate that broke a rule or fiduciary duty, was dishonest, or is a defendant or convicted in criminal proceedings; revoke charter	Yes, through court	Bar permanently, revoke license, expel member
Civil penalties through court	Yes	Yes, 3 tiers based on severity of fraud and impact: 1. to $5K for individual or $50K for legal person, or the gain 2. to $50K/$250K or the gain, if fraud, deceit, manipulation, or deliberate or reckless disregard of regulation	

(continued)

Table 8.2 (continued)

Enforcement Tool	Bank Regulators	SEC	SROs
		3. to $100K/$500K for a legal person, if #2 actions with substantial loss	
Criminal penalties (through the court)	Yes	Willful violations of law or willful and knowing, false and misleading statements: fine to $1m + 10 years in jail for individuals, to $2.5m for legal persons	

Source: GAO (2001), pp. 16–21; Securities and Exchange Act of 1934 and rules issued pursuant to it; NYSE Constitution n.d.; NYSE Hearing Board Procedures (undated) at 9.

Table 8.2 also shows the more limited enforcement tools of the SROs. They supervise mainly their members, although Congress extended their remit to parties in contractual relations with the members. The tools are those that work on members:[16] formal undertakings by the firm to refrain from similar wrongful activity in the future or to change internal systems to those that require further training or a new license; fines; and return of funds to affected people, such as investors;[17] public censure of the firm or officer, which affects reputation (and is therefore to be avoided);[18] prohibitions against working with other members; withdrawal of licenses; and expulsion from membership. The SROs do not have the power to initiate court action, civil or criminal. The SEC reviews their decisions.

Types of Tools Used

The way regulators use their enforcement tools reveals their priorities. They deploy tools in various combinations to achieve different goals. Bank regulators appear to downplay PCA as though it were forced on them. Securities regulators, in contrast, employ many more tools, allowing them to fine–tune their use.

Bank regulators include a standard set of requirements in their PCA directives, although the language varies. After stating the seriousness of the capital deficiency, they specify the increase needed. The Fed simply requires the bank to return to acceptable legislated levels. The FDIC specifies the dollar amount of the Tier 1 capital increase, the Tier 1 target ratio (or step-ups over time), and the methods to be used to increase capital, which require FDIC prior approval. If the bank fails to meet the targets in a specified time, it must merge or sell. The directive tells the bank to comply with the PCA statutory requirements, such as limiting interest rates to depositors, limiting senior officers' compensation, and restricting capital distributions, management fee payments, asset growth, acquisition of interests in other companies, new business, or new branches. The bank must disclose the PCA directive to its shareholders. About half the 10 banks that received PCA directives from FDIC recovered, and the other half closed.

The bank regulators have not used other tools at their disposal in conjunction with the PCA directives, at least so far. The exception occurred in 1999, when the FDIC used a PCA directive to remove the CEO of a bank as it closed the bank (Victory State Bank, South Carolina); thus, the FDIC at least is prepared to move beyond the standard directive. The Fed, in 1997, had issued a cease-and-desist order to Zia New Mexico Bank as it approached the 8% capital floor, and two years later it issued a PCA directive when the bank was significantly undercapitalized. So, other tools may be used before the FDIC issues a directive. In the abstract, however, PCA is required as soon as a bank is undercapitalized.

ANALYSIS OF ENFORCEMENT

The central question for this chapter is why the number of formal actions (see the following subsection) is so small. Perhaps regulators substitute informal actions for formal ones. Perhaps the strong economy during the period examined meant that few banks or securities firms encountered serious problems with their capital. It may be that supervisors prevent firms from hitting the ropes. The subsequent subsections explore these matters.

The Low Number of Formal Actions

The number of formal actions undertaken to enforce capital adequacy rules among both banks and securities firms has been small since the mid-1990s, when comparative data became available. Prior to that time, U.S. bank regulators reported enforcement actions for the composite CAMELS ratings,[19] not merely for capital adequacy. In 1991, the Federal Deposit Insurance Corporation Improvement Act (FDICIA) required regulators to act when capital reached specified levels, and shortly after that regulators began to post information about these actions on their web sites.

This aggregate evidence does not support the view that enforcement plays a significant role in maintaining capital adequacy of banks and securities companies. Even now, bank regulators rarely use formal actions to enforce capital adequacy rules alone. The Fed, the Federal Deposit Insurance Corporation (FDIC), and the Office of the Comptroller of the Currency (OCC) together reported on average three prompt corrective actions each year from 1993 to 2001, or a total of 27, for capital inadequacy. Of these, the OCC was responsible for 12, the FDIC for 10, and the Fed only for five, as listed in appendix 1. Not one concerned a major bank or a foreign one.

Securities regulators report a higher number of actions, but not a large number—182. The SEC and the self-regulatory organizations (SRO)—the NYSE and NASD—reported an average of 30 actions a year between 1996 and 2001 (a period for which comparable data are available) taken against broker-dealers for violating capital adequacy rules. The Securities and Exchange Commission (SEC) took action against 44 broker-dealers.[20] The New York Stock Exchange (NYSE) reported only 16 actions. The National Association of Securities Dealers (NASD) reported 122 actions, twice the combined total for the NYSE and the SEC.

The numbers for both the banking and the securities actions are small, given the size of the regulated population—a total of 209 for the periods covered. During the nine years from 1993, 8,700 banks, on average, were supervised (FDIC 2000). On the basis of this number, the three actions a year, on average, represent a minuscule percentage (0.003%) of banks. There are, on average, 7,500 broker-dealer firms.[21] The 30 actions a year, on average, over the six years, involve a very small percentage (0.4%) of this total. Only compared with the tiny ratio for banks does the ratio for broker-dealers look large.

The number of formal actions to deal with capital adequacy problems was small also in comparison with the overall number of problem and failed banks. Among banks, on average, the number of banks forced to take prompt corrective actions was only 4% of the number of problem and failed banks, which in turn constituted only a small portion of the entire population of banks. Securities regulators did not publish records of a comparable set of problem companies. The actions were also small in their potential impact on the stability of the financial system. None of these firms, had its condition worsened, was large enough to start a crisis.

This research finds that only a few U.S. firms controlling a small portion of total financial assets become the object of formal actions by U.S. bank and securities regulators to enforce capital adequacy rules. The underlying question is why these actions are so relatively rare. Is it because the problems are resolved by informal action? Is it because these data report enforcement only during good economic times? The following sections discuss these two possible explanations. Later, the chapter asks whether supervision contributes to the low level of actions in a positive or negative way.

Answers to these matters reveal the modest impact of prompt corrective action and net capital enforcement today. PCA may not have fulfilled its intended goal of forcing supervisors to act, rather than wait for problem banks to outgrow their troubles.

Informal Processes as Substitutes for Formal Actions

Informal actions do not appear to substitute substantially for formal ones, although they may prevent a firm's capital from deteriorating to a point that requires formal action; also, if the case for formal action is weak, a bank may convince its supervisor to accept informal solutions that avoid publicity. The different role of informal action, coupled with questions raised later about the effectiveness of supervision, suggests that the low number of formal capital adequacy enforcement actions is not due in any large measure to the widespread use of informal actions.

Informal actions serve a different function from formal ones. Rather than displacing formal action, they address problems that are not potentially fatal and that require much less adjustment by the company. For securities firms, a supervisory review may reveal minor, transient errors. The experience of NYSE and NASD is that most firms just require minor adjustments.[22] Many factors related to the firm's performance and situation and the violated rule itself can lead the regulators to decide to act informally. These factors may include the following:

- The amounts involved are not material.
- The violation is the first for the firm, not one in a history of repeated violations.
- The firm encountered glitches installing new systems.
- New hires have made mistakes that reflect their lack of institutional memory.
- New products may have generated unexpected problems.
- The relevant capital rule is complicated, and the firm may have misunderstood it.
- The firm immediately told the regulator of the problem and showed good faith by solving it quickly.

These circumstances may prompt the regulator to hold a compliance conference with the principals of the firm or to write a letter of caution and to
refrain from formal action. Both types of warnings are not recorded as
disciplinary actions. Informal actions are more frequent than formal ones,
according to interviews. A rough estimate by a person at NASD revealed
that informal actions may be three times as common as formal ones.

For banks, informal actions tend to apply to those with composite
CAMELS ratings of 3 out 6 (weak financially or operationally but with a
remote likelihood of failure). The actions include memoranda of understanding between bank and regulator, a commitment letter from the bank's
board of directors, or resolutions by the board designed to remedy these
problems (FDIC 1996).

Formal actions and informal ones move in tandem, according to a study
of nonpublic (informal) and public (formal) Fed actions from 1990 to 1997
(Gilbert and Vaughan 2000). The number of informal actions reached a
high of 288 in 1992 and fell steadily to 39 by 1997. Similarly, formal actions peaked at 364 in 1992 and fell steadily to 42 in 1997. If the Fed had
sought to hide the worsening condition of banks during the recession of
the early 1990s, one would expect the ratio of informal actions to formal
ones to be higher earlier in this period than at a later time, which was not the
case.

Economic Cycles and the Level of Formal Actions

It is likely that the low number of formal enforcement actions reflects at
least in part the economic strength of the middle and late 1990s; the number
of enforcements would be expected to be higher in periods of economic and
financial downturn. The periods reported, 1993–2001 for banks and 1996–
2001 for securities firms, span cyclical upswings and the start of a downswing. These are the periods for which comparable data are available. For
banks, the FDICIA took effect in 1991, directing prompt corrective action
and the publication of information. For securities companies, the web sites
present data about each action beginning around 1995. If the data extended
back (or forward) into recessions when banks were under more stress, there
would probably have been more formal actions to enforce capital rules. But,
while the absolute number of formal actions may rise substantially from a
low base, the new number is likely to involve a small portion of all problem
banks or the entire banking population, for reasons explained later.

Data from an earlier enforcement regime broadly support the relation
between formal actions generally and industry conditions, although a closer
look shows the two do not move in lock-step with each other or with
macroeconomic growth. Formal enforcement actions against banks during
the 1980s and early 1990s were related to the number of problem banks.
These earlier formal actions are broader than those examined here for the
period from the mid-1990s on. The earlier actions were based not only on
capital adequacy but also on the other elements in CAMELS (asset strength,

management, earnings, liquidity, sensitivity). The actions explored here are only those related to capital adequacy.

Figure 8.1 shows how, as problem loans grew dramatically during the early 1980s and then declined to 1994, the number of formal composite CAMELS enforcement actions also grew and eventually fell. The changes in formal enforcement actions lags slightly behind changes in the number of problem banks at the start and the end of the cycle. Over the nine mid-cycle years between 1983 and 1992, when the number of problem banks peaked at more than 400 and then fell, the number of formal actions fluctuated around 200. The number did not track the rise and fall in the number of problem banks. Regulators may have (and were accused of having) kept the lid on formal action then in the hope that the banks would grow out of their problems. Certainly the economy was stronger in the mid-1990s (see table 8.3), allowing observers to hold out the hope of recovery for the banks.

The inverse relation between economic growth and problem banks exists but is not exact. As real GDP growth worsened or turned negative, the number of both problem loans and formal composite CAMELS enforcement actions grew. They increased dramatically during the period of low and negative growth from 1980 to 1982 and increased a bit during the slowing and negative GDP growth in 1990–1991 (see table 8.3). The strong economic growth that started in 1983 may have helped cap the enforcement actions, but the number of problem banks continued to grow for two more years.

So one might expect relatively fewer problem loans and capital adequacy enforcement actions during the fat years of the 1990s but a growing number as growth slowed. Between 1996 and 2000, U.S. real GDP growth ranged between 3.6% and 4.4% each year (IMF 2002, p. 167). One would expect

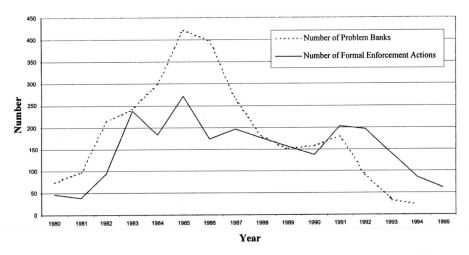

Figure 8.1. Relation of Formal FDIC Enforcement Actions to Number of Problem Banks, 1980–1995. Source: FDIC 1996, tables 12.5 and 12.7, pp. 443, 445.

Table 8.3. Real GDP Percentage Growth Per Year (for comparison)

1980	1981	1982	1983	1984	1985	1986	1987	1988	1989	1990	1991	1992	1993	1994	1995
-0.5%	1.8%	-2.2%	3.9%	6.2%	3.2%	2.9%	3.1%	3.9%	2.5%	0.8%	1.0%	2.7%	2.2%	3.5%	2.0%

Source: IMF (1997), p. 853.

that either in 2001, when real GDP grew only 0.8%, or in 2002, because of lags, the number of problem banks would rise compared to the number in the past. The FDIC, using a different time series from that in the chart, reported that, as expected, the number of FDIC-insured problem banks fell from 144 in 1995 to a low of 66 in 1999, then rose to 76 in 2000, 95 in 2001, and 119 in 2002 (FDIC 2003). But the number of PCAs did not change similarly. Actions by the OCC, the Fed, and the FDIC increased from one in 1998 to two each in 1999 and 2000 and to four in 2001, but there were only two in 2002. The number did not swell as the economy worsened. This is a puzzle.

For securities regulators, the number of actions to enforce the net capital rules rose one year and fell the next in no obvious pattern from the mid-1990s on. NASD, with by far the largest number of actions in comparison to other regulators, reported 24 actions in 1997, 17 in 1998, 22 in 1999, 32 in 2000, 22 in 2001, and only 13 in 2002 as the financial and economic trough deepened, or fewer actions than in any other year examined. One would expect the opposite in a downturn, as more firms find their capital is at the margin. But interviews suggested that different factors were at work. In today's downturn, firms are still living off their 10 fat years. Firms at the margin cannot afford to have the market see them being disciplined (e.g., forbidden to carry on their business even for three days), so they work even harder to comply. They try to avoid crossing the line into inadequate capitalization, since fines are published and customers check capital more now than in the past. Layoffs from securities companies during a downswing may lead to an increase in marginal securities firms as those fired try to work on their own, pulling the initial capital from their own savings. Regulatory capital is a lagging indicator of problems, even though it is presented as the central tool of supervision.

It is not obvious that the annual number of formal actions to enforce capital adequacy rules will rise dramatically. For banks, it may not rise much beyond the low double digits, even in a prolonged downturn. The FDIC study of the 1980s and 1990s concluded that "most banks that failed were closed within the time frame specified by FDICIA for critically undercapitalized banks." Only 21% "might have been closed earlier" (FDIC 1996, p. 454), and many of these were delayed because of limits on the OCC's ability to close them speedily, limits that have since been removed. For both banks and securities firms, the capital adequacy enforcement actions reach a very small portion of the problem firms. The action is elsewhere.

The Effect of Supervision on Enforcement

It may be that supervision makes formal enforcement largely unnecessary. Supervision may keep enforcement low either for positive reasons (supervisors catch the problems early) or negative ones (supervisors delay the use of formal action).

In this view, clear comprehensive rules, frequent and full reports and examinations, and explicit triggers for enforcement, as well as market incentives for firms to be well capitalized, may leave few violations to enforce. Supervisors do not need to catch 100% of all violations, and there is no harm to the system if a few small banks slip through.

The border between supervision and enforcement is fuzzy. Supervisors prepare for enforcement and help carry it out. When enforcement actions return the firm to health, the supervisors take up the reins again.

Most U.S. Finance Firms Are Reported to Be Well-capitalized

Among securities firms, at least, the largest ones, those that may threaten the system, hold capital that substantially exceeds the amount required by the regulators. This suggests that there is no or very limited need for enforcement.

Bank supervisors report that almost all banks in the United States are in fine shape. Regulatory capital ratios for banks published over the past decade suggest a very limited need for prompt corrective action. For all banks from 1990 to 2001, Tier 1 capital, Tiers 1 and 2 combined, and the leverage ratio rose to 1992; the first two then tapered off slightly and leverage plateaued. By end-2001, for all banks, Tier 1 capital was almost 10%, Tier 1+2 was 13%, and the leverage ratio was 7.75% (Federal Reserve Bulletin 2002, p. 269). On average, most banks look healthy.

Most U.S. banks placed in the well-capitalized category, the first and highest of the five (Federal Reserve Bulletin 2002, p. 269). During the period 1994 to 2001, the share of all banks' assets in these banks fluctuated between about 95.5% (1994 and 1998) and 98% (1996, 2000, 2001). Over the period, however, these banks' cushion of extra capital decreased. The average margins by which banks were well capitalized fell from a high of 2.2% in 1994 to about 1.75% in 2000, then rose to almost 2% in 2001. So, over the eight years, the well-capitalized banks got closer to the regulatory minimum.[23]

Among the largest securities firms, the practice is to hold capital above the regulatory levels, but the actual multiple may be substantially overstated in the literature. For example, in 2001, Merrill Lynch & Co., Inc., the parent company of the broker-dealer, stated in its annual report that it held capital of $88.5 billion, the sum of ownership equity and subordinated debt. This is more than 16 times the minimum regulatory capital of $5.4 billion it was obliged to hold by the SEC. But the SEC rule requires many adjustments to the gross capital figure given in the annual report. In fact, after those adjustments, Merrill Lynch held excess capital of $5.2 billion and total capital of $10.6 billion, still just over twice the minimum required but far short of the $88.5 billion stated in its annual report.[24]

Supervision of Firms That Later Failed

From the number of capital adequacy actions, it is not apparent that the more graduated triggers for banks catch noncompliance more effectively than the simpler ones for securities firms. Certainly, the securities regulators report significantly more formal actions than the number of prompt corrective actions reported by bank regulators. Perhaps the banks are stronger, of course. However, the graduated triggers for PCA directives used by bank supervisors did not identify moderately sized banks that failed since the mid-1990s. The next section addresses this.

One may question the sanguine view that the early work done by supervisors, either of banks or of securities firms, leaves enforcement officials less work than a Maytag repairman has. Firms are not candid. For example, expense-sharing agreements that remove liabilities from the books in corporate America are used by securities firms, too; lowering liabilities raises capital. Regulators may not have the resources to step up monitoring in hard times, so they may not catch these disguised transgressions. It is difficult for a regulator to show that a broker-dealer should have reported a liability transferred by an expense-sharing agreement.[25]

A closer look at some of the failed firms reveals supervisory lapses. Among banks, some of the largest firms that were closed in recent years went under without having received a PCA directive, and supervisors seem not to have tagged the capital beforehand for heightened risk.[26] Perhaps the supervisors missed important signals. Perhaps they were ignored when they said that a bank's loans were weak, only to see the bank fail later. If they identified weak loans as part of the "A" (for asset quality) in CAMELS, they also needed to use that information to determine whether capital was adequate.

This section is about the process of supervision and enforcement. It draws on case studies by the Office of Inspector General in the FDIC that examine the supervision of individual failed banks. The studies offer glimpses of how supervision works, or does not. Rarely is the curtain lifted as it is in the case of the failed banks described here. Similar studies of securities regulators were not available. Presumably the existence of these independent audits helps to motivate bank regulators to do their job well. Securities regulators are not subject to the same discipline, and they account for a much larger number of enforcement actions each year.

Possible Delays in Enforcement. Among the most costly failures from 1995 to 2002 are banks that suggest weak supervision of capital adequacy contributed to failure. *NextBank* failed on February 7, 2002, having lost 43% of its $700 million assets. Its problems developed after September 1999. In October 2000, the OCC insisted that the board remedy credit deficiencies, but the board failed to do so. Only on November 15, 2001, a year after requiring action and barely four months before the bank failed, did the OCC issue a PCA directive to restore Tier 1 capital (OCC 2002).

The OCC's enforcement actions against Hamilton Bank show that the supervisor deployed many enforcement tools against the bank over several years. In January 2002, the OCC closed Hamilton Bank after it had failed to meet most elements of CAMELS. By early 2002, the bank had lost 13% of its $1.3 billion assets. Its Tier 1 capital ratio, which had been about 6.5% in 2000, fell to 4.43% by September 30, 2001, and the bank was undercapitalized (Category 3 for PCA purposes) when it closed. The OCC sketched its actions to help the bank recover and described the nonresponsiveness of the board of directors and managers:[27]

- 1998: OCC issued a safety-and-soundness notice to the bank. The bank did not comply.
- 2000: OCC and the bank entered a consent cease-and-desist order. The bank "willfully violated the order by failing to make its books and records available to the OCC" and "concealed material information from OCC examiners."
- 2001: OCC failed to get the bank to consent to an amended cease-and-desist order, then issued a temporary cease-and-desist order that the U.S. District Court supported when the bank challenged it.

The OCC said that "The bank never achieved full compliance with the OCC's various enforcement actions and never met OCC-required capital levels." On its face, this appears to be a good example of deliberate enforcement, with actions escalating incrementally until the bank was finally closed as it limped across the boundary into the land of mandatory PCA. The regulators were ahead of PCA. But the process extended across three years. Did the supervisors move quickly enough? Did they evaluate loan quality well throughout the process? If not, the bank may have been undercapitalized for some time before it was closed, and prompt corrective action should have been instituted. These sorts of questions are not answered in press releases by supervisory agencies. They are addressed in the detailed studies that follow.

Three other banks—Connecticut Bank of Commerce, Superior Bank (a thrift), and BestBank—were the subject of detailed reviews by FDIC that were subsequently published. Background about them follows, and reveals why PCA did not work effectively for them.

Connecticut Bank of Commerce. The Connecticut Bank of Commerce lost 18% of its $399 million assets and failed June 26, 2002. A detailed study by the Office of Inspector General (OIG) documented how the FDIC examiners found and reported deficiencies to the bank's board during the 1990s. When the board did not act on the reports (because the chairman controlled the board), the FDIC did not follow up (OIG 2003). The CAMELS rating improved from the lowest 5 in 1991–1995 to a 4 in 1996–1997 and a 3 in 1998. Only in 2001 did it fall back to a 4. No new rating was given for more than a year, between December 1999 and March 2001, even though the bank was operating under an informal memorandum of understanding (MOU) replacing a cease-and-desist order from 1995 with which the bank had not complied in full.

Apparently the FDIC examiners concluded that, since the chairman was investing more in the bank (or seemed to be) during this period, it could rely on his assessment of the bank's prospects. FDIC issued a cease-and-desist order on November 30, 2001, to end weak credit administration, reduce credit concentrations, and reduce bad loans. The bank did not comply. The only PCA directive, dated June 25, 2002, ordered the bank to dismiss its chairman. At that time, the bank was already critically undercapitalized, the fifth and lowest category. Indeed, it appears that the bank should have been subject to PCA during much of the 1990s. FDIC later discovered that the chairman had fraudulently arranged for the bank to buy shares in another weak bank nearby during this period.

Superior Bank. The largest bank to fail during this period was Superior Bank, a thrift that failed July 27, 2001, having lost 20% of its $2.2 billion assets. In a report prepared at the request of Senator Paul Sarbanes, OIG concluded that Superior Bank's officers and board had concentrated the bank's funds in high-risk assets (the residuals from securitizing the bank's subprime loans), valuing them unrealistically, recognizing "enormous gains" that masked major operating losses, and paying dividends to the holding company that depleted bank capital. The chairman dominated the board of directors (OIG 2002).

The OIG faulted the bank's supervisor, the Office of Thrift Supervision (OTS), for identifying problems over many years but not ensuring that the bank had solved them.[28] The bank began overvaluing assets, inflating capital, and showing a return on assets far above the average for U.S. thrifts, beginning in 1993. OTS identified problems to the bank's board as early as 1993 but did not follow up by requiring the bank to implement solutions, and its board "regularly disregarded" the recommendations. The outside accountant supported the chairman in his incorrect interpretations of accounting practice. OTS believed that the bank's wealthy owners could, and would, inject capital. Not until July 2000 did OTS begin formal supervisory action.

Coordination between OTS, as primary supervisor, and FDIC, as the insurer, failed. OTS denied the request of the FDIC regional office to participate in the 1999 examination. The FDIC regional office did not ask its national office for support. When the two agencies worked together in January 2000, they began to see the valuation problems but relied on assurances from the bank managers and the accountant, Ernst & Young, that the problems would be remedied.

The OTS failed to identify the bank's capital as inadequate. It relied on the faulty valuation of assets that it criticized. So the OTS saw discrete failures by the bank but did not analyze their effect on the bank's condition.

OIG concluded that "PCA did not work in the case of Superior. The capital ratios at Superior did not accurately reflect the financial position of the institution" (OIG 2002, "Superior Bank," at ii.) OTS was complicit in the miscalculation. PCA was "untimely and ineffective." OIG said that "the failure of Superior Bank underscores one of the most difficult challenges facing bank regulators today—how to limit risk assumed by banks *when their profits and capital ratios make them appear financially strong*. The federal banking agencies have attempted to address this challenge through the adoption of risk-focused examination programs and risk-based capital requirements. However, the recent failures of Superior Bank, First National Bank of Keystone, and BestBank demonstrate that further improvement is needed" (emphasis added; OIG 2002, "Superior Bank," at 5.) The italicized phrase points up the weakness of PCA as an enforcement technique.

BestBank. BestBank lost 54% of its US$318 million in assets and closed July 23, 1998. The Bank Insurance Fund (BIF) lost US$172 million. A criminal investigation was under way into possible fraud—disguising delinquent accounts—but this was not included in the OIG report. BestBank concentrated its assets in a high-risk unsecured credit card travel program, while attracting deposits via the Internet by offering unusually high interest rates. The bank issued the cards to subprime borrowers with bad credit histories and delegated management of its assets in the credit card program to a nonaffiliated third party, Century. Two months before BestBank closed, this delegated lending accounted for 71% of all assets and 971% of Tier 1 capital. BestBank also paid large bonuses to its executives. The salaries of the CEO and president were "unusually large" compared with those offered by other banks.

The FDIC's Department of Supervision (DOS) expressed concern in 1996 and 1997 when BestBank lacked audited financials. As early as 1995, its Tier 1 capital ratios "began to falter." "Although the ratios were mathematically in line with regulatory standards, they were not sufficient to mitigate the level of risk in the bank's asset structure" (OIG 1999, "BestBank," at 8.) The DOS "oversight could have been more effective in controlling Best-Bank's undisciplined growth, concentration in unsecured subprime lending, and poor underwriting practices, which represent a significant risk to the BIF" (OIG 1999, BestBank, at 9.)

The DOS was denied access to Century's books, even though Century was managing the major source of BestBuy's income and risk and even though Century agreed, in its contract with BestBuy, to submit to any regulatory exam. The counsel to the Dallas office of FDIC said that the FDIC lacked statutory authority to examine Century, which was not affiliated with the bank. BestBuy managers also lacked similar information.

BestBank denied the DOS full access to BestBank's own books in 1996, and the DOS acquiesced, dropping its plan to inspect the books. BestBank, in 1996 and 1997, required the examiners to pass all requests to see the bank's books through one person, the risk manager. This considerably slowed the FDIC examiners, who accepted the restriction for two years. In 1998, they threatened to get a temporary restraining order, and the bank backed down.

Summary of Case Studies. These case studies reveal that supervisors did not fully implement the existing rules. These failures may help explain the low number of prompt corrective actions. Outright fraud, which is inevitable and is difficult for supervisors to catch, was not the whole story; it was a partial factor in only one of the failed banks. More common was behavior on the part of supervisors allowed the banks to obfuscate and delay. If it were a disease, it might be called Supervisory Operational Risk Syndrome (SORS). These primary supervisors fell short in the following areas:

- They failed to relate risk to capital, which may have been "mathematically in line" but was not adequate for the risk the bank had taken on (BestBank; Hamilton Bank, whose Tier 1 capital fell to 4.43% shortly before it collapsed, may be a second example). This is a danger inherent in the Basel 1 rules, which do not distinguish between concentrated and diversified portfolios.
- They failed to make sure assets were valued accurately. Firms in trouble often overstate the real value of loans or positions. If one lacks confidence in the accuracy of the accounting, enforcement of capital rules becomes meaningless.
- They relied on the major shareholder rather than do their own investigations, despite the history of weak capital (Connecticut Bank).
- They failed to recognize the full extent of risk in the banks' portfolio (BestBank).
- They identified the bank's noncompliance but failed to do the following:

  a. Make the bank's board resolve these problems (such as incorrect valuation of new instruments), sometimes for years (Nextbank, Connecticut Bank, Superior)
  b. Relate the individual problems to the bank's overall conditions (Superior)

- They failed to coordinate well with the insurer, FDIC (Superior).
- They accepted the bank's reluctance to open completely to the supervisor, thereby getting an incomplete picture of the bank's risks (BestBank).

Do these shortcomings matter? Surely the cost of achieving 100% success by supervisors would be too high. The system can afford relatively small problems, including these. If problems are limited only to these banks, then there is little concern. Yet, why assume that such supervisory failures apply only to these banks? We do not know what would be found if the curtain were lifted on supervisory activities at other, perhaps bigger banks.

These stories are not unique, according to a very interesting analysis of the entire population of U.S. banks, which suggests that, at the aggregate level, supervisors are at least easy on banks that are merely undercapitalized, in terms of CAMELS level 3. (See Gilbert 2003.) This is the level of informal supervisory action and is different from the "undercapitalized" category 3 of FDICIA. Supervisors do not press banks to return to healthy CAMELS levels 1 or 2. From 1993 to 1999, 147 banks on average were downgraded to level 3 each year. Yet, the author of the analysis found that, for banks in level 3, the following occurred:

- Supervisors slowed examinations for many banks. After 63% of the banks entered level 3, the interval between examinations became longer than when a bank had been at the higher level. The researcher expected the opposite because the banks in category 3 were in a worse state.

- Supervisors allowed asset growth for a substantial group: about 35% of the banks reported asset growth, and 12% reported asset growth of at least 10%. This works counter to efforts to strengthen the banks' capital relative to assets.
- Supervisors allowed the banks receiving new equity to pay dividends that were, in a significant number of cases, substantial. About 22% of the banks received new equity, 65% of this group paid dividends, and 58% of them paid more dividends than they received in new equity. Very roughly, this means that for the 147 banks that entered level 3 each year, 32 got equity injections, 21 paid dividends, and, of that 21, 12 paid out more to the shareholders than they received in new equity. This could also undermine the goal of strengthening capital.
- Supervisors allowed a substantial number of banks to remain in category 3 a long time. About half returned to levels 1 or 2 within 18 months, but another a quarter took up to three years, and about 5% more took four years. Over the seven-year period, 61 banks merged with other banks, and 8 failed. Most of the remainder continued to operate at a rating below 2.

This suggests the supervisors are not concerned about banks at level 3 and give them little incentive to improve. This is consistent with the story in the case studies, which are more specifically about capital.

Enforcement Rarely Targets Large Firms

Most enforcement reported here applied to small and medium-size firms that pose no systemic risk. The largest failed medium-size banks were described in the preceding section. Almost no very large banks or securities firms were the object of enforcement actions; those that were are described later. It is not clear if this happened because the large firms are well managed or because the capital rules do not apply to them as well.

Enforcement and Small Financial Firms

The banks and securities firms subject to capital adequacy enforcement actions were almost uniformly small or medium size. The asset size of each subject institution was not compiled because a simple look at the list of firms reveals that these were not on the list of top 100 commercial banks or major securities companies. Table 8.4 shows that problem banks tended to be smaller than average. The ratio of problem banks' assets to all banks' assets (line f of table 8.4) is always lower than the ratio of the number of problem banks to all banks (line c). That is, from 1994 to 2002, the assets of all problem banks, compared with the assets of all FDIC-insured banks, ranged

Table 8.4. Problem Banks' Number and Assets in Relation to All FDIC-Insured Commercial Banks, 1992–2002

Banks	2002	2001	2000	1999	1998	1997	1996	1995	1994	1993	1992
By number:											
a. All banks (number)	7887	8079	8315	8579	8773	9142	9527	9940	10451	10958	11462
b. Problem banks	119	95	76	66	69	71	82	144	247	426	787
c. (b) as % of (a)	1.5	1.2	0.9	0.8	0.8	0.8	0.9	1.4	2.4	3.9	6.9
By assets: (US$ bns)											
d. All banks	7,075	6,552	6,245	5,735	5,442	5,015	4,578	4,313	4,011	3,706	3,505
e. Problem banks	36	36	17	4	5	5	5	17	33	242	408
f. (e) as % of (d)	0.51	0.55	0.27	0.07	0.09	0.10	0.11	0.39	0.82	6.53	11.64

Source: FDIC (1998, 2003).

only from a low of 0.07% in 1999 to a high of 0.82% in 1994 (line f). The number of problem banks in proportion to all banks was consistently higher: from a low of 0.8% to a high of 2.4% (line c). Relatively more problem banks hold fewer assets. The regulators were taking action against small banks. This is consistent with the overall pattern of supervision, at least of banks. Most of the banks that were downgraded between 1993 and 2000 had assets of less than $500 million (Gilbert 2003 at 4).

About 50% of NASD's capital enforcement actions against securities firms involve capital consists of marginal firms, whose capital barely meets the minimum $5,000 required even in good times.[29] One or two mistakes can put them below the minimum capital requirement. The firms may not take these technical violations seriously, even though the regulators say they do.[30] But even the regulators know these individual firms do not threaten systemic risk because they do not hold customers' assets.

The exchanges are concerned primarily about brokers that hold customer funds and therefore need to be well capitalized. These brokers do not constitute a large share of the roughly 5,500 broker-dealers. NYSE regulates most of those that hold customer funds, about 400. Of these, only about 250 clear, and some do so only for themselves and their affiliates.[31] The NYSE had a very low number of capital enforcement actions.

Few Capital Enforcement Actions Involve Big Financial Firms

For all the hoopla about the increasingly sophisticated regulations for risk-based capital, no major firms have been closed or seriously disciplined because they were violating these rules. No big banks have been subject to PCA. The big banks whose capital was wiped out elsewhere at some point in the past decade failed despite the protection of the capital adequacy rules. In the United Kingdom, for example, a calamity in the form of employee fraud and a spectacular failure of supervision caused Barings Bank to lose all its capital. In Japan, two of the largest banks collapsed, but in the period leading up to their collapse they were not charged with having violated the capital adequacy regulations as applied in Japan. Long-Term Credit Bank and Nippon Credit Bank both lacked capital because their bad loans were huge; the Japanese government had to take them over.

The few big U.S. financial firms that were the object of capital enforcement actions caught regulators' attention in one case because of fraud involving another broker, but mainly because of technical glitches that alerted regulators to deteriorating asset quality or growing credit or market risk. All the cases were in securities markets, although some involved banks.

SEC and Bear, Stearns. The only SEC proceeding against a leading broker-dealer involved Bear, Stearns, one of the 10 largest firms in the United States (SIA 2001a). In 1995, Bear, Stearns became the clearing broker for another broker-dealer, A. R. Baron & Co., Inc., a member of NASD. Baron ran a boiler-room operation and was already in financial trouble. Within a year, Baron was cited by the SEC for fraud, saw its capital fall below the minimum, stopped business, was liquidated, and lost its broker-dealer registration.

Bear, Stearns aided Baron in its fraud and continued violation of the net capital rules. The SEC found that Bear, Stearns did the following:

> Charged unauthorized trades to Baron customers; repeatedly requested and obtained credit extensions without any inquiry sufficient to establish good faith; liquidated property in customer accounts to pay for unauthorized trades; refused to return customer property that had been liquidated to pay for unauthorized trades; and disregarded customer instructions.[32]

Bear, Stearns also did not keep books and records that would have revealed Baron's problems. The decision detailed these misdeeds.

The proceeding against Bear, Stearns cited it not specifically for holding inadequate capital but for helping another broker-dealer to do so. It resulted in a cease-and-desist order, a large civil fine of $5 million, and a hefty payment of $30 million into a fund to help meet claims of Baron's customers from the time that Bear, Stearns acted as the clearing broker. Bear, Stearns suffered a large financial hit, but, despite its direct participation in a customer's fraud, it did not incur a criminal penalty.

NYSE and Merrill Lynch. Only two large broker-dealers were subject to disciplinary proceedings before the NYSE for insufficient capital. Merrill Lynch owned one, and Deutsche Bank owned the other.

Merrill Lynch Pierce Fenner & Smith, Inc. (MLPF&S), a subsidiary of Merrill Lynch & Co., Inc. (Merrill & Co.), is the group's broker-dealer and an NYSE member since 1885. It is among the top 10 U.S. brokers, ranked by assets (SIA 2001a). At the end of 1999, it had about 64,000 employees worldwide, of which 25,000 were registered with the NYSE. The parent held $65 billion in capital (which is not regulatory capital) at the end of that year; MLPF&S held $2.78 billion in excess capital.[33]

Late in 1998, Merrill & Co. decided to centralize the group's cash holdings in itself so that it could respond with speed to crises like the one that had occurred in Asia the previous year. MLPF&S began transferring cash to its parent. But, unknown at the time to MLPF&S, a negative number was misread as a positive one. As a result, from then on, MLPF&S overestimated its assets and therefore its excess capital.

On October 27–30, 1999, MLPF&S ran a net capital deficit of from $1 billion to $3 billion without realizing that the deficit existed and therefore did not report it to the NYSE, as it was obliged by the exchange rules to do. Unaware that its account was in deficit at the end of October 1999, the firm continued to trade, violating SEC and NYSE rules.

MLPF&S compounded the problem by obtaining permission from NYSE to prepay $500 million of subordinated debt on October 29, during what turned out to be the period of net capital deficiency. Prepayment deepened the net capital shortfall.

When MLPF&S discovered the shortfall, on October 30, it reported the deficit that same day to the NYSE. NYSE observed that throughout the three deficit days, the group had had a large pool of cash in the coffers of Merrill & Co. that was available for transfer to its broker-dealer. The group was therefore liquid. The SRO noted that MLPF&S immediately notified it of the shortfall, another mark in the firm's favor. Finally, the group quickly took steps after the shortfall to remedy its management systems so that the problem would not happen again; for example, it set up an intercompany balance account of more than $4 billion for Merrill & Co. and its broker that included $1 billion as a cushion against low capital in MLPF&S. It built in careful reviews of the effect any cash transfer to Merrill & Co. would have on MLPF&S capital.

The penalties were censure, a fine of $250,000 and a requirement that the broker-dealer's general counsel review designated reporting procedures and take steps to improve them, submitting a copy to the NYSE within 120 days of the decision.

This appears to be a story of mere technical failure, rather than a sign of more serious capital problems.

NYSE and Deutsche Bank. Deutsche Bank Securities Inc. (DBSI) is the second NYSE member that is part of a major financial group and that was subject to a hearing for capital deficiencies during this period.[34,35] Under another name and as part of Morgan Grenfell, DBSI joined the NYSE in 1987. In September 1993, it merged with two other Deutsche Bank securities firms (Deutsche Bank Capital Corporation and Deutsche Bank Government Securities) and changed its name to Deutsche Bank Securities Corporation. In May 1998, it took its current name.

DBSI's parent is among the largest financial institutions in the world, a universal bank based in Germany. DBSI itself is not huge, however. From a New York City headquarters, it operated only four branches in three cities, and had 1,505 employees of whom 705 were registered with the NYSE and served institutional clients.

NYSE's Division of Member Firm Regulation examined DBSI annually in the fall of 1996, 1997, and 1998. Both the 1996 and 1997 examinations revealed violations of NYSE rules and U.S. securities laws, including accounting and reporting failures. DBSI responded to each report. In March 1998, DBSI installed a new computer system. Almost immediately, flaws in the new system revealed "a significant number of fails and breaks in its stock record and unreconciled cash items in its clearance account."[36] DBSI knew it faced major problems reconciling the books, which contained many inaccurate accounts and records. It did not know that the inaccuracies had caused it to underestimate required capital and that, as a result, it had a net capital deficiency.

DBSI continued to carry out securities transactions while its capital was below the minimum, and it failed to report the deficiency to the NYSE until April 30, 1998, more than a month after it occurred. Both action and nonaction violated NYSE and SEC rules.

After March 1998, DBSI hired consultants to help fix the problems and to help it meet its regulatory duties, which was accomplished "in three months without risk of loss or exposure to customers."[37]

DBSI did not contest the findings, so the decision took the form of a Stipulation of Facts and Consent to Penalty constituting neither an admission nor a denial of guilt by DBSI. The penalty was censure and a $175,000 fine.

This is the story is of a poorly managed broker-dealer subsidiary of one of the leading financial institutions in the world. A history of failures to comply with Exchange and SEC rules revealed the inadequate management. A transition to new equipment did not run smoothly. For eight days in March, the firm did not know that its capital was deficient. It took steps to fix the problem but, unlike Merrill, delayed reporting.

Again, the surface story suggests the kind of technical glitches that happen often and are managed without loss while they persist. The underlying problems are addressed with outside expertise and solutions put into place. These problems never posed a major threat to the broker-dealer.

On the other hand, the managerial and supervisory problems spread across three years, at which point they actually caused a capital deficiency. It is not clear from the proceedings how urgently the NYSE forced DBSI to respond to the shortcomings of the earlier years, 1997 and 1998. The fact that similar problems caused the capital deficiency in 1998 suggests that more aggressive enforcement earlier might have prevented the capital shortfall. If so, the NYSE's treatment of DBSI has the ring, on a smaller scale, of the Bank of England's friendly and nonurgent handling of the many managerial problems Barings Bank encountered in the three years leading up to the bank's collapse. There were so many problems that the regulators missed the deadly one, Mr. Leeson's fraud, and the bank collapsed. The DBSI story raises the question, much less dramatically, whether SROs tend to treat the big players more gently than the others. This review of medium-size bank failures raises the question of whether bank supervisors are also slow to enforce at that level.

NASD and Banc One Capital Markets. In April 2001, the regulatory arm of NASD fined Banc One Capital Markets, Inc., for holding inadequate net capital. The company was the broker-dealer subsidiary of Bank One Corporation, a financial holding company with assets of $269 billion at the end of June 1999. Beginning in early 1999, Banc One Capital had converted its software to process securities and manage accounts. Posting errors flourished, and by mid-1999 the transactions account and the general ledger differed by more than $1 billion in 4,000 accounts. As a result, between February and August, Banc One's net capital deficiencies ranged from $520 million to $1.27 billion. Its customer reserve accounts were similarly deficient.

Banc One Capital did not notify its securities regulators of the unreliable books or that it was operating with inadequate net capital. When the NASD's district office identified the deficiencies, however, Banc One Capital cooperated and restructured its operations. The fine was $1.8 million.[38] The Federal Reserve Board (FRB), which was the holding company's consolidated supervisor, did not report that it played any role in this enforcement action.

NASD and Merrill Lynch. In July 1997, in an action so insignificant that it was barely described, NASD fined Merrill Lynch Government Securities of Puerto Rico, S.A., for conducting "a securities business while failing to maintain its minimum required net capital."

Summary of Actions Involving the Largest Firms. Very few actions involve the largest firms, ones that are global in scale. None of the largest banks was subject to actions involving capital adequacy by their regulators. On the securities side, two NASD actions constituted a minuscule 1.6% of the NASD's 122 actions. The single SEC action involving a global firm accounts for barely 2% of all 44 actions by the SEC. The actions against two NYSE firms account for 13% of the actions against the 16 firms against which the NYSE brought action, but the universe is too small for the fraction to carry much meaning. The 13% share is noticeable but much lower than one might expect, since the big firms dominate dealer positions and broker-dealer capital in the NYSE. Relative to their market presence, the big firms are not highly represented in the NYSE enforcements.

There are several reasons why so few enforcement actions involve the largest financial firms. One is that their capital is a multiple of required regulatory capital and cushions them. The Merrill Lynch action, however, illustrates how easily even the biggest broker-dealers can discover that the cushion has disappeared.

The experience with Merrill and, to a lesser extent, Deutsche Bank raises a question about the conventional wisdom that the biggest securities companies always hold much more capital than the regulations require. We do not know Merrill's minimum regulatory capital in October 1999, so the deficiency cannot be compared to it, but at the end of 2001 the minimum was $5 billion for the parent, so the $3 billion deficit is significant. How did the company get so close to the minimum net level?

A second reason is that the large firms are technically competent, particularly when compared to their smaller brethren. It was technical mistakes, however, that got Merrill Lynch, Deutsche Bank, and Bank One into trouble. The deficiencies resulted from new policies introduced by management, one involving cash management across the group and the others involving conversion to new firmwide computer systems or software. Merrill's shortfall was portrayed as an internal communications glitch that was remedied by the introduction of better systems. The parent had adequate cash, and MLPF&S had a claim on the parent. Merrill played by the rules, notifying the Exchange within the time period, and the problem was solved fast. In general, transitions appear to be particularly vulnerable moments; Barings was destroyed during a much more profound transition, when it tried to merge an investment bank and a merchant bank with two very different cultures.

A third possibility is that the capital adequacy rules, or the supervisors who apply them, miss important problems or treat the big players lightly. To determine whether this is the case would require the kind of review carried out by the FDIC's Office of the Inspector General for banks. Perhaps the SRO treats large members with kid gloves compared to the way it treats smaller members. The fines of $250,000 for Merrill and $175,000 for Deutsche Bank are not the largest imposed for net capital deficiencies during the period, and their relative impact on these two large groups was much less than the impact of a comparable fine on the smaller broker-dealers that were the object of most enforcement actions. The impact of a fine in the $200,000 range on a Merrill, with assets of $310 billion at the end of 1999, or on a Deutsche Bank, with assets of $836 billion, was much less than its impact of the same fine on the much smaller firm Josephthal & Co. the same year. Josephthal's assets at that time are not available, but the firm had only about 900 employees at 24 offices in the United States and abroad.

The role of the broker-dealer's parent introduces a twist that is not faced by smaller banks outside financial holding companies. Obviously, the group has a strong incentive to hold down the cost of capital. But if a broker-dealer fails during a shortfall like Merrill's, can the parent be counted on to help? If the parent operates across many markets, this is a question that cannot be answered by an SRO present in only one of those markets.

If the big firms come closer to the line than conventional wisdom assumes, why are there not more actions taken against them? Is the NYSE right to rely on firms to self-report in exceptional circumstances and periodically? The Singapore Industrial Monetary Exchange (SIMEX) changed its rules after Barings, after all. But this goes to the area of overlap between supervision and enforcement. The Merrill and Deutsche Bank actions raise the question of whether the big firms operate much closer to the minimum than we customarily assume.

Enforcement by Type of Capital Violation

Since the Basel rules set capital adequacy front and center as perhaps the single most important tool for supervisors, one might expect a large proportion of the enforcement actions to involve credit risk for banks and market risk for securities firms, as well as for banks. This turns out not to be the case.

In accordance with the guidelines in FDICIA, bank regulators issue PCA directives to banks that are undercapitalized, seriously undercapitalized, or critically undercapitalized, as defined by the law. Earlier in this chapter, regulators were shown to move slowly in getting banks out of level 3 of CAMELS. Similarly, it is not clear that bank regulators institute PCA quickly, even though "P" stands for "prompt." For example, among the very small number of directives were two from the FDIC to small-state nonmember banks that were critically undercapitalized, one with total Tier I and II capital of 5.2% and the other with 4.8%. There was no record of earlier PCA directives as the banks passed through the prior two stages on their way to critical. Perhaps the banks collapsed so fast that the FDIC caught them only at the critical stage. The record is so slight that one cannot be sure, nor can one tell what caused the capital deficiency. The FDIC has all its actions on its web site, the Fed site contains those after 1995, and the OCC lists actions only from 2002, so the story one gleans for bank supervisors is thin and uneven.

The major problem that prompted action by securities regulators was low net capital. This was the cause of action in 155 actions, or 85% of the total of 182. Capital was wrongly reported in 84 actions, or 46% of these. Securities regulators give much fuller information.

All but one of the proceedings against broker-dealers for low levels of capital or for bad reporting address problems of operational risk, rather than market risk. From 1996 to 2001, 65% (119 actions) of the 182 actions against securities firms (see table 8.5) dealt with capital below the permitted threshold or with misreporting not due to fraud or theft (e.g., because of technical problems such as changes to the computer system, a CFO might not classify accounts correctly and might miscalculate the amount of capital needed). Another 34% (62 actions) concerned theft, fraud, or market manipulation; an example is the broker-dealer who steals customers' funds and misreports the firm's capital as adequate. These are all commonly treated as a form of operational risk.

Enforcing Capital Rules for Market Risk

Market risk is not the subject of significant enforcement action by securities regulators. Securities regulators reported finding and enforcing only one violation that occurred because adverse movements of the market forced capital below the threshold. This instance is described here.

The firm in question was David Blech & Company, Incorporated ("D. Blech & Co."), a broker-dealer registered with the SEC that was defunct by the time of the proceeding. The SEC decision described the facts as follows:[39] Blech was the chief executive officer of D. Blech & Co., which specialized in underwriting and making markets in biotechnology securities. In 1994, the biotechnology industry experienced a cyclical downturn, and the

Table 8.5. Securities Regulators Compared: Proceedings to Enforce Net Capital Rules—Summary Table of Actions and Penalties, 1996–2001

Type of Offense and Regulator	Percentage of Total	Net Capital Is	
		Too Low	Not Reported
A. Low capital and misreporting resulted from fraudulent schemes, theft, and market manipulation			
SEC (court, internal, SRO)	17	23	14
NYSE	0	0	0
NASD (only internal)	17	24	20
Subtotal A in percent	34	47	34
B. Low capital and misreporting were the main illegal acts			
SEC (court, internal, SRO)	7	9	9
NYSE (only internal)	9	15	15
NASD (only internal)	50	84	26
Subtotal B in percent	65	108	50
C. Low capital and misreporting resulted from declining market prices			
SEC (internal)	0.5	0	0
NYSE	0	0	0
NASD	0	0	0
Subtotal C in percent	0.5	0	0
D. Total in figures	182	155	84

Source: Regulators' web sites.

price of securities in which D. Blech & Co. made a market declined. Because D. Blech & Co. held large inventory positions in these biotechnology securities and the equity value of these securities had decreased, D. Blech & Co. experienced a net capital crisis. In an attempt to keep D. Blech & Co. afloat, from at least June 1, 1994, through September 22, 1994, Blech engaged in unlawful and unauthorized trading of seven biotechnology securities. D. Blech & Co. also failed to maintain adequate net capital and failed to keep accurate books and records from approximately March through September 1994. Blech, who controlled D. Blech & Co., was liable for these violations.

The penalty was to bar Blech from future association with any broker or dealer. His company had closed, and he had already pled guilty to two counts of securities fraud. The SEC turned to the U.S. District Court to prosecute his illegal trading in 1994 and, later, in biotechnology stocks, from November 1997 to January 1998.[40]

This proceeding is of particular interest for two reasons. First, it is the only one to deal with the effect of market risk. The broker-dealer was not one of the industry leaders. It was a well-known small niche player specializing in an industry that made it particularly vulnerable to market risk. No proceeding that involved market risk was found for any large firm.

Second, the capital adequacy rules were enforced by Blech's clearing broker, not by a regulator. Bear, Stearns Securities Corp., headquartered in New York City, concluded that Blech could not satisfactorily demonstrate that its capital met the regulatory minimum. Bear, Stearns "took D. Blech off the Automated Confirmation Transaction service, effectively barring D. Blech from posting bids and offers on the Nasdaq market's system." (See Calian 1994.) The collapse came fast. According to *The Wall Street Journal,* about six months before it closed, "D. Blech more than met the minimum net capital required by regulators' rules, records show. The firm reported regulatory net capital of $4.7 million, far above the required $298,325." (See Calian 1994.)

Noncompliance Due to Fraud and Theft

The SEC handled prosecutions of noncompliance due to fraud and theft more than the SROs. Thiryt-one of the SEC's 44 actions, or 70%, concerned fraud or theft; 31 of the SROs' 138 actions, or only 22%, did. Indeed, NYSE had none of the most serious actions; the SROs enforced the many more noncompliance actions that appear to be innocuous.

Securities regulators distinguish clearly between Type A noncompliance, meaning low capital or misreporting due to fraud or theft and Type B, which covers the less heinous mistakes. Appendix 2 expands table 8.5 to include comparisons of the enforcement tools used by the three securities regulators in both circumstances.

The 62 actions against brokers who broke the capital rules using fraud or theft carried heavier penalties than the other infractions, as one would expect. The SEC issued 17 cease-and-desist orders for Type A offenses, compared to only 3 for Type B. These include orders to correct conditions and related powers for specific reasons, notably mandamus, injunction, and orders to individuals to comply with the law and regulations and to exchanges, or securities associations, or clearers to make members comply. NASD and the SEC levied fines in 38 actions and censured or suspended the violators in 29. Permanent penalties (those that bar, revoke license, expel from membership, close, and liquidate) numbered 25, or 40%.

The tools used in the milder Type B infractions were themselves milder. The ubiquitous fine is the tool of choice, levied in 90% of the actions. NASD levied 80% of the fines, and its use of them—in 92% of all its Type B actions—surpassed the 88% occurrence in NYSE cases and the 75% occurrence in SEC cases. The fines ranged from a low of $25,000 (in 1998, for badly classified accounting) to a high of $400,000, for seriously deficient internal controls coupled with deliberately misleading statements (in 2000) and $1.35 million for numerous rule violations, including low net capital (in 1999). Most fines imposed by the NYSE were relatively small. The distribution was as follows:

- Under $100,000: 6 fines. These broker-dealers and their infractions were small; all but one were assessed before 1998, and that one in 2001.

- \$100,000 to under \$200,000: 2 fines. Both involved transitions in ownership; the problems occurred about that time and were not likely to be repeated.
- \$200,000 to under \$300,000: 4 fines. Multiple miscalculations of net capital or instances of bad supervision or major loss of net capital.
- \$400,000 and above: 2 fines. Many violations of many rules, of which net capital was one, and very bad internal controls, with many misleading statements.

The fines appear to reflect the seriousness of the infraction. Censure (67 cases, or 56% of all Type B actions), probably the most modest penalty, and suspension (49, or 41% of Type B cases) are well suited to dealing with SRO members without creating a lethal effect. The penalities in the 26 matters that required action by the malefactor were designed primarily to rehabilitate. Permanent penalties were imposed in just 34 cases, 29% of the total of Type B offenses, compared with more than 40% of Type A offenses.

Temporary restraining orders, issued pending the completion of proceedings, were used only three times. These are less useful because the respondent may, within 10 days, ask the court to review.[41]

Fines, censure, and suspension emerge as the preferred tools, far outstripping any other, because they are best imposed by SROs on their small members, who are the target of most capital adequacy enforcement. Faced with fraud, the SEC enters the fray to deploy injunctions and cease-and-desist orders, and the SROs apply terminal sanctions at a higher rate. Criminal actions are rare. This makes sense; fraud, theft, and manipulation are intentional and may not stop when a proceeding begins, so cease-and-desist orders are essential.

CONCLUSION

Several conclusions emerge from this review of formal capital adequacy enforcement.

Enforcement actions were very rare during the 1990s and in the early part of the next decade. This low rate does not seem to have occurred simply because enforcement took place by alternative, informal means. Formal and informal enforcement serve different functions. Certainly, one reason for the low rate of formal enforcement was that, for much of the period during which enforcement actions were examined, there was economic and financial growth. But even into the recession of 2001 the rates were relatively low.

Effective supervision may also account for the low rate of enforcement actions. Perhaps the supervisors caught banks that were heading toward violations of the capital adequacy rules and turned around many of the bad performers. After all, most of the banks, at least, are reported to be well capitalized.

Case studies raise questions about whether supervision is really that effective. The case studies do not demonstrate widespread failure by supervisors;

they do demonstrate a tendency of supervisors to identify certain problems but to fail to follow through. Combined with an underlying question about whether banks' assets are accurately valued, this tendency could suggest that weak banks, at least, are not the object of prompt corrective action as much as they should be.

The actions by securities regulators involve almost exclusively small or medium-size firms. The small firms populate the problem category. Many of the little guys are at the margin already and dip into noncompliance when their income falls a bit lower than usual. Most of the rest break the law (e.g., commit fraud or theft) and get caught, with capital infractions as a by-product. The processes and penalties are calibrated well enough to deal with these situations. Enforcement actions against large firms occur for technical reasons and are quickly remedied.

Enforcement of capital adequacy regulations in the United States deals almost exclusively with deficiencies that arise because of operational risk, rather than market or credit risk. At the very least, this suggests the importance of further work on operational risk. It also raises questions about the resources being devoted to refining regulatory regimes for market and credit risk. In both sectors, regulators seem to have fairly wide discretion in enforcing the rules.

The data examined here reveal that enforcement in the United States is by type of firm (i.e., bank or broker-dealer), and does not address the overall capital needs of an entire financial conglomerate. In the securities proceeding against Merrill Lynch by the NYSE, while the SRO was aware that the parent had substantial capital, the NYSE did not report that it had considered whether Merrill & Co.'s total capital was adequate for the needs of the entire group so that it could be a source of strength to the broker-dealer. This would not be within the scope of the NYSE hearing, in any case. No enforcement involves a study of the capital adequacy of BHCs or FHCs.

APPENDIX 1: PROMPT CORRECTIVE ACTIONS, 1993–2001

OCC PROMPT CORRECTIVE ACTIONS

Year	Bank and location
1993	American National Bank, Gonzales, TX
	Farmers And Merchants National Bank, Hamilton, VA
	First Charter Bank NA, Beverly Hills, CA
	Mechanics National Bank, Paramount, CA
1994	Merchants Bank of California, NA, Carson, CA
1998	Monument National Bank, Ridgecrest, CA
	The Malta National Bank, Malta, OH
	Western American National Bank, Bedford, TX
2000	Metropolitan Bank, New York, NY

2001   NextBank, N.A., Phoenix, AZ
                Prairie National Bank, Belle Plaine, MN
                Sinclair National Bank, Gravette, AZ

FDIC PROMPT CORRECTIVE ACTIONS

Year	*Bank and location*
1993	Provident Bank, Dallas, TX
	People Bank, Amite, LA
	Century Thrift and Loan Association, Los Angeles, CA
	Midland Bank, Kansas City, MS
	Bank of San Pedro, San Pedro, CA
1994	Capital Bank, Downey, CA
1995	Brentwood Bank of California, Los Angeles, CA
1996	American International Bank, Los Angeles, CA
1999	Victory State Bank, Columbia, SC
2001	The Salt Lick Deposit Bank, Salt Lick, KY

FRB PROMPT CORRECTIVE ACTIONS

Year	*Bank and location*
2000	New Century Bank, Southfield, MI
1999	Zia New Mexico Bank, Tucumcari, NM
1994	First Bank of Philadelphia, Philadelphia, PA
	Pioneer Bank, Fullerton, CA
1993	Country Hill Bank, Lenexa, KS

Sources: http://www.occ.treas.gov/scripts/enfsrch.cfm
            http://www.fdic.gov/bank/individual/enforcement
            http://www.federalreserve.gov/boarddocs/enforcement/search.cfm

Appendix 2. Securities Regulators Compared: Proceedings to Enforce Net Capital Rules—Summary Table of Actions and Penalties, 1996–2001

		Net Capital Is										Bar	Bar					
Regulators	Percentage of Total	Too Low	Not Reported	C&D	Injun	TRO	Act	Fine	Disgorge	Censure	Suspend	Temp.	Perm.	Revoke	Expel	Close	Liquidate	Criminal
A. Low capital and misreporting resulted from fraudulent schemes, theft, and market manipulation																		
SEC (court, internal, SRO)	17	23	14	17	2	3	13	2	4	4	4	0	0	1	0	1	1	3
NYSE	0	0	0	0	0	0	0	0	0	0	0	0	0	0	0	0	0	0
NASD (only internal)	17	24	20	0	0	7	25	3	10	10	11	2	15	0	7	0	0	0
Subtotal A	34	47	34	17	2	10	38	5	14	14	15	2	15	1	7	1	1	3
B. Low capital and misreporting were the main illegal acts																		
SEC (court, internal, SRO)	7	9	9	3	1	2	9	0	1	1	5	2	0	1	0	0	1	0
NYSE (only internal)	9	15	15	0	0	0	14	0	15	15	4	0	0	0	2*	0	0	0
NASD (only internal)	50	84	26	0	0	26	84	5	51	51	40	3	27	0	3	0	0	0
Subtotal B	65	108	50	3	1	28	107	5	67	67	49	5	27	1	5	0	1	0
C. Low capital and misreporting resulted from declining market prices																		
SEC (internal)	0.5	0	0	0	0	0	0	0	0	0	0	0	0	1	0	0	0	1
NYSE	0	0	0	0	0	0	0	0	0	0	0	0	0	0	0	0	0	0
NASD	0	0	0	0	0	0	0	0	0	0	0	0	0	0	0	0	0	0
Subtotal C	0.5	0	0	0	0	0	0	0	0	0	0	0	0	1	0	0	0	1
D. Total	182	155	84	20	3	38	145	10	81	81	64	7	42	3	12	1	2	4

Key to penalties:

C&D Injun.: Cease-and-desist, injunction; TRO: temporary restraining order; Act: broker-dealer agrees to actions that will improve its ability to prevent future violations; Fines (civil); Disgorge: repay gains; Censure; Suspend: temporarily withdraw license; Suspend: activities or association with members (temporarily); Bar: no association with NYSE members as principal; Temp. = temporary; Perm. = permanent; Revoke: end license to practice; Expel from NYSE membership (* = withdraw); Close firm; Liquidation; Criminal trial.

Source: Regulators's web sites.

Notes

1. For insurance companies, the regulatory goal is to "limit insurance company failures to ensure the long-run viability of insurance companies so that they can meet policyholders' claims in the future," according to the GAO (1998). Enforcement data analogous to those for bank and securities firms do not exist for the insurance industry. Fifty state regulator agencies regulate the capital of insurance firms in the United States. For this reason, insurance capital enforcement is not included in this chapter.

2. Informal actions include memoranda of understanding between bank and regulator, a commitment letter from the bank's board of directors, or resolutions by the board designed to remedy these problems. Informal actions are not systematically examined here, but are compared to formal actions.

3. See www.occ.treas.gov/enforce/enf_search.htm.

4. See www.fdic.gov/bank/individual/enforcement.

5. See www.federalreserve.gov/boarddocs/enforcement/search.cfm.

6. NASD Rule 3130(b)(1)(A), Regulation of Activities of Members Experiencing Financial and/or Operational Difficulties, NASD Manual Online, available at http://cchwallstreet.com/nasd/nasd.asp.

7. National Securities Clearing Corporation, Standards of Financial Responsibility and Operational Capacity, Rules and Regulations, Addendum B-2 and B-23, and Addendum S, available at NSCC web site www.nscc.com.

8. The OCC supervises national banks, which in 1998 (about midway through the period examined here) held 59% of all bank assets and included most of the biggest U.S. banks. Among the top 25 U.S. banks, the OCC supervised banks with 72% of the assets, 81% of the deposits, and 89% of U.S. offices. So the OCC supervises most of the largest U.S. banks (Greenspan 1999).

9. The FDICIA (1991, §1831o) and see Jackson and Symons (1999, p. 187). The five ratings in the text integrate the Federal Reserve's criteria and those of FDICIA. The next four elements of CAMELS (asset quality, management, earnings, and liquidity) are scored similarly. A sixth component was added in 1996—sensitivity to market risk, such as changes in interest rates, foreign exchange, commodity prices, or equity prices. All six elements are considered by U.S. regulators. Capital, asset quality, and market sensitivity are closely related and are important for enforcement.

10. The leverage ratio is "the ratio of Tier 1 capital to average tangible assets, [which] are equal to total assets less assets excluded from common equity in the calculation of Tier 1 capital" (Federal Reserve Bulletin 2001, p. 375).

11. 12 USC §371(c).

12. Other types of actions enforce more than capital. For example, as a bank's CAMELS rating drops, supervisors must act. These situations are not reviewed here thoroughly because they often do not involve capital adequacy directly.

13. Exchange Act Rule 17a-11(f).

14. I am indebted to Richard K. Kim for this point.

15. The International Lending Supervision Act of 1983.

16. See NYSE Constitution, Sec. 5, and Rule 476, Disciplinary Proceedings Involving Charges Against Members, Member Organizations, Allies, and NYSE Hearing Board Procedures (undated), at 9. Available at NYSE web site: www.nyse.com.

17. From 1988, NYSE could assess a fine in any amount (NYSE Rule 476). Available at: www.nyse.com.

18. Defined by Richard Bernard, General Counsel, New York Stock Exchange, in communications with the author. Censure is not defined in the Exchange Act rules, but it is mentioned without elaboration or definition as a possible penalty in the NYSE Constitution (Article IX, Sec. 5). Censure is also a penalty the SEC may impose on an SRO or its officer or director (Exchange Act, Section 19[h]).

19. CAMELS is the acronym for six categories of bank performance: capital adequacy, asset quality, management, earnings, liquidity, and sensitivity to market conditions.

20. The data come from a search for "net capital" on the SEC's web site. The search yielded 333 possible sources, which were then examined. This list shows administrative and court actions reported by that search. Only one action is recorded for an entity even if the search revealed multiple actions during the period.

21. NASD also reported that, on average in this period, 5,400 firms did business with the public and had more than 92,000 branches and 664,000 registered securities representatives. Against these 5,400 firms, the 20 actions a year on average gives a ratio of 0.4% a year.

22. Interview.

23. A bank's margin is the percentage point difference between the bank's ratio—either its actual Tiers 1+2, its Tier 1, or its leverage—closest to the corresponding regulatory ratio for a well-capitalized bank and that regulatory ratio. The average margin for all well-capitalized banks is the average of all the margins weighted by each bank's share of total assets of well-capitalized banks.

24. SIA 2001b. There are no aggregate data for all securities firms, or subsets, that separate minimum net capital and excess net capital. Interviews, SIA and SEC.

25. For example, NASD wants the authority to demand an annual audit at the firm's expense when its exam encounters unclear accounts. Interview.

26. I am grateful to Professor George G. Kaufman for this point, and to him and Alton Gilbert for related data and analysis.

27. OCC News Release, January 11, 2002.

28. This chapter does not examine the OTS systematically. The Superior Bank case is interesting here, however, because it reveals in more detail supervisory problems that are similar to those for the other banks.

29. Interview.

30. Interview.

31. Interview.

32. Securities Act of Release No. 7718, August 5, 1999, and Exchange Release No. 41707, August 5, 1999, Administrative Proceeding File No. 3_9962, *In the Matter of Bear, Stearns Securities Corp., Respondent.*

33. The information for this story comes from Exchange Hearing Panel Decision 00-109, June 29, 2000. It is a Stipulation of Facts and Consent to Penalty agreed to by MLPF&S without admitting or denying guilt.

34. In 2001, Deutsche Banc Alex Brown Inc. was one of the 10 largest broker-dealers in the United States (SIA 2001a).

35. The hearing is reported in Exchange Hearing Panel Decision 99-70, June 23, 1999 ("Decision 99").

36. Ibid., para. 19, at 5.

37. Ibid., para. 52b, p. 10.

38. NASD Enforcement Actions, NASD Regulation Fines Banc One Capital Markets, Inc. $1.8 Million For Net Capital, Customer Reserve, and Record Keeping Violations (April 2001).

39. United States of America Before the Securities and Exchange Commission, Exchange Act Release No. 43693, December 8, 2000, Administrative Proceeding File No. 3_10379, *In the Matter of David Blech, Respondent,* Order Instituting Public Administrative Proceedings, Making Findings, and Imposing Remedial Sanctions.

40. United States v. David Blech, 97 Crim. 403 (KTD) (S.D.N.Y.), March 28, 1998. This case involved criminal fraud for illegal trading, not net capital deficiencies, and is not recorded in the tables.

41. See Exchange Act §21C.

References

American Banker. Various years. Top 100 Banking Companies by Total Assets. Available at: www.americanbanker.com/rankings.html?ranking=/BTHC.html.

Board of Governors of the Federal Reserve System. 2002. Uniform Financial Institutions Rating System (December 26).

Calian, Sara. 1994. Blech Stumbles, and Some Biotech Stocks Tumble. *The Wall Street Journal* (September 23).

Federal Deposit Insurance Corporation (FDIC). 1996. History of the Eighties—Lessons for the Future. Vol. 1: An Examination of the Banking Crises of the 1980s and Early 1990s. Available at: www.fdic.gov/bank/historical/history/vol1.html.

———. 1998. Quarterly Banking Profile (December 31). Available at: http://www2.fdic.gov/qbp/1998dec/qbp.pdf.

———. 2002. Quarterly Banking Profile. Table 1-A. Selected Indicators. FDIC-Insured Commercial Banks (March 31). Available at: http://www2.fdic.gov/qbp/2002mar/qbp.pdf.

———. 2003. Quarterly Banking Profile, Table 1-A. Selected Indicators. FDIC-Insured Commercial Banks. Available at: http://www2.fdic.gov/qbp/qbpSelect.asp?menuItem=QBP.

Federal Deposit Insurance Corporation Improvement Act (FDICIA). 1991. Available at: http://www.fdic.gov/regulations/laws/rules/8000-2400.html.

Federal Reserve Bulletin. 2001. Profits and Balance Sheet Developments at U.S. Commercial Banks in 2000. Washington, D.C. (June).

———. 2002. Profits and Balance Sheet Developments at U.S. Commercial Banks in 2001. Washington, D.C. (June).

General Accounting Office (GAO). 1998. Risk-Based Capital: Regulatory and Industry Approaches to Capital and Risk. Report to the Chairman, Committee on Banking, Housing, and Urban Affairs, U.S. Senate, and the Chairman, Committee on Banking and Financial Services, House of Representatives, Washington, D.C. (GAO/GGD-98-153) (July). Available at: http://www.gao.gov/archive/1998/gg98153.pdf.

———. 2001. Comparison of Financial Institution Regulators' Enforcement and Prompt Corrective Action Authorities. Washington, D.C. (January 31). Available at: http://www.gao.gov/new.items/d01322r.pdf.

Gilbert, R. Alton. 2003. Surprising Observations about the Supervision of Banks Downgraded to CAMELS 3. Unpublished paper.

Gilbert, R. Alton., and M. D. Vaughan. 2000. Do Depositors Care About Enforcement Actions? Working Paper 2000-020A, Table 1, at 40. Federal Reserve

Bank of St. Louis, (July 1). Available at: http://research.stlouisfed.org/wp/2000/2000-020.pdf.

Greenspan, Alan. 1999. H.R. 10 and Financial Modernization. Appendix B, Table 2. Testimony of Chairman of the Federal Reserve Board before the Subcommittee on Finance and Hazardous Materials, Committee on Commerce, U.S. House of Representatives, April 28. Washington, D.C. Available at: http://www.federalreserve.gov/boarddocs/testimony/1999/19990428.htm.

International Monetary Fund (IMF). 1997. *International Financial Statistics Yearbook*. Washington, D.C.: IMF.

———. 2002. World Economic Outlook. Washington, D.C.: IMF (September).

Jackson, Howell, and E. Symons. 1999. *Regulation of Financial Institutions*. American Casebook Series. St. Paul, Minn.: West Group.

Office of the Comptroller of the Currency (OCC). 2002. OCC Prompt Corrective Action Directive, November 15, 2001. Press Release (February 7).

Office of Inspector General, FDIC (OIG). 1999. The Failure of BestBank, Boulder, Colorado. Audit Report No. 99-005 (January 22). Available at: www.fdic.gov/oig/a-rep99/99-005.html.

———. 2002. Issues Related to the Failure of Superior Bank, FSB, Hinsdale, Illinois. Audit Report No. 02-005 (February 6). Available at: www.fdic.gov/oig/a-rep02/02-005.pdf.

———. 2003. Material Loss Review of the Failure of the Connecticut Bank of Commerce, Stamford, Connecticut. Audit Report No. 03-017 (March 10). Available at: www.fdic.gov/oig/a-rep03/03-017.pdf.

Securities Industry Association (SIA). 2001a. Broker Dealer Categories.

———. 2001b. *Yearbook Report on Capital Adequacy*.

Index